AF576683

Let it Shine

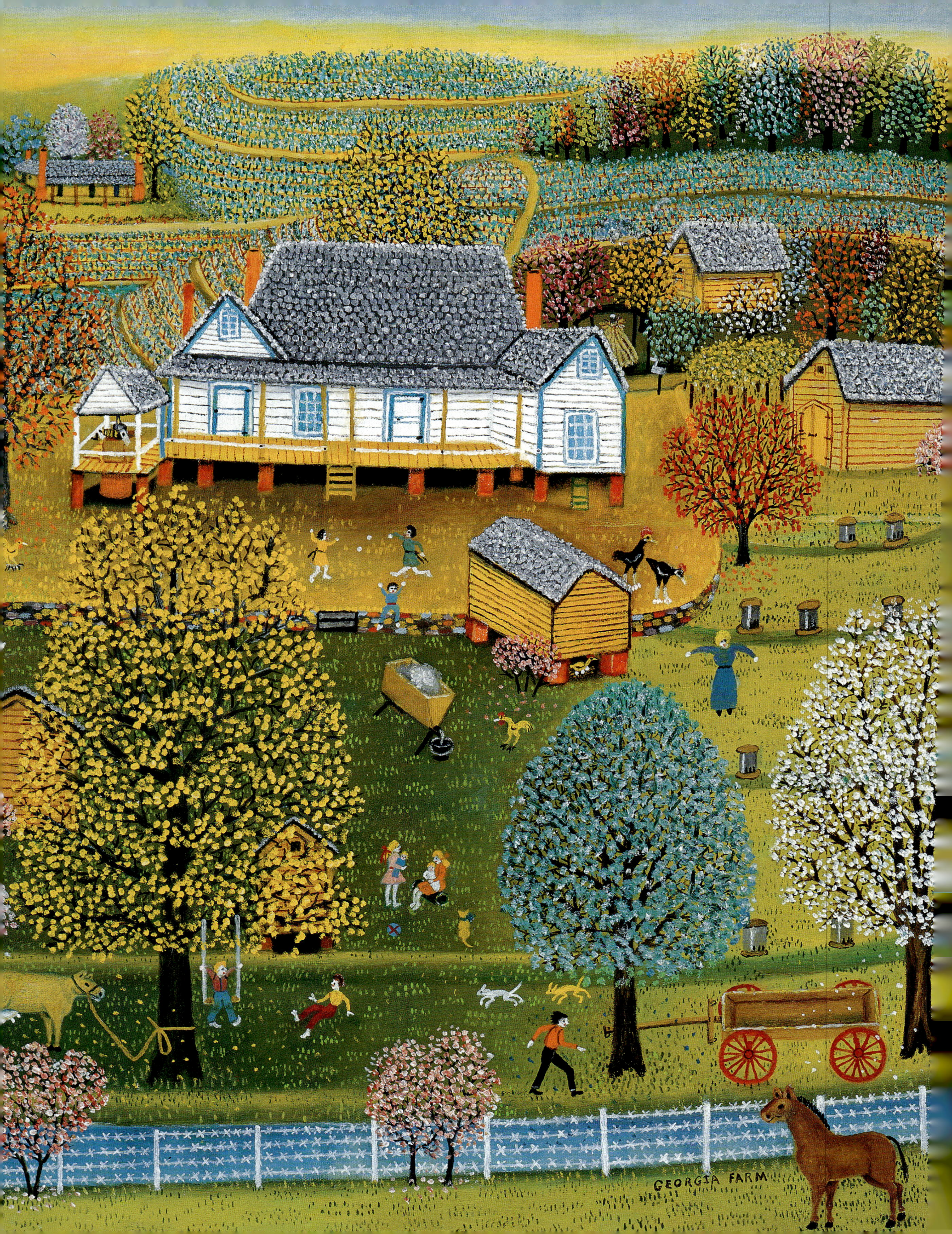
GEORGIA FARM

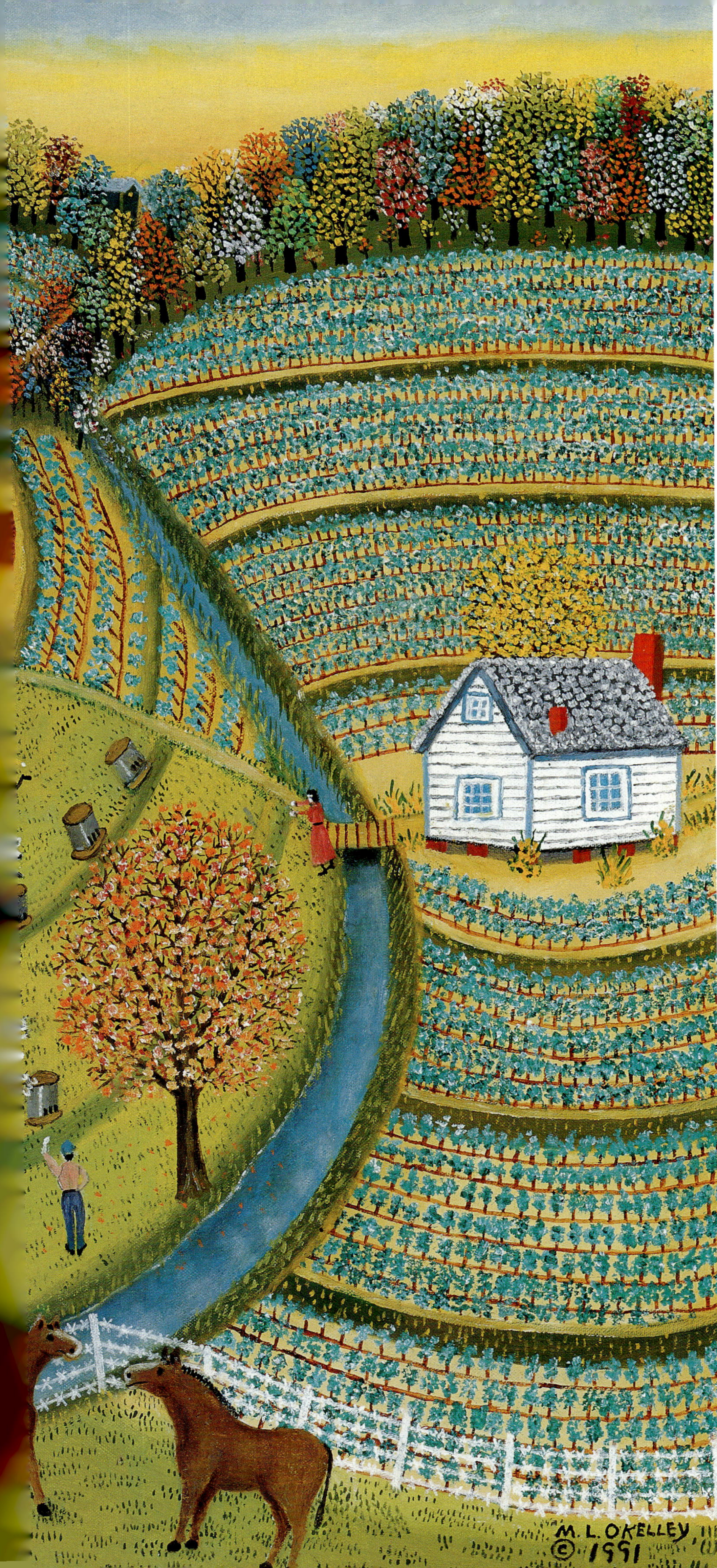

Let it Shine

Self-Taught Art from the T. Marshall Hahn Collection

Essays by
Lynne E. Spriggs
Joanne Cubbs
Lynda Roscoe Hartigan

Catalogue by
Susan Mitchell Crawley

Photography by
Peter Harholdt

High Museum of Art, Atlanta

Distributed by the
University Press of Mississippi

Let it Shine: Self-Taught Art from the T. Marshall Hahn Collection was organized by the High Museum of Art.

Generous support was provided by Georgia-Pacific Corporation.

Additional support was provided by Sun Trust.

Let it Shine: Self-Taught Art from the T. Marshall Hahn Collection was on view at the High Museum of Art, Atlanta, from June 23 to September 2, 2001.

Library of Congress Control Number: 00-136380
ISBN 1-57806-363-9

For the High Museum of Art
Kelly Morris, Manager of Publications
Nora E. Poling, Associate Editor
Janet S. Rauscher, Assistant Editor
Melissa Duffes Wargo, Assistant Editor

Distributed by
University Press of Mississippi
3825 Ridgewood Road
Jackson, Mississippi 39211-6492
1-800-737-7788

Designed by Susan E. Kelly
Proofread by Sharon Vonasch
Produced by Marquand Books, Inc., Seattle
www.marquand.com

Printed by CS Graphics Pte., Ltd., Singapore

Pages 2–3: Mattie Lou O'Kelley, *Georgia Farm* (cat. 60, detail)
Page 5: Leroy Almon, *God's Commandments to Man* (cat. 3, detail)
Page 8: Marshall Hahn in his Atlanta home, 1996

Every effort has been made to contact the proper copyright holder for all images.

Photograph Credits

Cats. 1–85: Peter Harholdt
Page 13, fig. 2: Mike Jensen
Page 13, fig. 3: Mike Jensen
Page 14, fig. 4: Mike Jensen
Page 15, fig. 5: Mike Jensen
Page 18, fig. 11: Georgia-Pacific Corporation, Jim Robinson
Page 26, fig. 6: Judith Alexander Augustine
Page 29, fig. 8: Roger Manley
Page 31, fig. 10: Arthur Rothstein, Farm Security Administration, Prints and Photographs Division, Library of Congress, Washington, D.C.
Page 36, fig. 13: Courtesy Luise Ross Gallery, New York
Page 37, fig. 14: John F. Turner
Page 38, fig. 15: Victor Faccinto
Page 39, fig. 16: Norinne Betjemann, Courtesy Fleisher/Ollman Gallery
Page 44, fig. 1: Doris Ullman, used with special permission from the Berea College Art Department, Berea, Kentucky
Page 44, fig. 2: Dorothea Lange, Farm Security Administration, Prints and Photographs Division, Library of Congress, Washington, D.C.
Page 48, fig. 4: Michael D. Hall
Page 48, fig. 5: Jeffrey T. Camp
Page 49, fig. 6: Jeffrey T. Camp
Page 51, fig. 9: Courtesy of the Corcoran Gallery and College of Art Archives
Page 52, fig. 10: Andy Nasisse, Andy Nasisse Papers, Archives of American Art, Smithsonian Institution
Page 53, fig. 11: Liza Kirwin, Archives of American Art, Smithsonian Institution
Page 53, fig. 12: Liza Kirwin, Archives of American Art, Smithsonian Institution
Page 54, fig. 13: James Allen
Page 55, fig. 14: Lucinda Bunnen
Page 55, fig. 15: Allen Huffman
Page 56, fig. 16: Chuck Rosenak, Chuck and Jan Rosenak Research Material on American Folk Art, Archives of American Art, Smithsonian Institution

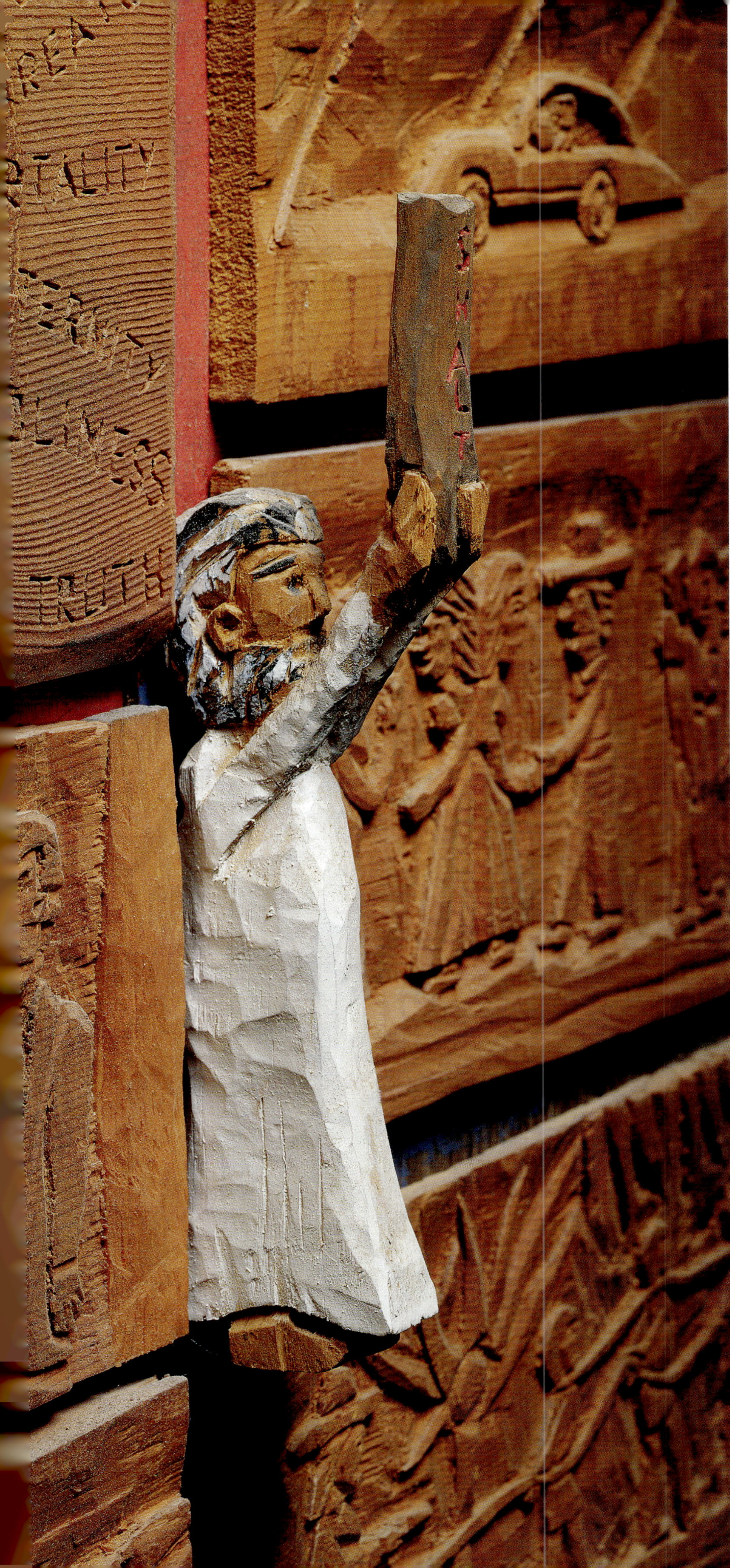

Contents

Acknowledgments

Gratitude of the first order goes to Marshall Hahn for giving his extraordinary collection to the High Museum of Art, encouraging the Museum and our public to embrace self-taught art and inspiring this exhibition. Marshall has been extraordinarily generous; over the years, he has graciously opened his homes to guests, has made his works of art and his records readily available, and has never been too busy to share his knowledge, memories, enthusiasm, and vision. Marshall's leadership has helped bring the High's department of folk art to life. During his many years of service as Chairman and CEO, then Director and Honorary Chairman of the Board of the Georgia-Pacific Corporation, Marshall has maintained an unwavering personal and professional commitment to support of the arts.

I am particularly grateful to Michael E. Shapiro, the High's director, for his support of this project. I am also indebted to the High's previous directors: a working relationship with Marshall Hahn first took root during Gudmund Vigtel's tenure, and grew significantly under Ned Rifkin's leadership. Thanks also to Philip Verre, Deputy Director of the High Museum of Art.

This publication is the result of many concerted efforts. Susan Mitchell Crawley's refreshing enthusiasm and well-honed research skills have been invaluable. She has ferreted out all manner of fugitive information and has translated extensive research into eloquent and illuminating catalogue entries. I commend Susan, Janet Rauscher, Melissa Greven, Nicole Smith, and Joslyn Chandler for their organizational skills and good-humored efforts that have supported and assisted me with the production of this catalogue. I extend a personal thanks to Marshall and his family for the opportunity to come to know them. Special thanks to Marshall's assistant Lori Hudson for her reliable and graceful help in all matters. My predecessor Joanne Cubbs also worked closely with Marshall and is intimately familiar with the collection. In her essay for this catalogue, Joanne weaves considerations of specific artists into a tapestry of themes and concerns common to many works of southern self-taught art. Lynda Roscoe Hartigan, Chief Curator of the Smithsonian American Art Museum, brings her expertise to focus on the history of collecting folk art in the South. Although the American South is acknowledged as one of the nation's richest regions for folk and self-taught art, comprehensive examinations of this legacy are just beginning.

Artists and their relatives who were interviewed for this project include Ned Cartledge, Thornton Dial Sr., Howard Finster, Lonnie Bradley Holley, Joe Light, Annie Lucas, Charlie Lucas, Mary Michael Shelley, Jimmy Lee Sudduth, O. C. Sudduth, and Mose Tolliver. A heartfelt thanks to all of these individuals for sharing such memorable insights. Special thanks to Robert Reeves, who conducted thorough and invaluable interviews with the following individuals: Shari Cavin and Randall Morris, Larry Hackley, Barry and Allen Huffman, Jane and Bert Hunecke, Louanne LaRoche, Roger Manley, Judith McWillie, Andy Nasisse, Tom Patterson, Tony and Marie Shank, Willem Volkersz, and Jonathan Williams. Judith Alexander, James Allen, William S. Arnett, Peter J. Brownlee, William Ferris, Estelle Friedman, Baron and Ellin Gordon, Liza Kirwin, and Chuck and Jan Rosenak were also consulted. I thank all of them for their candor and assistance.

I also thank the following people for contributing their knowledge, research, memories, inventories, and photographs to the contents of this catalogue: Harvie B. and Charles L. Abney; Parker Agelasto; Judith Alexander; McKinley Alexander; James Allen; Mary Almon; Andy P. Antippas; Barbara Archer; Paul Arnett; William S. Arnett; Judith Alexander Augustine; Hildegard Bachert; Gordon W. Bailey; Talis Bergmani; Rick Berman; Margaret Bodell; David Brenneman; Barbara Brogden; Lucinda Bunnen; Jeffrey T. Camp; Robert Cargo; J. B. Coins; Nicole Cottles; Melody Barnett Deusner; Thornton Dial Sr.; Margaret Doan; Beverly Finster; Tim Flinn; Randy Franklin; Richard Gasperi; Shelby Gilley; Anton Haardt; Larry Hackley; Michael D. Hall; Jimmy Hedges; Barry and Allen Huffman; Mike Jensen; Jane Kallir; Marissa Keller; Tim Keny; Hazel Kinney; Louanne LaRoche; Yoon Lee; Michael and Kiyoko Lerner; Joe Light; Jim Linderman; S. H. Lockett; John M. MacGregor; S. Major; Roger Manley; Frank Maresca; Ruth Mekel;

Eugene W. Metcalf Jr.; Frank Miele; Randall Morris; Andy Nasisse; John Ollman; Tom Patterson; Regenia Perry; Anthony J. Petullo; Jay S. Potter; Doralee Ratliff; Robert Reeves; Roger Ricco; Luise Ross; Elizabeth Sackton; Pam Sechant; Eugenia Shannon; Thomas Silliman; Mike Smith; Suzanne Stephens; Michael Stevens; Tracye Stormer; Michael Thompson; Mildred Thompson; Paul Tolson; John F. Turner; Gudmund Vigtel; Carolyn Walsh; Marcia Weber; Richard and Maggie Wenstrup; Ruth West; Lucy Chase Williams; Lois Zetter; Anne Motley and Barbara Luck, Abby Aldrich Rockefeller Folk Art Museum; Mark Pascale, Curator of Prints and Drawings, The Art Institute of Chicago; Robert Boyce, Director, Doris Ullman Galleries, Berea College; Miriam Fowler, Curator of Education, Birmingham Museum of Art; Kim Davis, Assistant Registrar, the Corcoran Gallery of Art; Michael Watts, Tarble Arts Center, Eastern Illinois University; Emmanuelle Delmas-Glass, Folk Art Society of America; Jim Robinson, Senior Photographer, Georgia-Pacific Corporation; Zhi-Yong Yin, Professor of Geography, Georgia State University; Adrian Swain, Curator, Kentucky Folk Art Center; Brooke Davis Anderson, Janey Fire, Stacey Hollander, and Lee Kogan, Museum of American Folk Art; Bill Fagaly, Assistant Director of Art, New Orleans Museum of Art; Victor Coonin, Professor of Art History, Rhodes College; Dennis Preisler, Sears Corporate Historian, Sears Archives; Liza Kirwin, Curator of Manuscripts, Archives of American Art, Smithsonian Institution; Cindy Regal, *Southern Living* magazine; Judith McWillie, Chair and Professor of Painting and Drawing, The Lamar Dodd School of Art, University of Georgia; Tamara Kennelly, University Archivist, Virginia Tech; and Robert Knott, Professor of Nineteenth- and Twentieth-Century Art, Wake Forest University. Additional assistance was provided by research librarians at Emory University, Georgia State University, and the Kansas State Historical Society.

Editing and production of this catalogue were orchestrated by Kelly Morris with Janet Rauscher and Nora Poling. In particular, Janet Rauscher has gracefully devoted long hours, considerable knowledge of this material, and meticulous editing skills to ensure excellence. Many thanks to Ed Marquand and Susan Kelly of Marquand Books for designing this handsome volume, printed at CS Graphics in Singapore. Color photography was beautifully executed by Peter Harholdt.

On the High's staff, Frances Francis and Maureen Morrisette have once again demonstrated their skills as registrars-par-excellence, ably assisted by Lannie Ethridge, Kelly Ziegler, Saskia Benjamin, and Keith Knox. Jody Cohen, Marjorie Harvey, Linda Boyte, Jim Waters, and Angela Jaeger have combined their talents to create a remarkable installation. Jim Waters and our preparators have readied dozens of artworks to facilitate curatorial inquiries. Larry Miller has overseen the challenging task of reframing our work by Martin Ramirez. Thanks to Sheldon Wolf, Nancy Gaddy, Roanne Katcher, and Sally Corbett for their support. Special gratitude goes to Nick Clark, Joy Patty, Pat Rodewald, and Jena Sibille, who have helped give volume and form to this project's educational initiatives. Many other staff members have also contributed their time and talents to ensure the success of this endeavor.

It is with gratitude that I acknowledge the contributions of every person whose wisdom and enthusiasm have added immeasurably to the realization of this project.

Lynne E. Spriggs
Curator of Folk Art

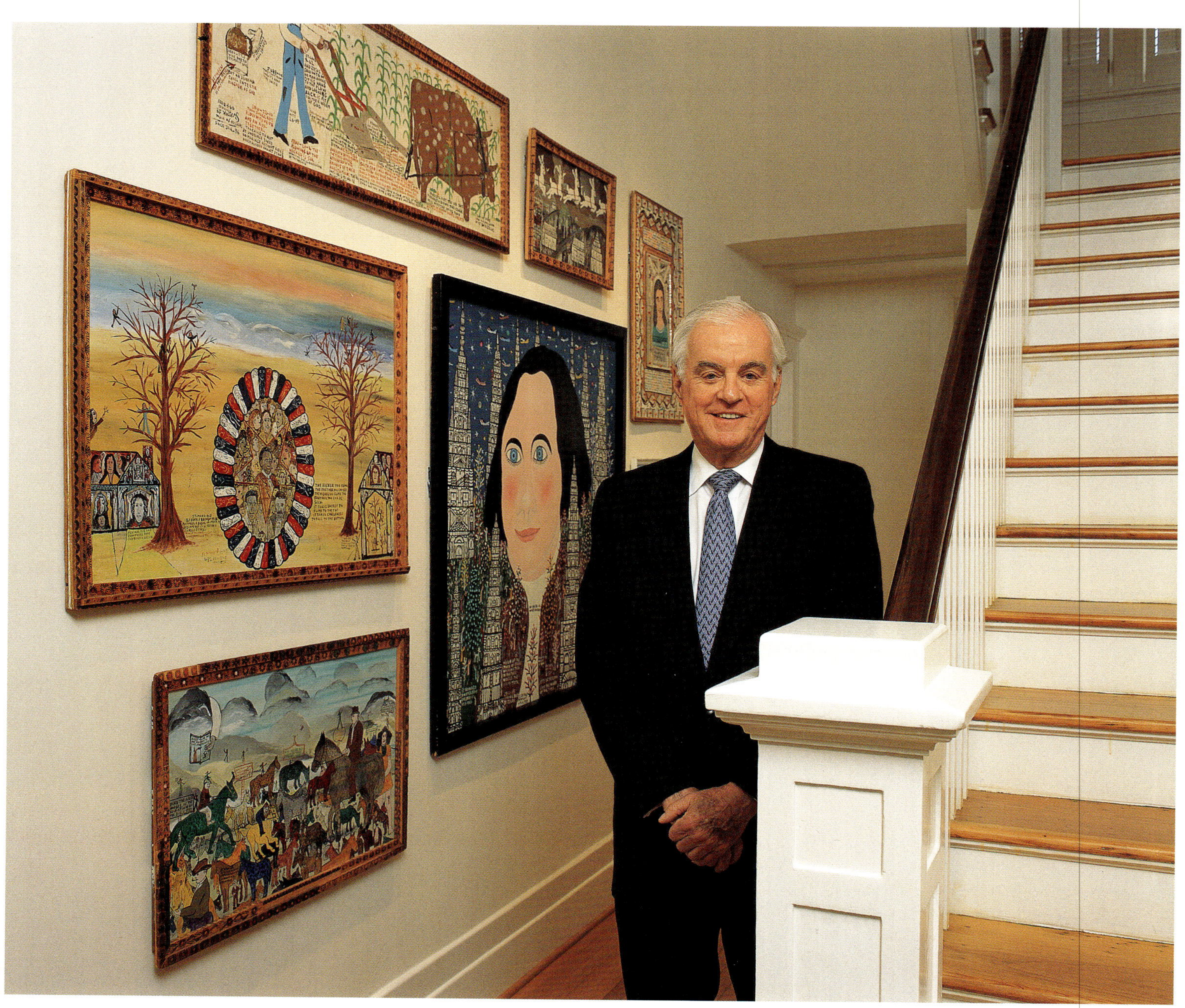

Foreword

T. Marshall Hahn is the first American collector to focus his attention on twentieth-century self-taught art from the American South and to give the majority of his collection to a major fine arts museum. The decision to place this collection in a general art museum rather than a museum devoted solely to folk art follows in the footsteps of Bert Hemphill and Michael and Julie Hall, who housed the majority of their own collections in the Smithsonian American Art Museum and the Milwaukee Art Museum. Thanks to the remarkable generosity and vision of Marshall's gift, the High Museum of Art is now one of the country's most important repositories of contemporary American self-taught art.

Forty years ago Marshall made his first art acquisition, a painting by Streeter Blair purchased from the artist. It is the storytelling that most attracts Marshall to the artists represented here. He knew little about many of these individuals when he first became interested in their works. But as a born-and-raised Southerner, he identified with the artists themselves; as a man who thrives on challenges, he quickly went to work learning about the artists' lives, techniques, and creations. Marshall's curiosity led him to visit Atlanta galleries and the High Museum of Art and to take road trips to meet artists during the 1980s and 1990s. The resulting collection is now permanently housed at the High Museum of Art.

The Hahn Collection recognizes American artists who have worked without formal academic art training or, in many cases, financial reward and critical acclaim. These artists employ common, often recycled materials to produce works prized for their originality. In collecting, researching, preserving, and exhibiting these works, we are called upon to stretch our understanding of art to encompass expressions that are at once fascinating, curious, unconventional, and familiar.

The essays in this catalogue explore Hahn's collecting legacy from three vantage points. Reflections about his personal relationships with the artists and works in his collection are shared in a conversation between Marshall and Lynne E. Spriggs, the High Museum of Art's Curator of Folk Art, who has brought this exhibition to life. Joanne Cubbs, who served as the Museum's first curator of folk art, provides an eloquent discussion of specific works and artists in Hahn's collection. Lynda Roscoe Hartigan, Chief Curator at the Smithsonian American Art Museum, offers a useful overview of some of the most significant moments in the history of the field, enabling us to understand Hahn's place within the larger story of collecting self-taught art in the American South.

The High Museum of Art has been the recipient of many benefits as a result of Marshall Hahn's philanthropic spirit and professional leadership in supporting the arts and education. In the presentation of this exhibition and catalogue, we are also grateful for generous support from Georgia-Pacific Corporation and Sun Trust.

With growing scholarship and increasing public recognition, self-taught art is claiming its place in American art history. Marshall Hahn's gift to the High Museum of Art ensures that this remarkable American legacy will endure for all to enjoy.

Michael E. Shapiro
Nancy and Holcombe T. Green, Jr. Director

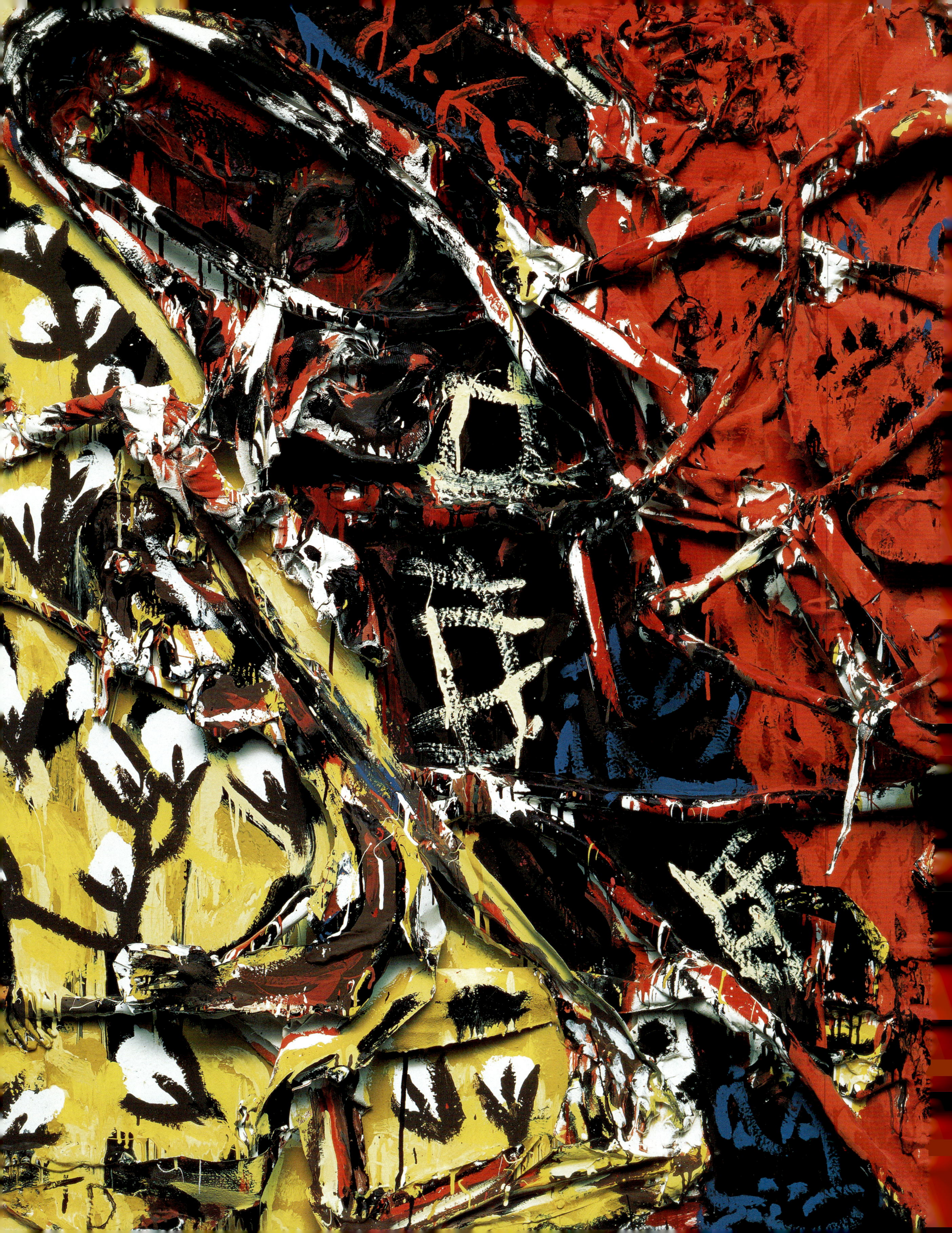

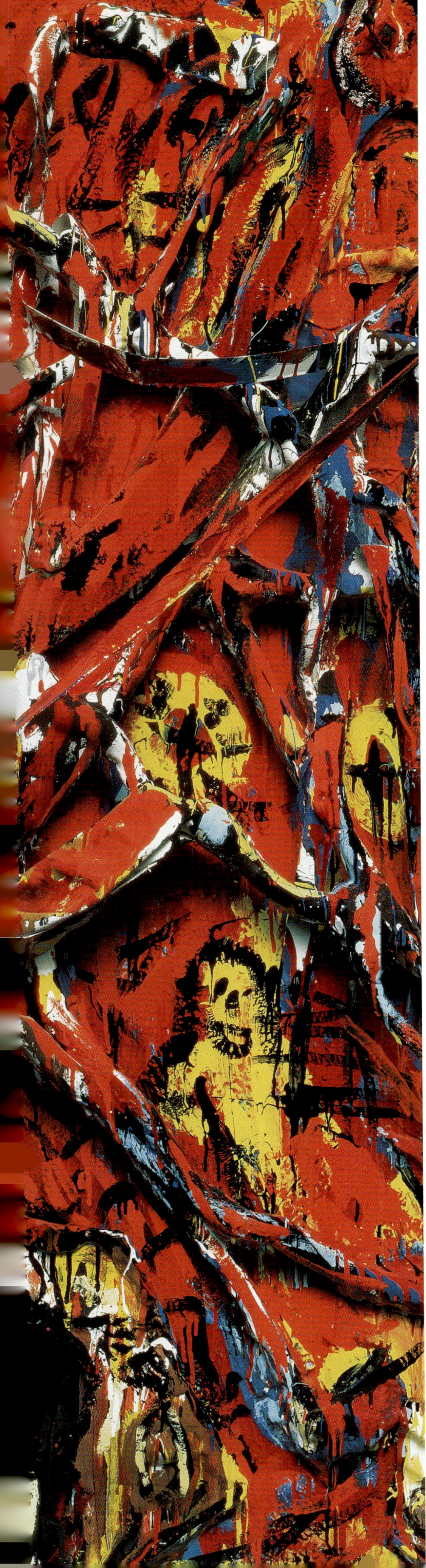

Remembering the Road

T. Marshall Hahn and the High Museum of Art

Lynne E. Spriggs

T. Marshall Hahn Jr. was born in Lexington, Kentucky, on December 2, 1926, the first of three children. He grew up in a home in which education was highly valued and, at the young age of eighteen, graduated from the University of Kentucky with a Bachelor of Science in Physics. Following two years of service with the Navy, Hahn moved to Boston. While there, he married Margaret Lee and received a doctorate in Physics from Massachusetts Institute of Technology in 1950. Hahn returned to the University of Kentucky to teach as Associate Professor and, later, Professor of Physics. Leaving Kentucky to become head of the Physics Department at Virginia Polytechnic Institute and State University (Virginia Tech) in Blacksburg, Virginia, Hahn continued to build a career in academic administration. He served as Dean of the College of Arts and Sciences at Kansas State University before being named President of Virginia Tech at thirty-five years of age. He was the youngest state university president in the country at that time.

In 1975, the Hahn family, which by then included children Betty, Anne, and Bill, moved to Portland, Oregon. A friend who was Chief Executive Officer of the Georgia-Pacific corporation encouraged Hahn to join him. Hahn accepted the offer and advanced rapidly, moving with the company's headquarters to Atlanta, where he became Chief Executive Officer in 1983. Ten years later he retired as Chairman and CEO, serving as Director and Honorary Chairman of the Board until May 1999.

In the spring of 1996, Marshall Hahn announced his intention to donate a substantial portion of his collection of contemporary folk art to the High Museum of Art. This gift became the first major collection of contemporary self-taught art largely from the South to be given to an American museum. The collection highlights works by African American artists whose vernacular expressions revolutionized the field of twentieth-century self-taught art. Today, the Hahn Collection comprises over 140 paintings, works on paper, and sculptures created by more than forty artists, including Ned Cartledge, Thornton Dial, Sam Doyle, Howard Finster, William Hawkins, Mattie Lou O'Kelley, Elijah Pierce, Nellie Mae Rowe, and Bill Traylor, all of whom are represented in depth. The collection also features significant works by Raymond Coins, Henry Darger, Minnie Evans, Lonnie Holley, Sister Gertrude Morgan, John Perates, Martin Ramirez, Herbert Singleton, and Joseph Yoakum.[1]

Thornton Dial, *Heading for the Higher Paying Jobs* (cat. 23, detail)

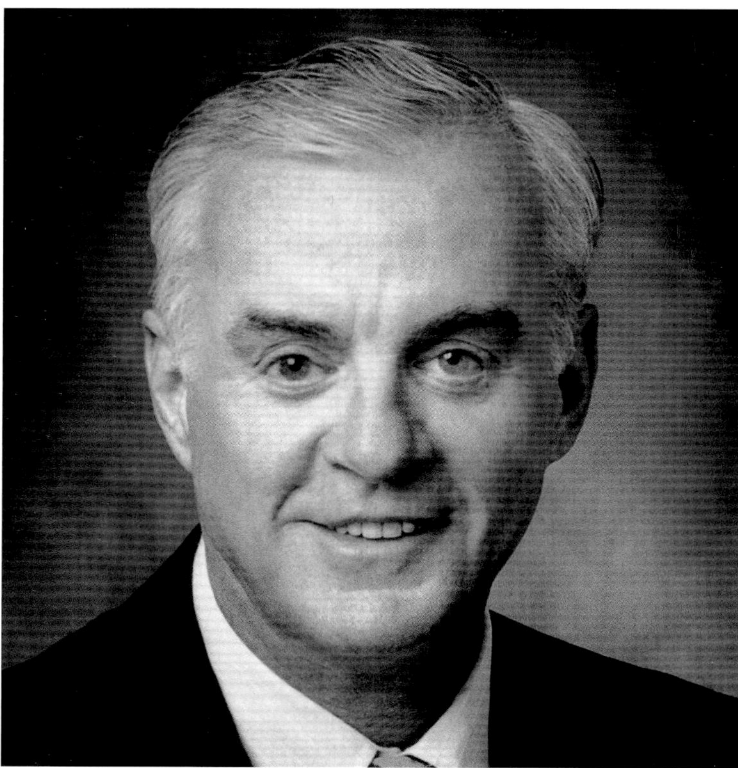

Figure 1. Marshall Hahn, 1986.

Marshall Hahn's gift reflects his ongoing commitment to the High Museum of Art and to the field of self-taught art as a means of public education. A consummate folk art collector, advocate, fund-raiser, and philanthropist, Hahn led the effort to establish the Museum's downtown branch in 1985 and was instrumental in a 1993 decision to devote those galleries to exhibitions of folk art and photography. Thanks to Hahn's uncompromising vision, in 1994 the High became the first (and only) major, general interest fine arts museum in North America to establish a curatorial department devoted to folk art. In 1998, Hahn was elected a lifetime member of the High's board of directors. He now spends the majority of his time on the family's farm in Blacksburg, Virginia, but Hahn's legacy of tireless ambition and generosity lives on in Atlanta. The High Museum of Art continues to present a broad range of exhibitions and educational programming dedicated to folk art and fosters an expanding collection of more than five hundred works of contemporary self-taught art.

An Interview with Marshall Hahn

Lynne Spriggs: You began collecting self-taught art forty years ago, in the early 1960s. What artists were you first interested in, and how did you become aware of their work?

Marshall Hahn: When I was Dean of Arts and Sciences at Kansas State University from 1959 to 1962, I spent time visiting each department, and the School of Art was part of my jurisdiction. They were working with the Hall family of Hallmark Cards, who were acquiring works of self-taught art, particularly memory painters, and using them as a basis for greeting cards. My interest was really sparked when I visited their collection and decided I wanted to buy an original Grandma Moses. The Halls were going to help me find one, but Moses died and the prices soared far beyond what I thought I could afford as an academician.

Shortly after, I was speaking at the University of Kansas in Lawrence one day. I visited a show there of works by Streeter Blair and was really drawn to the work. At that time, Blair was referred to as "Grandpa Moses." The first piece I ever bought was Blair's *Stage Is Coming* (fig. 2) in 1961. This is a painting of Hook House Inn, the first stagecoach stop out of St. Joseph, Missouri. Blair had grown up in Kansas and was very interested in painting the history of the Midwest. He would describe how you could see the stage as it was crossing the prairie, when the sun was low on the horizon. The inn owners would see the stage coming and start getting dinner ready. Blair painted the scene so you can see what each of the family members is doing to help with the dinner preparations. In all, I purchased twelve to fifteen of Blair's paintings from Blair himself or from Ross Peacock in New York for anywhere from $500 up to $7,500. During that period, his works really experienced a surge of popularity. Vincent Price initiated and curated his Sears, Roebuck & Co. exhibition of the Vincent Price Collection of Fine Art. I believe the show was called *Art for the People*, and it traveled across the country. This show drove prices up to $5,000 to $10,000, and Blairs were selling for the same price as Salvador Dalis traveling in the same show. For a while he was very popular.[2]

Spriggs: You got to know Streeter Blair and established a friendship over the years?

Hahn: Yes, Streeter was a charming guy. From Kansas, my wife and I moved to Blacksburg, Virginia, where I served for thirteen years as president of Virginia Polytechnic Institute and State University. While I was at Virginia Tech, I invited several interesting people in as part of a visiting scholars program—people who would have a broad appeal—to address both students and faculty. Streeter Blair came and spoke as part of this program and stayed with us in our home. He was a former high school principal and advertising executive—so he knew how to tell a good story—and when he spoke to students, they loved it. He came with a whole slide show of his paintings that he had photographed at various stages, so he could sequentially demonstrate his process. He said he didn't know how to paint a wagon load of watermelons without painting the wagon first, placing all the boards in to construct the bottom of the wagon, and then gradually piling watermelons in, and that was the way he painted it—a very practical approach! He also knew how to bake bread—a great houseguest. He would get up in the morning—early, before anyone was up—go down to the kitchen, make himself at home, and start baking bread before he went to his class.

I invited others to come as visiting scholars during those years, including David Brinkley and Vincent Price. Vincent stayed with us for three to four days. He was also a charming fellow who was in love with self-taught art, particularly memory painting. He wasn't just a monster character actor. So many people didn't recognize his interest and expertise in art, and I was aware of it only because he and I were the two biggest Streeter Blair collectors. He admired Blair's storytelling talents.

Spriggs: Price seems to have been particularly interested in the relationship between collecting and educating.

Hahn: That was his thrust when I had him as a visiting scholar. That was what interested me. He was very much concerned that more people ought to appreciate art. I liked Vincent Price immensely, and I'm sure that his sensibility had some influence on me.

Spriggs: Most of the works you gave to the High are by Southern artists, and your family roots are here in the South.

Hahn: That's right. I was born in Lexington, Kentucky. At that time, my father was a physics professor at the University of Kentucky, where my mother had also gone to school. I grew up in Lexington and graduated from the same university before leaving for the Navy.

Spriggs: At what point did your collecting interests begin to focus on visionary and self-taught artists of the Southeast?

Hahn: My perspective of the field and my interests have definitely changed over the years. When I first started out, my primary interest was memory painters. I started with Blair because it was an opportunity, an exciting first encounter with art. He was creating paintings about his memories of growing up in Kansas, where I was living at the time. He also did historically based paintings of places like Kentucky and Virginia. When I came to Atlanta in 1982, it became very clear to me that the Southeast was important as a source of fine self-taught art. I saw self-taught paintings at the High and then began going to local galleries—Modern Primitive, David Knoke, Rick Berman. I would ask about an artist and learn that they worked in Alabama, Georgia, Louisiana. Then when I was in New Orleans, for instance, I would go to the galleries there. I'd visit Barrister's Gallery and Gilley's or Gasperi's. That's where I got the Herbert Singleton carved door (cat. 70) and work by David Butler. There was Jay Johnson's gallery and the Outsider Art Fair in New York. Pretty soon after arriving in Atlanta, I began to travel all over, went to galleries, and then I started visiting the artists.

I suppose the next self-taught artist I had a lot of contact with after Streeter was Georgia artist Mattie Lou O'Kelley, another memory painter (figs. 3–5). I also got more and more interested in other Southern self-taught artists like Thornton Dial, Lonnie Holley, Bill Traylor, Elijah Pierce, and also William Hawkins.

Spriggs: The High has a special history with Mattie Lou O'Kelley. In 1975, director Gudmund Vigtel bought a still life by her when she was still unknown, and that became the Museum's first work by a contemporary self-taught artist. She later donated a painting of her parents' farm in north Georgia. You gave the Museum some tremendous examples of her work—tell me about O'Kelley.

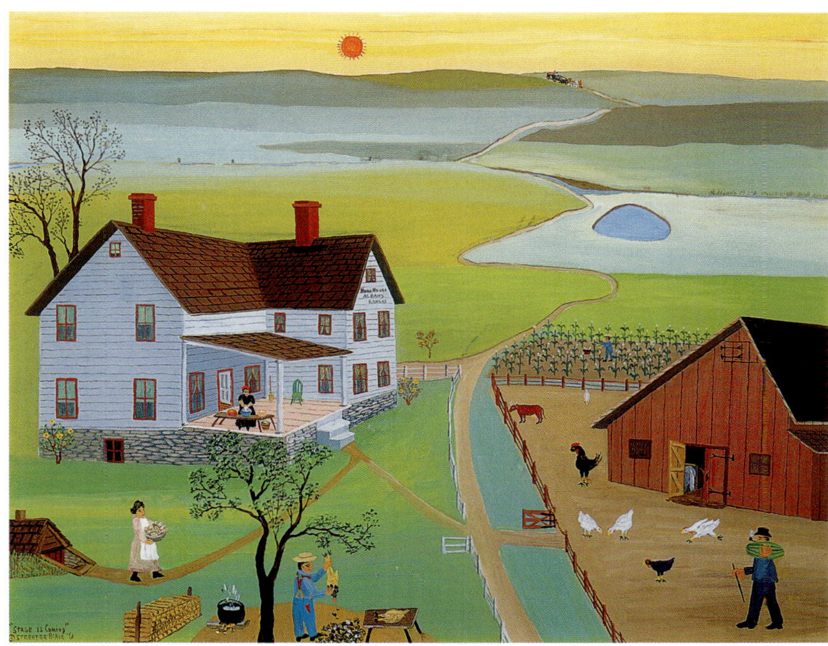

Figure 2. Streeter Blair, *Stage Is Coming*, 1961, oil on canvas, 19¾ x 25¾ inches, collection of T. Marshall Hahn.

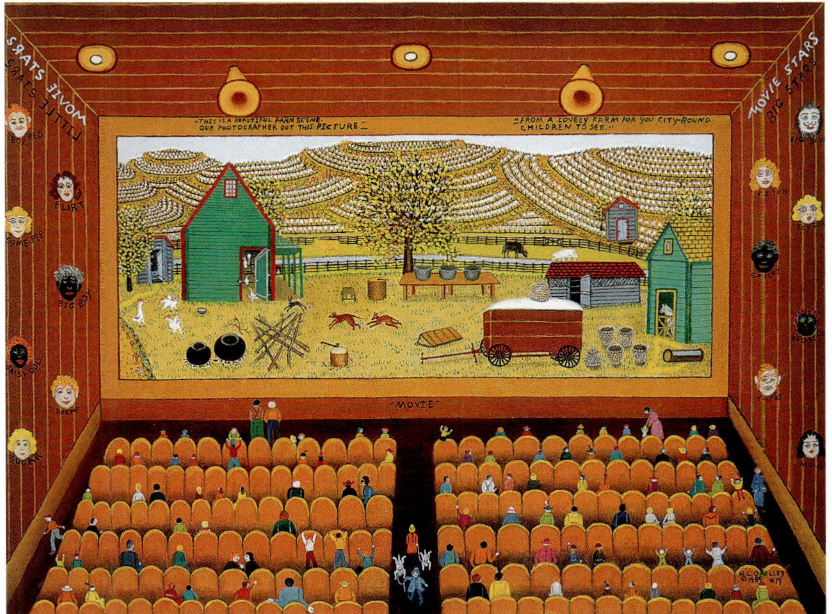

Figure 3. Mattie Lou O'Kelley, *Movie*, 1989, oil on canvas, 24⅛ x 31½ inches, collection of T. Marshall Hahn.

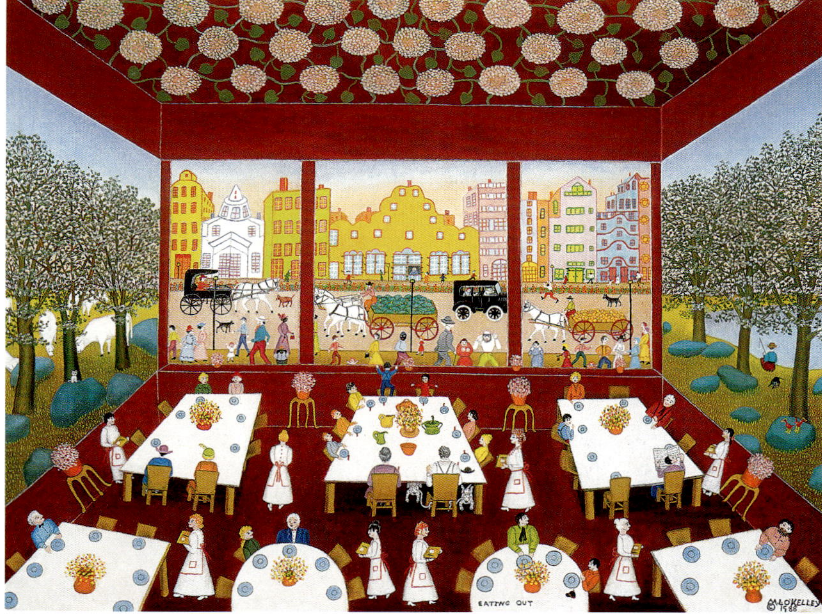

Figure 4. Mattie Lou O'Kelley, *Eating Out*, 1988, oil on canvas, 23¾ x 32⅛ inches, collection of T. Marshall Hahn.

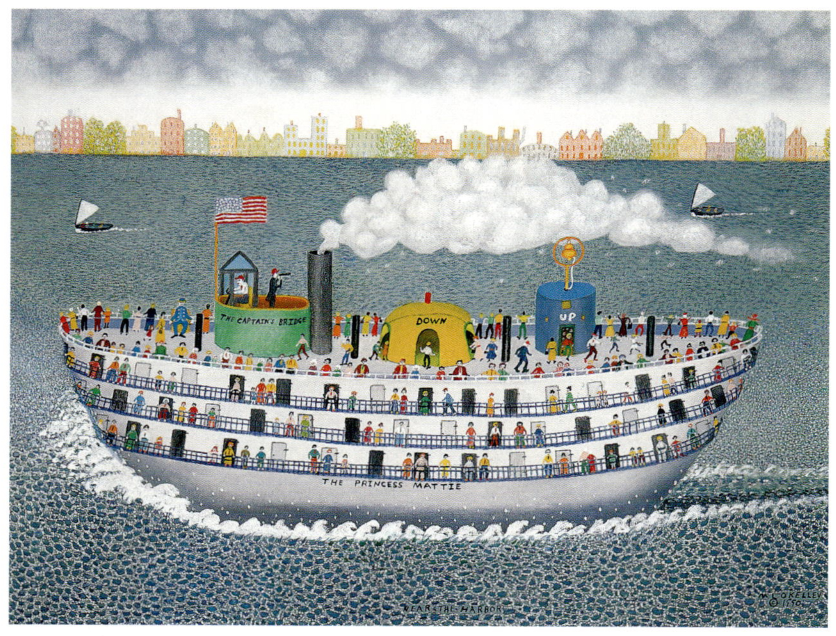

Figure 5. Mattie Lou O'Kelley, *Near the Harbor*, 1990, oil on canvas, 23½ x 31¼ inches, collection of T. Marshall Hahn.

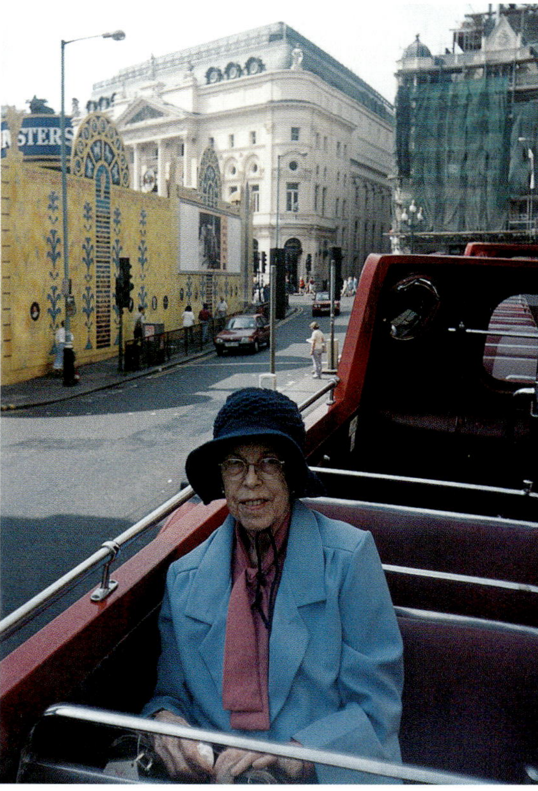

Figure 6. Mattie Lou O'Kelley in London, ca. 1990.

Hahn: Mattie was different. A wonderful person. I think I was one of the few people who could really get along with her. When I saw two of her pieces at the High, I decided I wanted some. So I went to dealers and kept inquiring, and everyone who had a Mattie Lou was hanging on to it. And that still seems to be largely the case. There's just never been a lot of liquidity in the market for her works, which is how I got to meet her in the beginning. I couldn't find any to buy, so I finally tracked her down myself.

When I went to see her, she had painted two of the works for her book *Moving to Town*, was painting the third, and wouldn't sell any of them to me unless I bought all twenty-four, including the twenty-one that hadn't even been done yet. That's how I ended up with all the images from that book. Later, I mentioned that I'd like to have a portrait of her, and she did a self-portrait (cat. 61)—wearing a cameo I gave her—which the High now owns. Many of the works I got from her date from 1987 to 1990.

Spriggs: I know you still own a very large commissioned painting O'Kelley did of your Virginia farm.

Hahn: I took her up there. She got out in front of the house. We set up a card table for her. She put on a little sunbonnet. She took my photograph [of the farm], laid her sketching pad along with her canvas out flat on the card table, then started to draw, sketching out all the forms. What she liked to do first was a pencil drawing, and then she'd go to the canvas and do the sketch on the canvas, still looking at the subject, but referring to her pencil sketch, too. Then she would paint it. Flat. She didn't use an easel.

This was her process, and I saw her do it a number of times: she would visualize a painting and sketch it in pencil on transparent paper. Sometimes she would write a verse on the back of these preliminary drawings, something approximating the text she wrote for the book. Mattie gave me a box of drawings that I gave the High. She was going to throw them out.

Spriggs: What was it that attracted you to some of the other artists and works you began to collect?

Hahn: My decision to continue collecting self-taught art was partly opportunistic, in that I was from the South and living in the South, and this region is such a fount of so many great self-taught artists. There were so many people in this part of the country who were relatively cut off from the rest of the country for so long. These people didn't have a lot of others around telling them they couldn't paint. They were just trying to tell a story that was burning to get out. So there's real passion in the art, and I love that.

But with an attraction to carving, you're certainly not going to miss Elijah Pierce; it isn't going to matter whether he's a Yankee or a Southerner. At the same time, if you like works that are raw, flat, and bold, you're not going to miss William Hawkins. Mattie had a bold, outspoken personality on canvas and in person. Although I didn't meet him, Hawkins was the same way. That's one of the things I like about so many of these artists—they're enthusiastically unconventional. They're uninhibited and free to express themselves, and they do it in a bold manner. I think this work encourages new ways of doing things and looking at things without treading on anyone. No one has to look at it. But it's great that it's often so vibrant and direct; it almost forces you to deal with it.

Spriggs: That sense of boldness you admire comes through in colors, forms, compositions, even in the articulation of details.

Hahn: When people would come to see O'Kelley and want to buy one of her paintings, they would say, "And we particularly want one that has a lot of *things* in it." She said she liked to put a lot of things in, meaning a profusion of detail. I've always been attracted to impressive details and intricate drawing.

Spriggs: Someone like William Adkins also displays an appreciation of detail work, but he is calling on a very different kind of sensibility. His works seem to be more about invention than memory.

Hahn: Sort of a cross between Leonardo da Vinci and Dwight Mackintosh. I liked them [Adkins's works], maybe because of my engineering background. They just appealed to me.

Spriggs: He seems fascinated with the structure of things and how they fit together. I suppose the same could be said for other artists in your collection, from someone like Lonnie Holley or Streeter Blair to Mattie Lou O'Kelley.

Hahn: That's right. O'Kelley was uneducated, but she really understood things. Take her painting *Near the Harbor* (fig. 5). She was disappointed when she finally took a trip on the Queen Elizabeth II

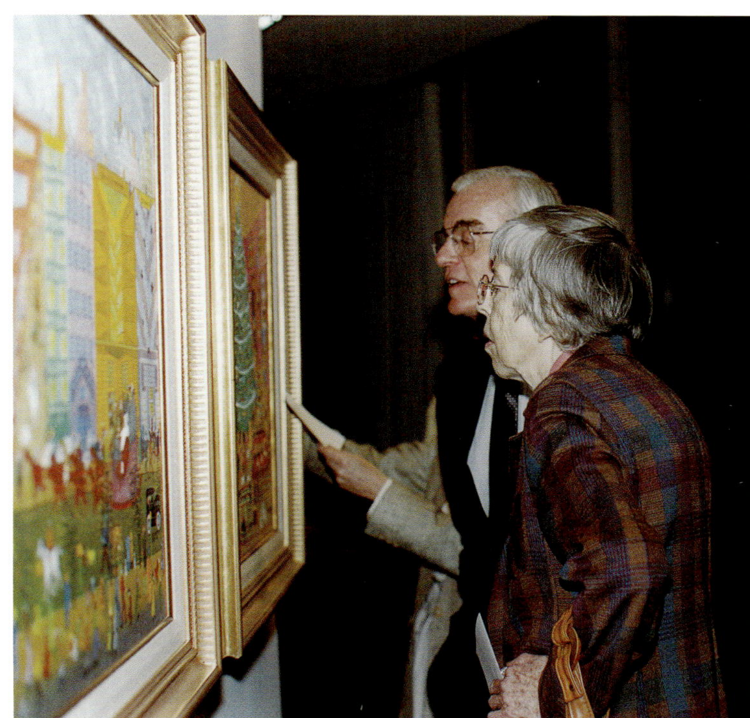

Figure 7. Marshall Hahn and Mattie Lou O'Kelley, ca. 1987.

because the ship's layout wasn't consistent with her mental picture of how it would be. So when she returned home, she went ahead and designed the ship her way, and painted it as she thought it should be. With a sixth grade education, she reengineered it in her own imagination. *Moving to Town* was entirely a product of her memory, but it also included fantasy—remembering things as she thought they ought to be.

Spriggs: That ability to imagine something in the mind's eye is a powerful thing. She really used her imagination when it came to color, too.

Hahn: O'Kelley was one of the very best colorists, really creative. I'd kid her and say, "I never saw a purple tree, or a purple mountain." And she'd say, "No, but look how pretty it is. Maybe there should be purple trees." She liked purple and was going to have purple trees if she wanted to. She was a character and a great lady. Her paintings were so vibrant and animated; her passion was definitely in her art. She was pretty much a recluse, but she took great joy in seeing her work displayed. If you could get her in front of a painting, that was one of the few times she would become very willing to talk. She would really light up and tell you all about it—why she painted it the way she did.

Spriggs: It was in large measure thanks to your close friendship with O'Kelley that she was also able to leave a financial legacy to the High. How did that happen?

Hahn: Mattie Lou and I became good friends over the years and as she became frailer I looked after her. She had no close friends. She was constantly worried about her finances. She'd obviously been

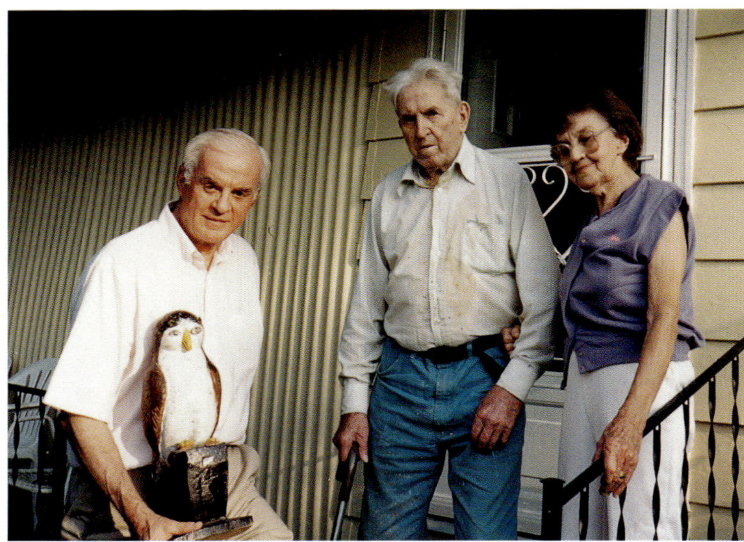

Figure 8. Marshall Hahn and Mr. and Mrs. S. L. Jones, ca. 1996.

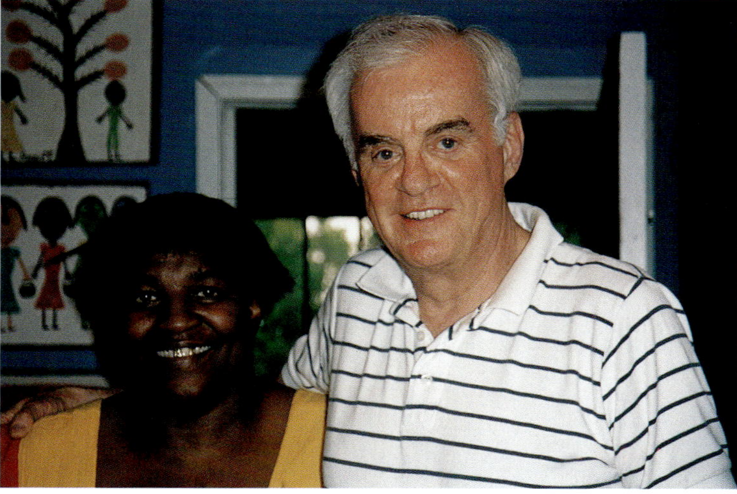

Figure 9. Annie Tolliver and Marshall Hahn, ca. 1996.

exploited by people, and it took a while for her to learn she could trust me. For a while, each time she would finish three paintings she would call and say to me, "Well, I've got three more ready, bring me a cashier's check." And she finally got to the point where she would let me write her a personal check. Even when I first went to see her it took a number of calls—and she called two or three people, to see if I wouldn't try and beat her out of something.

But we became good friends, and I worried about her declining ability to handle her finances. I arranged to set up a trust fund for her own benefit. The bank would do two things: pay her bills and manage her money. The market was very strong at that time and, eventually, her estate became substantial. She had helped her nieces and nephews to the point that she didn't want to do that any more, and she wanted to provide for her mother's grave. Then she got it in her head that she was going to leave her estate to me. I said I didn't want that to happen. She could be a very stubborn lady, and she would say, "Well, I'm going to do it anyway. You can give it to whomever you want." I told her I would give it away, and that was not a tax-effective way to do it. She would say, "Well, who would you give it to?" And I'd say, "Well, you're interested in self-taught art, I'm interested in self-taught art. I would give it to, say, the High Museum." And she would say, "Well, what about the Museum of American Folk Art?" I'd say, "Well, that's fine, too. Maybe give it half and half." So finally we worked it out that she wouldn't leave it to me, she would leave it to the two of them. What ended up happening for Mattie Lou was a fortuitous set of circumstances that worked out well for everybody.

Spriggs: Your purchases over the years involved personal visits with other artists in their homes. Tell me about the carved owl (cat. 51) you bought from S. L. Jones.

Hahn: He did that piece as a gift to his wife about ten years ago. He was a wonderful man. A few years ago, I saw his name on a rural mailbox. I just stopped and asked if I could visit him, and I saw the owl. I was trying to get carvings, and his little living room was just covered with drawings, all of which I bought. I said, "What about the owl?" And he said, "That's not mine, it's my wife's. I gave that to her, did that for her, so you'd have to ask her." She told me, "Well, no, I wouldn't want to sell it. I look at it every day." I said, "Suppose I bought it and had a really good, big color photograph made and framed and sent that to you and paid you for the owl?" Mrs. Jones jumped right on that, "Oh, well, I'd like that."

Spriggs: What other artists did you come to know?

Hahn: I'd spend time with Ned Cartledge. He's a wonderful guy. I got to know Ned well. We'd go to lunch together, dinner, and became good friends. Many times when I'd visit their house, Amy, his wife, fixed dinner for us. She was a wonderful cook, and Ned raised the vegetables in their garden. During those visits, I'd admire pieces on the wall that were not for sale. Ned would say those were his personal collection, the pieces he liked and kept. But then Amy had a very disabling stroke, and she was hospitalized until her death. One day Ned called me up and said that because of her condition and some of the requirements of Medicaid, he needed to sell his personal collection. He asked if I would buy the entire collection and named a price. I gave him twice what he asked.

I met Mose Tolliver and Annie Tolliver. I knew Leroy Almon and went to see him frequently. He was a good friend. I remember meeting Bessie Harvey just before she died. She was just great—warm and charming. She was frail at that point, though. Her health was poor. I remember her telling me, "People don't understand my art. They'll send me a root and say, 'Make me something.' It doesn't work that way. I see a root in the woods, and I either see there's something there, or I don't. You can't just send me a piece of root and say, 'Make something.' "

I liked being able to read the art, and the ability to talk to the artist about what he or she was trying to say really enhanced that sense. *Heading for the Higher Paying Jobs* (cat. 23), for instance, is an easy painting to read and understand. But that understanding was certainly enhanced a lot—and was one reason I bought it—visiting with Bill Arnett and having Thornton Dial explain it to me in his own words. Lonnie Holley's descriptions of his work—very articulate, passionate descriptions—add another dimension to that work. And the more time you would spend with Lonnie listening to him talk, the greater your ability to read his work and to understand it, whether he was talking to you or to a classroom full of kids. You can begin to understand something about what makes him tick, his life philosophies and experiences.

Spriggs: Have you spent much time with Lonnie Holley?

Hahn: I went to see Lonnie once on my own and took about a thousand of his children and him to lunch somewhere—as many as a big car would hold. Just beautiful children. His life is his art and his children. I understand why he had such a hard time relocating.[3] I think Lonnie recognized his environment as one piece of art, a total environment. It was a part of his home and his life. So when he had to relocate, he didn't see it as simply moving singular pieces of art. I like Lonnie. He's very much a showman. Put him in a room with a piece of his art and the work will have a bigger impact when he is there to talk about it and interact with it.

Thornton, on the other hand, is a very quiet, dignified, low-key man—but with a lot of presence. An impressive man. I also really like Ronald Lockett's works. I had about fifteen at one point. His work was quiet, gentle, serious—very much like he was.

Spriggs: I know you have a personal connection with Howard Finster.

Hahn: Finster and I have the same birthday. He's eleven years older. He did a birthday present for me a couple of times. He is an institution, an icon. Howard's a minister, and his art is his gospel, his pulpit—at least it started out that way.

Spriggs: Didn't you commission a piece by Finster?

Hahn: Yes. Doug Ivester, who was the chairman of Coca-Cola, and I and the other board members of Coca-Cola Enterprises were off on a tour. I saw one of those soft drink coolers shaped like a Coke bottle. It was about six feet tall. I said "Wouldn't that be great painted by Howard Finster?" and Doug said, "Yes. I'll send you one." He did, he gave it to me. It was just clear plastic. We worked with Howard's daughter, Beverly, and she agreed that he would paint it. So he painted it for me on the bottle given to me by Coca-Cola Enterprises (cat. 38).

Of the pieces I had, I always liked *In My Father's House Are Many Mansions* (cat. 36). I'm sorry I didn't go down early on and get more of those wonderful boxes. There was another piece [*Take My Yoke Upon You and Learn of Me Saith Jesus* (cat. 35)] I gave to the Museum that I know was hanging outside. It fits in with what the Museum already had from Paradise Garden.

Spriggs: That piece is a wonderful example of Finster's early paintings from the Garden. Before you decided to give your collection,

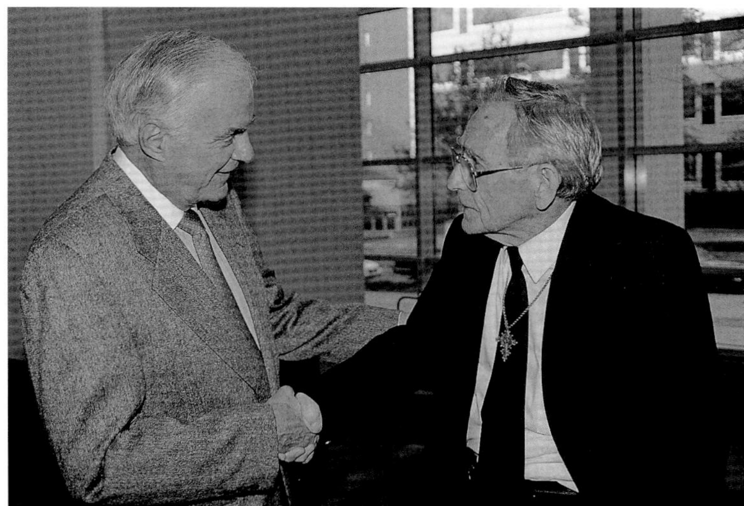

Figure 10. Marshall Hahn and Howard Finster, ca. 1996.

you played a central role in helping to establish what eventually became the Museum's Folk Art and Photography Galleries. How did that idea come about?

Hahn: The gallery space in the Georgia-Pacific building now occupied by the High was originally designed with the idea that it would become an industrial museum to display the history of Georgia-Pacific and its mills. When I became CEO of G-P in 1983, that space still had not been developed, and I thought we had a real opportunity. Here was the Southeast, a region so rich in self-taught art. We were in a major Southern metropolis with the best access to all that material, and not much was being done about it. So I jumped on it and started trying to do a few things. I felt certain there would be more broad-based interest in a downtown art museum featuring self-taught art than in an industrial museum.

I talked with Michael Lomax, then chairman of the Fulton County Board of Commissioners, and Gudmund Vigtel, the High's director, and we put the pieces together. That was in 1985. Metropolitan Life, which owns the building with Georgia-Pacific, also agreed. It was exciting because this was truly a cooperative three-way partnership between major corporations, a major museum, and a major governmental body.

Once the branch was open and operating, the High showed all sorts of art down there, but the most popular and well-attended show was one featuring the works of self-taught artists, *Outside the Main Stream*, which Barbara Archer organized in 1988. There were whirligigs placed outside in green spaces, which helped draw people in. It created a level of enthusiasm that was really impressive. I started talking to the Museum's new director, Ned Rifkin, about making the G-P satellite into the self-taught art focal point of the High. I was actively collecting and had Ned over to the house for a series of dinners with other local folk art collectors. I introduced him to some of the art and tried to sell the whole idea. Apparently, people interested in photography were making similar proposals, so

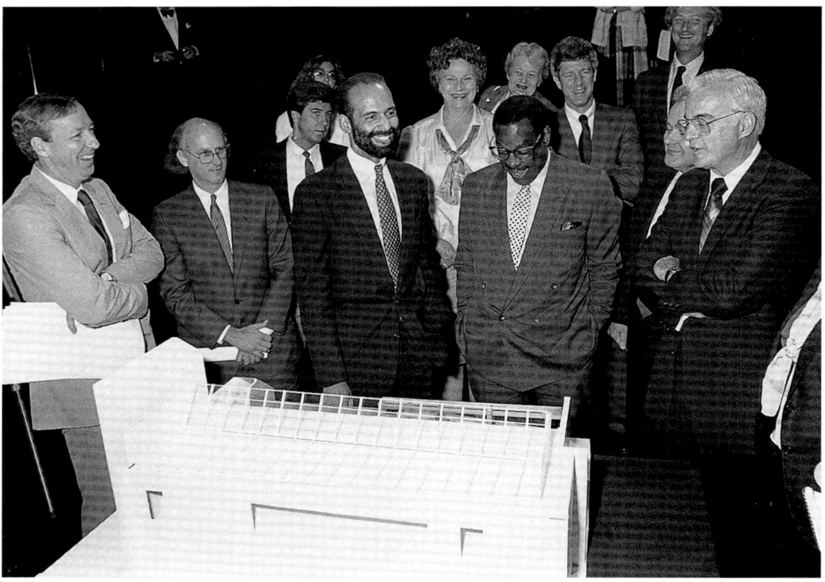

Figure 11. From left: Kermit Birchfield, Senior Vice President, Law Department, Georgia-Pacific; architect Mack Scoggin; Michael Lomax, chairman of the Fulton County Board of Commissioners; Marvin Arrington, president of the Atlanta City Council; Gudmund Vigtel, director of the High Museum of Art; and Marshall Hahn with a model of the High Museum of Art's downtown galleries, June 1985.

we eventually compromised and designated the space to be the folk art and photography galleries of the High in 1993.

Spriggs: That was the same year you helped the Museum add sixty works by Southern self-taught artists from collector and artist Andy Nasisse to the permanent collection.

Hahn: That collection was particularly strong in artists like Bessie Harvey, J. B. Murry, and Dilmus Hall, and his pieces gave the High a good early group of important material.

Spriggs: And one year later, you helped the High become the first general fine arts museum in the country to establish a folk art department.

Hahn: As Ned and the Museum focused more on self-taught art, I went to one of the local foundations and proposed that they make a grant to fund a full-time curator, which was done. Joanne Cubbs arrived that year, and we worked a lot together. I'd sold the home where I had previously displayed my personal collection and thought the best place for the major part of the collection would be the High, so more people could enjoy it. I also helped the Museum gain funding from Norfolk Southern for acquisitions, so the folk art collection could continue to grow.

Spriggs: As CEO of a major corporation, you set a tremendous model for supporting the arts.

Hahn: I think corporations play an important role in contributing to the quality of life in any city. G-P is an example of a major corporation that moved its headquarters to Atlanta. We moved because, among other things, the quality of life was important in attracting and retaining top people. That included educational opportunities and the whole range of cultural opportunities: the symphony and, obviously, the High. You can be penny-wise and pound-foolish if you cut funding for the arts, causing a significant impact on the quality of life and perhaps adversely affecting a corporation's decision to move here or stay here. The city has been good to us, and I've encouraged executives and managers to put something back into the city. I think all corporations and the people who manage those corporations tend to have the resources to contribute personally, and it makes a lot of sense to focus on those areas about which you're passionate. The way I saw it, the High had a golden opportunity. Given the locale and given where so much of the art originated, I thought the High should be a world center of self-taught art, so I did what I could to encourage them in that direction.

Spriggs: The gift of your personal collection to the Museum certainly boosted momentum in that direction! In 1981, one year before your arrival in Atlanta, the High staged its first exhibition of works by a self-taught artist, Carlton Garrett from Georgia. The next year, Peter Morrin [then curator of twentieth-century art] bought thirty works by Bill Traylor for the collection. You came to own some extraordinary Traylors yourself.

Hahn: Like so many other collectors, I regret not having bought more Traylors early on. But two of the ones I gave you—the elephant with the brown ear (cat. 80) and the black and brown dogs fighting (cat. 79)—are really significant additions to an already world-class Traylor collection.

Spriggs: In addition to the High, pieces from your collection were given to two other institutions.

Hahn: Yes. I had worked with the Museum of American Folk Art, and I had always had an interest in Colonial Williamsburg. We decided to give a small number of pieces from the collection to those two museums: eleven to the Abby Aldrich Rockefeller Folk Art Museum and eight to the Museum of American Folk Art in New York. The High got everything else except what we kept in the family.

Spriggs: You decided to hold on to a few favorite paintings by Howard Finster, Mattie Lou O'Kelley, Grandma Moses, and Streeter Blair. You still love works by memory painters.

Hahn: Well, I think that even though I moved beyond memory painters to become interested in other artists, I'm still most attracted to works that have impressive detail, intriguing colors, and tell a story—so they resonate with memories.

Spriggs: Was there much art in your home when you were growing up?

Hahn: There were three large portraits of my great-great-great-grandmother and my great-great-grandmother and grandfather done by Kentucky itinerant painters. I still have those. They're in our home in Virginia. That's about it for art. There were a lot of books in the house. I remember my father reading to my brother and me from H. G. Wells when we were really little. I also remember loving Frank Baum's Oz books. Even when we were poor, my parents made sure that I always got an Oz book for my birthday and for Christmas. That was a series of twenty-five volumes, and I had them all.

Spriggs: That story had enormous appeal for so many. The contrast between the fantasy of Oz and life in Kansas captured the imagination of Henry Darger, too. I believe his personal library contained first editions of all the Oz series, and I know there are references to characters from those books in his story *The Realms of the Unreal* (see cat. 19). He's an artist you collected whose works combine real and imagined worlds.

Hahn: All of his images were created as illustrations for an elaborate story he wanted to convey. That's really what draws me to any work of art: I've always enjoyed good stories.

During my years at MIT, apart from the unparalleled opportunity to learn from great scientists and Nobel Prize winners, I remember listening to Robert Frost, who was a poet-in-residence while I was there. On many Thursday afternoons he would talk about his work in one of the auditorium-type classrooms. I would go no matter how busy I was or where I was in my studies. You talk about drawing a picture, "red as a child's mittens," "soft as a colt's nose," now that's painting. I was in love with his work. He'd talk and tell stories. Maybe that resonated and reinforced something and made me more susceptible to the storytelling of folk artists. He used those crisp little verses to re-create certain memories. He painted pictures with his words.

Notes

Conversations and interviews were conducted with Marshall Hahn in Atlanta, Georgia, on March 3, May 20, July 1, August 5, and November 12, 1998, and March 9, April 14, and October 18, 1999. Tape recordings and transcriptions, High Museum of Art, curatorial files.

The title of this essay comes from a 1992 work by Thornton Dial, illustrated in Baraka et al. 1993, p. 155.

1. As stipulated by Hahn, proceeds from the sale of works not added to the High's permanent collection are used to purchase new works, as are his ongoing gifts. Recent additions to the T. Marshall Hahn Collection include works by Martin Ramirez, Joseph Yoakum, John Perates, Sister Gertrude Morgan, and Elijah Pierce.

2. As early as the 1940s, stage, film, and radio actor Vincent Price was acknowledged as a dedicated art collector. Committed to educating the public he published and lectured across the country on what he termed "the battle of bringing art to people in their daily lives." "Vincent Price on Art," *The Vincent Price Gallery Official Website*, http://members.aol.com/vpgallery/Art.html (23 November 1998).

Beginning in 1962, Price became active in an unusual program sponsored by Sears, Roebuck & Co. to make art accessible to the general public and readily available at reasonable prices throughout the country. Price bought over fifty-five thousand works of art for Sears to sell throughout the 1960s. In all eleven Sears stores, the Vincent Price Collection of Fine Art experienced great success, along with a dozen different exhibits that toured Sears stores and other venues, including schools and universities. See Parish and Whitney 1974.

3. For five years, Lonnie Holley and his family fought an expansion of the Birmingham airport that caused them to leave their home and abandon Holley's one-acre sculpture environment in 1998.

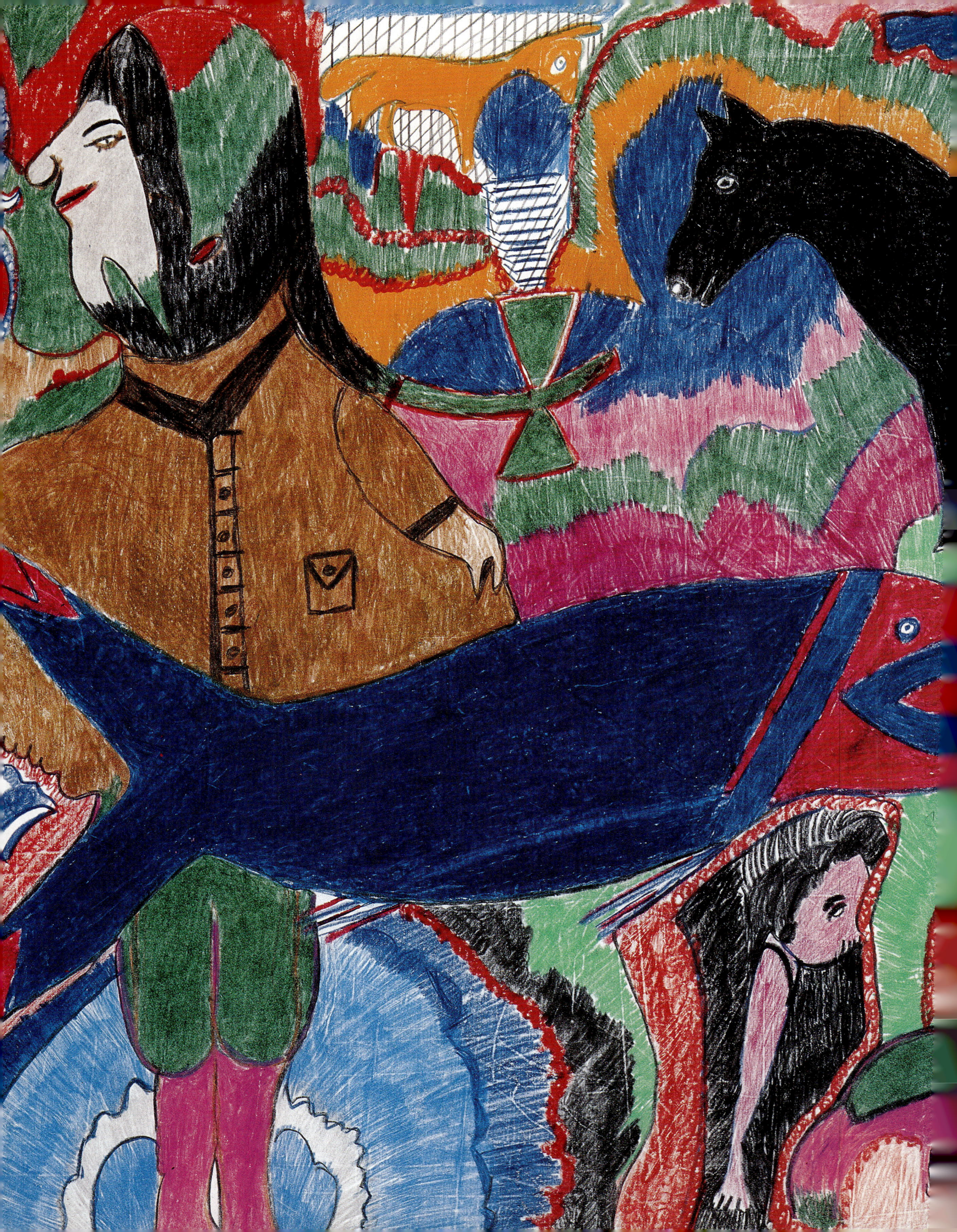

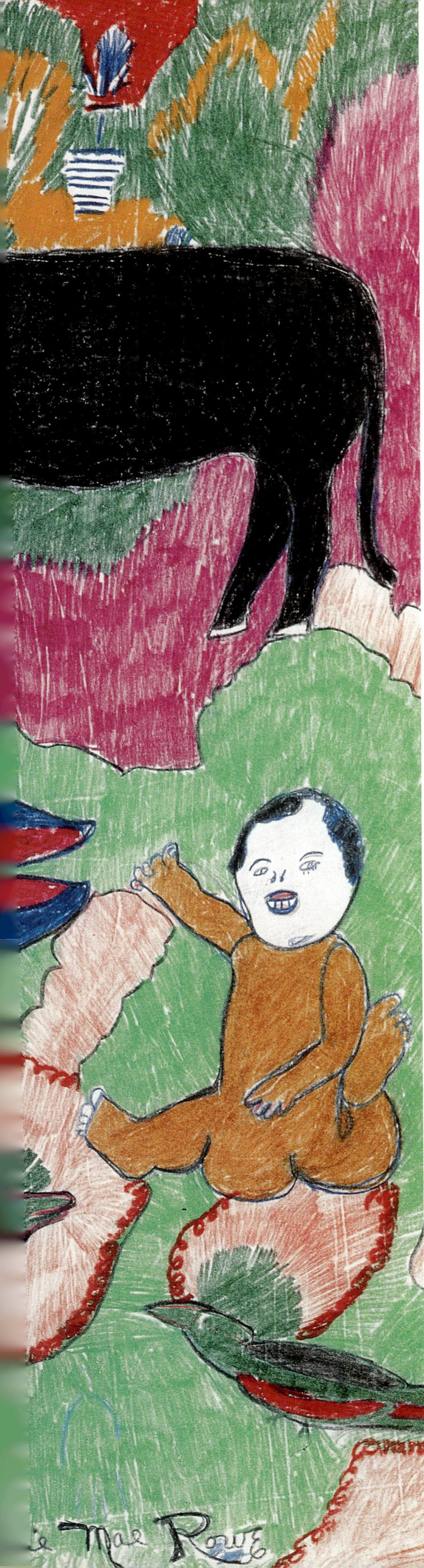

New Geography

Mapping Meaning in Self-Taught Art from the South

Joanne Cubbs

For a long time, most self-taught artists from the South were known only to a few individuals, and, with few exceptions, their works remained absent from the official chartings of twentieth-century art and culture. But during the last two decades, much of this has begun to change. A historic flurry of exhibitions, touring extravaganzas, publications, collecting, marketing, and critical acclaim has brought increasing recognition to Southern self-taught art and, more particularly, to the vernacular expressions of those African American artists who continue to be such a significant part of the phenomenon.

Now, in the midst of this long-awaited approbation, there is much to be done in mapping meaning within the works of these artists and in tracing the critical relationships between their personal creative worlds and the larger universe of cultural forms and ideas. This essay ponders the aesthetic practices and conceptual concerns of major makers within this newly acknowledged territory of the American visual imagination.

"I Paint What I See": The Rhetoric of the Everyday

The most fundamental source of inspiration for artists has always been the everyday visual world—the familiar universe of objects, characters, and events that compose daily existence. Within this discourse on the ordinary, some individuals have the ability to turn the mundane into the marvelous, to shape a distinctive aesthetic vision from the commonplace, or to imbue the simplest subject matter with significance. In the South, Charley Kinney's renderings of deer, hoot owls, haunted houses, tornadoes, and bear attacks capture the ethos of Appalachian mountain life. Using mud for paint, Jimmy Lee Sudduth has created surprisingly expressive works from a repertory of such prosaic subjects as cowboys, city buildings, dancing girls, cows, and his beloved dog Toto. Mose Tolliver continues to paint everything from turtles, birds, lizards, and his house dog Spot to women riding scooters and his own self-portrait, transforming nearly all that he has seen or experienced into a vast body of surreal imaginings and erotic fantasies. Embellishing his small home in an otherwise undistinguished Louisiana neighborhood, David Butler once turned an elementary iconography of tin-snipped and polka-dotted stars, roosters, bicycles, trains, and alligators into a magnificent yard art spectacle.

Nellie Mae Rowe, *Red and Blue Fish* (cat. 66, detail)

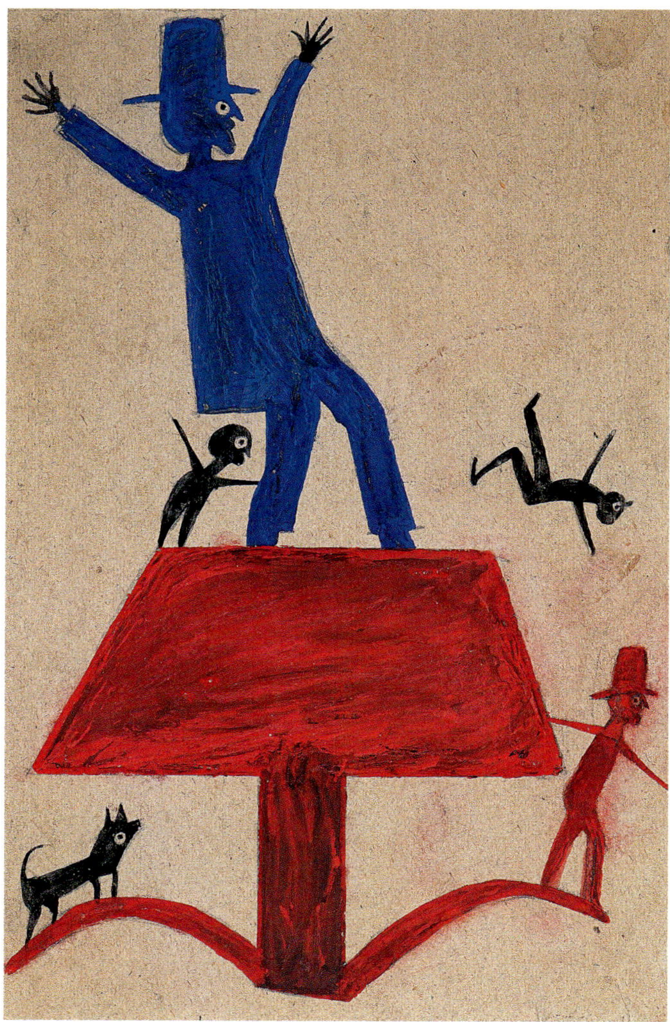

Figure 1. Bill Traylor, *Untitled*, 1939–1948, tempera and pencil on cardboard, 11¾ × 7¾ inches, High Museum of Art, purchase with funds from Mrs. Lindsey Hopkins, Jr., Edith G. and Philip A. Rhodes, and the Members Guild, 1982.93.

Among the most renowned Southern artists who have drawn their subjects from everyday life is Bill Traylor (fig. 1). A master of the quotidian, Traylor possessed a special genius for snatching poignant bits of human drama from the course of the ordinary. The immediate setting for Traylor's art-making was the bustling market district of Montgomery, Alabama, from around 1939 to 1948. There, sitting on a wooden box, often in the doorway of a pool hall, he observed and recorded the urban characters that passed before him—a woman admonishing a one-legged man, a transient Mexican worker looking for a hotel, a street preacher wildly pointing and pontificating, and the ambling figure of a grand old gentleman with a stovepipe hat walking bent over a cane. In many other drawings that feature multiple actors, Traylor's scenes become even more theatrical. Figures scramble frantically after a runaway goat cart, scurry amidst barking dogs to catch sight of an airplane, chase one another angrily with hatchets and sticks, and scamper up ladders in pursuit of a chicken on a rooftop (see cat. 82).

Prominent among the artist's vignettes of animated street life are depictions of drunkenness (fig. 2). There are images of country folk creating a Saturday night ruckus in the big city; drinkers performing graceful backbends, leaps, and other acrobatic feats to balance themselves and their bottles; and bands of smaller sprite-like figures forever attempting to poke, scold, and chastise these self-absorbed revelers out of their debauchery. Here, and throughout his work, Traylor comments on the nature and foibles of humanity. Inspired by an affection for our struggles and shortcomings, his drawings capture a sense of the human spirit that is both comic and compassionate, satiric yet sympathetic.

To portray his subjects, Traylor developed an idiosyncratic style of figuration. He began each drawing by depicting a few geometric shapes—a man's rectangular torso, a woman's trapezoidal skirt, or a horse's triangular neck and legs. With skilled economy, he elaborated

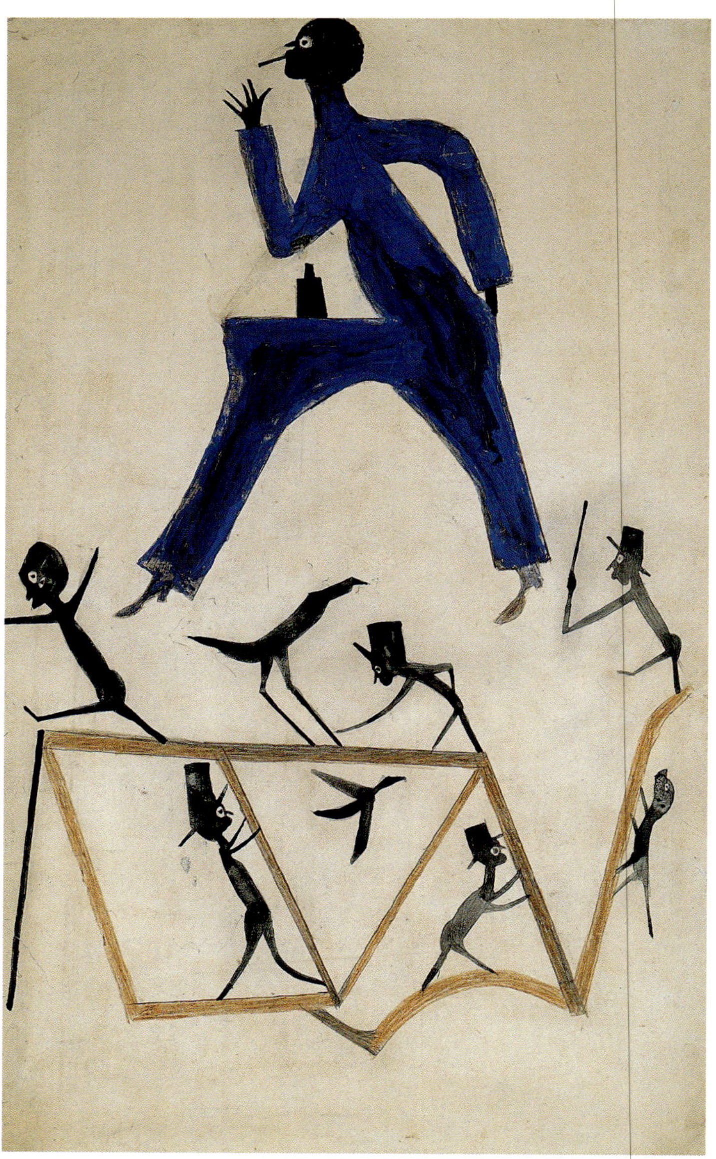

Figure 2. Bill Traylor, *Untitled*, 1939–1948, tempera and pencil on cardboard, 22¼ × 14 inches, High Museum of Art, purchase with funds from Mrs. Lindsey Hopkins, Jr., Edith G. and Philip A. Rhodes, and the Members Guild, 1982.114.

upon these elemental forms until he caught the essential qualities of his characters. The simple, silhouetted figures that emerged from this process are a potent combination of abstraction and representation. Despite a minimum of formal means, they render all the nuances of narrative gesture in a manner that is most eloquent.

Like many artists who recount tales of the everyday, Traylor's facility in constructing the narrative realms of his drawings underscores his talents as a storyteller and inspires speculation on the roots of his image-making in the oral traditions of the rural South. In contrast to the homey view of storytelling as a quaint and peripheral form of entertainment, folklore scholars point to the central role of such narrative practices within Southern culture and emphasize their power to dramatize life meanings and comment upon the surrounding social world, even when transposed to a new modern setting.[1] Traylor, who often muttered stories and reminiscences to himself as he drew, chronicled his surroundings with the keen observation, humor, and inventiveness of a gifted yarn-spinner. His work also demonstrates links to the indigenous black Southern musical form of the blues. In particular, his drawings share the rich pathos and tragicomic sentiments of the blues aesthetic and its themes of love gone bad, boozing and losing, and down-on-their-luck individuals endlessly at odds with a world of trouble and adversity.

Still another impetus behind Traylor's art was his late-life move from the country to the city. As the tale goes, Traylor was born into slavery around 1854 on an outlying Alabama plantation and remained there as a farmhand for most of his life. By the mid-1930s, when he was in his early eighties, the "scattering" of his children and the death of his "white folks" prompted his move to Montgomery.[2] In the city, he found brief employment in a shoe factory, until difficulties with rheumatism placed him on relief and on the streets. Sleeping in the back room of a funeral parlor, he spent his days seated on the sidewalk or under the shed roof of a nearby fruit stand creating his drawings. Between 1939 and 1942 alone, he produced an astounding fifteen hundred images.

The artist's journey to the city became the precipitating moment for a flurry of creative activity. His new urban surroundings provided him with a ringside seat at the teeming social life that he so loved to restage within his images. Amidst the detritus of this environment, he found an assortment of art materials—scraps of cardboard from old window displays, advertisements, street posters, and discarded boxes whose random cracks, stains, and tears inspired the initial inflections of his pencil and crayon marks. The urban environs, particularly the ubiquitous visual language of commercial street art, also seemed to influence the development of his abstract style. On the reverse sides of some of his salvaged drawing surfaces are vestiges of the era's sleek modernist graphics and cartoon-like advertising figures that may have served as sources for his schematized aesthetic.

Finally, it was Traylor's relocation to the city that ironically prompted the many scenes of rural life that he created alongside his more urban narratives. Among these are images of men driving mules, women milking cows, dogfights (see cat. 79), possum hunts,

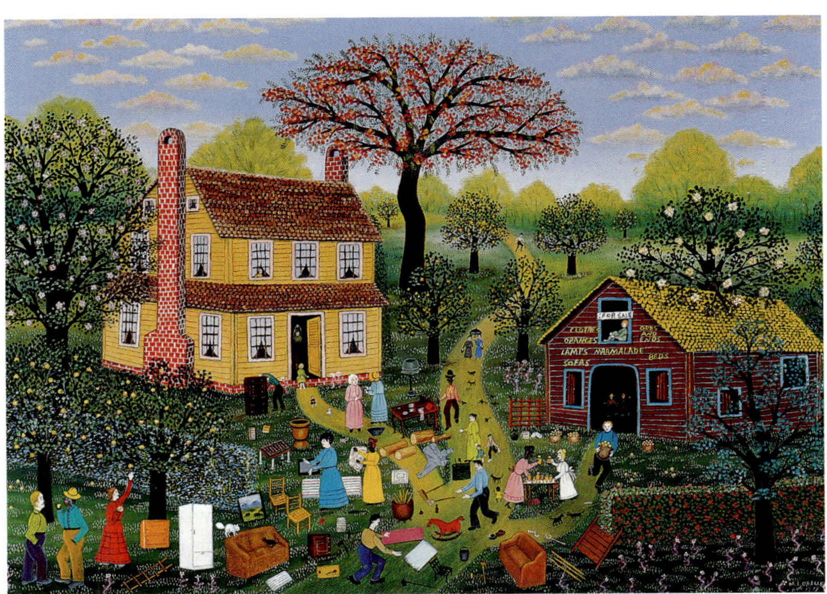

Figure 3. Mattie Lou O'Kelley, *Yard Sale*, 1979, oil on canvas, 28 x 40 inches, High Museum of Art, purchase with funds from the Mattie Lou O'Kelley Endowment, 1999.94.

and plantation owners. His most repeated subjects are animals—"sullen" mules, sinister snakes, giant purple pigs, chickens, owls, whippoorwills, and old horses "turned out to pasture to die"—all portrayed with the kind of individuality that issues from a rich repository of memory and experience. In fact, a feeling of longing for his rural past often underlies Traylor's art. As the artist himself once remarked about one of his drawings, "I wanted to be plowing so badly today that I made me a man plowing."

Such recollections of the vanishing rural world have inspired works by numerous other self-taught artists from the South. One of them is Clementine Hunter, whose widely acclaimed paintings document the everyday rituals of Southern plantation life in the early twentieth century. Often referred to as "the black Grandma Moses," Hunter worked for most of her life as a field hand and later as a domestic for Melrose Plantation, a deteriorated eighteenth-century Louisiana manor that was finally converted into a cultural center and retreat for artists and writers. According to legend, Hunter's first painting, around 1940, was prompted by her discovery of discarded tubes of pigment while cleaning one of the visiting artist's rooms. Over the next four decades, until her death in 1988 at around the age of 102, she produced over five thousand images documenting black rural existence, including scenes of picking cotton, harvesting pecans, and gathering figs; weddings (see cat. 50), baptisms, and funerals; and honky-tonk dances and church dinners. In addition to her oil paintings, Hunter created figurative cloth-appliqué wall hangings in the tradition of African American story quilts.

Hunter's southern plantation imagery finds a European American counterpart in the agrarian visions of Mattie Lou O'Kelley (fig. 3). The seventh of eight children born to a farming family in the hills of northeastern Georgia, O'Kelley began to devote more time to painting in the late 1960s, following her retirement from a series of city jobs as a seamstress, cook, waitress, and millworker. Evoking the idyllic memories of her childhood, her work records the details of rural life against a backdrop of visual enchantment. Glowing prismatic skies and green swelling hills lined with dots of pointillist color rise above scenes of cotton picking, wheat threshing, butter churning, chicken plucking, blueberry picking, and sauerkraut making. Endlessly flowering trees appear amid the tasks of plowing the fields, sharpening tools, dredging the river, and "hiving" the bees. Storybook autumns with purple barns and golden fields are the setting for the harvesting of melons, the making of cider, and the slaughtering of hogs during the "killing frost" of late November.

Like many artists referred to as "memory painters," both Hunter and O'Kelley drew inspiration from vernacular traditions of representational painting, transforming the mundane practice of conventional realism with their use of highly simplified forms, vivid patterning, spatial flattening, and a vibrant palette. Marked by a disinterest in more naturalistic techniques of rendering, their works have been historically mischaracterized as naïve or primitive and charged with a false innocence that overlooks their historical content, tongue-in-cheek humor, and aesthetic fluency. Often these artists are also accused of being incessantly nostalgic, of idealizing and sentimentalizing the past in a way that denies its real-life tragedies, horrors, and hardships. This is for the most part true, especially in the case of O'Kelley, whose overtly romanticized images might even be viewed as a form of sugary escapism. Of course, nostalgia tends to censor recollections and to offer a sense of solace or detachment from the world in the place of historical truth and social insight, but it can also be argued that such placid reminiscences sometimes play an important role in maintaining the human spirit. Among those possessing a greater familiarity with the artist, O'Kelley's arcadian fantasies have been understood as beguiling antidotes to difficult times, palliatives to the loneliness, impoverishment, and menial labor that is said to have characterized much of her adult life.[3] Here, nostalgia becomes an act of rapture, a reveling in the discourse of memory as pure pleasure.

A curious exception to O'Kelley's idealized picture-making is a striking self-portrait entitled *Mattie in the Morning Glories* (cat. 61), which she produced in 1992 at the age of eighty-four. At first glance, the image appears to be a contemporary replica of early American limner paintings, which were characterized by the same restrained facial cast, stiff frontal pose, flattened picture plane, and symmetrical design. The seated artist wears a treasured cameo pin and appears surrounded by morning glories, a favorite flower that O'Kelley frequently admired for its "charm and beauty."[4] But, conspiring against such romantic allusions—and endowing the painting with a surreal edge—are aspects of the artist's likeness that have been rendered with strange candor and realism. Her aged hands, posed prominently on her lap, are grotesquely veined and unapologetically displayed with brilliant red nail polish against the acid green background of her dress. The stoic, tight-lipped expression on her face evokes O'Kelley's well-documented tenacity of spirit. More significantly, it seems to betray a restrained and prim personality not always comfortable revealing itself. Perhaps beyond the artist's conscious intentions, O'Kelley's own image becomes surprisingly confessional. Unlike her pastoral landscapes, it refuses to retreat into the imaginary.

In sharp contrast to O'Kelley's rural idealism, the sensibility underlying the painted relief carvings of Herbert Singleton might be described as urban cynicism. The everyday world portrayed by Singleton is the impoverished black ghetto and its universe of crime, violence, and brutality. An ex-con and reformed drug user who has lived all his life in one of the roughest neighborhoods in New Orleans, Singleton draws upon his own life experiences as sources for his dark depictions of black street culture. Among his subjects are such neighborhood familiars as "Big Hat Willie," a notorious pimp known for his flamboyant chapeaus; "Fat Zeano," a big bully who gestured the sign of the "evil eye" before knocking out his adversaries; and "Roach," a.k.a. "Dr. Kalicky," whose special street talent was assisting small-veined "users" with the techniques of shooting up.[5] In various renderings of "Joe Horseshoes Grocery," where Singleton reportedly swept floors as a youth, other characters are shown rolling dice, playing cards, and dancing to the music of a jukebox as Joe threatens to shoot someone trying to steal his pinball machine. Conjuring scenes from a nighttime haunt called Club 27, the artist re-creates a disturbing vision of drinking, prostitution, drug abuse, gambling, pistols, skulls, and bloody knives.

Jazz funerals, especially those held for friends who met with a premature demise, are also among the repertoire of black street life recorded by Singleton. One of his most spectacular examples is the *Hallelujah Door* (cat. 70). Carved in 1993 on a nearly ten-feet-tall discarded church door, this work documents a New Orleans–style funerary ritual in all its pageantry. In one panel, a grave digger toils at his work; in another, the body of the departed lies solemnly in his coffin as onlookers utter the words, "Lord, here lay a good man." Other panels present the march of bereaved mourners to the grave site, the raising of colored handkerchiefs and parasols high in the air to signify the flight of the spirit at the moment of "cutting the body loose," and the "second line" dancers, acrobats, and musicians that transform the formal ceremony into the ecstatic celebration that jazz player Jelly Roll Morton referred to as "the end of a perfect death." Rising above the entire scene appear a trio of angels and Christ himself, arms open, welcoming the deceased home (fig. 4). Finally, scrawled at the very top of the door is the statement "Glad you dead you old rascal you." Quoted from an old street song often played at jazz funerals, this comic remark reflects the farcical spirit used to lighten the expressions of grief at such events. The irreverent comment is also an oblique reference to the essential pessimism underlying Singleton's view of humanity and its endless struggle between good and evil. According to the artist, "People nothing but trouble," and "we're all looking in the mirror, and it casts sinful reflections."[6]

The artist whose work, although rooted in the everyday, most challenges its boundaries is Nellie Mae Rowe. Most of Rowe's

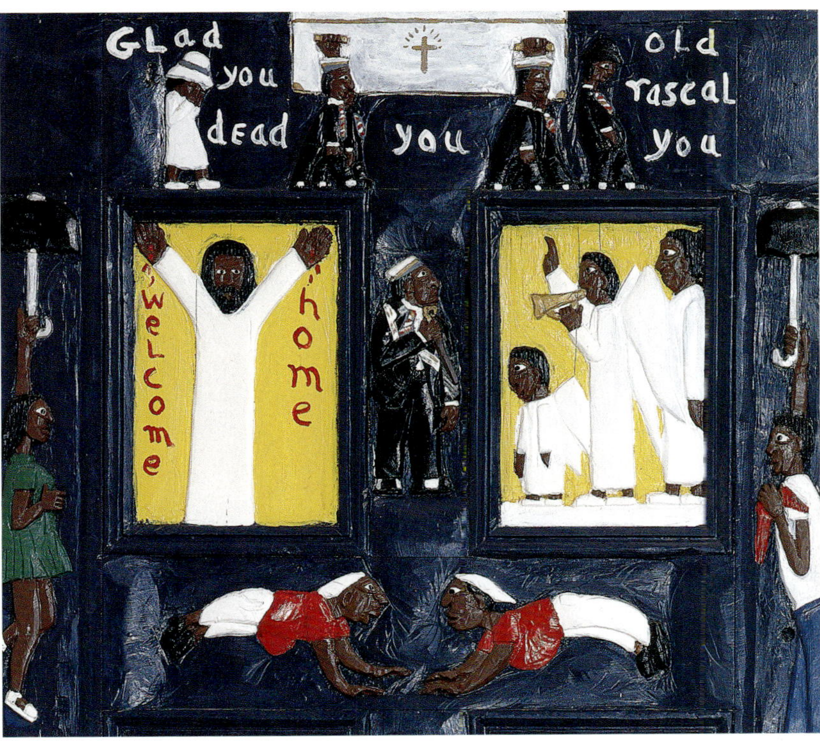

Figure 4. Herbert Singleton, *Hallelujah Door* (cat. 70, detail).

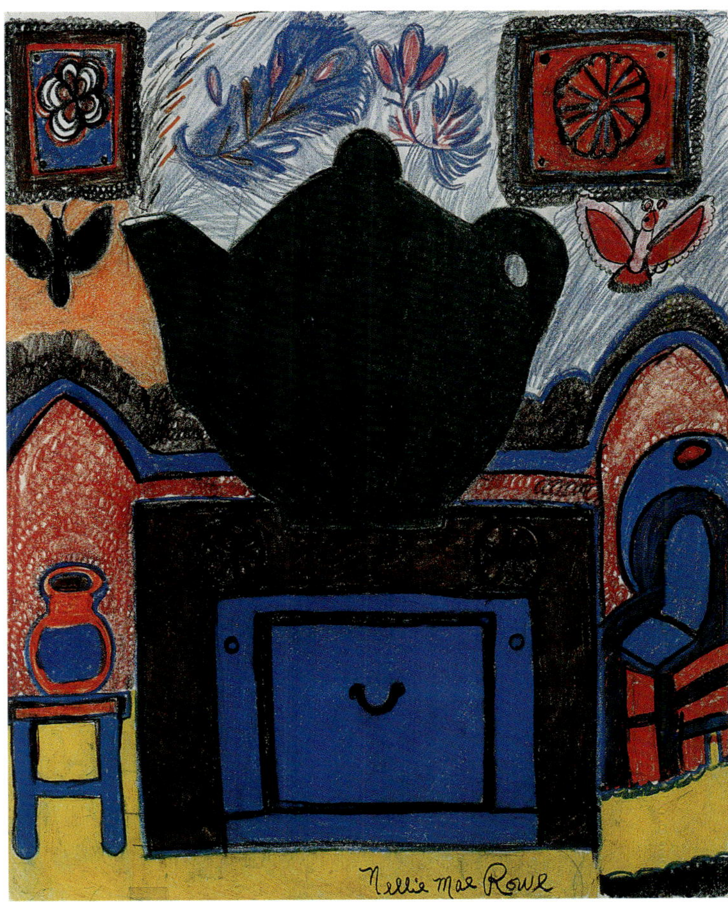

Figure 5. Nellie Mae Rowe, *Nellie's Teapot*, 1979, crayon and colored pencil on paper, 17 × 14 inches, collection of Harvie B. and Charles L. Abney, promised gift to the High Museum of Art.

images arose from her everyday musings and recollections, but her drawings often transpose familiar subjects into a world poised between the real and the imaginary. Sometimes, the commonplace dissolves into the purely fantastic, as hybrid combinations of ordinary images turn into "things that you haven't seen born into this world yet."[7]

Many of Rowe's depictions seem to be products of errant observation—the free-form play of her creative consciousness on the myriad of potential subjects that surrounded her. So it is possible to imagine how a stranger passing by her window one day might have inspired her vivid rendering of the *Woman in Orange and Red* (cat. 67), how an ordinary trip on the interstate would have prompted the striped comic frenzy of her famous *Pig on Expressway*, or how a glimpse around her own kitchen could have turned an innocent domestic object into the giant black apparition that looms in the center of a piece simply entitled *Nellie's Teapot* (fig. 5).

Frequently, Rowe's imagery is autobiographical. Numerous drawings of architectural whimsies document her own resplendently decorated house and yard, once located in the Vinings community just outside Atlanta. Other works refer to the rural world of her youth, including a portrait of the family mule Molly, whose black silhouette is now rendered in memory upon the rowdy checkerboard of a country quilt. The artist's spiritual life is reflected in repeated depictions of her own hands raised in solemn blessing and in such works as *Nellie Mae Making It to Church Barefoot*. A surreal portrayal of two giant footprints on their way to worship, this image conjures a sense of her religious humility and serves as a clever image-pun for the linking of "soul" with "sole." On the lighthearted side are pictures of husky wrestlers, ruby-feathered fan dancers, and the ever-strange alligator man, which offer a peek into Rowe's pop culture fascinations.

There is much about Rowe's underlying narratives that may be intriguing, but at the heart of her work are the unusual formal strategies that brilliantly shape their representation. As soon as the first outlines of Rowe's subjects were laid to paper, they became engulfed in the riotous patterns, exuberant color, and surging forms that constitute her dynamic pictorial world. It is as if her drawings transport the unsuspecting things of this universe into a curious make-believe realm. Plants and trees sprout exotic plumage. Some human figures don bright attire, fancy hats, and elaborate hairdos, while others metamorphose into butterflies, parrots, or the cow that jumped over the moon. Flight-of-fancy birds, dogs, lions, snakes, and beasts of all kinds meander through her scenes amidst the arabesque lines and cloud-like contours that inscribe what has been aptly described as Rowe's "teeming amalgamation of life forms."[8]

While pondering the nature of Rowe's unusual aesthetic, one detects the influence of those expressive practices referred to as the "domestic" or "decorative" arts. The realm of the decorative has been the subject of similar theoretical considerations since the 1970s,

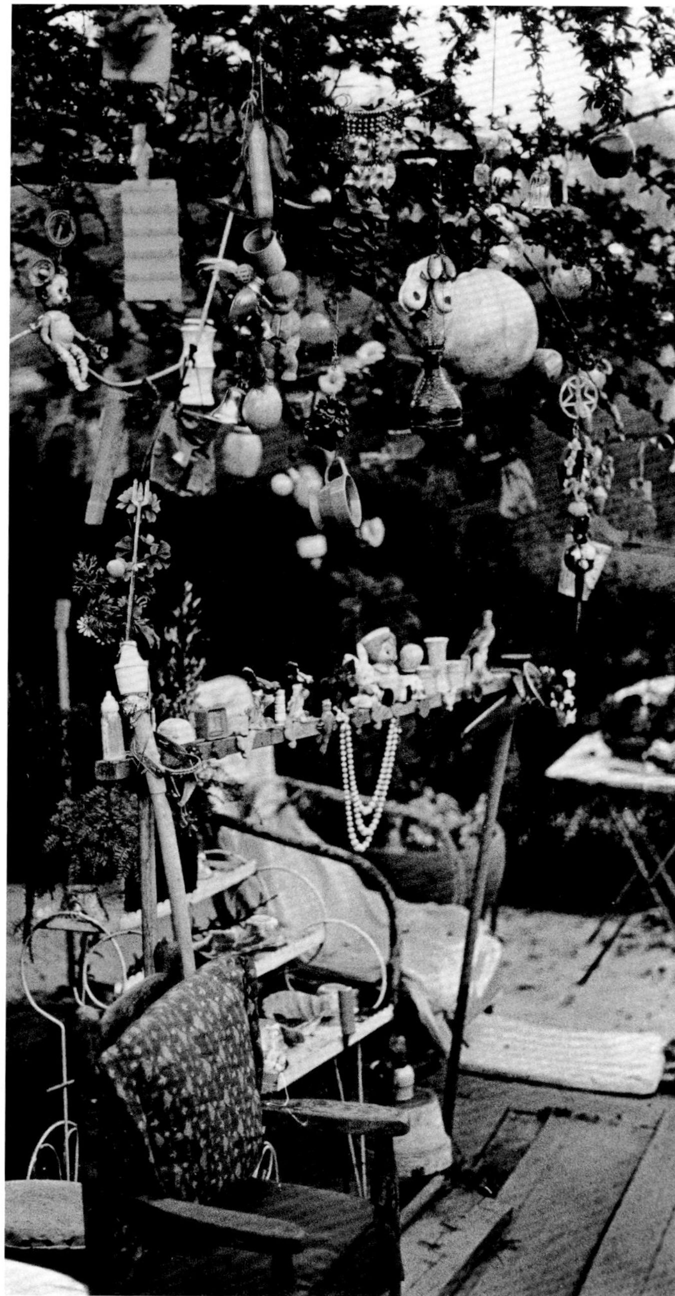

Figure 6. Nellie Mae Rowe's yard, 1971.

when the work of women artists began to garner long-awaited recognition within mainstream art discourse. While searching for an overarching aesthetic explanation for such creativity, it was often argued that women's art was grounded in the domestic craft traditions historically associated with their gender. Suddenly, the visual vocabularies of quilts, rugs, needlework, and painted china were credited as sources for a wide range of contemporary artistic expressions. More significantly, the belief arose that women had access to a distinct critical intelligence arising from their experience of the decorative, a special aesthetic insight into the pleasures of color, the complex beauty of pattern, and the delights of the sensual. The obvious fallacy of this essentializing notion, applied across the diversity of art made by women, is now well understood. But in the case of some artists, including Nellie Mae Rowe, there is a bit of truth to the hypothesis.

In Rowe's work, all content is subject to the potent authority of her strong decorative sensibility. She "sewed" together complicated visual patterns in the same formidable way that her mother, an accomplished quiltmaker, combined the multicolored pieces of fabric in her own handiwork. And she orchestrated the shapes and masses of her crowded images with the same skills demanded in the artful arrangement of domestic spaces stuffed with striped rugs, swirling wallpaper, dotted chairs, ceramic figurines, and potted plants. In fact, the dense decorative domain of Rowe's drawings seems to replicate the thickly arrayed environment of her own house and yard.

Often while describing the tasks that she performed during her many decades as a domestic worker, the artist referred to her talent for rearranging the furnishings in the rooms where it was merely her job to sweep and dust. She described this practice, which earned mixed reactions from her employers, as her special God-given gift or "power" for "placing things."[9] This nearly irresistible imperative to create aesthetic structure inspired the fascinating spatial strategies of her drawings and found full expression in the elaborate embellishment of her own small home.

Many years before Rowe produced her acclaimed body of larger-scale colored drawings in the late 1970s and early 1980s, she had begun to adorn the interior of her single-story frame house and its surrounding property. Inside her home, she covered walls, lined shelves, and festooned windows with displays of altered photographs, plaques, religious pictures and statuary, drawings, plaster-cast owls, Christmas ornaments, jewelry, plastic fruit, and countless other decorative items. Sitting amidst the bric-a-brac, pillows, crocheted afghans, and flower-covered chairs were the artist's own creations—her series of stuffed-cloth portrait figures, or "dolls," as well as an amazing assortment of small human and animal sculptures fashioned from chewing gum and embedded with glass marbles, beads, and hair. In her yard (fig. 6), Rowe mounted similar displays. She posed stuffed "guardian" dogs at the threshold; trimmed her bushes to form topiary images of sheep, elephants, and other creatures; and suspended toys, bottles, painted egg cartons, and countless found-object assemblages from railings, bushes, and tree limbs.[10]

Commingling the tradition of African American yard art with the popular ethic of *House Beautiful*, Rowe dressed up her entire universe. As in her drawings, her acts of embellishment turned things ordinary into realms wondrous, and she called her new world Nellie's Playhouse. Translated into the rubric of aesthetics, Rowe's notion of "play" was the perfect metaphor for the free-form inventiveness and exuberant spirit that characterized her art-making. Especially in her later years, this designation also symbolically protested the life of hard work that she felt had always limited the realization of her strong artistic ambitions, and it proclaimed her final freedom to pursue her artistic whims and desires in a place of creative refuge. Following a painful recounting of the life events that had often denied her the opportunity to make art, Rowe once asserted: "Now it is time for me to rest and play. I've worked my days, now I want to play these other days out. And God will let me do it, too. I'm goin' to play in my playhouse. I love it!"[11]

"The Past Is Never Past": The Shapes of History

In many ways, the artists who document the everyday world are engaged in depicting small bits of history. They are diarists, biographers, and storytellers recounting visual tales that are closely tethered to the familiar details, anecdotes, and experiences of their own lives. But beyond such intimate historians are others who cast a wider net for their subjects, portraying characters and events from further outside their own personal worlds. These artists work to capture the larger shapes of history.

One such artist, William Hawkins, possessed what might be described as a roving sense of history. He traveled imaginatively to diverse times and places, searching out the most sensational subjects for his paintings. A teller of prehistoric tall tales, he captured images of larger-than-life characters from the earth's evolutionary past—a snarling mastodon, monstrous black "man-eaters," and a growling, red-scaled tyrannosaurus rex trampling past fiery volcanoes (see cat. 41). Hawkins chronicled the birth of Christ and the death of George Washington, and he documented bullfighting in Mexico, buffalo hunting in the Wild West, and the building of the Statue of Liberty in New York City. Sometimes his affection for the wonders of the world led him home. A Kentucky farm boy turned city dweller, Hawkins also recorded the landmark architecture of his adopted town of Columbus, Ohio, turning such historic structures as the Billy James Theatre, the Willard Hotel, and the Huntington Bank into geometric portraits.

Hawkins's means of transport to realms far and near were the images of popular culture, which served as visual source material for his nearly encyclopedic range of subjects. Even his local city scenes were typically drawn from printed photographs or newspaper clippings. A pop culture *bricoleur*, he refashioned the familiar and often mundane imagery of postcards, picture books, calendars, advertisements, newspapers, and magazines into startlingly novel depictions.

One of the most amazing examples of Hawkins's artistic alchemy is his masterpiece *Con[q]uest of the Moon #1* (fig. 7, cat. 39). Chronicling

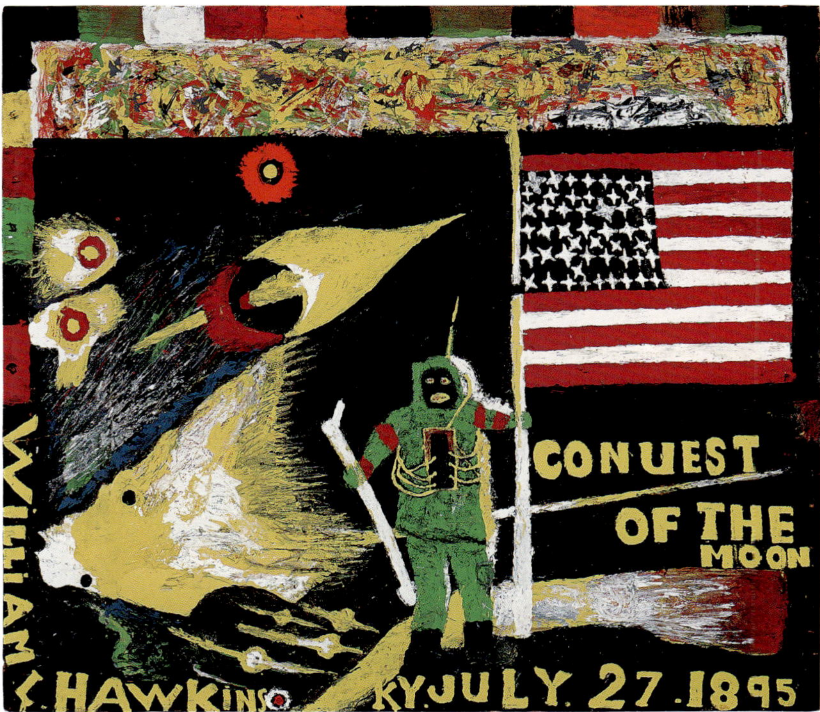

Figure 7. William Hawkins, *Con[q]uest of the Moon #1* (cat. 39).

the first manned landing on the moon, the painting was inspired by a series of now famous lunar photographs showing the Apollo astronauts raising the U.S. flag on the Sea of Tranquility. These widely disseminated photographs, which were reproduced in 1969 in *Life* magazine, *National Geographic*, and countless newspapers across the country, soon became icons of the popular imagination. Years later, in 1984, they incited Hawkins to create his own vision of this monumental moment in the history of the twentieth century.

In Hawkins's rendering of the event, a lone astronaut plants a giant U.S. flag on the moon's surface. Adorning the figure are details of space technology—air supply hoses, backpacks, radio antennae, and even the staff-like core tube used to gather rock and soil samples. Beyond these historical details, however, Hawkins's account departs dramatically from its sources. The grayed tones of the original photograph have been replaced with brilliant color, and within the astronaut's darkened face visor there glows an eerie, mask-like visage. The scene is set within the stark black background of endless space, conjuring a sense of what Neil Armstrong described as the moon's "magnificent desolation," but exploding out of the dark are blazing comets, expressionistic bursts of light, and a flurry of cosmic fireworks that evoke the patriotic, pyrotechnic zeal of an earthbound Fourth of July celebration.

In terms of expressive precedents, Hawkins's *Con[q]uest of the Moon* reflects the hyperbolic text of space adventure stories and the apocalyptic spectacles of modern science-fiction movies. It also calls to mind the heightened drama of American grand manner history paintings from the nineteenth century, which Hawkins came to know through the assorted fine art reproductions that made their way into his collection of salvaged images. Even the work's heroic title, triumphantly inscribed within the scene, mirrors the epic spirit and grandiose aspirations of Western historical narratives.

The theatricality that Hawkins shared with conventional history painting was, in fact, a central tenet of his creative work. Believing that great art should surprise and astonish its viewers, he created dazzling pictorial effects through the use of bold abstract forms, strident color combinations, energetic brushstrokes, and flamboyant decorative patterns. Much of his art's affective power arises from the way he handled the paint itself. Employing a free-form, improvisational method of image-making, he worked with pigment directly from the can, pushing, mixing, dripping, swirling, and scumbling paint to create stunning visual textures as he shaped his subjects.

Another way in which Hawkins created aesthetic impact was to add three-dimensional elements to his work. A homemade modeling compound provided areas of low relief or surface texture. Found materials affixed to his paintings enhance the physical presence of his subjects. Even more innovative, however, was a technique that the artist began to employ around 1986: instead of quoting images from his archive of popular pictures, he began to incorporate actual printed sources directly into his paintings. This use of collage, the sudden contrast of photographic realism with the artist's more abstract, painterly depictions, produced a new level of visual and conceptual intrigue.

A major work in Hawkins's later collage series is his 1989 *Tiger and Bear* (cat. 48). In this primal scene of conflict, a ferocious tiger, taken from the illustration of a circus advertisement or movie poster, lunges to attack a giant black bear. Appearing between the two beasts is a magazine photograph of a nesting bird, which juxtaposes the delicate symbols of birth and new life with those of predatory violence and death. In other pasted images that look as if they have been torn from the pages of a travel guide to the tropics, monkeys scurry excitedly up palm trees, fleeing the threat of carnage. Combining found images to create a kind of conceptual puzzle, Hawkins's mortal contest between the tiger and the bear comments on the random brutality of nature, its elemental forces, and its life-and-death dramas. One of a number of the artist's paintings that depict animals fighting, it also seems to serve as a more distant metaphor for the struggles, conflicts, and savageries of human history.

In several works, Hawkins appropriated imagery from famous paintings by other artists. In one nativity scene, he used a tiny reproduction of the Mona Lisa to depict the figure of the Holy Mother, wrinkling the face of da Vinci's portrait in order to exaggerate her infamous smile. In another work, he used a small headshot of Stevie Wonder to represent Christ in a black remake of da Vinci's *Last Supper*. Recycling even the hallowed icons of high art, Hawkins expressed a great passion for picture-making. Through his ingenious use of cast-off images and other formal inventions, he transformed his vernacular sources and turned the flotsam and jetsam of our time into remarkable artistic visions.

In contrast to William Hawkins's wide-angled approach to subject matter, Sam Doyle's portrayal of history was highly focused. Although Doyle mined popular culture for his paintings of famous African Americans like Joe Louis, Jackie Robinson, and Ray Charles, the majority of his work concentrated on more local characters. While Hawkins was roaming about the world via his treasure trove of mass media images, Doyle found a wealth of historical subjects right in his own backyard within the community of St. Helena Island, where he spent all of his life.

A barrier island off the South Carolina coast, St. Helena was predominantly inhabited by former slaves and their descendants. The isolation of the island nurtured the preservation of African and African American memories and traditions, and while St. Helena would become increasingly integrated into mainland culture as the century progressed, the island of Doyle's youth was steeped in the African American cultural tales and historical accounts that would inspire the artist's paintings.

From the late 1960s until his death in 1985, Doyle worked to depict the life and lore of St. Helena. He captured its most colorful personages, chronicled its struggle to survive the atrocities of slavery, and even documented its supernatural inhabitants. Among his favorite subjects were the island's root doctors—traditional healers like Dr. Buzzard, who consulted the spirit world and received divinatory messages through a conch shell held to his ear. Doyle also painted many portraits of his relative, Adelaide Washington, a former slave whose representation with a field hoe, sun hat, and cotton basket recalls the history of bondage and commemorates the endless labor and physical hardships of farming life on St. Helena both during slavery and after. His otherworldly figures include such specters as Old Hag, a malevolent spirit from Gullah folk tradition who "rides" her sleeping victims at night, and Whooping Boy, the ghost of a beheaded slave who protests his murder by raising himself out of his grave every seven years to run about the island crying mournfully.[12]

In another major series of works, Doyle documented the first individuals within the island's African American community to assume particular vocations. He depicted the first black physician, Dr. York Bailey (see cat. 27), and painted portraits of Paul Holmes, *First Black Mailman*, Frank Capers, *First Black Barber*, and James Doyle, *First Black Truck Driver*. He created other likenesses of the first black dry cleaner, bus driver, policeman, and passenger ship captain. Doyle also chronicled, with particular fascination, the practitioners who assisted the life transitions of birth and death. He made many images of his grandmother Lucinda Ladson who, as a slave, was trained by a plantation owner named Dr. White to become St. Helena's first black midwife. He also portrayed David Chisholm, the first black undertaker, and, in *John Chisolem, St. Helena's First Embalmer* (cat. 28), David's nephew John. While a young boy, Doyle had witnessed John Chisholm prepare Doyle's brother for burial.[13] Many years later, the artist's depiction of this unconventional subject—a figure in a white lab coat, posed with a giant embalmer's needle over a draped cadaver—captures an eerie sense of historical authenticity.

More than a group of individual portraits, Doyle's "First Blacks" series was clearly intended as a larger symbol of black achievement. Created in the wake of the Civil Rights era, it reflects the ideology of the black consciousness movement and its call to celebrate the contributions of African Americans within American social life. Another influence may have been the widespread preoccupation in the mid- to late 1970s with documenting one's family or ethnic community. Known popularly as the "Roots phenomenon," this passion for genealogy created a particular enthusiasm for African American history and culture.[14] But there may have been a local impetus as well. The belief in social self-betterment through the accomplishment of a trade had been a strong aspect of St. Helena's history since 1862, when the island became the site for the well-known Penn School. One of the first educational institutions established in the South for freed slaves, Penn's program of industrial and agricultural training dignified even the most common forms of labor and proffered individual initiative and the nobility of one's work as a means of triumph over the past oppressions of slavery and the ongoing injustices of racism.[15]

At the same time, Doyle did not limit himself to chronicling just those industrious inhabitants of St. Helena who might be held in high esteem. In fact, a group of his most intriguing paintings depicts characters from the social margins. Among his repertoire of misfits and outsiders are free spirits like Ramblin' Rose (see cat. 29), who wandered from place to place with a beer can in her hand, and Rockin' Mary, who smoked a corncob pipe and liked to "rock" to the music. An attraction to carnivalesque extremes inspired other portraits: Le Bit, the island's smallest woman; Miss Full Back, a woman of ample proportions; Siptoor, the dwarfed prankster; and a man nicknamed Frip, who reportedly had the island's longest penis (see cat. 32). Other figures transgressed sexual taboos and mores. Promiscuity is the subject of portraits entitled *Good Time Girl* and *Try Me* (cat. 31). Doyle repeatedly painted a cross-dresser whom he called Miss Boy, and in *Two Ladies* depicted a lesbian couple who "didn't have much need of men." He also painted a series of half-female/half-male characters, whom he called He/She or Two in One, describing these individuals as "sometimes a woman, sometimes a man. They can go both ways."[16]

There is often a comic or mischievous quality to Doyle's depiction of such nonconformists that calls to mind the puckish antics of the trickster. A pan-cultural figure with particular resonance in African and African American traditions, the trickster delights in violating social proprieties. But beyond their affinity with the trickster personality, Doyle's eccentric characters serve an even more critical function within his conception of community. In his conspicuous embrace of social outsiders, Doyle expressed a radicalized view of history, a vision that encompassed both the lofty and the licentious, those we exalt and those we debase. His generous understanding of community welcomed the figures of its territorial edge and challenged the dominant designations of high and low, superior and inferior, normal and deviant, that otherwise encode our social world.[17] Finally, Doyle effects a powerful form of symbolic reversal, inverting the system of hegemony that not only rendered such personalities outside the bounds of history but supported his own disenfranchisement as a black man as well.

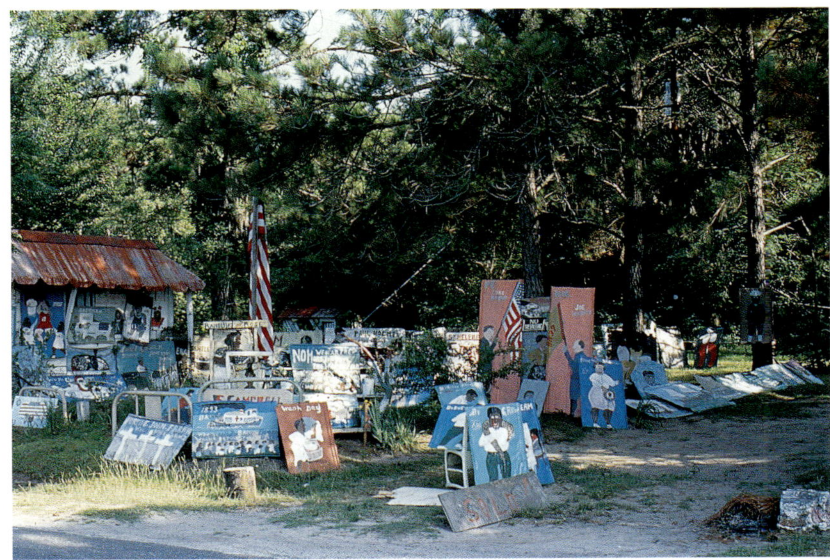

Figure 8. Sam Doyle's yard, ca. 1983.

Given Doyle's strong relationship to his community, it is not surprising that he put his works on public display. He painted his characters with house enamel on large sheets of corrugated roofing tin and exhibited them in his front yard (fig. 8). Hanging his pieces on clotheslines and leaning them against trees, along a bedpost fence, and on the side of his house, he created an outdoor portrait gallery that linked his work to the local universe he sought to depict.

The aesthetic of Doyle's painting might best be described as raw and abstracted. Employing a blunt style of figuration, he avoided background details and reduced the shapes and gestures of his subjects to their essence. As Doyle himself once explained, "I paint the spirit of the person."[18] But despite the simplicity of their forms, Doyle's paintings possess a sense of historical potency, a feeling of heightened knowledge that issues from a longtime connection to a place and its past. Over the years, Doyle himself became a bit of a celebrity on the island of St. Helena, a part of the larger history that he portrayed. As one neighbor mused after the artist's death in 1985, "Sam be one missing person around here."[19]

Doyle's historical portraits are part of a long tradition of self-documentation within African American culture. The call to record history and to counter the invisibility of African Americans within this country's retrospective consciousness has always figured prominently within black critical discourse. During the 1880s, Frederick Douglass asserted, "It is not well to forget the past. Memory was given to man for some wise purpose. The past is . . . the mirror in which we may discern the dim outlines of the future . . . The colored people of this country are bound to keep the past in lively memory till justice shall be done them."[20] One hundred years later, in 1985, author James Baldwin exhorted, "Go back to where you started, or as far back as you can, examine all of it, travel your road again and tell the truth about it. Sing or shout or testify or keep it to yourself; but *know whence you came*."[21]

It is perhaps this desire to testify in the void between African

American experience and mainstream history that underlies the fascination with the past and continues to influence the work of so many contemporary black artists. As art historian Richard Powell explains, "Because of the 'peculiar' institution of slavery and its legacy of segregation, discrimination, and historical discontinuity for blacks, artists within the African American cultural complex have long valued the didactic and spiritual role that the historical past can play in creative work. Unlike the ambivalent, love/hate relationship that many contemporary postmodernists have with the past, many African Americanists incorporate into their work—usually without discomfort or satire—issues of heritage, lineage, and other historical markers."[22]

Critic Michael Brenson further describes the antagonistic and even adversarial relationship with history that has characterized both avant-garde and late modernist art, and he contrasts these sentiments with those of much African American art practice in which the passion to remember becomes part of the impetus to create: "Black artists through much of this century have assumed the existence of a viable and indispensable community that they had no desire to reject. What a strange idea that advanced art could, in effect, ask them to forget where they had come from, what they had been cut off from, and what their history had been! An aesthetic of newness that glorified originality and rupture could not do justice to the experience of a history that was endangered. How could a past be overturned that had not yet even been fully allowed to exist? How could memory be the enemy when everything that had to be remembered was threatened with being erased?"[23]

Thornton Dial is an artist for whom art serves to represent the complexity of his historical experience as an African American. In a prodigious body of paintings produced over the last ten years, Dial captures major moments in black memory—from the history of enslavement, life in the antebellum South, and Jim Crowism to the pursuit of desegregation, the Civil Rights movement, and contemporary race relations. But his work offers more than a mere recollection of the past. Now in his early seventies, Dial chronicles African American survival with a social prescience and criticality wrought from decades of struggle as a black, working-class man in the racial hotbed of the South. Together, Dial's images explore the political, economic, and ideological forces that shape social reality, revealing what he refers to as the "strategy of the world."[24]

Mirroring the allegorical structure of fables and African American folktales, Dial often employs a cast of animal characters to enact his narratives of human corruption and folly, triumph and moral strength. In his repertoire of symbolic beasts, birds denote the capacity for flight, escape, and spiritual redemption. Monkeys are exploiters and oppressors who jump on the backs of others. They are agitated agents of misfortune and the tyranny of the status quo. "Wild dogs" signify violence and the unknown, while deer symbolize the ability to move through social and political bramble with stealth, caution, and alertness. The "horned, hard-headed goat" is stubborn and "butt-headed," but also possesses the determination, perseverance, and sheer force of will to overcome any obstacles in the path of its desired achievements. Finally, the major protagonist in many of Dial's historical dramas is the tiger. This "proud-stepping" character represents the spirit of the African American man as he struggles to make his way in an often antagonistic world. Noted for its ability to "spring back" from adversity and land on its feet, the tiger is the perfect figure to negotiate society's imbalances of power and to leap with fury toward the jobs, education, and justice otherwise denied him.[25]

Throughout Dial's work, the tiger assumes many identities and meanings. In the most basic sense, the tiger is Dial himself, the artist's social and political alter ego. It is also an image used to invoke Civil Rights leader Martin Luther King Jr., the "freedom cat," as he crosses Selma bridge during the famous 1965 voting rights protest march to Montgomery and as he is later assassinated and martyred. The tiger further embodies a more local historical reference to a man named Perry L. "Tiger" Thompson, whom Dial came to know as a fellow worker at the Pullman Standard Plant in Bessemer, Alabama. A former prizefighter and strident labor organizer, Tiger Thompson became for Dial a heroic emblem of social uplift and "fighting for the rights of people" in a pre–Civil Rights era.[26]

Dial's tiger invites still further associations. In black parlance, "cat" is a common appellation for an African American man. It is linked to the term of high regard for "a devotee of hot jazz, appearing early as 'hepcat' and later 'cool cat,' when cool meant hot, slick and unruffled."[27] The striped suit of the tiger evokes a prison uniform, an allusion to the frequent criminalization of black men, as well as to the more widespread predicament of all African Americans who are "locked" in a racist society. The interlocking black and white patterning of the tiger also signifies Dial's oft-stated conviction that we are all part of the same struggle and, finally, that our fates are joined in the need for interracial cooperation. Borrowing a more popular source, Dial once likened his mythic creature to the well-known advertising slogan for Exxon gas that urged, "Put a tiger in your tank." Here he imposes a punning and humorous guise on the tragic historical dilemma of African Americans who invisibly "fueled" the industrial "engine" of the United States with their labors while receiving none of the credit or benefits.[28] Finally, there is the trickster aspect of the tiger that manifests itself in the minstrel-like personae of both the caged circus beast and the obsequious household pet, characters whose trained antics and domesticated grins serve to mask the jungle cat's rage and power.

Dial's tiger imagery exemplifies the fluid and open-ended play of meaning that is the central strategy of his creative work. His ability to lay symbol upon symbol creates a rich figurative language that inspires deep and proliferate readings. Scholar Henry Louis Gates has identified this manner of embedding multiple sign systems within a single text as a major rhetorical practice of African American expressive culture. Referred to as "signifying," this sophisticated form of encoded "speaking" is rooted in black vernacular storytelling traditions, or "lying" sessions, of the rural American South.[29] In contrast to the explicitness and surface clarity that is a requirement for "truth" in conventional Western discourse, signifying, also known as "double voicing," opts for plurality, ambiguity, intertextuality, and double statement.[30] To paraphrase poet and activist Amiri Baraka on the complexity of Dial's iconography, the tiger's got many tales.[31]

More than just a poetic device, however, the techniques of signifying developed in response to a social exigency, the need both to camouflage and disclose one's messages concurrently. As Gates explains, "Black people have always been masters of the figurative: saying one thing to mean something quite other has always been basic to black survival in oppressive Western cultures. Misreading signs could be, and indeed often was, fatal. 'Reading' in this sense, was not play; it was an essential aspect of the 'literacy' training of a child. This sort of metaphorical literacy, the learning to decipher complex codes, is just about the blackest aspect of the black tradition."[32]

Until the mid-1980s, Dial maintained a secrecy about his work that has now become legendary. Fearing reprisals from both whites and blacks who might resent or misunderstand his social commentary, he reportedly hid, destroyed, recycled, or buried all of his early creations. Even more significantly, many elements of his current aesthetic practice have been shaped by the rhetoric of disguise. His telling of "benign" animal tales helps to conceal the socially and politically charged nature of his paintings. His characteristic use of bold expressive brushstrokes and thick encrusted surfaces engulfs his subjects in a world of masterfully orchestrated chaos. Each giant canvas is a dense symbolic field of enigmatic images, accumulated material fragments, vestigial faces, and vague tortured forms that seem to dissolve in and out of comprehension.

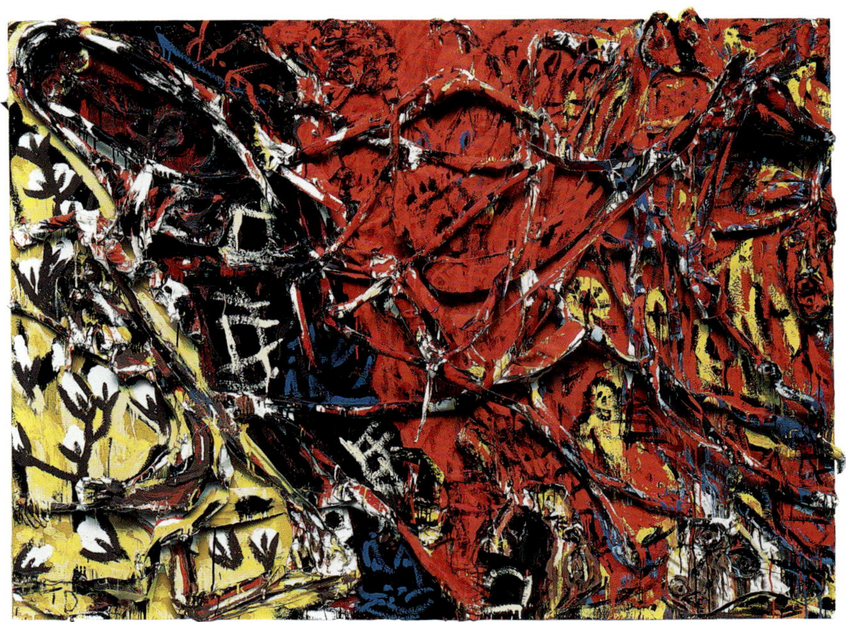

Figure 9. Thornton Dial, *Heading for the Higher Paying Jobs* (cat. 23).

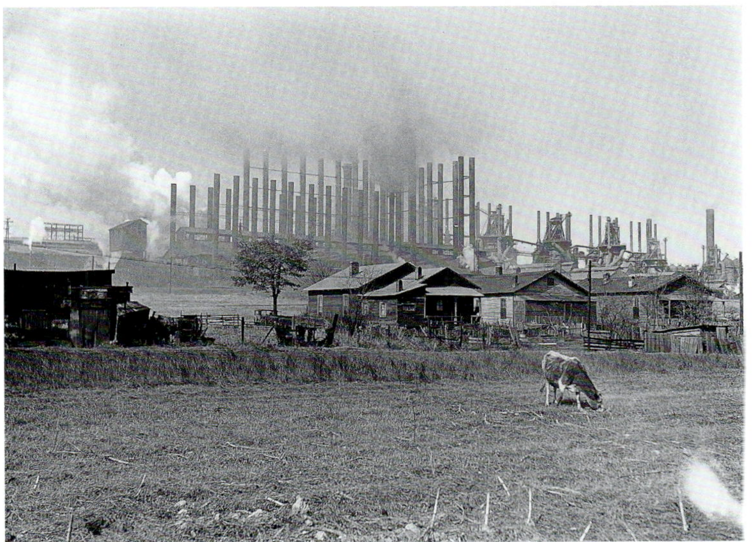

Figure 10. Workers' living quarters and Ensley steel plant, Birmingham, Alabama, ca. 1937.

In a major work from 1992 entitled *Heading for the Higher Paying Jobs* (fig. 9, cat. 23), Dial illustrates his potent style of picture-making. Dial's paintings typically spring from his own experiences. His move from rural Emelle to industrialized Bessemer (outside Birmingham, Alabama) paralleled the Great Migration—the historic journey of African Americans during the first part of the century as they moved from the rural South to the industrial cities of the North. To depict this epic passage, Dial divided his canvas into four progressive scenes. The piece begins with a stylized rendering of yellow cotton fields and a large bent figure, signifying both the labors of slavery and the backbreaking, postplantation era of sharecropping and tenant farming. After World War I, assailed by boll weevils, storms, and floods, the Southern cotton economy began to collapse. Black farmers, already on the edge of subsistence, sought other work, including labor in the region's mines, harvesting raw materials for the country's burgeoning industrial empire (fig. 10).

Dial comments on the harsh realities of coal mining in the second section of his painting. Slowly emerging from subterranean darkness is the outline of a blackened figure whose elongated face appears mule-like. Bred for hard physical labor and worked to death in the mines, mules are often used by Dial as symbols for African Americans who were forced to toil in dangerous and dehumanizing circumstances. Nearby, crosshatched marks evoke the appearance of human vertebrae and simultaneously serve as ladders descending into the earth. In the next segment of the work, Dial portrays the mining of iron ore. Using an avalanche of crimson brushstrokes to depict the hills of mineral deposits, he forecasts the fiery drama of his fourth and culminating scene, which portrays the steel mills and factories of the city.

To capture the effects of urban industry on African American lives, Dial re-created the image of Hell's inferno. Labor is represented by a chorus of tormented faces and tiny, twisted figures reduced to mere specters by the blazing factory furnaces. Dripped paint within the texture of the rendering conjures an allusion to both melted flesh and the spilling of lifeblood. Hovering within the flames are images of farm animals, a reference to black workers as "beasts of burden" and a harkening back to the African American traditions of the Southern agrarian past that had been uprooted to make way for a more modern life. Graffiti-like drawings of tigers are inscribed here and elsewhere in the painting, phantom witnesses to the litany of physical toil and the historic colonization of black bodies.

The exploitation of African American labor is a recurring theme in Dial's work, perhaps because it so poignantly represents the paradoxes within black American experience—the contradictions between the rhetoric of democracy and the tyranny of racism, between the "triumph of civil rights" and the day-to-day struggle for real equality. In many ways, Dial's portrayal of African American history underscores the frequent irony of the American Dream and its simplistic promise of progress. While the Emancipation Proclamation brought freedom to the postslavery South, most black farmers still had to work under the oppressive dictates of white planters, who continued to control the land and resources. Coal mining was a treacherous occupation for both black and white workers before the introduction of coal-loading machinery in the 1930s, but during the most dangerous decades preceding this invention, the number of black miners went up precipitously in relation to a decrease in the number of white coworkers.[33] Finally, while the movement to urban factories did indeed bring higher paying jobs for many, African Americans suffered the lowest wages, the most menial tasks, and the most expendable, dead-end positions. As one steelworker recalls, "The blacks had the dirtiest, the lowest, the filthiest man-killing jobs in the mill. They were in the flue holes, they worked the blast furnaces, the coke plants, eating up all that smoke and dust."[34] Recalling his own years as an industrial metalworker and offering a metaphor for taking strength from such adversity, Dial once asserted, "You can't harden the iron without the fire."[35]

In later works, Dial creates another generation of morality tales on the politics of race, taking on such controversial contemporary subjects as the Rodney King verdict and the L.A. riots, the hearings of Supreme Court Justice Clarence Thomas, and the O. J. Simpson trial. He also reflects upon a wide range of issues confronting the late twentieth century that exceed the boundaries of race. He compares the historical dilemmas of African Americans with those of women and the impoverished underclass, who strive similarly for opportunity and equality. And he links his accounts of black struggle to a body of diverse concerns from homelessness, unemployment, and the failings of capitalism to global pollution, the plight of the American city, and the AIDS epidemic.

Among the many found materials that Dial incorporates into his paintings are ropes and straps, which stretch like thick membranes across the surfaces of his canvases. Most commonly, these objects are interpreted as symbols of black oppression, recalling the bondage of slavery, the violence of Southern lynchings, and the binding of human possibilities. But they also seem to be a larger metaphor for the knotted threads of history itself. For Dial envisions the world and its past as a labyrinth of social and political relationships in which all of our destinies are entangled. It is his ability to unravel and spin these strands of human connection that gives his art its power.

"Remembering as Revolution": The Passions of Politics

Dial's socially inspired work demonstrates the powerful correlation between memory and politics. It has been a relatively recent admission on the part of mainstream Western scholarship that all history is political and that accounts of the past are highly variable and always constructed in a way that reinforces the beliefs, values, and desires of their author. Dominant conceptions of history, told by those who have the power to achieve the illusion of social consensus, work to buttress the authority and ascendancy of some over others.[36] Conversely, as the once-excluded voices of artists like Dial begin to render a different vision of history, remembering becomes revolutionary.

There is a strong political dimension in the works of a number of self-taught artists from the South. Like Dial, Alabama artist Ronald Lockett often used covert animal metaphors to express his social views. In his "Traps" series from the late 1980s and early 1990s, Lockett painted naturalistic likenesses of deer ensnared in netted traps and caged behind real wire fences (see cat. 55). These images of struggle and entrapment have been interpreted as symbols of sociopolitical oppression that link the theme of cultural domination with the abuse and exploitation of the natural world. In another group of more enigmatic deer landscapes, Lockett's pastoral scenes are enshrouded in metaphysical darkness, and shadow-like animal figures pose in delicate white outline against an environment of enveloping blackness (see cat. 56). The wire fencing appears again, but now its tangled mesh serves to represent the textured hides of the deer themselves. Formed from the materials that once imprisoned them, these mysterious creatures seem to comment paradoxically on the vulnerability and despair as well as the strength and adaptability of the human spirit.

Passionate social commentary also drives the painted relief carvings of Atlanta artist Ned Cartledge. With a biting sense of humor and sardonic wit, Cartledge creates cartoon-like critiques of contemporary American politics. He mocks government corruption, lampoons presidents, and editorializes on a broad menu of current affairs from the Vietnam War, the Iran-Contra Scandal, and the follies of foreign policy to nuclear proliferation, "trickle-down" economics, "televangelism," and the religious right. At the heart of his own

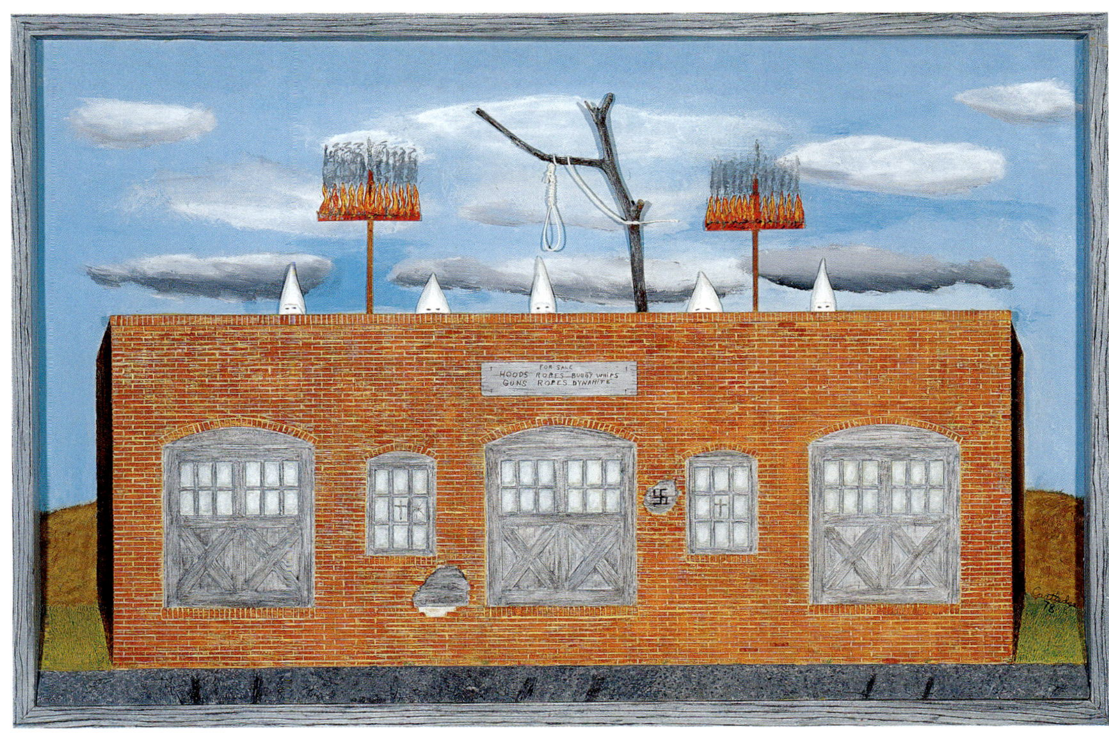

Figure 11. Ned Cartledge, *Coming Back* (K.K.K.), 1978, carved wood with acrylic paint, fabric, wood, and twine, 23½ x 37 inches, High Museum of Art, gift of the artist, 1980.29.

political convictions are the principles of liberal democracy as well as the tenets of fellowship and tolerance espoused by his Unitarian Universalist faith. The artist also cites his early exposure to racism as a major impetus behind his political commentaries. According to Cartledge, the experience of growing up in the segregated South of the 1930s and 1940s served to foster his strong social consciousness.[37]

As for many artists from the region, bigotry and racism are the focus for some of Cartledge's most powerful images. In a piece from 1978 entitled *Coming Back* (K.K.K.) (fig. 11), he represents an old warehouse that was part of the original headquarters for the Ku Klux Klan in Atlanta. An eerie portrayal, it pictures five hooded Klansmen, a pair of burning crosses, and a lynching tree emerging like grisly apparitions above the roofline of an otherwise ordinary city building. In another major work, *The Flag Waver* (cat. 11) from 1970, Cartledge presents a scathing satire of school segregation and state-sanctioned racism. The central character in this carving is a gun-slinging bigot who screams racial epithets, tramples the figure of an innocent social protestor, and flaunts his false patriotism by waving a giant Confederate flag. In the background are other symbols of racist oppression—a dwarfed likeness of the U.S. flag signals the triumph of bigoted provincialism over the national good, an overturned school bus symbolizes the region's resistance to integration, and the barred doors of a closed schoolhouse echo the X-shaped design of the looming Confederate banner. Intended to represent former Georgia governor Lester Maddox, the portrait of the flag waver is framed by axe handles, a popular emblem of segregationist fervor that Maddox handed out as souvenirs, which Cartledge associates with slave mistreatment in the antebellum South. In a now-famous statement about the inspiration behind such highly charged and controversial works, Cartledge once explained, "I am not inspired, I am provoked."[38]

Another example of socially informed art is the work of Lonnie Holley, who transforms broken typewriters, discarded kitchen appliances, abandoned TV sets, worn furniture, and a vast collection of other cast-off materials into poignant metaphors for the world's social and political dilemmas. In his found-object assemblages, an old soccer ball trapped in a rusty wire cage comments on the social and economic obstacles that restrain some from achieving success or "making the goal" (fig. 12). A junk tire—combined with a toy gun and a plastic flower—cites the increasing incidence of urban drive-by shootings and memorializes the victims of youth gang violence. And a pair of dilapidated "soldier" boots, affixed with a scavenged circuit board to a cross-shaped grave marker, invokes the horror and absurdity of contemporary technological warfare. In countless other works, Holley addresses an even wider panoply of sociopolitical subjects, from the problems of drug addiction, the health care crisis, black-on-black crime, racial injustice, and the tragedy of unwanted children to the Persian Gulf conflict, world hunger, religious hypocrisy, and the fate of the natural environment.

The originating site for Holley's symbolic constructions was the elaborate sculpture environment that the Alabama artist created over the last fifteen years on an acre of wooded land near the Birmingham airport. Recently dismantled, the constantly changing yard installation was a wondrous maze of object clusters that hung

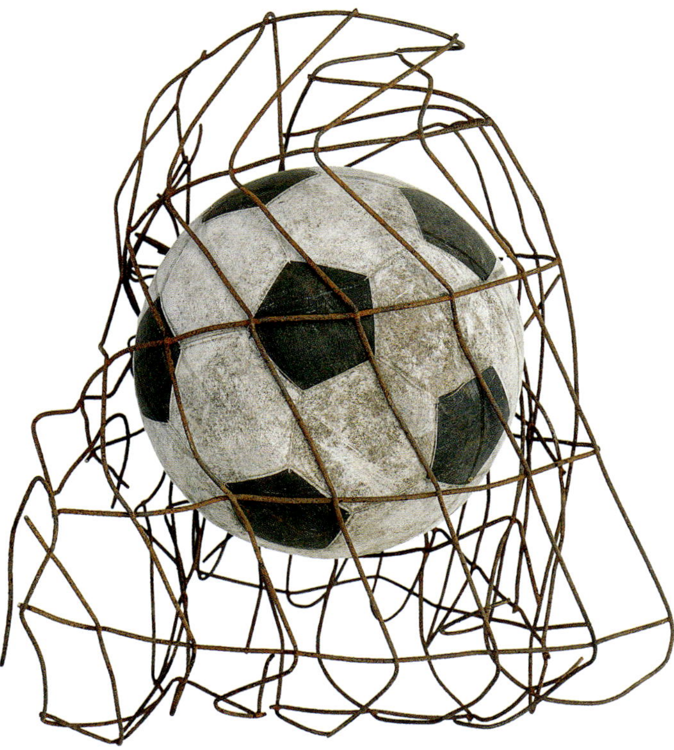

Figure 12. Lonnie Holley, *Obstacles Before the Goal*, 1994, metal fencing and soccer ball, 15½ × 14 inches, High Museum of Art, gift of William Arnett, 1996.41.

from trees, appeared moored to wires, and sat perched amidst mounds of unassembled debris and material remnants awaiting their own metamorphosis into Holley's world of ideas.[39] Although Holley's work synthesizes many cultural sources, his visionary landscape was most closely linked to the vernacular tradition of found-object assemblages that have long embellished African American yards, gardens, and gravesites. Particularly common in the rural South, African American "yard shows" manifest the same practice of elaborate object encoding that characterizes Holley's allegorical sculptures. Often intended to give material expression to a repertoire of philosophical principles, these shrine-like displays are also infused with a spiritual iconography that mirrors the more cosmic concerns underlying Holley's creations, including his frequent allusions to memory, the necessity of honoring one's ancestors, the cyclical process of life and death, and the ongoing transformation of matter into spirit.

In a 1994 piece entitled *Blown Out Black Mama's Belly* (cat. 49), Holley fashions an icon of human birth and continuity that embodies many of these larger themes. Here, a giant, stretched-out inner tube from an old transfer truck tire represents a female torso that has been tugged and pulled, deformed and distended, by the repeated rigors of childbearing. Intended to represent a maternal figure who has symbolically endured one of life's "rougher roads," the punning likeness is enhanced by the use of the tire's inflation hole to depict a navel and by the presence of a hanging loop that has been strategically tied to create the outline of a head above. Trailing from the assemblage is a long umbilical cord formed from upholstery stuffing and tied with scraps of varicolored fabric. Such wrapped and tied elements appear frequently in Holley's work as well as throughout the Afro-Atlantic world, where they serve as traditional ways of binding charms and containing spiritual energies. In *Blown Out Black Mama's Belly*, the wrapped cloths inscribe the figure with a sense of accumulated power and underscore the widespread belief in the sacred role of mothers as the originators of life.

Many other meanings may be attributed to this piece as well. Cueing and channeling multiple interpretations of his works, Holley effects the same open-ended play of signification that characterizes the creative strategy of other artists like Thornton Dial and the literacy code of much African American expressive practice. According to one of Holley's own improvised readings, *Blown Out Black Mama's Belly* is a tribute to "any woman who suffered to have a baby."[40] It further symbolizes a sort of universal mother, the primordial womb from which all human beings descended and whose multicolored umbilical ties symbolize the diverse peoples of the world. The figure also seems to signify the moral force of black matriarchy, and, finally, it serves as a bittersweet memorial to the struggles of the artist's own mother Dorothy Mae Holley, a woman who reportedly gave birth to twenty-seven children and died at the age of sixty-nine.[41]

In an earlier work from 1987 entitled *The Spirit of the Man by the Chicken House Door*, Holley created a similar reminiscence of his grandfather. Included in this found-object vignette is an old wooden chair that was his grandfather's favorite place to sit and think. Although empty now, it still bears the worn imprint of his body. Within the context of African American yard displays, such chair imagery alludes to visionary powers, spiritual presence, and "the continuing influence in this world of deceased leaders and ancestors."[42] Next to the chair is a weathered door with a silhouette of the aged patriarch carved at the top. Posed together, the chair and door recall the grandfather's patient watch over the family's chicken house, which was its primary source of food. A rusty oilcan filled with lantern fuel sits at the foot of the chair. Playing upon the association of lamplight with wakeful vigil, it symbolizes the quality of quiet care and duty that the old man possessed.

Such memorial tableaux and countless other homages to the past are among the predominant concerns of Holley's art, which he creates not only from the resources of his own life, but from what he perceives to be the energies and understandings accrued in previous generations.[43] His fascination with loss and preservation and with recollection and the passage of time is also reflected in his adoption of used, broken, and discarded objects as the material for his work. According to Holley, timeworn objects serve as "points of power for memory."[44] And, in the most metaphysical sense, junkyards are graveyards, places of access to the dead and to the knowledge and powers of a world long gone.

For Holley, however, junk is also a means to reaffirm life in the here and now. In his work, the reinvestment of artistic meaning in throwaway objects serves as a metaphor for redeeming the socially dispossessed or human castaways of this world. Finally, the social merges with the spiritual, and recycling becomes a quasi-religious imperative—a potent symbol for the promise of spiritual regeneration in the face of overwhelming world problems—that echoes the Christian resurrection ethos. As scholar Grey Gundaker has explained, "Junk is the emergent stuff of rebirth."[45]

Finally, Holley's work functions as a series of "spiritual object-lessons."[46] It forwards the belief that life can be transformed through the "ritual intentionality" of art.[47] Not simply attempting to comment on history, Holley has a political mission to alter its often destructive path, to effect real-world change in the human social condition. As the artist has remarked, "The purpose of my art is to heal the human mind . . . everything is medicine."[48]

"God Is Not Dead": The Worlds of the Spirit

It is often argued that religion is the most powerful force in the social and cultural life of the South. Perhaps more than anywhere else, the South is the place where people go to church, read the Bible, listen to popular gospel hymns, await a conversion experience, encounter roadside warnings on the wages of sin, and hear politicians using scriptural metaphors to express their impassioned views of the world. Despite the presence of many religious faiths and denominations, evangelical Protestantism has always been at the heart of the South's religious culture. Among the tenets of this popular religion is a belief in the absolute moral authority of the Bible and its divine revelations as well as a propensity for individualized and highly emotional religious experiences that begin with a life-transforming moment of personal conversion. To evangelical Southern Protestants, salvation and the truth of one's faith are obtained not through liturgies, sacraments, creeds, and the performance of good works but rather through the direct and intimate presence of God in one's life. Within charismatic religious forms arising out of such evangelicalism, the infusion of God's grace becomes manifest in ecstatic encounters with the Holy Ghost and other expressions of spiritual rapture.

Although sharing a common origin in the region's evangelicalism, the religious practices of black and white Southerners have traditionally remained distinct from one another. Overlapping and synthesizing Anglo-Protestantism with the spiritual systems of West and Central Africa, African Americans forged their own sacred history and celebratory worship style, rooted in the traditions of both worlds.[49] According to scholar Cornel West, this history of interaction between black people and evangelical Christianity began "when African slaves, laboring in the sweltering heat of plantations owned and ruled primarily by white American Christians, tried to understand their lives and servitude in the light of Biblical texts, Protestant hymns, and Christian testimonies."[50] Christianity, in general, tendered a theodicy of triumph over evil that struck deeply among oppressed black people, for it promised spiritual solace and moral rectitude for those refused wordly justice. Evangelical Protestantism was particularly attractive within early African American communities because its emphasis on an intimate and holy relationship with God fostered a sense of self-worth in individuals otherwise denied social status and empowerment. The emotional drama of "getting the spirit" and the "holy dance" of evangelicalism also appealed to Southern slaves because it recalled the unrestrained ecstasy of the "ring shout" and other African ritual expressions.[51] Such religious Africanisms, joined with the adapted forms of white Protestantism, would remain the underlying spiritual resource for the formidable constellation of Southern Christian communities that collectively became known as the Black Church.

Given the centrality of religious belief within Southern life, for both blacks and whites, it is not surprising that much self-taught art from the region draws upon the spiritual lives of its makers. Of course, art and religion have frequently been connected, as evidenced by the association of human creativity with divine inspiration that appears within the cultural thought of many times and places. In the South and particularly within the individualistic ethos of the Southern evangelist faith, art and spiritual awakening are often inextricably linked, and religion serves as a framework for understanding and appreciating the works of even the most unconventional artists. As Southern writer Tom Patterson explains, "Whereas in many cultures the kind of obsessive creativity exhibited by these artists might tend to be seen as signs of madness, in the South—and particularly in its rural areas—they're more likely to be regarded as demonstrators of intense religious faith, signs of prophesy, or evidence that artists are somehow 'touched' by God and therefore deserving of special respect."[52] Recalling her youth in the segregated black communities of the South, cultural critic bell hooks also describes the theological underpinnings of art-making: "Our aesthetics were informed by religious experience. Within our all-black churches we were taught to value talent, what old folks called 'the gift.' We were taught that no matter the circumstance, class, gender, or race, if the divine spirit had given one the 'gift'—the capacity to create art—then one had to yield, to surrender to that calling."[53]

Many self-taught artists view their creative work as a spiritual calling, and they attribute their talents to God with the same fervent rhetoric that characterizes Southern church testimonials and other public exhortations of faith. Sam Doyle said, "Art is my calling, and the Good Lord guides my hand."[54] Nellie Mae Rowe asserted, "He gave me this gift," and "I just have to keep drawing until He says, 'Well done, Nellie, you have been faithful.'"[55] Mary T. Smith painted abstract portraits on large pieces of corrugated roofing tin that included iconic images of Christ, angels, and "praise figures" posed with their arms reaching up in an attitude of worship. She mounted her works around her Mississippi house and property, explaining, "I did it to brighten up the yard, and please the Lord."[56] About his limestone sculptures, Tennessee artist William Edmondson declared, "Jesus has planted the seed of carving in me," and "It's the work of Jesus speaking his mind."[57]

Strong religious convictions have also produced an abundance of sacred subject matter. In New Orleans, Sister Gertrude Morgan portrayed passages from the Book of Revelation, rendering apocalyptic

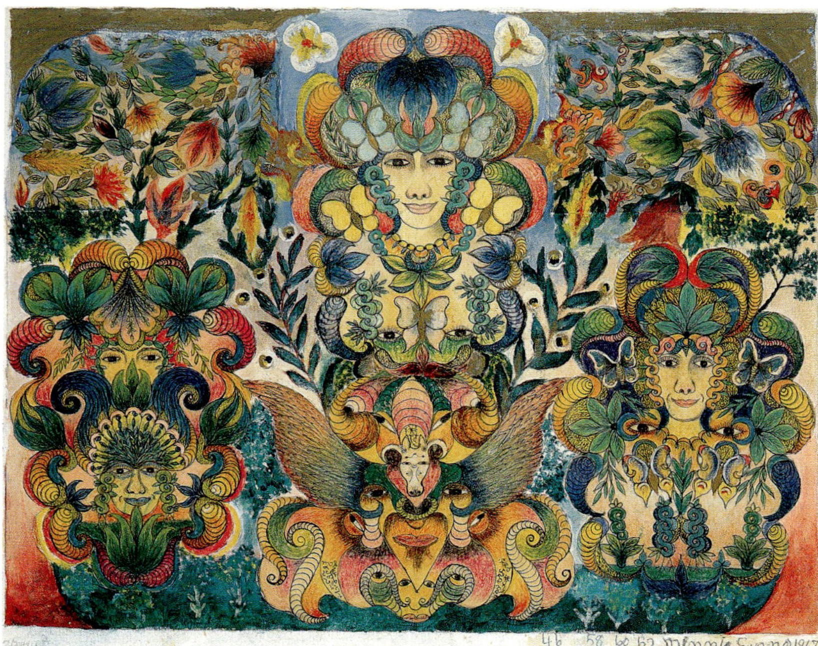

Figure 13. Minnie Evans, *Untitled* (Composite with Female Face), 1945–1967, graphite, oil, wax crayon, and collage on canvas board, 21 x 26½ inches, collection of the Dorothea M. Silverman family.

scenes of flying angels, winged beasts, and Christ in his final glory. Drawing from scriptural accounts of Genesis, Kentucky carver Edgar Tolson created a series of existentially charged meditations on the Fall of Man, while Mississippi-born artist Elijah Pierce recounted numerous other biblical tales in the wood reliefs that he fashioned between giving haircuts in his barbershop in Columbus, Ohio. Like a number of other spiritually motivated artists, these makers viewed their art as vehicles for their religious ministries. Morgan, a self-proclaimed street preacher, Tolson, a lay preacher, and Pierce, a licensed Baptist preacher, all created visual sermons to spread the word of God and fulfill divine missions.

Especially prominent among the religiously inspired artists of the South are those who have been beckoned by dreams, visions, and celestial voices. These individuals are agents of unbidden miracles and spiritual revelations that instruct and direct them in their creations. Raymond Coins professed to have highly symbolic and sometimes prophetic dreams that he illustrated in images cut from pieces of an unusual blue rock found near his home in a rural area of North Carolina. William Edmonson attested to personal encounters with angels who contacted him like a "swish of wings fluttering up under the eaves of my house,"[58] and he began his stonework after seeing the image of a tombstone in the sky and hearing the disembodied voice of God commanding him to carve. J. B. Murry, a sharecropper from Georgia, was similarly compelled by a divine vision to begin his spirit writings. Recording communications directly from God, his expressive calligraphy and abstracted ghost figures reveal warnings of evil and messages of salvation when decoded through the reading lens of a bottle of holy water drawn from the artist's own well.

Among all the religious artists from the South, Minnie Evans is one of the best-known. Like many other authors of sacred art, she was guided by visions in her work. Evans had already begun to experience apparitions as a child and often exclaimed, "My whole life has been nothing but dreams." She began to transcribe the mystical imagery of her revelations into pictures after hearing the voice of God prompting her to "draw or die." Assisted by divine forces in a kind of meditative art practice, she commingled her dream iconography with biblical subject matter to conjure scenes of a heavenly domain lushly grown with mysterious vegetation and inhabited by angels, serpents, unicorns, griffins, and winged devils.[59]

In her major drawings and paintings from the late 1950s to the early 1970s, Evans borrowed most frequently from the colorful imagery of Revelation prose, recasting the cosmic wonders, trumpeting seraphim, and strange beasts of the apocalypse into her Edenic fantasies. The artist's fascination with ancient history and mythology also influenced her image-making, as evidenced by the disembodied faces of gods, goddesses, kings, queens, and prophets that hover like giant specters amidst her otherworld greenery. Festooned in feathers, enshrined in floral wreathes, or crowned in rainbow light, these divine figures gaze serenely out of the arabesque foliage that entwines them (fig. 13). Enigmatic characters transported from distant times and foreign places, they are signifiers of exotic realms and of the essential mystery underlying Evans's religious belief.

Evans imbued her work with a further sense of religious mystery by incorporating passages of cryptic text into her images. Attempting to summon the sacred, her secret hieroglyphics mimic the mediumistic writings and graphic invocations of spiritual power found in many religious traditions. The compositional structures of Evans's work encodes still other spiritual ideas. Organizing her sensual garden imagery into highly symmetrical designs, the artist portrayed a universe that was not random or chaotic but subject to the order and harmony of God's divine plan.[60] Some commentators have also likened the artist's flatly patterned, hieratic drawings to the schematized world vision that characterizes the meditative mandalas of India, while others connect her strong axial arrangements to the cross-shaped diagram of intersecting spiritual and earthly spheres known within Afro-Atlantic religious philosophy as the Kongo cosmogram.

Among the most haunting spiritual elements in Evans's work are the eyes that appear within the markings on butterfly wings, emerge from the feathered backs of birds, and peer out from the artist's forest of floral forms. These hypnotic images allude to the power of an all-seeing God and to the divine spirit that animates all creation. They are also symbols for spiritual vision itself and for the quality of deep discernment possessed by Evans and other religious seers. In the artist's favorite accounts of Revelation, there is a reference to "four beasts full of eyes before and behind," who prophesy the coming of the Lord (Revelation 4:6). The terms "four-eyed" or "double-sighted" are also used within African American culture to describe those individuals who are able to perceive more than one plane of existence at a time.[61]

While such mysticism may seem extraordinary, the visionary experiences that inspired Evans's art-making are familiar occurrences within the Christian supernatural and many African American spiritual practices. The embrace of biblical miracles within these traditions as well as the belief in the dreams and revelations that underlie the scriptural accounts of Daniel, the prophet Ezekiel, and St. John the Divine precondition the acceptance of personal visions among the faithful. In black churches in the South, when a member of the congregation is suffering a personal crisis, he or she is encouraged to pray for an instructive dream or apparition.[62] And during services, the mark of a successful preacher is his or her ability to bring about the arrival of the Holy Spirit and to inspire direct communion with God among receptive and divinely chosen worshipers.[63] Similarly, the pastor of Evans's church sanctioned her dreams as God's doing, a special gift of the spirit. In one sense, her art was simply a productive means of dealing with the demands and rigors of her religious visions.[64]

The overarching theme of Evans's art—the divine in nature—is also a prevailing convention of Western religious thought, rooted in Adam and Eve's sacred garden. Within this theological scheme, nature becomes a metaphor for the sublime and a reflection of God's grace and glory in the world. Evans captured a feeling of beatific splendor in her highly sensuous renderings of butterflies and blossoms, snails and seedpods, leaves, vines, and tendrils. Often cited as a source of inspiration for her botanical marvels were the opulent natural surroundings of the Airlie Gardens estate in Wilmington, North Carolina, where Evans worked as a gatekeeper for almost thirty years. But even more significant were the impulses of her religious imagination. The iconography of nature intimately connected Evans with the divine. As she once explained, "God dressed this world in green. . . . Green is God's color. He has six hundred and some shades of [it]."[65]

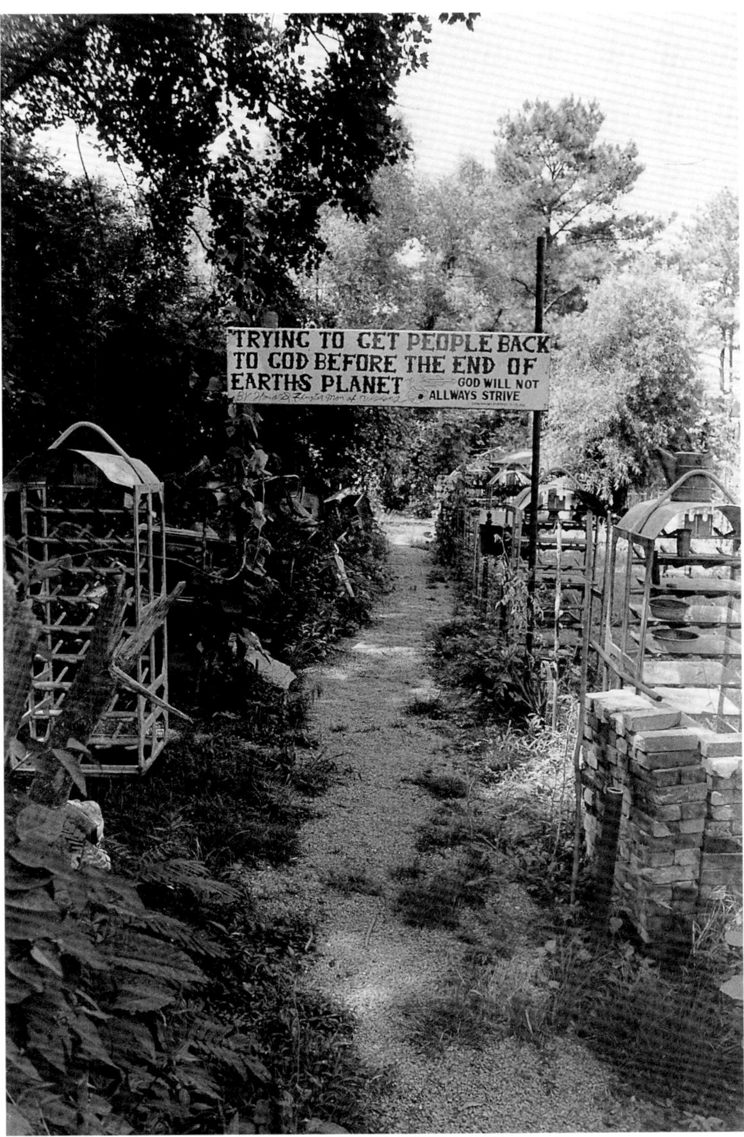

Figure 14. The back gate to Paradise Garden, 1987.

While Evans was drawing her heavenly jungles, Howard Finster, another artist a few hundred miles away, was building his own vision of Eden in a fabulous environmental creation that he called Paradise Garden (fig. 14). Begun in the 1960s and developed over two decades, Finster's two-acre site in Pennville, Georgia, gradually evolved into a labyrinth of horticultural wonders, homemade waterways, and glass-encrusted walls and sidewalks. Within his garden universe appeared a growing collection of idiosyncratic monuments, painted concrete sculptures, architectural whimsies, and found-object constructions, including his *Bible House*, *Serpents of the Wilderness Mound*, bicycle tower, floating tin angel, and spired wedding-cake chapel dubbed the World's Folk Art Church.[66]

Hoping to represent every verse of the Bible in his environment, Finster mounted countless signboards with scriptural quotations and spiritual exhortations. Linked to the tradition of roadside evangelism, his displays of religious text resembled those frequently seen outside rural churches, on hillsides, and in yards across what Flannery O'Connor described as the "Christ-haunted" landscape of the South.[67] According to Finster, his written messages are also a means of replicating the voice of God as it spoke within the original Garden of Eden. At times, the artist's passages from the holy book assume dramatic sculptural form—a life-size lion and two calves conjured the biblical notion of the peaceable kingdom; a giant's eight-foot-long shoe referred to a warning from the Ephesians to have "your feet shod with the preparation of the Gospel of Peace" (6:15); an ornamented figure called the "Coin Man" commented on the perils of greed decried in the book of James as the root of all evil (5:1–4); and the likeness of a small child posed atop a den of snakes illustrated a passage in the book of Isaiah on the power of faith to protect the innocent from harm (11:8–9). Finally, suspended from the trees and rafters above were silver garlands, plastic bottles, and shimmering, mirror-studded "suncatchers" that cast bits of reflected light throughout the sacred setting.

Like Evans, Finster views nature as a portal to the spirit and as a place to experience the mysteries of the divine by contemplating the wonders of creation itself. In his garden, he expanded this sacred cosmology to include the products of the human imagination and placed on elaborate display a wide array of man-made inventions

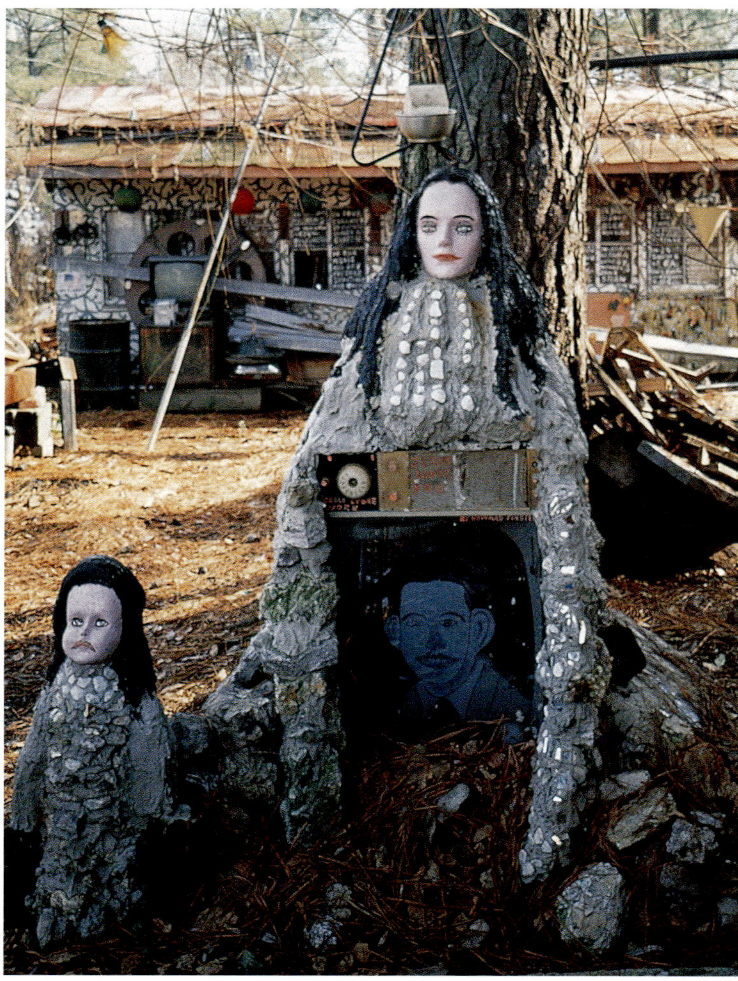

Figure 15. *Mother and Child,* which incorporates a used TV set, in Paradise Garden, 1980.

(see fig. 15) that he viewed as a kind of extension of God's own handiwork.[68] Among the remarkable artifacts on exhibit was a pair of tonsils in a jar of formaldehyde. Donated by a local boy, the unusual specimen was placed by the artist in one of his object-encrusted walls in order to celebrate the marvels of modern surgery. Other symbols of human innovation included a heart machine, a John Deere tractor, a case of dental molds, a yo-yo, a bazooka rocket, a wooden shoe cast, a mole trap designed by Mr. and Mrs. Elmer L. Sprayberry, and a wooden chair carved in a bottle by "a crippled boy in school."

In one way, Finster's garden was simply a vast reclamation project. He had built the park itself from an overgrown piece of swampland that took seven years to clear and fill. And, after joking that he was "trying to get one of everything in the world," he proceeded to collect and preserve what were at least the most curious examples. He even provided sanctuary for the remains of a Civil War victim found on a neighbor's property and encased the anonymous skeleton in a glass-topped concrete attraction entitled *Tomb of the Unknown Body of this Country*. By the time he had completed the major parts of his site, he had also incorporated literally thousands of everyday found objects into his cement structures—from silverware, jewelry, and broken watches to hubcaps, television parts, license plates, and valentine boxes.

In a poem that once hung from his garden's fence, Finster described his recycling ethos: "I took the pieces you threw away, and put them together, by night and day. Washed by rain, dried by sun, a million pieces, all in one." But more than the saving of lost things, the real purpose of his work was the retrieving of lost souls. As he explained in another sign, "I built this park of broken pieces to try and mend a broken world of people who are traveling their last road." At still another moment, he extolled, "Come see the spirit that is in even the despised of the earth and repent, the end is near."[69]

This urgent sermon of redemption, which echoed metaphorically throughout every inch of his rambling make-do environment, was a message that Finster had preached for many years. Called to God's work at the age of sixteen, he became a Baptist preacher in the early 1930s, conducting tent revivals and river baptisms, writing religious poems and homilies for local newspapers, hosting a radio prayer show, and serving as pastor to many rural congregations in the region. Often, his sermons recounted the numerous spiritual visions that he had experienced since seeing his first apparition at the age of three. Not surprisingly, it was an encounter with an otherworld specter that convinced him to concentrate his efforts on the construction of Paradise Garden. In 1976 another vision directed him even more emphatically to make art the focus of his holy ministry.

The oft-told story of this momentous event begins with Finster, then around sixty years old, at work painting one of the bicycles that he regularly repaired in order to earn extra income as a sort of fix-it man. Suddenly, after getting some paint on the tip of his finger, he looked down and, in the paint smudge, he saw a face. The face spoke to him and said, "Give up the repair of lawn mowers. Give up the repair of bicycles. Give up the preaching of sermons. Paint my pictures. Make sacred art."[70] From this divine command came the endless body of visionary paintings (see fig. 16) that would bring Finster wide recognition as an artist, spread his religious missives across vast populations, and inspire his own self-characterization as "Man of Visions, Earth's Cartoonist from God."[71]

As a painter, Finster has developed a fantastic narrative style with only a vague resemblance to illustrations in Bible books, popular comics, and other vernacular sources, which seemed to provide some initial guidance. Of course, much of his iconography was derived from Scripture, particularly the dramatic imagery of bloody seas, fiery deaths, and winged monsters in the Revelation text favored by so many Southern visionaries. To this millenialist imagery, the artist adds his own fantasies of global disaster—scenes of destruction by floods, storms, giant insects, nuclear holocaust, a dying sun, or the falling of great stars from the heavens—all mimicking the proselytizing horrors of the biblical apocalypse. Beyond such wrathful prophesies, he also paints images of the "New Jerusalem," a heavenly universe of white-robed angels, sparkling celestial mansions, and smiley-faced clouds augured to rise in the aftermath of world cataclysm. Within his holy firmaments, there sometimes appear mysterious spacecraft, unknown stars, and extraterrestrial creatures—a repertoire of less orthodox religious subjects inspired by Finster's

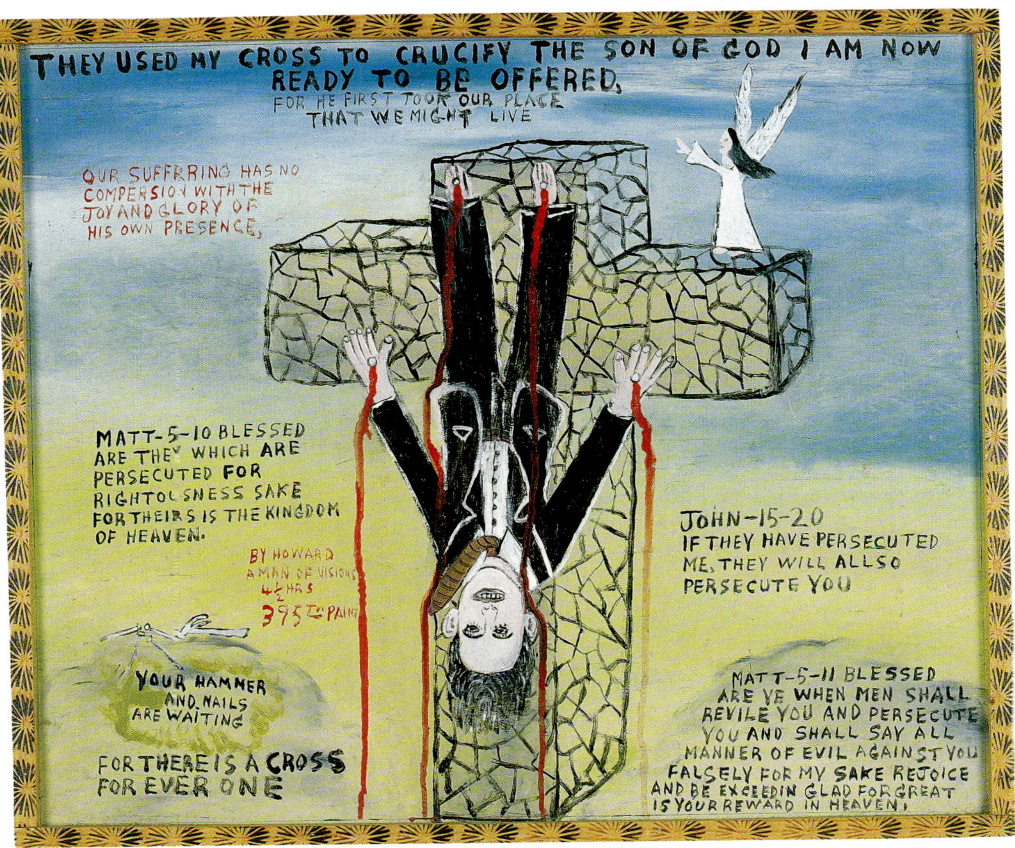

Figure 16. Howard Finster, *They Used My Cross to Crucify the Son of God*, #395, 1977, enamel on plywood, 15¼ x 18½ inches, collection of Linda and William Stoudt, promised gift to the High Museum of Art.

visions of life on other planets and his belief that he himself is a visitor from another world reincarnated here to enlighten and convert the faithless.

Finster's all-encompassing religious vision also embraces emblems of modern popular culture. He incorporates images of Delta airplanes, Coca-Cola bottles (see cat. 38), and Greyhound buses into his spiritual landscapes, and he juxtaposes the holy likeness of Jesus Christ with portraits of Elvis Presley, Santa Claus, Marilyn Monroe, Hank Williams, and other figures sanctified by their celebrity. His visual parables further include such historical personages as Leonardo daVinci, George Washington (see cat. 37), Henry Ford, and Charles Lindbergh, a pantheon of inventors, artists, explorers, and statesmen representing the creative will of God in the world. Finally, filling the spaces between his surreal imagery, Finster prints apocryphal text, a tireless outpouring of scriptural quotations, personal anecdotes, harsh moralisms, and doomsday warnings, all scrawled with the same free-form fervor that characterized his evangelist preaching.

According to some estimates, Finster has produced well over 45,000 works of art, imparting his religious messages on everything from painted gourds to Cadillac hoods. Few can rival his prolific creative efforts or the notoriety that he has garnered from an audience composed of churchgoers and rock stars, politicians and art students, folklorists and art critics. But what is even more remarkable is the consistency of purpose that has characterized Finster's work in the world. Through decades of sermons spoken and forgotten, through the building and deterioration of a holy garden, through the painting of countless visions and the fame they brought, and finally, through the recent years of mass-produced cut-outs and laundry-marker drawings, which have been said by some to mark his decline as an artist, Finster has always held close his first and only real concern—the soul of humanity and its salvation.

Appearing on a Finster self-portrait from 1987 is an excerpt from the book of Proverbs that might be regarded as a mission statement for this maker, as well as a tribute to the many other self-taught artists from the South who have contributed so richly to the landscape of contemporary art and culture: "Where there is no vision, the people perish." (29:18)

Notes

1. Simon Bronner, "Folklife, Storytelling," in Wilson and Ferris 1989, p. 488.

2. The sources for quotations from and biographical information on Traylor are Shannon 1988; and "Remembering Bill Traylor: An Interview with Charles Shannon," in Maresca and Ricco 1991, pp. 3–31.

3. Luck 1995, pp. 3–4.

4. O'Kelley, undated document, collection of the artist's papers, High Museum of Art.

5. Robert Knott, "Herbert Singleton: Between Good and Evil" (paper presented at the annual meeting of the College Art Association, San Antonio, Tex., January 1995).

6. Quoted in Artists' Alliance 1992, p. 71; and Knott 1992, p. 13.

7. Rowe entitled a small 1978 portrait drawing *Something That Ain't Been Born into this World Yet*, and she said, "I draw things you haven't seen born into this world." Quoted in "Nellie Mae Rowe in Her Own Words," in Alexander 1983, p. 11.

8. Xenia Zed, "Nellie's Hagiography," in Gruber and Zed 1996, p. 22.

9. *Nellie's Playhouse*, prod. and dir. Linda Connelly, 13 min., Center for Southern Folklore, 1983, videocassette.

10. Kogan 1998, p. 19.

11. *Nellie Mae Rowe: Folk Artist—Vinings, GA*, prod. Charles Brown, 13 min., Charleston Communication Center, 1975, videocassette. Quoted in Kogan 1998, p. 31.

12. For information on the identities of Doyle's subjects, I am primarily indebted to LaRoche 1989; and Spriggs 2000.

13. Spriggs 2000, p. 19.

14. In his book *Mystic Chords of Memory*, Michael Kammen discusses Alex Haley's 1976 book *Roots* and its later television adaptation in terms of their impact on the search for African American heritage during the 1970s. He writes, "The social and cultural impact of Haley's *Roots* was incalculable. Its twelve-hour adaptation televised in January 1977 broke all audience records in the medium, won nine Emmy awards, and most important, was believed to have a salutary effect on race relations in the United States. A little more than a year later ABC offered *Roots: The Next Generations*, a fourteen-hour sequel. The spillover effect was immediate: enthusiasm for African-American genealogy; diverse exhibitions pertaining to black family life; a new home in Harlem for the Schomburg Center for Research in Black Culture, prompted in part by the immense increase in the use of its facilities." Kammen 1993, see pp. 641–643.

15. Doyle himself attended the Penn School through the ninth grade, studying literature and carpentry. It was there that his talents as an artist were first recognized. Reportedly, he was even offered an opportunity to study art in New York by the sister of one of his instructors, an opportunity that he declined because he had to go to work. "Sam Doyle," in Livingston, Beardsley, and Perry 1982, p. 82.

16. Quoted in Spriggs 2000, p. 25.

17. For more information on the play of symbolic hierarchies in culture, see Stallybrass and White 1986.

18. Quoted in LaRoche 1989, unpaginated.

19. Quoted in Diego Cortez, "One Missing Person," in *Sam Doyle* (New York: Pat Hearn Gallery, 1986, brochure), unpaginated.

20. Quoted in Kammen 1993, pp. 121–122.

21. Baldwin, "The Price of the Ticket," in Baldwin 1985, p. xix. Quoted in Kogan 1998, p. 15.

22. Powell, "African American Postmodernism and David Hammons," in Driskell 1995, pp. 123–124.

23. Brenson, "The Pressure of Voices," in Weld, Serikawa, and Smalls 1992, p. 7.

24. "Thornton Dial Talks About His Work," in Arnett and Arnett 1990, p. 4.

25. The primary source for information on Dial's animal imagery is Paul Arnett and William Arnett, "Notes on Works," in Baraka et al. 1993, pp. 66–156.

26. Thornton Dial first described Tiger Thompson as an inspiration for his tiger imagery in *Thornton Dial: Image of the Tiger*, dir. Robert Richardson, Jr., prod. Tommie Dell Smith, 27 min., Verite Productions and Riverside Film and TV Productions, 1993, videocassette. For a further discussion of the influence of Tiger Thompson in Dial's work, see Robert Hobbs, *Thornton Dial: The Tiger Looking In* (Richmond: Virginia Union University, 1997, brochure), unpaginated.

27. Ibid. For many suggestions of tiger interpretations, I am grateful to Hobbs as well as to Amiri Baraka, "Fearful Symmetry: The Art of Thornton Dial," in Baraka et al. 1993.

28. While the interpretation here is mine, based on numerous works and statements made by Dial on the subject, it was Robert Hobbs who confirmed the artist's specific reference to the Exxon slogan. Telephone conversation with Joanne Cubbs, 11 September 1999.

29. Gates, "Criticism in the Jungle," in Gates 1984, pp. 1–24; and Gates 1988.

30. Gundaker 1998, pp. 52–55.

31. Baraka, "Fearful Symmetry," in Baraka et al. 1993, p. 49.

32. Gates, "Criticism in the Jungle," in Gates 1984, p. 6.

33. Berry and Blassingame 1982, p. 204.

34. Oliver Montgomery in *Struggles in Steel: A Story of African American Steelworkers*, prod. Tony Baba and Raymond Henderson, 58 min., California Newsreel, 1996, videocassette.

35. Interview by Lynne Spriggs and Susan Crawley, Bessemer, Ala., 5 May 1999, tape recording and transcription, High Museum of Art, curatorial files.

36. Kammen 1993, pp. 4–5.

37. Donna Gordon, "Folk Art with a Conscience: The Work of Ned Cartledge," *The World* (March/April 1993), p. 35.

38. Sources for information on Cartledge's *The Flag Waver* include Ned Cartledge, "Artist's Commentary," in Westervelt 1986, p. 12; Muller 1994, pp. 18–19; and Oppenhimer 1995–96.

39. In spring of 1998, after five years of fighting a drawn-out condemnation procedure and despite protests from the local art community, Holley's environment was destroyed to accommodate a runway extension for the Birmingham International Airport. Approximately half of his pieces were

moved in trucks to the artist's new home in Harpersville, Alabama, and the remaining works were leveled by bulldozers.

40. Conversations with Joanne Cubbs and Monique Curnen, Birmingham and Atlanta, fall 1995.

41. This work's symbolic connection to Holley's mother was verified by the artist in an interview by Lynne Spriggs and Susan Crawley, Harpersville, Ala., 7 May 1999, tape recording and transcription, High Museum of Art, curatorial files.

42. Gundaker 1993, p. 68.

43. McWillie 1987, p. 46.

44. Interview by Lynne Spriggs and Susan Crawley, Harpersville, Ala., 7 May 1999, tape recording and transcription, High Museum of Art, curatorial files.

45. Grey Gundaker, "What Goes Around Comes Around: Temporal Cycles and Recycling in African-American Yard Work," in Cerny and Seriff 1996, p. 81.

46. Patterson 1993, p. 18.

47. McWillie 1988, p. 10.

48. Conversation with Joanne Cubbs, Atlanta, 9 October 1995; and quoted in McWillie 1992, p. 83.

49. Wilson 1991–92, p. 9.

50. West 1982, p. 15.

51. Ibid., pp. 35–36; and Albert J. Raboteau, "Black Religion, Black Life," in Wilson and Ferris 1989, p. 191.

52. Quoted in Gail Trechsel, introduction to Kemp and Boyer 1994, p. 17.

53. Hooks 1995, pp. 116–117.

54. Quoted by C. E. McLaurin, 1983, Beaufort, S.C., newspaper article, High Museum of Art, curatorial files.

55. Quoted in Alexander 1983, pp. 9, 11.

56. Quoted in Kimberly Nichols, "Artists' Biographies," in Yelen 1993, p. 328.

57. Quoted in Fuller 1973, p. 3.

58. Quoted in LeQuire 1981, p. 54.

59. *The Angel That Stands By Me: Minnie Evans' Paintings*, dirs. Allie Light and Irving Saraf, 29 min., Light-Saraf Films, 1982, videocassette.

60. Kahan 1986, p. 13.

61. Gundaker 1998, p. 22.

62. McWillie 1988, p. 50.

63. Gundaker 1998, pp. 24–25.

64. Kahan 1986, p. 21.

65. Quoted in Barbara Rogers, "To Draw or Die," *Wilmington Star News*, January 19, 1969, sec. B, p. 1; and MacAdam 1990, p. 34.

66. Although Finster's Paradise Garden still stands and remains open to the public, many of the original works have deteriorated, been vandalized, or been removed from the site.

67. Quoted in Ketchin 1994, p. xi.

68. Many of the "inventions of mankind" put on display in Paradise Garden were previously assembled by Finster for a smaller "museum park" that he had begun to build in Trion, Georgia, in the late 1940s.

69. Quoted in Norman J. Girardot, "Howard Finster," in Longhauser and Szeemann 1998, p. 164.

70. Quoted in George Spencer, "American-Made: God-Inspired Art Thrives in the Nation's Heartland," in *Aspire* (June/July 1995), p. 34.

71. Finster frequently signed his paintings from the 1970s and 1980s with one or another of these appellations.

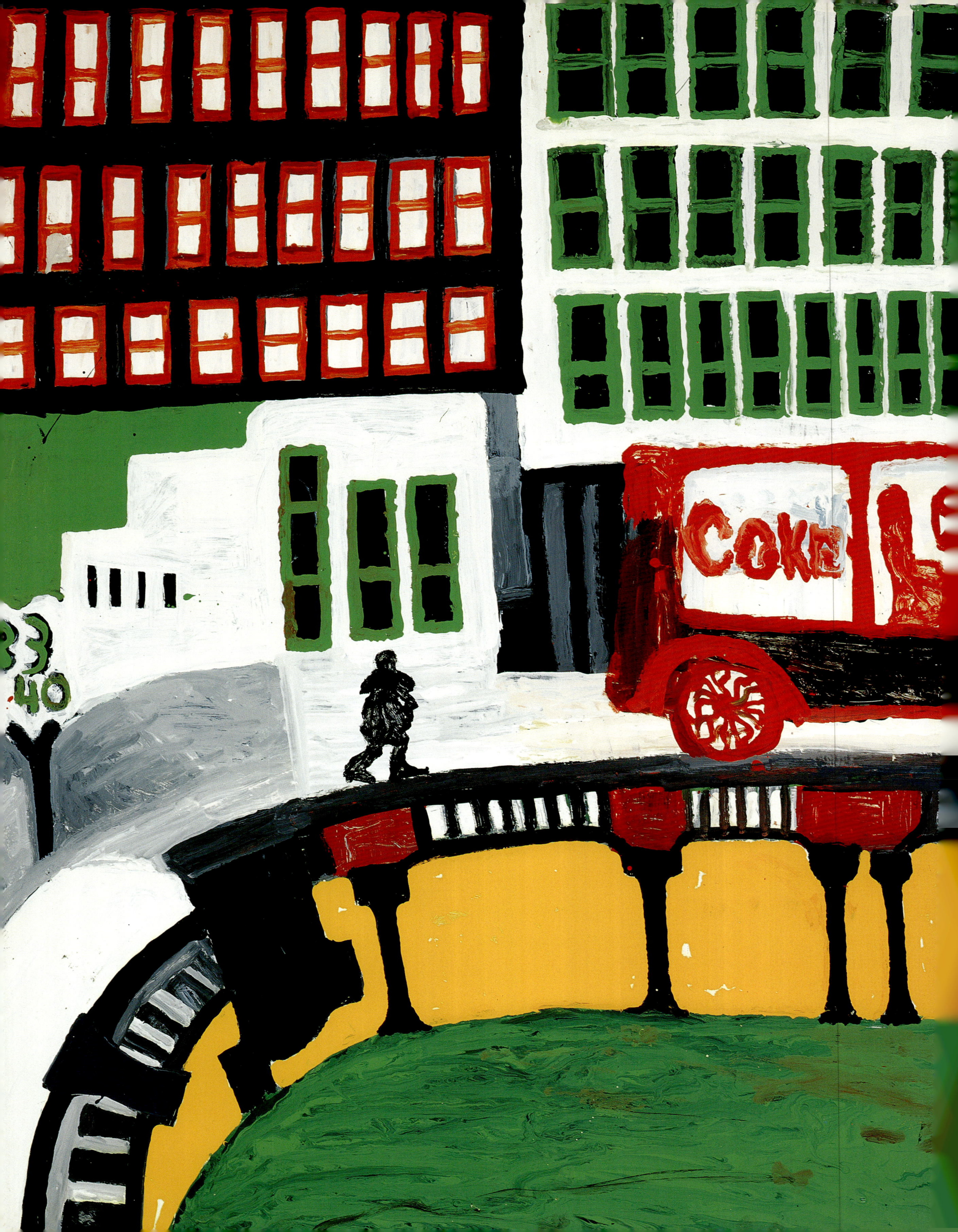
COKE
40

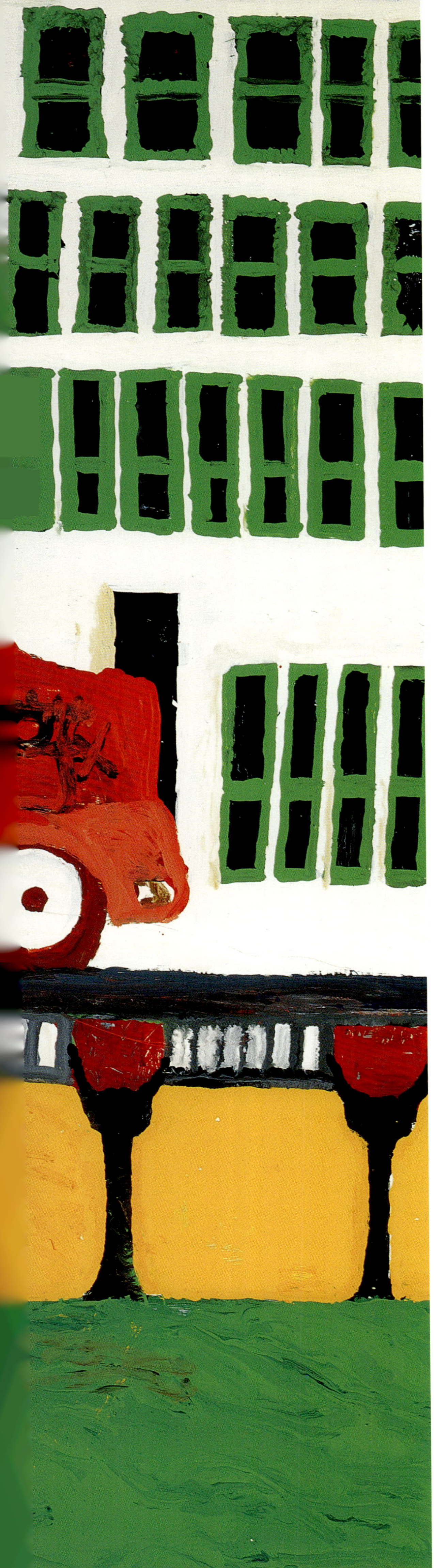

From the Sahara of the Bozart to the Shoe That Rode the Howling Tornado

Collecting Folk Art in the South

Lynda Roscoe Hartigan

Baltimore's H. L. Mencken—a bitingly perceptive essayist and editor—provoked anger, dismay, and embarrassment among his fellow Southerners when he published "The Sahara of the Bozart" in his book *Prejudices, Second Series* in 1920. Mencken's essay summarized his crusade against American tendencies toward the provincial and puritanical and indicted the South as being "almost as sterile, artistically, intellectually, culturally, as the Sahara Desert." As proof, he asserted that "in all that gargantuan paradise of the fourth-rate, there is not a single picture gallery worth going into, or a single orchestra capable of playing the nine symphonies of Beethoven, or a single opera-house, or a single theater devoted to decent plays . . . and when you come to critics, musical composers, painters, sculptors, architects, and the like, you will have to give it up, for there is not even a bad one between the Potomac mud-flats and the Gulf."[1]

This characterization underscores a dynamic that has played a large role in the evolution of collecting Southern folk art: the South's often defensive obsession with culture as the locus of its identity, countered by equal parts of ambivalence, disdain, and fascination that the Northeast has historically demonstrated toward the South. Mencken was misguided, however, in his estimation of Southern culture, which, as other writers have revealed, is rich in traditions and resources. The energy that has gathered around Southern folk art since the 1930s, for example, argues forcefully against his assertion of aridity.

A thoughtful analysis, let alone a thorough history, of collecting Southern folk art covers terrain vast enough for a book. "The wise explorer," acccording to Lytton Strachey, "will row out over the great ocean of material and lower down into it, here and there, a little bucket which will bring up to the light of day some characteristic specimen . . . to be examined with a careful curiosity."[2] This essay brings up "little buckets" of events, issues, and personalities that I regard as seminal, characteristic, or overlooked.

The 1930s

Documenting Traditional Southern Folklife and Architecture

Initiated almost immediately after the Civil War, documentation of traditional Southern folklife was pursued aggressively during the 1930s. Writers William

William Hawkins, *State Office Building #2* (cat. 40, detail)

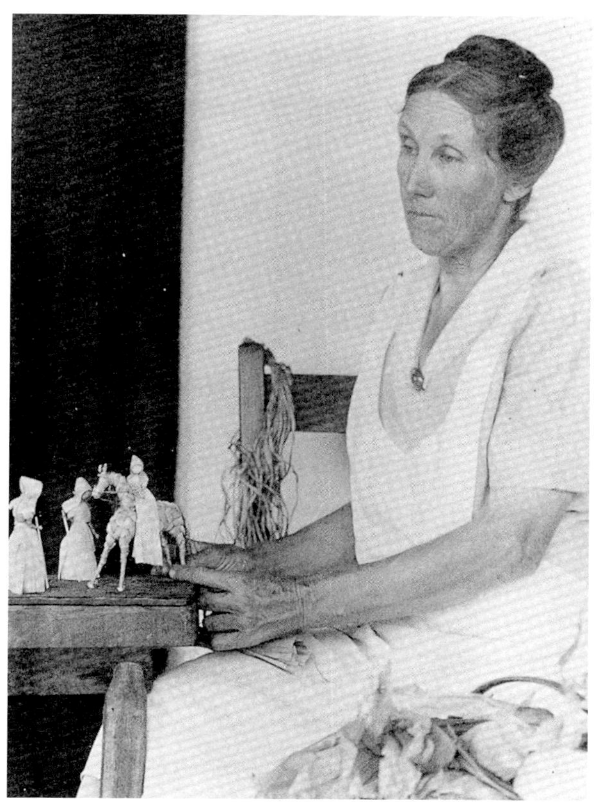

Figure 1. Mrs. Rosalie Pless, craftswoman from Russellville, Tennessee, ca. 1930. Photograph in *Handicrafts of the Southern Highlands.*

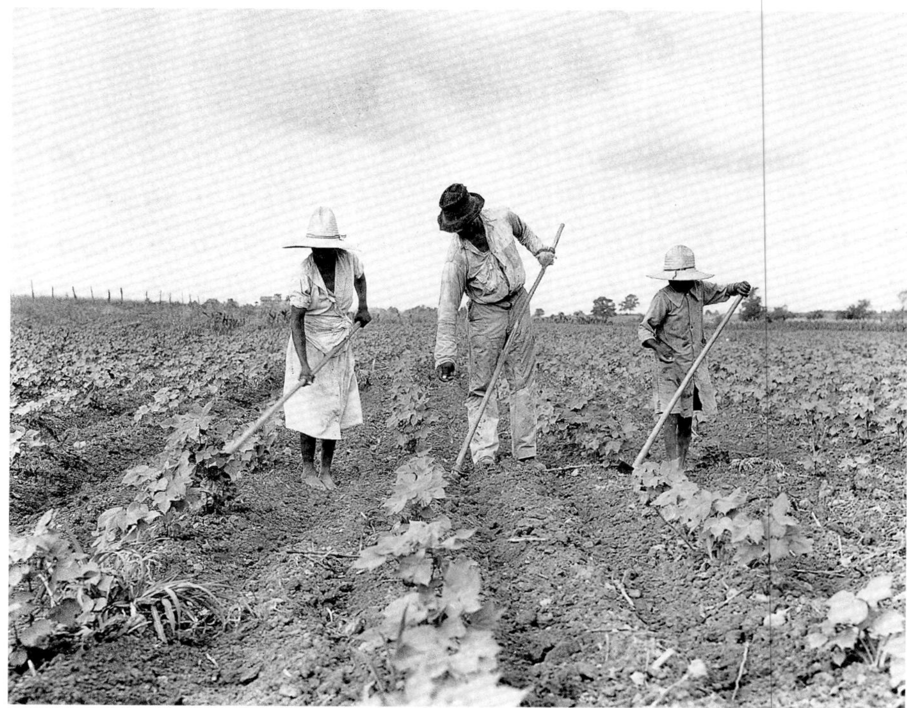

Figure 2. Tenant farmer and his family cultivating cotton, Eutaw, Alabama, July 1936.

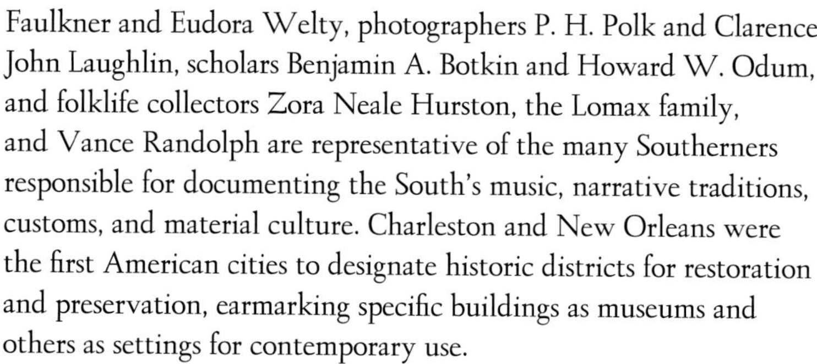

Faulkner and Eudora Welty, photographers P. H. Polk and Clarence John Laughlin, scholars Benjamin A. Botkin and Howard W. Odum, and folklife collectors Zora Neale Hurston, the Lomax family, and Vance Randolph are representative of the many Southerners responsible for documenting the South's music, narrative traditions, customs, and material culture. Charleston and New Orleans were the first American cities to designate historic districts for restoration and preservation, earmarking specific buildings as museums and others as settings for contemporary use.

Allen H. Eaton and the Craft Revival

Sociologist Allen Eaton typifies the complex role non-Southerners began to play in the documentation, revival, and distribution of Southern crafts for a national audience during the 1930s. His book *Handicrafts of the Southern Highlands* (fig. 1), which the New York–based Russell Sage Foundation published in 1937, is considered the first comprehensive study of southern Appalachian crafts. Despite Eaton's nostalgia for the rural, he provided scholars and the general public with information on regional crafts (including folk carving but emphasizing quilts, baskets, and the like), connoisseurship, techniques, materials, and designs. Aspiring to promote self-sufficiency in the region, Eaton extolled the educational and socioeconomic benefits of the South's historical craft revival programs, such as those at Berea College in Kentucky since 1893 and at North Carolina's Penland School of Crafts, the country's oldest and largest craft school, founded in 1923.[3]

The Depression, the FSA, and Photography

In 1929, the South was all too familiar with poverty, inescapable after the Civil War and exacerbated by the agricultural system's decline after World War I. President Franklin D. Roosevelt identified the region's poverty as the "nation's number one economic problem" as he inaugurated New Deal programs such as the Civilian Conservation Corps and Works Progress Administration during the mid-1930s. These programs provided direct relief, especially in the South. Simultaneously, the Federal Writers' and Music Projects—geared toward employment, uplift, and preservation—collected priceless records of everything from slave narratives to folksongs and produced publications from state guidebooks to anthologies of folktales and life histories of Southern farmers and workers.

The federal program that had the greatest impact on the country's image of the South was the Resettlement Administration, later renamed the Farm Security Administration (FSA). Building on the social reform example of Lewis Hine's photographs of Southern working conditions in 1907, FSA administrator Roy Stryker dispersed photographers across America to document the conditions of farming communities. The South's agrarian economy took center stage in many FSA photographs (fig. 2). Dorothea Lange, Marion Post Wolcott, Arthur Rothstein, Ben Shahn, and Walker Evans—primarily non-Southerners—captured the region's disenfranchised farmers to empathetic effect. Although North Carolina's pioneering publisher W. T. Couch argued in 1933 against stereotyping the

South as having an agrarian, anti-industrial culture, he and others of like mind could do little to offset that image as it achieved iconic status in James Agee's words and Walker Evans's photographs for their 1941 book *Let Us Now Praise Famous Men*.[4]

Holger Cahill

A naturalized citizen who changed his name to disguise his Icelandic heritage, Holger Cahill was American folk art's principal missionary in the 1930s. He created a picture of the common man different from that offered by FSA photographers. The craftspeople (primarily New Englanders) whose functional and decorative achievements he celebrated—in historic exhibitions at the Newark Museum, The Museum of Modern Art, and Colonial Williamsburg between 1930 and 1938—were presented as sturdy, productive Americans during the eighteenth and nineteenth centuries.

Cahill traveled extensively to build Abby Aldrich Rockefeller's folk art collection, and in 1934 he headed south on a buying trip at her request. Years later he recalled that, "I didn't buy enough in the South ever to send it by truck," even after four months of canvassing in search of the ceramics, furniture, and paintings he had expected to find in a part of the country he considered older and more established than the Midwest, where he was raised.[5] When Cahill visited Jacksonville, Florida, he began "to gather the impression that the South had been left behind in the cultural development of the United States because of the poverty after the Civil War." Heartened by a few choice discoveries in Charleston and Savannah, Cahill was disappointed in Atlanta, where he found almost nothing "with the exception of a glass painting in the German style." While he considered Tennessee's and Kentucky's mountain crafts charming, the trip's greatest find—a rare watercolor of eighteenth-century African American life—occurred in Orangeburg, South Carolina. Although Cahill and those documenting Southern folklife at the time were focused on the past, their impressions and results were worlds apart, the curator coming away almost empty-handed, the documentarians filling volumes and photo files.

William Edmondson

New York fashion photographer Louise Dahl-Wolfe photographed William Edmondson's stone carvings (fig. 3) in Nashville between 1934 and 1937 and shared them with The Museum of Modern Art's founding director, Alfred Barr.[6] Like Cahill, Barr was involved in the period's discussion of modernism and primitivism. In 1937, Dahl-Wolfe's advocacy earned Edmondson a one-person exhibition that Dorothy Miller (Cahill's wife) organized at the Modern. It was the first such honor the museum accorded an African American artist. A blizzard of press in the art world, popular magazines, the African American community, and wire-service newspapers covered the occasion. Although Edmondson's public profile had receded considerably on the national level by the mid-1940s, the celebrity that he experienced was historic, at the time outdoing Horace Pippin's in sheer volume and condescending fascination and preceding Grandma Moses's well-managed rise to sustained fame by 1946. The twentieth-century's first folk art star rose, it would seem, from the black South.

The 1940s

The Folk Art World, Dead or Alive?

Busy directing the Works Progress Administration's federal art program between 1935 and 1942, Cahill unofficially ceded the role of folk art champion to a fellow New Yorker, Sidney Janis, a modern art dealer, collector, curator, and writer. Janis gravitated toward living folk artists, especially painters, and in 1942 published *They Taught Themselves: American Primitive Painters of the 20th Century*. By 1946, when reproductions of memory paintings by Grandma Moses began appearing on Hallmark Christmas cards, Moses and American folk art were inseparable for the public, convinced as never before that the rural Northeast was folk art's domain. The window of opportunity that Janis had opened for contemporary folk artists otherwise closed: the folk art world was more comfortable in the realm of antiques and the art world turned away from the discourse about European Modernism and folk art and toward Abstract Expressionism as America's new art.

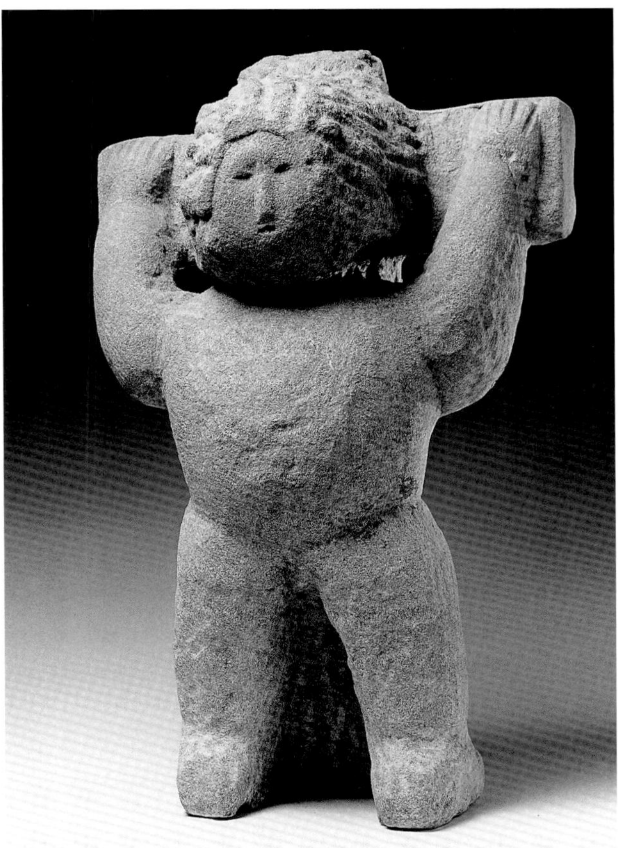

Figure 3. William Edmondson, *Crucifixion*, 1932–1937, limestone, 18 x 11⅞ x 6¼ inches, Smithsonian American Art Museum, gift of Elizabeth Gibbons-Hanson. One of nine sculptures in Edmondson's 1937 one-person show at The Museum of Modern Art.

Bill Traylor

In 1942 Victor d'Amico, The Museum of Modern Art's pioneering director of museum education, organized Traylor's first one-person show outside of his native Alabama at the Fieldston School of the Ethical Culture Schools in Riverdale, New York. D'Amico subsequently offered some of Traylor's drawings to Alfred Barr for the Modern's collection and to private collectors. He had not, however, consulted his source, Charles Shannon, the Montgomery painter who had befriended Traylor and collected many of the fifteen hundred or more drawings he created between 1939 and 1942. Incensed by the paltry sum suggested, Shannon demanded their return and retreated from his efforts to bring attention to Traylor until 1979. The exchange between d'Amico and Shannon marked the first controversy surrounding the patronage of an African American self-taught artist, a controversy that foreshadowed issues of ownership, access, and equity that returned to plague not just Shannon but the contemporary folk art field in the early 1990s.

Melville J. Herskovits and James Porter

Anthropologist Melville Herskovits published his landmark work, *The Myth of the Negro Past*, in 1941. Although he argued that diverse black American cultural forms retained African characteristics, he maintained that visual manifestations of African American folk art and crafts were long lost. For the next three decades, Herskovits's findings and theories went unnoticed by art historians disinterested in African American art, folk art, and material culture.

African American painter and art historian James Porter invoked adjectives like eccentric and inexplainable in "Naïve and Popular Painting and Sculpture," a chapter in his 1943 book, *Modern Negro Art*. Writing about Edmondson, Porter aligned the carver's efforts with the intuitive and child-like, as did many of the period's mainstream writers on folk art. He also suggested that Edmondson's "stammerings of the imaginative intelligence" evoked "symbols of half-articulated meaning familiar to the race-mind."[7] Porter was ambivalent about claiming an intuitive kinship between African art and black folk artists, an attitude he shared with Harlem Renaissance philosopher Alain Locke. Both believed that this assumption slowed access to the mainstream for trained African American artists. In the 1920s Locke had recognized the contributions of early black artisans, who were associated with the South, but refused to equate African art's "discipline," "style," and "technical control" with the work of black self-taught artists and craftsmen.[8] Locke and Porter helped set in motion the sense of conflict that has surrounded the perception of black folk art in African American cultural circles.

The 1950s

Black Mountain College

During its short-lived existence between 1933 and 1956, Black Mountain College mingled North and South, black and white, American and European in its rural North Carolina setting. Its avant-garde approach to the arts and education reached its zenith between 1951 and 1956 under the direction of poet Charles Olson. Among the students he attracted was painter Robert Rauschenberg, a native of rural Texas. Rauschenberg's combine paintings, which feature everything from a paint-spattered family quilt to old tire treads, introduced the contemporary art world to the improvisational aspects of Southern vernacular culture during the mid- and late 1950s.

Shades of Mencken and Cahill

In 1952, Colonial Williamsburg, the magazine *Antiques*, and The Virginia Museum of Fine Arts in Richmond organized *Southern Furniture, 1640–1820*, the exhibition that inaugurated serious interest in Southern decorative arts. Its success contradicted Edgar P. Richardson's damning assessment, "very little of artistic merit was made south of Baltimore," which he had delivered in his capacity as the Metropolitan Museum's American art curator at Colonial Williamsburg's first Antiques Forum in 1949.[9] Eight years later Nina Fletcher Little, the noted folk art collector in Massachusetts, asserted that "New England was the richest center of folk art because it was richest in craftsmen" and that "in the South there is less evidence of folk art" in her publication on the Abby Aldrich Rockefeller Folk Art Museum's collection.[10] The Northeast still dominated folk art's rural, preindustrial stereotype, delaying appreciation of the South's contributions, but the collaborative project devoted to Southern furniture signaled an impending revision of this limited perspective.

The Abby Aldrich Rockefeller Folk Art Museum

The Abby Aldrich Rockefeller Folk Art Museum (AARFAM) opened in 1959 as the country's first folk art museum, located adjacent to the Historic Area of Colonial Williamsburg. In operation since 1926, Colonial Williamsburg was the nation's first major outdoor museum. It was already an extraordinary demonstration of the Rockefeller family's interest in preserving early America's heritage when Abby Aldrich decided in 1939 to place the bulk of her folk art collection there.

The original nucleus of 424 works, dating primarily from 1740 to 1865, has since grown to almost three thousand. Although the Museum retains a historical focus for its collection, it began acquiring twentieth-century examples in 1957, earlier than is usually assumed.[11] Edgar A. McKillop, William Edmondson, Miles Carpenter, Eddie Arning, Edgar Tolson, and Mattie Lou O'Kelley—from North Carolina, Tennessee, Virginia, Texas, Kentucky, and Georgia—are some of the modern Southerners represented. AARFAM's exhibitions, publications, and interpretive programming devoted to the folk arts of eighteenth- and nineteenth-century America have provided models of scholarship. Less known is the Museum's adventuresome efforts on behalf of contemporary Southern self-taught artists. As early as 1972, it exhibited James Hampton's mid-century visionary environment, *The Throne of the Third Heaven of the Nations Millennium General Assembly* (fig. 8). In the mid-1970s AARFAM supported efforts to document Walter Flax's personal fleet of homemade ships in nearby Yorktowne, Virginia, establishing it as an early force in the preservation of environments by self-taught artists.

The 1960s

The Corcoran Gallery of Art

American Painters of the South—with sixty-six artists represented by 124 works created from about 1710 to 1860—opened in the spring of 1960 at the Corcoran Gallery of Art in Washington, D.C. Its modest catalogue opened with a bold assessment:

> A history of painting in the American South has yet to be written. . . . Since, for a variety of reasons, the Southern states have not been combed for native works of art to the extent, for instance, that the Northeast has, the average museum visitor may be acquainted with only half a dozen names of painters of the South, and may have a very lopsided view of the history of American art as a result.[12]

The portraits, landscapes, and genre scenes in the show compared favorably to those produced elsewhere in the country, and the mix of regional and visiting artists, including Europeans, was also characteristic. Folk art and works by academically trained artists were intermingled to demonstrate the range of American talent. Claiming little about regional traditions or characteristics, the exhibition made the first serious attempt to add the South's early folk and fine arts to the history of American art, itself a fledgling topic among scholars and collectors at the time.

Minnie Evans

In 1962, Nina Howell Starr encountered the colorful visionary drawings of Minnie Evans, an African American gatekeeper for Airlie Gardens in Wilmington, North Carolina. A photography student at the University of Florida, Starr documented roadside folk art and began photographing and interviewing Evans, who had started drawing in 1935. Over the course of their twenty-five year friendship, Starr purchased approximately five hundred works. She also arranged for the artist's first show in New York in 1966, and, nine years later, curated her one-person show at the Whitney Museum of American Art; Evans was the first contemporary folk artist the Whitney so honored.

Museum of Early Southern Decorative Arts

The country's only museum dedicated to the early South's regional decorative arts opened in 1965 in Winston-Salem, North Carolina. The Museum of Early Southern Decorative Arts (MESDA) is part of Old Salem, Inc., incorporated in 1950 as a historic restoration of an eighteenth-century town founded by Moravian settlers from Pennsylvania. Like Colonial Williamsburg, Old Salem combines scholarly research, educational outreach, and tourism. MESDA features paintings, furniture, ceramics, textiles, silver, and metalwork made and used in Maryland, Virginia, the Carolinas, Kentucky, Georgia, and Tennessee through 1820. Its surveys of the South have advanced efforts to locate, catalogue, and preserve traditional crafts.

Grassroots Revival and Preservation Efforts

America's sense of itself as a world power after World War II contributed to a nationwide folk revival during the 1950s and 1960s; popular and scholarly interest in the South's musical and craft traditions ran high. In the early 1960s, for example, New Orleans artist and dealer Larry Borenstein persuaded Allan and Sandra Jaffe to found Preservation Hall in the French Quarter. There, classic New Orleans jazz came alive again, and the achievements of elderly black musicians were introduced to new audiences. In 1969, the nonprofit New Orleans Jazz and Heritage Foundation, Inc., was organized to preserve and promote the area's indigenous culture. An annual pilgrimage for many, the New Orleans Jazz and Heritage Festival is the Foundation's principal fundraiser for its community-oriented goals. Borenstein, the Jaffes, and the Festival provided support and exposure in the 1970s for a key New Orleans figure: the African American missionary, musician, and self-taught painter Sister Gertrude Morgan.

In March 1967, B. Eliot Wigginton's high school English students in rural Clayton, Georgia, published *Foxfire*, a "homegrown" magazine of their poems and short stories interspersed with tales and home remedies gleaned from the community. Wigginton and his students continued issuing the magazine and established a nonprofit foundation oriented toward regional educational enrichment. In 1972 Doubleday published *The Foxfire Book*, an anthology that sold more than three million copies, a company record at the time, and a series of *Foxfire* volumes—featuring topics such as folk carving—proved equally successful over the next decade.

Founded in rural Lechter County, Kentucky, in 1969, Appalshop is a nonprofit arts and education center that provides training opportunities for the region's poor and minorities through a wide range of programs: film, television, and theater production, noncommercial radio programming, musical recordings, and books. Appalshop has earned national acclaim for producing and distributing materials about Southern mountain culture.

Edgar Tolson

Government-sponsored cooperatives since the 1920s have stimulated regional economies, especially in Appalachia. There, workers for Volunteers in Service to America (VISTA) and Appalachian Volunteers (AV)—programs organized as part of President Lyndon B. Johnson's War on Poverty and Great Society initiatives—began organizing new co-ops in 1965. They identified local craft traditions, recruited active craftspeople, trained new practitioners, and developed marketing strategies and outlets. Late in 1966, VISTA/AV staff encountered Edgar Tolson's small carved dolls and animals (fig. 4) just outside of hilly Campton, Kentucky, and by 1967 secured his participation in the Grassroots Craftsmen cooperative.

That same year the co-op brought its crafts, including Tolson's carvings, to the attention of Carl Fox, who oversaw Smithsonian Institution museum shops. Fox and Ralph Rinzler, a founder of the Smithsonian's Festival of American Folklife in 1967, were determined to provide a national showcase for "authentic handmade crafts."[13] Tolson sold his carvings in Smithsonian shops and demonstrated his skills at the Folklife Festival in 1968 and 1973. The Smithsonian also featured several of his sculptures between 1968 and 1976 in *American Folk Craft Survivals*, a small but prominent display at the National Museum of American History.[14]

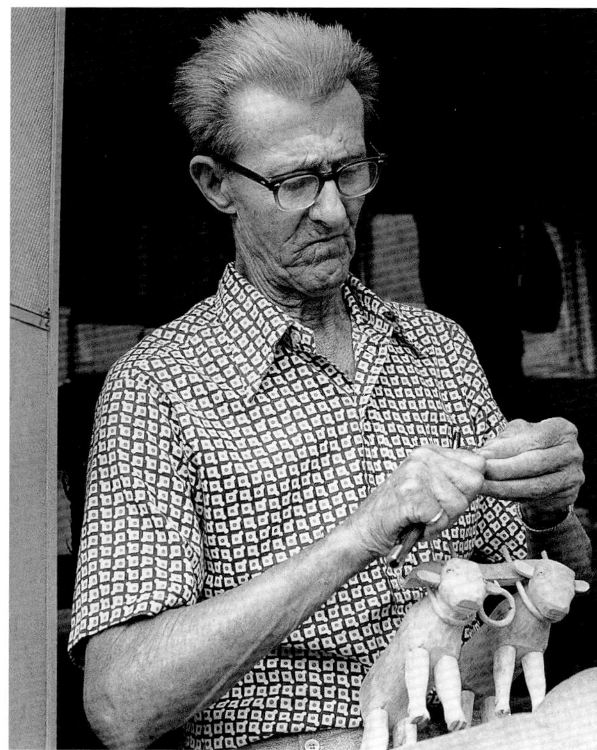

Figure 4. Edgar Tolson, Campton, Kentucky, 1979.

The 1970s

Bert Hemphill

This dapper rebel, with roots in Atlantic City, New Jersey, and Columbus, Georgia, credited Tolson with inspiring his belief that "folk art is flourishing in the U.S.A. today."[15] After acquiring Tolson's carvings in 1968 and visiting with the artist in 1970, Bert Hemphill set aside his interest in nineteenth-century folk art to focus on contemporary self-taught artists. In 1970 he organized *Twentieth-Century Folk Art and Artists* for New York's Museum of American Folk Art; in 1974 he and Julia Weissman wrote a book bearing the same title. These projects established Hemphill as the leading advocate of contemporary folk art. Even today, many collectors, curators, and dealers consider his book the major pictorial anthology of twentieth-century folk art in its selection of two hundred artists, including a healthy representation of Southerners.

Heading south came naturally to Hemphill, who had spent part of his childhood in Columbus, Georgia. Road trips between 1972 and 1977—into Virginia, West Virginia, Kentucky, Alabama, Georgia, and the Carolinas—unearthed significant additions to his collection (fig. 5), such as carvings by S. L. Jones, drawings by Nellie Mae Rowe, paintings by Howard Finster, and Southern ceramics. He made a point of sharing his collection, contacts, and knowledge —whether on the road or in his Manhattan apartment—through exhibitions, publications, and mentoring relationships until his death in 1998.

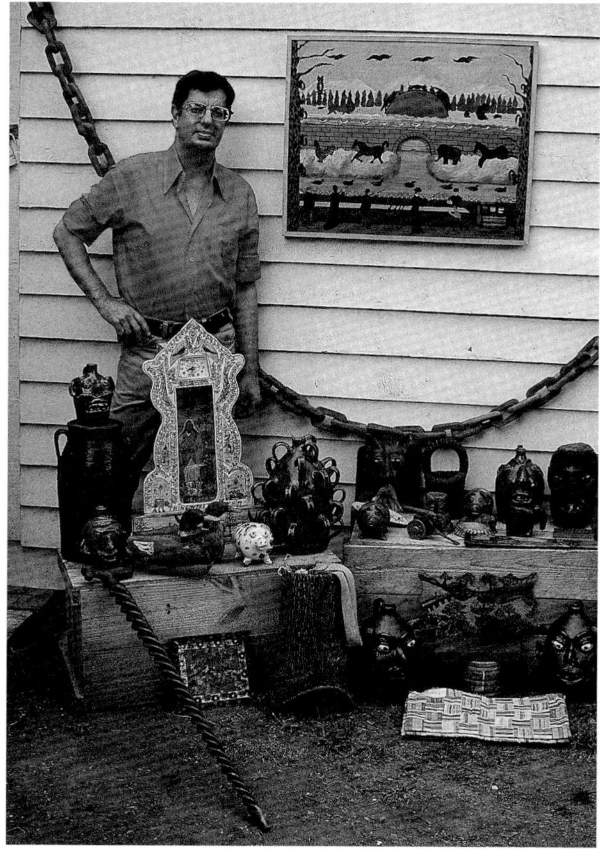

Figure 5. Bert Hemphill with ceramics, carvings, a Howard Finster clock, and other objects gathered on a Southern trip, ca. 1977.

Michael and Julie Hall

Opportunity knocked twice in the summer of 1968 as the Halls of California and Tennessee met Edgar Tolson and Bert Hemphill. They introduced Hemphill to Tolson's streamlined carvings, and he initiated them into the folk art world. Emerging in the 1970s as astute collectors, the Halls became ardent supporters of Tolson. In 1973, he was included in the Whitney Museum of American Art's biennial (the first self-taught artist accorded the honor) thanks to Michael Hall, a sculptor participating in the same exhibition. Like the painters and sculptors who recognized folk art's creative potential earlier in the century, Hall exemplifies the contemporary American artists who have responded to recent folk art, frequently documenting and collecting it in the process. Over the last three decades he has been an articulate voice for contemporary folk art in university teaching, publications, exhibitions, and public speaking.

Jeffrey Camp

On July 30, 1974, the *Wall Street Journal* published Barry Newman's "Folk Art Finders: Uncovering the Works of Untrained Artists

Takes Lots of Looking." It was the first high-profile piece in what has become widespread coverage of trends in collecting contemporary folk art. Newman alerted a new generation of collectors to the adventures and acquisitions awaiting them if they traveled the South's country roads. Written in a style that evoked Charles Kuralt's popular television series *On the Road*, the story followed Jeff Camp driving his van throughout the South on a marathon buying trip. Formerly in public relations in the Richmond, Virginia, area, Camp sold everything from quilts to country cookbooks—"the folk art experience under one roof"—between 1972 and the mid-1980s.[16] His inventory also included paintings, sculpture, and drawings by Southern self-taught artists, notably carver Miles Carpenter from nearby Waverly, Virginia, and visionary jack-of-all-media Howard Finster from Pennville, Georgia. Camp soon counted Hemphill among his clients and began sending works to pioneering dealers Janet Fleisher and John Ollman in Philadelphia and Phyllis Kind in Chicago and New York (fig. 6). A decade later, Camp was eclipsed, in part by his freewheeling style, in part by stronger players in contemporary folk art's escalating market.

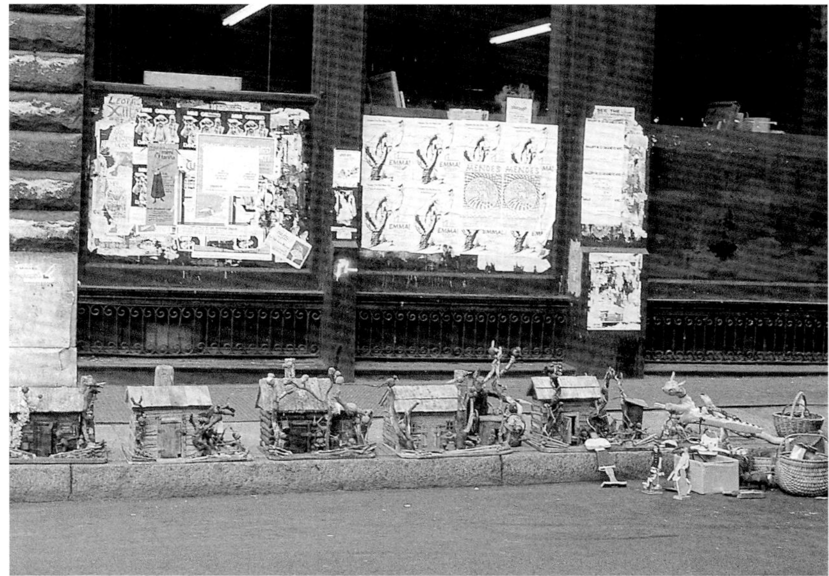

Figure 6. Contemporary Southern folk art (mostly wood tableaux by Russell Gillespie) comes to SoHo, outside Phyllis Kind Gallery, summer 1976.

The New South

Folk art collectors were not the only ones heading south. Recurring in the region's history since the 1880s, the concept of a "New South" has implied change and progress, yet has also connoted upholding a strong sense of pride in traditions and values. Even as the South continued to struggle with poverty in the early 1970s, journalists, investors, and urban studies experts pronounced a shift in urban development from the Northeast to the country's southern half from coast to coast. After World War II, pleasant weather, lower taxes, and cheap labor had attracted new businesses and industries to an area described as the "New South" or the "Sunbelt."

In 1966 the Progressive Farmer Company, then a Birmingham-based publisher, responded to this trend and elevated *Southern Living* from a one-page feature to a full-fledged magazine, which rapidly became the country's largest regional monthly. Metropolitan Atlanta became the Southeast's commercial, financial, and industrial center. The South's expanding population included many African Americans during the 1970s and 1980s. Encouraged by civil rights advances, they responded to the "Go South" and "Stay South" call, reversing the Great Migration of black Southerners who had moved north after World War I.[17]

New Centers for Southern Folklore and Culture

Since 1972, the Center for Southern Folklore in Memphis has produced internationally acclaimed films, publications, exhibitions, and festivals featuring the traditions of the mid-South region. Cofounders Judy Peiser and William Ferris spearheaded many of these efforts, which have helped revitalize Beale Street, an influential site of African American music and the heart of the city's historically black community. With Peiser as executive director, the Center has also been an important crossroads for artists, craftspeople, photographers, writers, and scholars. *Folk Art and Crafts: The Deep South*, which the Center organized in 1977 for the Smithsonian Institution Traveling Exhibition Service, provided the first national exposure for black artists such as James "Son Ford" Thomas and Luster Willis.

The Center for the Study of Southern Culture opened in 1977 at the University of Mississippi in Oxford. Under the leadership of William Ferris, Ann Abadie, and Charles Reagan Wilson, the Center's education, research, and outreach activities have integrated the arts, humanities, and social sciences for academic and popular audiences. The ambitious *Encyclopedia of Southern Culture*, published in 1989, epitomizes the Center's breadth. The encyclopedia's contributors address the South's visual arts, craft traditions, and folklife with a refreshing and authoritative variety.

William Ferris

Current chairman of the National Endowment for the Humanities, Vicksburg's William Ferris is the preeminent scholar of Mississippi folklife. His fieldwork in the late 1960s focused on the blues and Southern storytelling traditions, and he has written eloquently on the sense of place that is a hallmark of Southern folk art. After meeting Mississippi's black blues musician and self-taught sculptor James "Son Ford" Thomas in 1967, Ferris "began to look more broadly at [the] basket-making and quilting and folk painting that I had discovered in the course of my travels, and realized that this was in many ways an untapped well of creativity that had very clear connections to the oral traditions which were originally my focus."[18]

Missing Pieces

Interest in the regional and handmade reached new heights during the Bicentennial decade, when universities and government agencies also increased support of folklife programs. State surveys of folk art were particularly popular. In 1976, Georgia's survey culminated

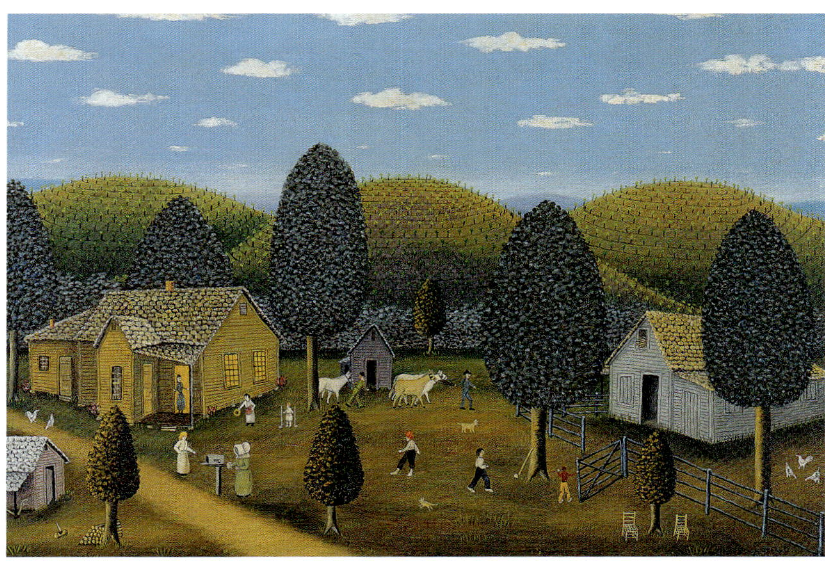

Figure 7. Mattie Lou O'Kelley, *Farm Landscape*, 1975, oil on canvas, 24 x 36¼ inches, Smithsonian American Art Museum, gift of Herbert Waide Hemphill, Jr. One of the works featured in *Missing Pieces*.

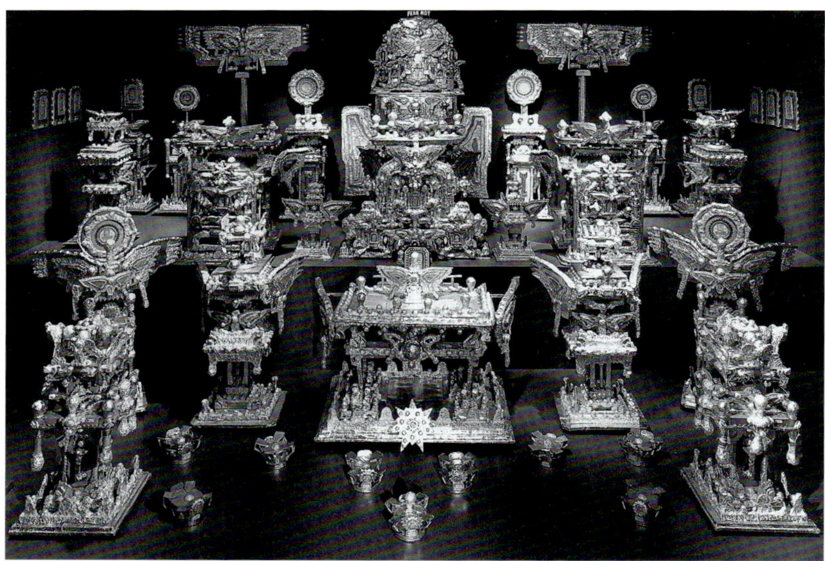

Figure 8. James Hampton, *The Throne of the Third Heaven of the Nations Millennium General Assembly*, ca. 1950–1964, gold and silver tinfoil, Kraft paper, and plastic over wood furniture, paperboard, and glass, 10½ x 27 x 14½ feet, Smithsonian American Art Museum, gift of anonymous donors.

in the exhibition *Missing Pieces: Georgia Folk Art* (1770–1976), which opened at the Atlanta Historical Society and traveled to museums in Savannah and Columbus over the next year. The Library of Congress presented it in 1978 under the auspices of its American Folklife Center, directed by Alan Jabbour since opening in 1976.

Nothing short of "discovering Southern pieces missing, until now, from the continuum of American folk art" was Anna Wadsworth's goal as she, Georganne Fletcher, and consultants prepared the exhibition, catalogue, and film.[19] The impressive team included Bert Hemphill, Alan Jabbour, Eliot Wigginton, and William Ferris, as well as John A. Burrison and Gladys-Marie Fry, experts in ceramics and textiles. A stunning group of early Georgia pottery and an ambitiously narrative Bible quilt by African American Harriet Powers distinguished the historical selection. Twenty-two contemporary self-taught sculptors and painters—Ulysses Davis, Howard Finster, Eddie "St. EOM" Martin, Mattie Lou O'Kelley (fig. 7), and Nellie Mae Rowe among them—stole the show, marking their public debut and identifying Georgia as a motherlode of living folk artists.

Judith Alexander

Atlanta dealer and collector Judith Alexander visited Nellie Mae Rowe in Vinings, Georgia, shortly after her appearance in *Missing Pieces*. Alexander was a former student of Hans Hofmann and the city's first dealer in modern expressionist art. In 1978 she opened Atlanta's first gallery devoted to Southern self-taught artists, including Rowe, Georgia Blizzard, Juanita Rogers, Bill Traylor, and Carlton Garrett. She remains Rowe's greatest advocate. Although Alexander; Marcia Weber and Anton Haardt in Montgomery, Alabama; Louanne LaRoche in Bluffton, South Carolina; and Luise Ross in New York would not align themselves in this fashion, their support of Rowe, Mose Tolliver, Juanita Rogers, Sam Doyle, Bill Traylor, and Minnie Evans, respectively, delineates the important role that women have played as collectors and dealers devoted to Southern folk artists over the past two decades.

The Mainstreaming of African American Art and Crafts Begins

When the Whitney Museum of American Art presented *Two Hundred Years of American Sculpture* as one of its Bicentennial exhibitions, critics and the NAACP decried the glaring absense of minority artists. Yet one work in the show—*The Throne of the Third Heaven of the Nations Millennium General Assembly* by African American James Hampton (fig. 8)—shone in its silver-and-gold foil glory, especially when *Time* art maven Robert Hughes described it as "the finest work of visionary religious art produced by an American."[20] After touring to the Museum of Fine Arts in Boston and the Montgomery Museum of Art in Alabama in 1977, *The Throne* went on permanent view at the Smithsonian American Art Museum in Washington, D.C. In November 1964, Hampton, formerly of South Carolina, died in Washington, leaving behind the monumental sanctuary that he had worked on since the late 1940s. In 1970, the Museum acquired the work, the first major example of American folk art in its collection.

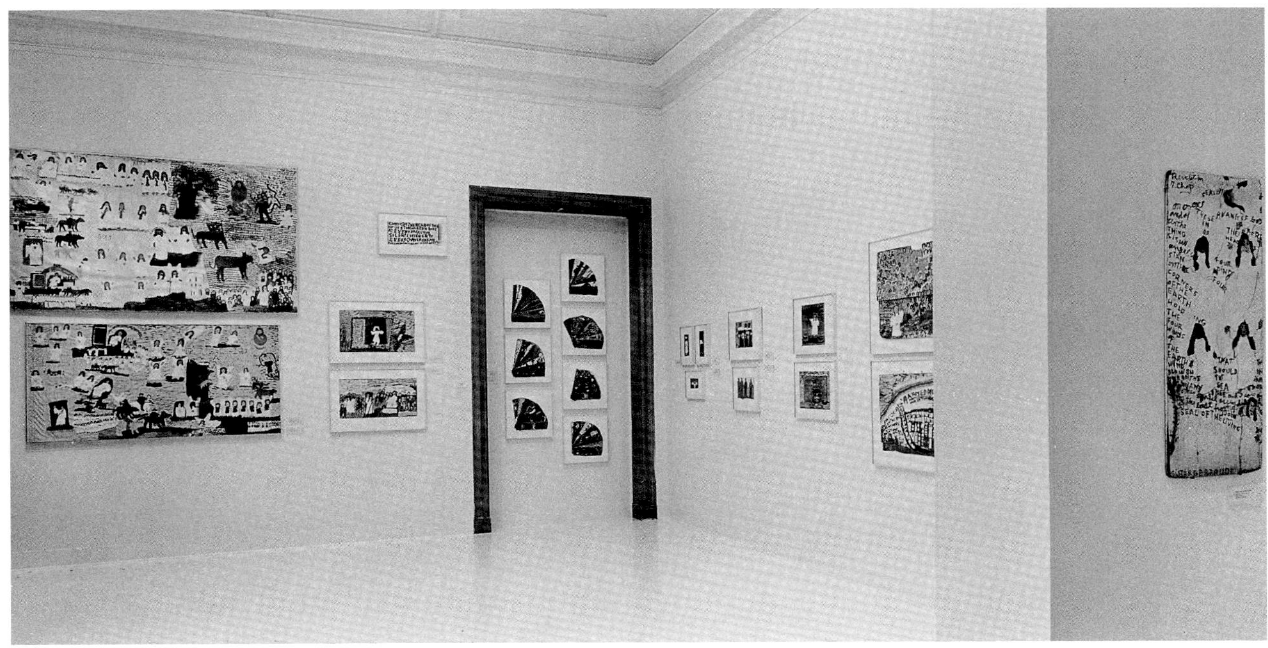

Figure 9. Sister Gertrude Morgan installation, *Black Folk Art in America, 1930–1980*, exhibited at the Corcoran Gallery of Art in 1982.

In 1976 the Los Angeles County Museum of Art presented *Two Centuries of Black American Art*. Organized by the eminent black painter and educator David C. Driskell, this survey was unprecedented in its ambitious scale and national exposure in Los Angeles, Atlanta (at the High Museum of Art), Dallas, and Brooklyn. Driskell, like Locke and Porter before him, emphasized the contributions of black artists to America's fine arts traditions. Presenting crafts, folk paintings, and sculpture made primarily in the South, the show also acquainted the general public with this underappreciated vein of African American creativity.[21]

Robert Farris Thompson and John Michael Vlach

In 1969, Yale University art historian Robert Farris Thompson published "African Influences on the Art of the United States," the first substantive documentation of African culture's transmission to and transformation in the Americas. Subsequently, his scholarship has unfolded in publications and exhibitions, exploring not just African art but also the work of modern black artists, especially self-taught African Americans throughout the South.[22] Maude Southwell Wahlman, Ramona Austin, and Grey Gundaker—dealing with textiles, walking sticks and staffs, and yard decoration, respectively—exemplify those who reflect the legacy of his teaching in their own careers as scholars of African and African American art and material culture.

Published in 1978, *The Afro-American Tradition in Decorative Arts* by folklorist John Michael Vlach is the subject's authoritative study, documenting expressions as diverse as musical instruments and graveyard decoration. Accompanying a nationally circulated exhibition that Vlach organized for the Cleveland Museum of Art, the book emphasizes utilitarian artifacts and traditional crafts made by African Americans since their arrival as slaves and into contemporary times. Like Robert Farris Thompson, he argues persuasively that African Americans are "culturally competent immigrants" with a tradition of innovation born of necessity.[23] Vlach, however, considers paintings, drawings, and sculpture by black self-taught artists as expressions of personal resources and does not include them in his axiomatic view of folk art as the socially useful art of a community.

The 1980s

Black Folk Art in America, 1930–1980

By any standards, the 1982–1983 exhibition *Black Folk Art in America, 1930–1980* was a blockbuster, with twenty artists represented by 391 paintings, sculptures, and drawings, lent by seventy-eight individuals and institutions, and hosted over two years by six major museums (fig. 9). The exhibition's emphasis on the South and the region's struggle with the old and the new was unmistakable, for all but one of the twenty artists were born and raised in the rural South, and eighteen were born before World War I and the Great Migration.

The co-curators, modern art historians Jane Livingston and John Beardsley, maintained that while black folk art is unrelated to traditional utilitarian crafts, its aesthetic reflects the communal nature of African American culture. In the companion publication, Regenia Perry, Southern black scholar of African and African American art and a pioneering collector of works by contemporary black self-taught artists, discussed black folk art's links to an "African-inspired stylistic chain" four centuries long.[24] Livingston reasoned in her introduction, however, that black folk art has flourished among

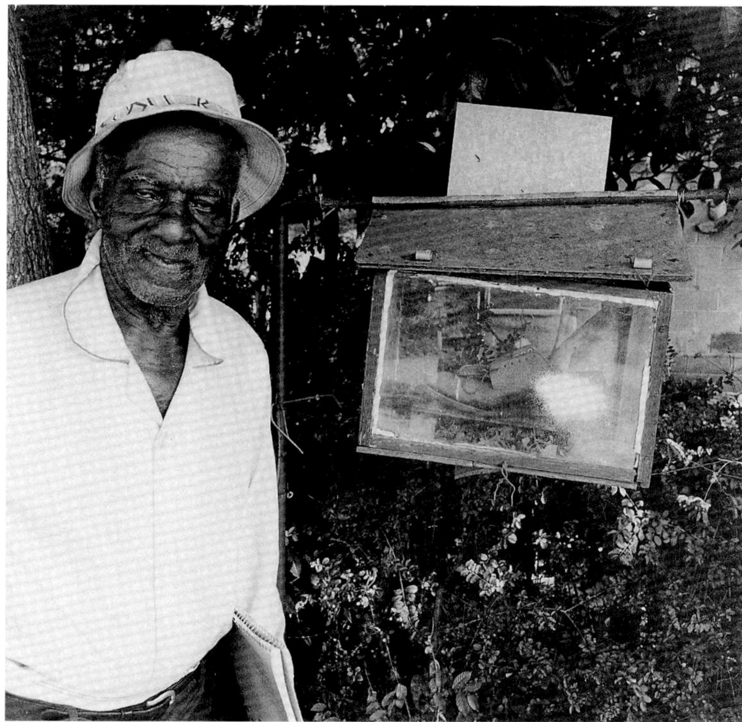

Figure 10. Dilmus Hall with his work *The Shoe That Rode the Howling Tornado*, ca. 1984.

"relatively few" individuals whose physical isolation has prevented external influences.[25] She also argued that Southern black folk artists have generated a distinctive style that dominates twentieth-century folk art. Livingston and Beardsley asserted that recognition of this phenomenon and its achievement was long overdue.

Although Dilmus Hall of Athens, Georgia, was not among the artists selected, the title of one of his found-object sculptures—*The Shoe That Rode the Howling Tornado* (fig. 10)—captures this project's tumultuous impact and legacy.[26] Art critics, folklorists, specialists in African American art and material culture—not to mention collectors and dealers—applauded the exhibition's daring and the power of the works themselves. However, many openly, even contentiously, questioned the compatibility of the show's claims for a distinctive Southern black folk art aesthetic with its recurring assertion of each artist's individuality.[27] "What It Is"—the title of Livingston's essay—posed issues that remain unresolved to this day. The excitement that the art generated is still palpable among those who saw the show or encountered the book. Almost all of the twenty artists have become widely collected, exhibited, and published, and William Edmondson and Bill Traylor, their careers resurrected by the show, have ascended to the greatest acclaim. Moreover, the list of seventy-eight lenders suggests that a small, quiet army had been at work, contributing greatly to the impression of an overnight sensation. Like Hemphill's earlier exhibition and book, the Corcoran's project issued a clarion call, refreshing or recruiting collectors, dealers, and scholars, inciting head-over-heels efforts to discover new artists, creating a market, and inspiring the contemporary art world to reexamine its assumptions and priorities.

Shari Cavin and Randall Morris

Meeting Bert Hemphill through Jeff Camp and seeing *Black Folk Art in America* in 1982, Shari Cavin and Randall Morris experienced epiphanies that took them beyond their previous interests (ethnographic materials primarily from Haiti and Mexico).[28] As the young New York–based couple began dealing heavily in the works of Howard Finster, Bessie Harvey, and other Southern self-taught artists, they brought to the art an interest in the relationship between the anthropological and the aesthetic, an approach that reflects their respect for Robert Farris Thompson's work. Cavin and Morris have advanced a dialogue between Western and non-Western forms, old and recent, in their capacity as dealers and writers since the early 1980s.

Judith McWillie and Andy Nasisse

Paging through *Black Folk Art in America* in 1982, artist Judith McWillie recognized kindred spirits. Born and educated in Memphis, she grew up understanding that "whether it's music or whether it's visual, it's always been the vernacular culture of Memphis that's put it on the map."[29] McWillie began photographing black vernacular artists in Tennessee around 1969. Joining the University of Georgia's faculty in 1974, she expanded her search to include Mississippi, Georgia, and Alabama. Familiarity with Robert Farris Thompson's writings and encouragement from Thompson himself spurred McWillie into writing, and she has specialized in interpreting visual manifestations of Afro-Atlantic religious traditions. Her exhibition and companion catalogue, *Another Face of the Diamond: Pathways Through the Black Atlantic South* (1988), exemplify her effectiveness on both fronts.

Andy Nasisse, fellow University of Georgia faculty member, cites childhood exposure to folk art environments and "object makers" in his native Colorado, throughout the Southwest, and in Mexico.[30] By the time he arrived in Athens, Georgia, around 1975, Nasisse had read Greg Blasdel's 1968 cover story on Midwestern folk art environments in *Art in America* and Roger Cardinal's landmark book *Outsider Art* (1972). He had also seen the Watts Towers in Los Angeles and soaked up outsider art in Phyllis Kind's gallery and the collections of "Hairy Who" artists in Chicago. Having traveled in the South with Bert Hemphill, Kind told Nasisse where he could find Southern folk art and referred him to a 1975 article in *Esquire* about Howard Finster. With *Missing Pieces* came new revelations. Nasisse devoted considerable time to photographing Southern self-taught artists and their environments into the 1980s. Like McWillie's, his admiration for the artists has permeated his teaching and international lecturing and inspired him to organize *MoJo Working*, an exhibition about contemporary Southern folk art, for the University of Indiana in 1988.

The Archives of American Art

Dedicated to documenting the country's visual history through primary sources, the Smithsonian's Archives of American Art expanded its activities into the Southeast during the early 1980s under the initiative of Kentucky-born art historian Estill Curtis Pennington. Inspired by the living artists and resources revealed by *Black Folk Art in America*, Liza Kirwin began augmenting the Archives's historical folk art materials (such as Holger Cahill's and Edith Halpert's) with papers, recordings, and photographs (fig. 11) from a roster that includes Jeff Camp, Howard Finster, Bert Hemphill, Judith McWillie, Andy Nasisse, Chuck and Jan Rosenak, and Willem Volkersz. The range of artists covered by these holdings establishes the Archives as a major research center for contemporary folk art.[31]

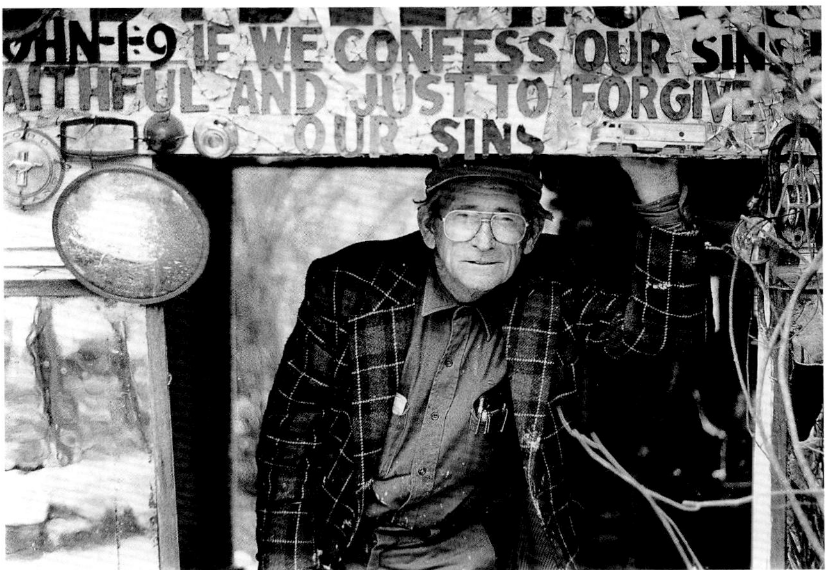

Figure 12. Howard Finster in Paradise Garden, Pennville, Georgia, April 5, 1985.

The Mainstreaming of Southern Art Begins

In 1983, two ambitious publications redressed the neglect of Southern art. From Tulane University in New Orleans, art historian Jessie Poesch focused on paintings, sculpture, architecture, and crafts in her detailed study *The Art of the Old South, 1560–1860*. The Virginia Museum of Fine Arts tackled a broader period in its nationally touring exhibition and companion book *Painting in the South, 1564–1980*, the subject's first comprehensive survey. Each book includes early examples of folk art, and the Virginia Museum's volume cites Bill Traylor as the twentieth-century exemplar.

Two years later, Cynthia Elyse Rubin published *Southern Folk Art* in conjunction with an exhibition at the Museum of American Folk Art, which has mounted exhibitions devoted to William Edmondson, Sister Gertrude Morgan, and other Southern folk artists since the mid-1960s. With the exception of Edmondson's carvings, modern self-taught artists did not figure in Rubin's study. Attending the Institute of the Museum of Early Southern Decorative Arts in 1981 inspired her art historical overview of pottery, decorated furniture, and textiles, as well as folk paintings and sculpture from the late eighteenth to early twentieth centuries. Like Poesch and the Virginia Museum's curatorial team, Rubin surveyed developments and contributors. All three books, however, resisted defining a distinctly Southern aesthetic.

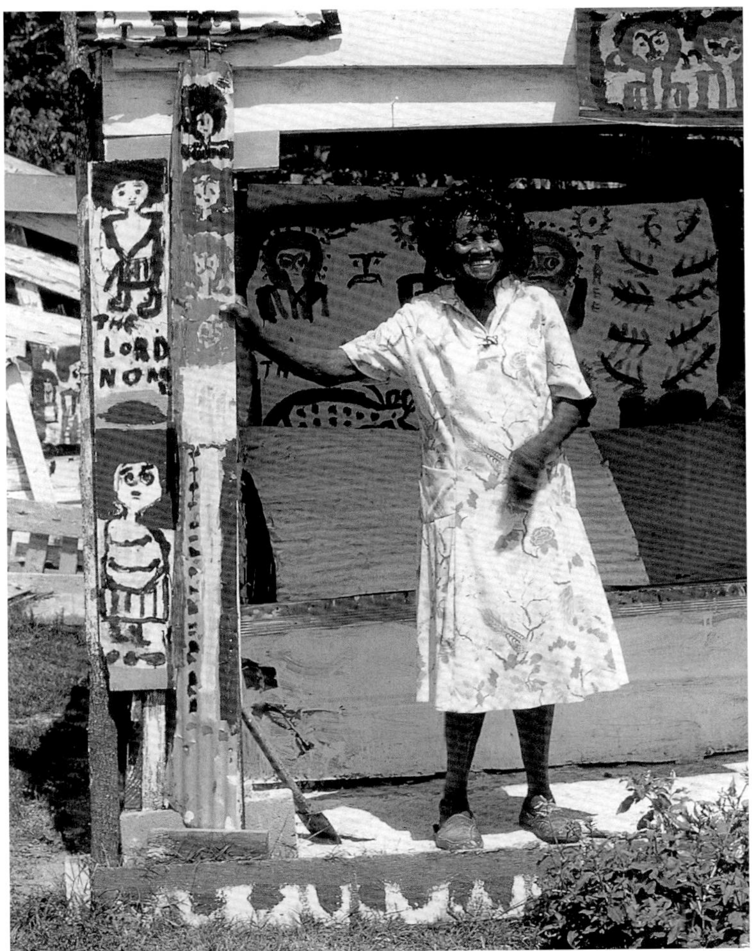

Figure 11. Mary T. Smith in front of her home in Hazelhurst, Mississippi, June 1, 1985.

Howard Finster

Georgia's "Man of Visions" Howard Finster (fig. 12) is arguably the country's most famous living folk artist. Public outreach comes naturally to this charismatic, entrepreneurial evangelist, who began building his sprawling grotto, Paradise Garden, in 1970 and creating "sermons in paint"—tens of thousands of them—in 1976. Finster's accomplishments are voluminous, but the high points say it all. *Life* magazine's June 1980 cover story on contemporary folk artists featured Finster, Miles Carpenter, Ralph Fasanella, and Mattie Lou O'Kelley. In 1982, Finster received a Visual Artist Fellowship for Sculpture from the National Endowment for the Arts and was given a solo show at the New Museum in New York; each event was a first for contemporary folk artists. The following year, Finster appeared on the *Tonight* show, rendering host Johnny Carson speechless, and the rock group REM—from Athens, Georgia—released its video, *Radio Free Europe*, filmed in Paradise Garden. Finster's inclusion in the American section of the Venice Biennale in 1984 was another milestone for contemporary folk artists. David Byrne commissioned Finster's trademark combination of words and images for the cover of *Little Creatures*, a 1985 Talking Heads album that

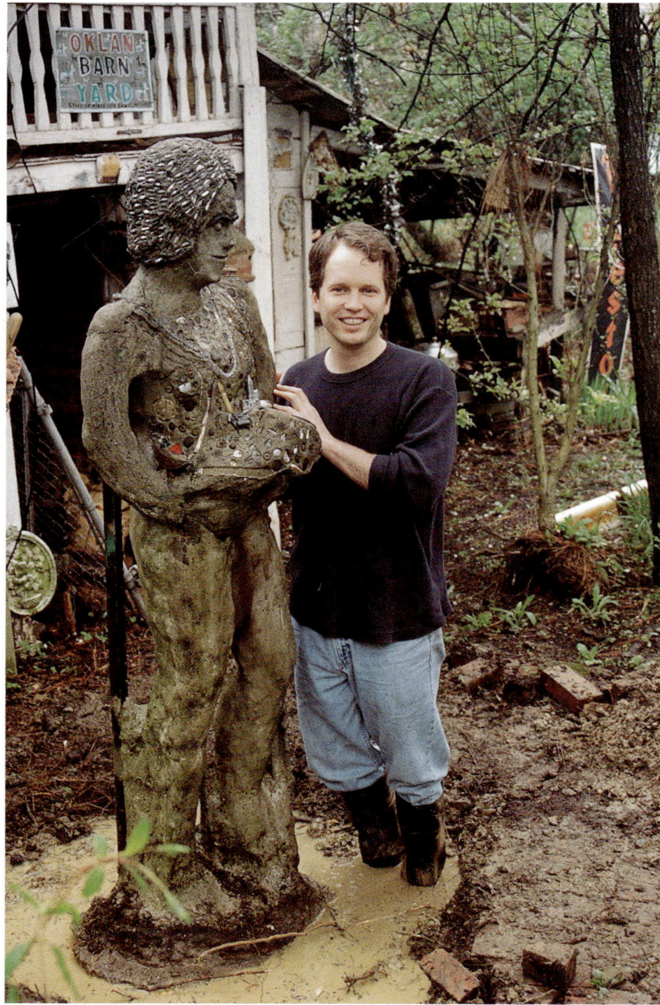

Figure 13. Bert Hunecke with *Coin Man* in Paradise Garden, ca. 1993.

sold a million copies; *Rolling Stone* magazine named it the year's best album cover. The celebrity of this man of multiple trades has swept folk art, along with collectors, dealers, curators, and the press, into the maelstrom of popular culture and contemporary art.

Jane and Bert Hunecke

Janeand Bert Hunecke of Atlanta met Howard Finster around 1983: "If we hadn't spent a day with Howard, we wouldn't be collecting this. We were collecting ethnographic material from central Asia. We're a long way from central Asia. . . . But to go and visit Howard, two hours away, and realize, 'Hey, this is our ethnographic material and we need to document this.' . . . That changed everything about the way we lived our lives outside of our careers."[32] Assembling one of the country's largest collections of Finster's works and archival materials, the Huneckes were also instrumental in the Paradise Project, a nonprofit effort begun in the mid-1990s to preserve selections from Paradise Garden (fig. 13) in the collection of the High Museum of Art. The Huneckes have combined connoisseurship and ethnographic integrity in their thoughtful collection of Southern decorative arts, plain furniture, and works by self-taught artists.

T. Marshall Hahn

A chance encounter with Streeter Blair's scenes of Americana in 1961 inspired Marshall Hahn to collect memory painting during his tenure as Dean of the College of Arts and Sciences at Kansas State University. In 1982, when Hahn moved to Atlanta, local memory painter Mattie Lou O'Kelley immediately caught his eye. Hahn also dove into the South's brand of outsider art and became a vigorous force in Atlanta's folk art scene while building a massive collection.

Signs and Wonders in North Carolina

North Carolina poet Jonathan Williams started his alternative press, The Jargon Society, while attending Black Mountain College in 1951. The 120 books Williams has published reflect his philosophy: "I just do the things that I think need to be done that probably nobody else is going to do."[33] The Jargon Society's pamphlet *Southern Visionary Artists*, written by Tom Patterson and Roger Manley in 1985, is one of its most underappreciated publications. Williams has cut a wide swath through the South, documenting the environments of folk artists and introducing other writers, photographers, and contemporary artists to unorthodox forms of creativity.

Stephen Syke's three-story pipe-and-hubcap tower and the "Goat Man's" decorated wagon flashed through Tom Patterson's mind as guest poet Jonathan Williams showed slides of outdoor environments to senior writing students at North Carolina's St. Andrews Presbyterian College in 1974.[34] Patterson has been attracted to roadside art and eccentric characters since his childhood in Mississippi and Georgia. Based in Winston-Salem, he has devoted much of his writing career to Southern visionary artists.[35] The December 1981 issue of *Brown's Guide to Georgia* featured Patterson's first lengthy piece on the subject. He has published two particularly insightful books: *St. EOM in the Land of Pasaquan: The Life and Times and Art of Eddie Owens Martin* with The Jargon Society in 1987 (see fig. 14) and *Howard Finster, Stranger from Another World* in 1989.

Both books feature Roger Manley's photographs of the artists and their environments, a passion of Manley's since his chance encounter with Annie Hooper's house overrun with sculptures on the Outer Banks in 1970.[36] Jonathan Williams introduced Manley and Patterson around 1983 and the three have shared adventures ever since. Trained as a folklorist at the University of North Carolina during the early 1980s, Manley has forged a peripatetic career as a folklorist, photographer, writer, curator, and filmmaker with diverse interests: outsider artists and their "self-made worlds," "hoaxes, humbugs, and spectacles," tribal peoples, and fairytales.[37] Throughout these pursuits runs Manley's respect for the primacy of creativity and his desire to instill that respect in others. In 1989, he produced an eloquent model, *Signs and Wonders: Outsider Art Inside North Carolina*, the publication for a traveling exhibition organized by the North Carolina Museum of Art in Raleigh.

In 1975, Allen and Barry Huffman attended a lecture on Southern pottery at the Museum of Early Southern Decorative Arts. The

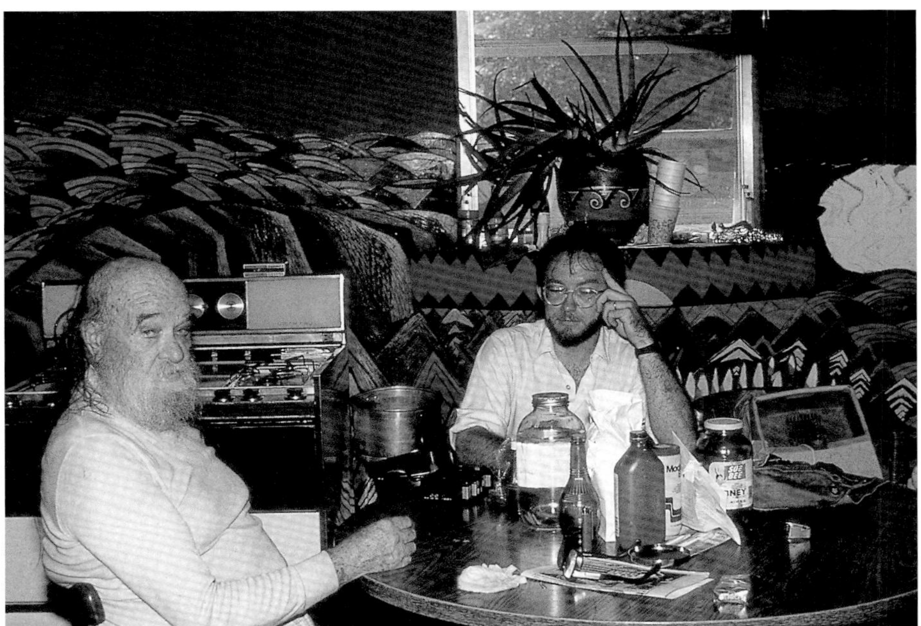

Figure 14. St. EOM (left) being interviewed by Tom Patterson at Pasaquan, October 1983.

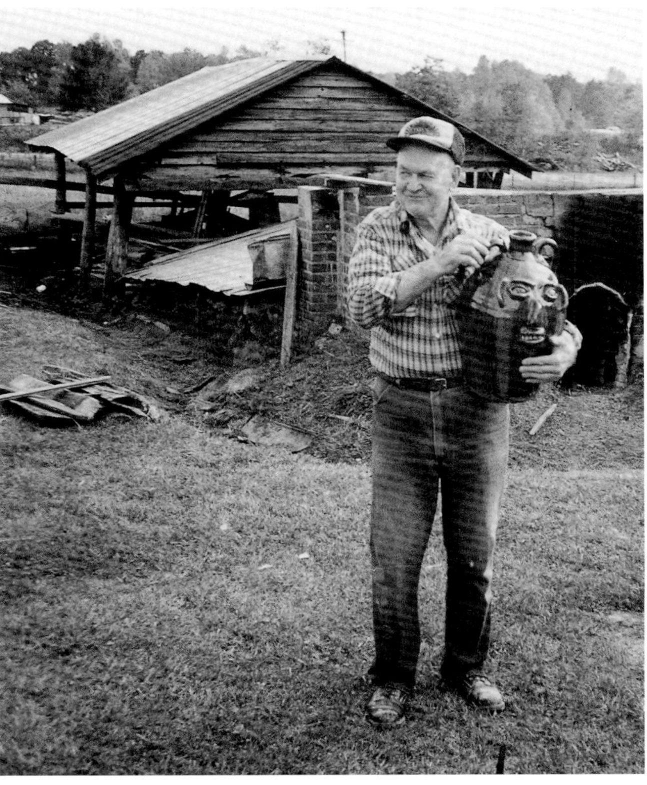

Figure 15. Burlon Craig at a kiln opening, 1992.

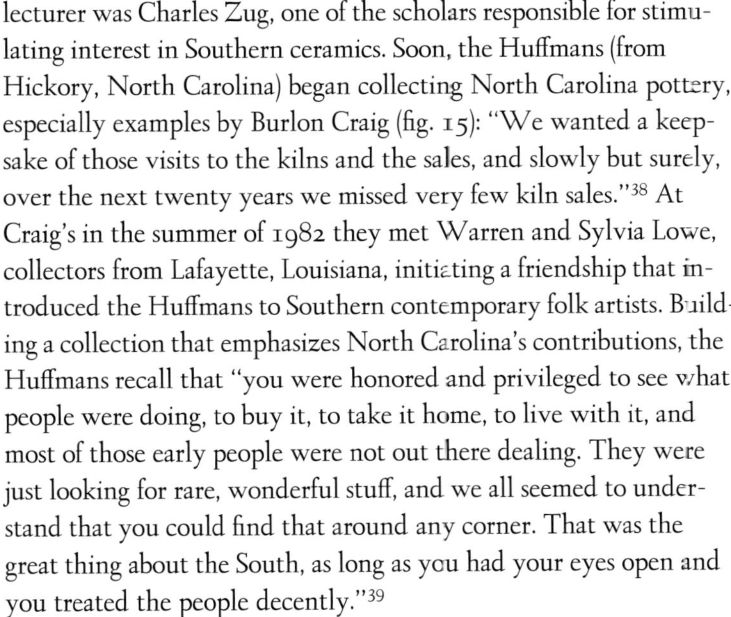

lecturer was Charles Zug, one of the scholars responsible for stimulating interest in Southern ceramics. Soon, the Huffmans (from Hickory, North Carolina) began collecting North Carolina pottery, especially examples by Burlon Craig (fig. 15): "We wanted a keepsake of those visits to the kilns and the sales, and slowly but surely, over the next twenty years we missed very few kiln sales."[38] At Craig's in the summer of 1982 they met Warren and Sylvia Lowe, collectors from Lafayette, Louisiana, initiating a friendship that introduced the Huffmans to Southern contemporary folk artists. Building a collection that emphasizes North Carolina's contributions, the Huffmans recall that "you were honored and privileged to see what people were doing, to buy it, to take it home, to live with it, and most of those early people were not out there dealing. They were just looking for rare, wonderful stuff, and we all seemed to understand that you could find that around any corner. That was the great thing about the South, as long as you had your eyes open and you treated the people decently."[39]

North Carolina's universities have also proven hospitable to contemporary folk art. In 1993, Tom Patterson collaborated with Brooke Anderson, then Director of the Diggs Gallery at Winston-Salem State University, to present *ASHE: Improvisation and Recycling in African-American Visionary Art*, an exhibition and catalogue that established the Diggs as a venue for innovative projects. In 1996 the Daisy Thorp Gallery at Wesleyan College in Rocky Mount became the formal repository for the Robert Lynch Collection of Outsider Art, comprising almost five hundred works from the greater Eastern Carolina region. Among the few African American collectors of contemporary folk art, Lynch collected works by artists such as Leroy Person, Herman Bridgers, and Vernon Burwell in depth.

New Trails in Appalachia

Early in his graduate fine arts studies at the University of Kentucky, Larry Hackley met Edgar Tolson in 1971. Today, Hackley is a dealer and curator devoted to Kentucky's contemporary folk artists, including Tolson, Earnest Patton, Evan Decker, and Charley and Noah Kinney. The 1970s, he recalls, were casual times, as he used Skip Taylor's *Kentucky Folk Art*, a 1976 state survey, to locate walking sticks and sculptures.[40] They were also lean times for finding buyers; he had his best luck sending works to dealers John Ollman in Philadelphia and Carl Hammer in Chicago. By the mid-1980s, Hackley sensed that the folk art market was looking up. He began organizing exhibitions, such as *Remembrances: Recent Memory Art by Kentucky Folk Artists* for the Kentucky Art and Craft Foundation Gallery in 1986 in Louisville. The Foundation was organized in 1981 to provide educational opportunities and marketplace exposure for the state's artists and craftspeople.

Adrian Swain came to the United States from England in 1971. He settled in Kentucky as a potter and began meeting folk artists such as Edgar Tolson, Charley and Noah Kinney, and Minnie Adkins between 1973 and 1978. Swain has been the curator of Morehead State University's Kentucky Folk Art Center since 1987, building a strong regional collection, providing a model retail program for area artists, and emphasizing community-oriented educational services. Stereotyped as highly decorative and craft-oriented, however, contemporary Appalachian folk artists have not been as widely embraced as their outsider counterparts elsewhere in the South.

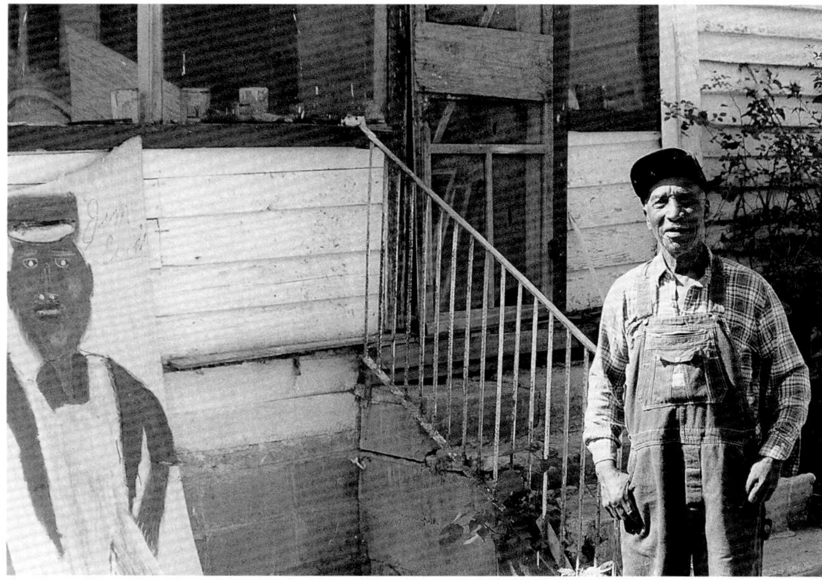

Figure 16. Jimmy Lee Sudduth with one of his mud paintings at his home in Fayette, Alabama, ca. 1992.

Baking in the Sun with Warren and Sylvia Lowe
Disaffected from the contemporary art they had been collecting, Louisiana natives Warren and Sylvia Lowe shifted gears in 1982, when they realized that they were surrounded by living folk artists. They started traveling throughout Louisiana and east Texas and then into Georgia, Alabama, and North Carolina. In just five years, they amassed a collection that included memory paintings, works by the South's obsessive visionaries, dramatic African American quilts, and Southern pottery. The collection made its public debut in 1987, when *Baking in the Sun: Visionary Images from the South*, a traveling exhibition and catalogue, was organized by the University Art Museum at the University of Southwestern Louisiana in Lafayette with Andy Nasisse and Maude Southwell Wahlman. During the 1990s, as their collecting interests and leisure time gravitated to the Southwest, the Lowes began dispersing their folk art holdings to university museums in Florida and Louisiana and through auctions.

The Hemphill and Hall Collections
Under the curatorial advocacy of Lynda Roscoe Hartigan, the Smithsonian American Art Museum acquired more than five hundred works from Bert Hemphill, "Mr. American Folk Art."[41] Representing his catholicity of interests, the selections also reflected a trend toward expanding the canon of the country's visual arts to include folk art as well as decorative arts, crafts, photography, and works by artists once marginalized because of gender, race, or ethnic background. The Museum's director, Elizabeth Broun, summed up the acquisition's significance: "For those who championed its cause through decades of offical neglect, finding folk art in museum galleries next to Hudson River landscapes and Abstract Expressionist canvases is a long-awaited legitimization, affirming the collector's independent judgment and giving overdue recognition to artists who worked without formal training, critical acclaim, or financial reward."[42]

In 1989 the Milwaukee Art Museum acquired 233 works from Michael and Julie Hall's collection, with strengths in sculpture, decoys, and twentieth-century self-taught artists. An avid supporter of contemporary self-taught artists since the 1970s, the Museum's director, Russell Bowman, described the occasion as "the single most important event" in the Museum's lengthy involvement with American folk art.[43] Hemphill and the Halls chose to place their collections in museums with concentrations in American and modern art. Positioning folk art in the "big picture," away from its stereotypical association with the Northeast and folk art-specific organizations, was a motivation in both instances. The Smithsonian American Art Museum in 1990 and the Milwaukee Art Museum in 1993 produced exhibitions and publications that celebrated their acquisitions and advanced scholarship in the field's historiography and object-oriented connoisseurship.

The Folk Art Society of America
Ann and William Oppenhimer, collectors of Southern folk art, and a small group of fellow enthusiasts founded the Folk Art Society of America in 1987 in Richmond, Virginia. The international membership now includes artists, educators, historians, writers, collectors, dealers, curators, and librarians. Its quarterly publication, *The Folk Art Messenger*, annual conference, and research library serve these constituencies.

The 1990s

Chuck and Jan Rosenak
The 1990s were busy for Chuck and Jan Rosenak, who have lived in Tesuque, New Mexico, since 1984. Between 1990 and 1992 the Museum of American Folk Art nationally circulated *The Cutting Edge: Contemporary American Folk Art from the Rosenak Collection*, the culmination of years of support from the Museum's director Robert A. Bishop. Published in conjunction with the exhibition was *Museum of American Folk Art Encyclopedia of Twentieth-Century American Folk Art and Artists*, the first in a series of four books that have established the Rosenaks as tireless chroniclers, "ambassadors of folk art," as they put it.[44] *The People Speak: Navajo Folk Art* (1994), *Contemporary American Folk Art: A Collector's Guide* (1996), and *The Saint Makers: Contemporary Santeras y Santeros* (1998) followed in rapid succession.

The Rosenaks' publications reflect a nationwide odyssey of collecting, interviewing, and photographing (fig. 16) that began in 1973, when the couple encountered Tolson's work in the Whitney biennial as well as the Smithsonian's small display *American Folk Craft Survivals*.[45] They have also ventured into new territories for the field itself, particularly nontraditional Native American weavings, pottery, and sculpture as well as an innovative, young generation of Southwestern Hispanic carvers. In 1997, the Smithsonian American Art Museum acquired 220 works that reflect the excellence of the

Southern, Native American, and Hispanic works in the Rosenaks' collection of some five thousand objects, an event that confirmed the Museum as the foremost repository of contemporary folk art.

William Arnett

In 1986, twenty years of world travel and thousands of hard-won objects—Chinese jade and porcelains, African and pre-Columbian art—already stretched behind legendary Atlanta dealer and collector William Arnett, as his interests turned to Southern black self-taught artists of a younger generation than those included in *Black Folk Art in America*. He has embraced Alabama's Thornton Dial and Lonnie Holley, each innovative in their handling of materials and masterful in their exploration of social and political content. In 1992, *Thornton Dial: Image of the Tiger*—an exhibition shared by the Museum of American Folk Art and the New Museum—established Dial as a key figure in the debate about where folk art ends and contemporary art begins. Zealous, articulate, and aggressively acquisitive, Arnett has upped the ante intellectually and commercially, pushing hard for a crossover into contemporary art.

The title of one of Dial's paintings—*Coming Out of Darkness, Looking for the Light*—hints at Arnett's goals, which he outlined in 1998: "The first was to create a collection of African-American vernacular art whose quality is on a par with other, better known art movements of our era. The second was to take that collection's message into what is called the 'dialogue' of art history."[46] Arnett and a team of consultants delivered eloquent testimony to the work that inspired these goals in *Souls Grown Deep: African American Vernacular Art of the South*, an exhibition of five hundred works organized during the Olympic Games in Atlanta in 1996. Four years later, Arnett published volume one of an anthology under the same title, an ambitious series of publications to be devoted to the South's African American vernacular art. Acclaimed in the national press, the project has established Southern black vernacular artists as bearers of Civil Rights empowerment and cultural meaning so powerful that they can no longer be marginalized.

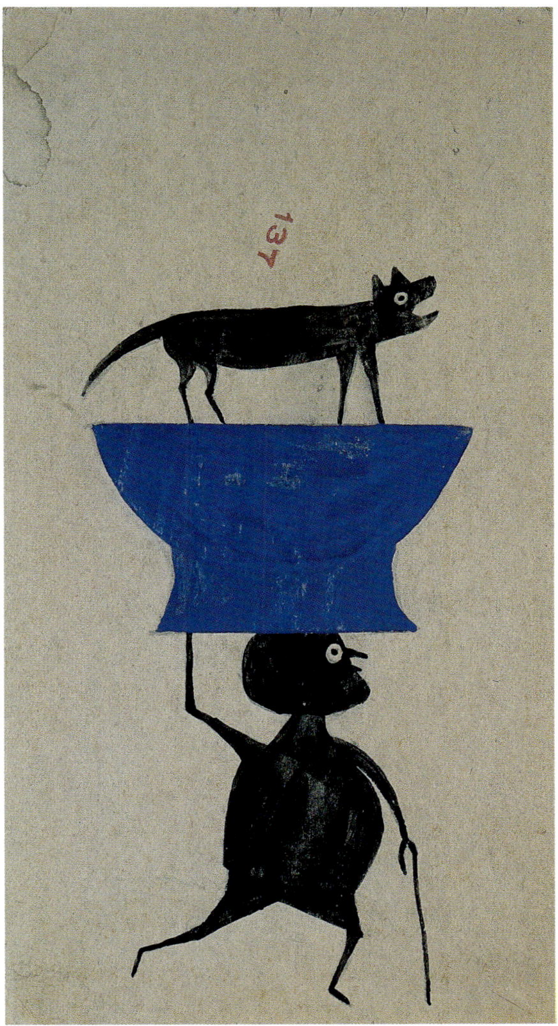

Figure 17. Bill Traylor, *Untitled*, ca. 1939–1948, tempera and pencil on cardboard, 13⅜ × 7⅜ inches, High Museum of Art, purchase with funds from Mrs. Lindsey Hopkins, Jr., Edith G. and Philip A. Rhodes, and the Members Guild, 1982.90.

The High Museum of Art

Since 1993 the High Museum of Art has emerged as a leader in the field of contemporary folk art. That year, it renamed its downtown branch at the Georgia-Pacific Center the High Museum of Art Folk Art and Photography Galleries, and in 1994 it established the country's first folk art department in a general art museum under the curatorial direction of Joanne Cubbs; Lynne Spriggs assumed the position three years later. Collecting early American folk art and decorative arts since 1956, the High has made a series of astute acquisitions of contemporary Southern folk art over the past two decades: in 1982, thirty Traylor drawings (fig. 17) from Charles Shannon; in 1993, sixty-eight works by Dilmus Hall, Bessie Harvey, J. B. Murry, Nellie Mae Rowe, Mose Tolliver, and others from Andy Nasisse; and in 1996, Marshall Hahn's gift of more than 140 objects. Securing a significant portion of Howard Finster's Paradise Garden in 1994, the High undertook an ambitious effort to preserve and exhibit a monumental outdoor environment. This major collection of more than five hundred works—mostly by Southern contemporary self-taught artists—is complemented by the Museum's strengths in Southern decorative arts, including painted furniture, Edgefield pottery, and Gullah baskets acquired from the collection of South Carolina's Tony and Marie Shank between 1996 and 1998.

The High has exhibited twentieth-century Southern folk artists such as Mattie Lou O'Kelley since 1975, and its first solo exhibition of a regional folk artist featured Carlton Garrett's mechanical tableaux six years later. Barbara Archer, the Museum's associate curator of education in 1988, celebrated over sixty folk artists from the Southeast in *Outside the Mainstream: Folk Art in Our Time*. This show alerted the High to a growing audience, which has benefited from its accelerated program of folk art exhibitions since the early 1990s. The Museum is one of several that have made concerted efforts to mingle the works of self-taught and trained artists in its galleries, and it has also provided a lively dialogue between folk art and the decorative arts in its installations.

New Doors Open

The Tree of Life, Wind in My Hair, The End Is Near—these catchy exhibition titles convey the spirit of adventure and public outreach of the American Visionary Art Museum, which opened in Baltimore in 1995. Its founder, Rebecca Hoffberger, emphasizes "big picture" thematic exhibitions organized by consulting curators such as Roger Manley, and the program has afforded contemporary folk artists, many of them Southern, considerable exposure.

From Edgecomb, Maine, to Orlando, Florida, from his Overfork Gallery filled with curios to the Mennello Museum of American Folk Art, Earl Cunningham's paintings of the American scene have come a long way. Founded in cooperation with the city of Orlando in 1998, the Museum is the brainchild of Marilyn and Michael Mennello, the principal collectors of Cunningham's work since the early 1970s. In addition to a stunning display of his paintings, the new museum showcases Florida's folk artists—another longstanding interest for the Mennellos—and hosts contemporary folk art exhibitions for its growing audience.

The Marketplace

Early in 1989 the investment trade paper *Barron's* published "Who Needs Picasso? Some Alternatives to $36 Million Paintings."[47] The alternatives were works by self-taught artists such as Bill Traylor. The article was one of the first in the national press to note that collecting outsider art was escalating during a period in which the market for contemporary art was faltering. Interest makes a market, and a market makes interest. In January 1992, New York art and antiques impresario Sanford Smith opened the newest of his trade shows, the Outsider Art Fair, in SoHo, then the heart of the contemporary art scene. Juried in the tradition of fairs that first became popular in art and antique circles during the 1970s, the Outsider Art Fair has grown in attendance, success, and media coverage each year. Like the art itself, the dealers hail from across the country and Europe and include veterans such as Phyllis Kind, Luise Ross, Frank Maresca, and Roger Ricco—all with well-established galleries in New York—Carl Hammer from Chicago, and Bonnie Grossman from Berkeley, as well as aspiring newcomers to the trade.

Mississippi-born, Harvard-educated Isaac Tigret has a keen eye for moneymaking trends. His success as the founder of Hard Rock Cafe served him well when he opened the first House of the Blues in Cambridge, Massachusetts, in 1992. Each of its sites is installed inside and out with works either commissioned or purchased in bulk from self-taught artists, primarily from the South. The atmosphere equates blues greats with great visual artists, but the operation's scale has raised questions for those who fear that work for hire diminishes passion and originality.

Based in Buford, Georgia, just outside of Atlanta, auctioneer Steve Slotin founded Folk Fest—billed as the world's greatest self-taught art show and sale—in 1994, and established the first auction house dedicated to folk art in 1999. Like Kimball Sterling, a seasoned auctioneer from Tennessee, Slotin is helping to build a Southern-based market for contemporary folk art.

In the midst of these public arenas, private dealers have also seeded important private and public collections. In 1995, "The Home Section" of the *New York Times* profiled Atlanta-based Jimmy Allen as a "folk-art scout extraordinaire."[48] Since the mid-1970s, he has specialized in retrieving Southern rural material culture—quilts, vernacular clothing and photographs, and African American furniture and art—as he travels thousands of backcountry miles. Allen's description of himself as a "picker" belies the often extraordinary quality of the objects that he has shepherded into public collections, the High Museum of Art, the Smithsonian American Art Museum, and the Abby Aldrich Rockefeller Folk Art Museum among them. Allen was also instrumental in persuading Atlanta-based Robert Reeves to join the ranks of private dealers during the 1980s.[49] In addition to working with Southern collectors to build appreciation of artists such as Dilmus Hall and Sam Doyle, Reeves has effectively moved the region's folk art and crafts into New York collections, including those of William Greenspon and Dorothea and Leo Rabkin.

Stormy Weather

Success comes at a price, as the contemporary folk art world abruptly discovered in 1992. In its "Legal Beat" column, the *Wall Street Journal* reported that Bill Traylor's heirs were filing suit against his lifelong supporter Charles Shannon and Hirschl & Adler Modern, the New York gallery credited with increasing Traylor's posthumous reputation and commercial success. Before the parties reached a sealed, out-of-court settlement, the case raised difficult "questions about just who owns an artist's work, especially against the backdrop of alleged racial exploitation."[50]

A year later, the CBS program *60 Minutes* aired Morley Safer's segment about alleged exploitation of Southern black self-taught artists. The story focused on the dynamics of William Arnett's financial arrangements with artists such as Thornton Dial, Bessie Harvey, and Charlie Lucas. Allegations of mistreatment and misrepresentation flew on and off camera, primarily between Safer and Arnett, with the artists caught in between.[51]

The issues and consternation raised by the high-stakes Traylor lawsuit and *60 Minutes* have recurred most recently for Purvis Young, Miami's painter of the streets. In May of 1999, the *Miami New Times* chronicled his ups and downs in the burgeoning outsider art market.[52] In 1994, Young and his Miami dealer Joy Moos, who had successfully promoted his work in contemporary art circles since 1989, settled a contractual dispute out of court. In March of 1999, Don and Mera Rubell, prominent contemporary art collectors who had moved from New York to Miami five years earlier, bought the contents of Young's studio—thousands of works at the time—for an undisclosed sum. Despite the artist's acknowledged satisfaction with the arrangement, the *Miami New Times* reported differing interpretations of the acquisition from exploitation to enlightened patronage.

Passions in New Orleans

In 1993, the New Orleans Museum of Art organized the nationally touring exhibition *Passionate Visions of the American South: Self-Taught Artists from 1940 to the Present.* The Museum's interest in contemporary folk art dates from the 1950s, when it exhibited artists such as Grandma Moses. In the 1960s, it began acquiring works under the leadership of its African art specialist William A. Fagaly, who maintained friendships with David Butler and Sister Gertrude Morgan, two of Louisiana's most inventive self-taught artists.

Seeing Fagaly's exhibition of Morgan's visionary paintings at the Museum in 1988, Dr. Kurt Gitter and his wife Alice Rae Yelen began collecting contemporary folk art in earnest. Gitter had been a devoted patron of Japanese art since the 1960s and Yelen an experienced educator at the New Orleans Museum of Art; both describe themselves as transplanted Northerners. The couple's first folk art acquisition was a group of Morgan's paintings and archival materials from Regenia Perry.

Yelen organized *Passionate Visions* and drew upon the expertise of William Ferris and modern art curators Susan Larsen, Jane Livingston, and Lowery Stokes Sims, also an African American specialist, for the companion publication. The project was the first "to provide an overview of painting and sculpture by Southern contemporary self-taught artists," approaching the topic as a regional phenomenon and emphasizing aesthetic merit in its selection.[53] In 1995, Gail Andrews Trechsel, a steady supporter of Southern folk art, curated *Pictured in My Mind: Contemporary American Self-Taught Art from the Collection of Dr. Kurt Gitter and Alice Rae Yelen* for the Birmingham Museum of Art. Trechsel's survey highlighted the couple's interest in balancing national scope and Southern touchstones in their holdings.

Flying Free in Virginia

Baron and Ellin Gordon, from Norfolk, Virginia, and Westchester County, New York, collected books, German Expressionist paintings, and early American painted furniture and decorative arts before moving to Williamsburg in the late 1970s. In 1997, the Abby Aldrich Rockefeller Folk Art Museum opened *Flying Free: Twentieth-Century Self-Taught Art from the Collection of Ellin and Baron Gordon,* evidence of a new love that had evolved in the interim. Dramatic upswings in the cost of early folk art, Bert Hemphill's persuasive friendship, early access to Jeff Camp, and an "eye-opening" visit to the Cavin-Morris Gallery in New York were among the factors that propelled them into collecting contemporary folk art. Their efforts are ongoing, visiting with artists, supporting AARFAM's efforts to expand its twentieth-century program, consulting the field's ever-widening array of dealers and curators, and shopping for folk art online.

Spirited Journeys in Texas

On a trip to Africa led by William Fagaly in 1988, Houston's Stephanie Smither met Bert Hemphill, and they became fast friends. Stephanie and her husband John, often with their grown children, traveled frequently with Hemphill throughout Texas and the South during the 1990s. The Smithers' transition from ethnographic material to contemporary folk art was swift under Hemphill's tutelage, and they reunited him with the South. Hemphill's collection took on new depth as he and the Smithers visited artists, dealers, and flea markets. The Smithers, however, were not strangers to folk art; cousin Murray Smither of Huntsville is a dealer who has been involved with Texas folk artists since the 1960s. Particularly supportive of Reverend Johnnie Swearingen's expressionistic paintings, the Smithers have developed a thoughtful collection that mingles the best of Southern folk art with increasing representation of artists nationwide and select examples by European outsider artists.

Two books, Cecelia Steinfeldt's *Texas Folk Art: One Hundred Fifty Years of the Southwestern Tradition* (1981) and *Folk Art in Texas,* edited by Francis Abernethy in 1985, have helped to establish the state's rich resources for folk art collectors, who have previously focused on other parts of the South. In 1997, Lynne Adele's exhibition *Spirited Journeys: Self-Taught Texas Artists of the Twentieth Century* and its catalogue for the Archer M. Huntington Art Gallery in Austin demonstrated this trajectory of appreciation.

The New Millennium

Observations of a Veteran

These are heady times for the appreciation of contemporary folk art. The first Whitney biennial of the millennium includes Thornton Dial, and James Hampton's millennial monument has returned to the Abby Aldrich Rockefeller Folk Art Museum. Nellie Mae Rowe and William Edmondson are the subjects of major publications and traveling exhibitions, organized by the Museum of American Folk Art and Nashville's Cheekwood Museum of Art, respectively. Five decades after Charles Shannon withdrew Bill Traylor's drawings from The Museum of Modern Art because they had been priced too low, Sotheby's auctioned one of his drawings for more than $170,000 in 1997 and The Museum of Modern Art recently acquired a choice selection of Traylors, courtesy of Shannon and his wife.[54] Seasoned and emerging collectors no longer need to rely on a grassroots network and can instead search for acquisitions at a plethora of galleries, art fairs, and auctions or test their skills (and luck) as they bid online, through eBay or through Kimball Sterling's, Steve Slotin's, and Sotheby's websites.

These are challenging times for the appreciation of contemporary folk art. Competition has increasingly supplanted camaraderie in the search for new artists, and the ethical dilemmas posed by the artists' race, age, poverty, isolation, or condition (physical or mental) have prompted disturbing trends in exploitation, acrimony, and legal contests. The first spate of aspersions on the authenticity of works has occurred, muddied sometimes by the role of artists' family members, exacerbated at other times by faulty connoisseurship, particularly when attributing anonymous examples to a race or region. Recognition of the self-awareness that shapes the form and content of work by self-taught artists is slowly emerging, as is its corollorary—sensitivity to the roles that we play as collectors, curators, documenters, and interpreters interacting in the artists' lives and bringing their work into the public domain.

The heady times and challenges apply to collecting contemporary American folk art regardless of region, yet they resonate most at this point in the history of collecting Southern folk art, which has steadily grown in presence in farflung exhibitions, publications, and collections private and public, since the 1970s. Mencken's Sahara is a mirage and Dilmus Hall's shoe still rides a metaphorical tornado; their respective turns of phrase suggest the South's association with a strong sense of place. Much within the covers of *Souls Grown Deep*, for example, reminds us that the region's black folk artists have distilled a cultural and racial dynamic of place in their work, and collecting Southern folk art has felt the impact of this dynamic as well. In a more universal vein, Eudora Welty once suggested that "one place comprehended can make us understand other places better."[55] It is difficult to ignore a human sense of place and community, a psychic and spiritual sense of place, as the emotive source of Southern folk art and the acquisitiveness (and inquisitiveness) it has inspired.

Notes

Since the late 1980s Robert Reeves has helped me iron out my understanding of Southern folk art's complex universe. I am most recently indebted to him for the incisive interviews that he conducted for this essay's preparation. I would also like to thank Estelle Friedman and Peter J. Brownlee for their research assistance.

1. Quoted in Fred Hobson, "Mencken, H. L.," in Wilson and Ferris 1989, p. 890. Mencken first published the essay in the *New York Mail* in 1917.

2. Quoted in Saarinen 1958, p. xix.

3. In 1920, Eaton joined the Foundation's Surveys and Exhibits Division. Nine years later, he was instrumental in establishing the Southern Highlands Handicraft Guild to acquaint the country with the area's diverse crafts through retail opportunities and traveling exhibitions. The American Federation of the Arts opened the Guild's first nationally touring exhibition at the Corcoran Gallery of Art in Washington, D.C., in 1933.

4. William T. Couch was the director of the University of North Carolina Press from 1932 to 1945. He promoted a publishing program to encourage Southerners to value books, particularly during a period in which the South was so heavily stereotyped as rural and therefore backward. See Couch 1935.

5. "Reminiscences of Holger Cahill," interview by Joan Pring, 1957, Holger Cahill Papers, Archives of American Art, Smithsonian Institution, Washington, D.C., p. 253. See pp. 251–277 for the full account of his Southern trip. All quotations of Cahill are from this interview.

6. Judith McWillie, "William Edmondson with Edward Weston and Louise Dahl-Wolfe, 1934–1941," in Thompson et al. 1999, pp. 45–48.

7. Porter 1969, pp. 135–136.

8. Alain Locke, ed., *The New Negro: An Interpretation*, quoted in Dover 1960, p. 33.

9. Quoted in Thomas Dewey, "Decorative Arts," in Wilson and Ferris 1989, p. 62.

10. Little 1957, p. xiv.

11. Steve W. Harley's oil on canvas *Wallowa Lake, Oregon*, 1927–1928 was the first work by a twentieth-century self-taught artist to enter AARFAM's collection, in 1957.

12. Eleanor Swenson Quandt, introduction to Corcoran Gallery of Art 1960, p. 6.

13. Ralph Rinzler, quoted in Ardery 1998, p. 82.

14. The case installation was in the Museum's "Hall of Everyday Life" and was organized by Joan Watkins, filmmaker, potter, and wife of cultural historian Malcolm Watkins at the Smithsonian Institution. The case also included carvings by George López of Cordova, New Mexico.

15. Quoted in press release, *Twentieth-Century Folk Art and Artists*, Museum of American Folk Art, Herbert Waide Hemphill, Jr., Papers, Archives of American Art, Smithsonian Institution, Washington, D.C., unpaginated.

16. Jeff and Jane Camp, telephone interview by Lynda Hartigan, 27 December 1988, tape recording, author's collection. Newspaper accounts such as Newman's were soon followed by books in this same vein. For an example, see Horwitz 1975, which includes profiles on twenty-two artists, many of them Southern.

17. For discussions of the "New South" and "Sunbelt" concepts, see Bernard and Rice 1983; Brownell 1975; and Woodward 1951. For a discussion of the relationship between Southern black self-taught artists and the urban experience, see Hartigan 2000.

18. William Ferris, telephone interview by Robert Reeves, 18 January 2000, tape recording and transcription, High Museum of Art, curatorial files. For Ferris's discussion of a sense of place, see Ferris 1982.

19. Wadsworth 1976, p. 5.

20. Robert Hughes, "Overdressing for the Occasion," *Time*, 5 April 1976, p. 42.

21. The exhibition included the following twentieth-century self-taught artists: David Butler, William Edmondson, Minnie Evans, Clementine Hunter, and Horace Pippin.

22. For Thompson's 1969 article, see Robinson, Foster, and Ogilvie 1969, pp. 122–170. Thompson's discussion of cultural transmission and transformation in Thompson 1984 is widely regarded as a seminal study.

23. Vlach 1991, p. 20.

24. Regenia A. Perry, "Black American Folk Art: Origins and Early Manifestations," in Livingston, Beardsley, and Perry 1982, p. 37. Perry has collected contemporary folk art since the 1970s and has organized several exhibitions on the topic.

25. Jane Livingston, "What It Is," in Livingston, Beardsley, and Perry 1982, p. 11. For a discussion of issues related to black folk art, see Hartigan 1994.

26. Robert Reeves mentioned this 1970s work in his self-interview, 21 January 2000, tape recording and transcription, High Museum of Art, curatorial files. Hall salvaged a shoe that had been through a tornado and placed it outdoors in a decorated aquarium with a sign that read, "the shoe that rode the howling tornado."

27. For a cogent discussion of the issues surrounding the exhibition, see Metcalf 1983.

28. Shari Cavin and Randall Morris, telephone interview by Robert Reeves, 20 January 2000, tape recording and transcription, High Museum of Art, curatorial files.

29. Judith McWillie, telephone interview by Robert Reeves, 7 January 2000, tape recording and transcription, High Museum of Art, curatorial files.

30. Andy Nasisse, telephone interview by Robert Reeves, 13 January 2000, tape recording and transcription, High Museum of Art, curatorial files.

31. For a discussion of the Archives of American Art's efforts, see Kirwin 1987.

32. Jane and Bert Hunecke, telephone interview by Robert Reeves, 26 December 1999, tape recording and transcription, High Museum of Art, curatorial files.

33. Jonathan Williams, telephone interview by Robert Reeves, 23 December 1999, tape recording and transcription, High Museum of Art, curatorial files.

34. Tom Patterson, telephone interview by Robert Reeves, 22 December 1999, tape recording and transcription, High Museum of Art, curatorial files.

35. Patterson has been a regular contributor to *Raw Vision* and Atlanta-based *Art Papers*. For an example of his approach to self-taught artists, see Patterson and Ingram 1993.

36. Roger Manley, telephone interview by Robert Reeves, 3 January 2000, tape recording and transcription, High Museum of Art, curatorial files.

37. The titles of two of Manley's books are the sources for the quoted phrases: *Self-Made Worlds: Visionary Folk Art Environments* (with an introduction by Jonathan Williams) and *Hoaxes, Humbugs, and Spectacles: Astonishing Photographs of Smelt Wrestlers, Human Projectiles, Giant Hailstones, Contortionists, Elephant Impersonators, and Much Much More!*

38. Allen and Barry Huffman, telephone interview by Robert Reeves, 28 December 1999, tape recording and transcription, High Museum of Art, curatorial files.

39. Ibid.

40. Larry Hackley, telephone interview by Robert Reeves, 6 January 2000, tape recording and transcription, High Museum of Art, curatorial files.

41. Helen Dudar, "Mr. American Folk Art," *Connoisseur* 210 (June 1982), pp. 70–78.

42. Elizabeth Broun, foreword to Hartigan 1990, pp. ix–x.

43. Russell Bowman, preface to Milwaukee Art Museum 1993, p. 9.

44. Chuck and Jan Rosenak, telephone interview by Lynda Hartigan, 1997, tape recording, author's collection.

45. Ibid.

46. Quoted in Cullum 1998, p. 26.

47. Peter C. Du Bois, "Who Needs Picasso? Some Alternatives to $36 Million Paintings," *Barron's*, 2 January 1989, p. 42.

48. Patricia Leigh Brown, "42,000 Miles a Year on the Antiques Track," *New York Times*, 9 November 1995, sec. C, p. 1.

49. Robert Reeves, self-interview, 21 January 2000, tape recording and transcription, High Museum of Art, curatorial files.

50. Jonathan M. Moses, "Heirs of Ex-Slave and Folk Artist Sue Collector for Rights to Work," *Wall Street Journal*, 30 November 1992, sec. B, p. 5.

51. For an account of Arnett's reactions to the *60 Minutes* segment, see Cullum 1998.

52. Judy Cantor, "From Outsider to Insider," *Miami New Times*. http://www.miaminewtimes.com/issues/1999-05-20/feature.html (20 May 1999).

53. Yelen 1993, p. 7.

54. Traylor's drawing *Blue Man, Black Mule* set the record for his work on 3 December 1997 at Sotheby's auction *Bill Traylor Drawings from the Collection of Joe and Pat Wilkinson*.

55. Quoted in Charles Reagan Wilson, "Sense of Place," in Wilson and Ferris 1989, p. 1137.

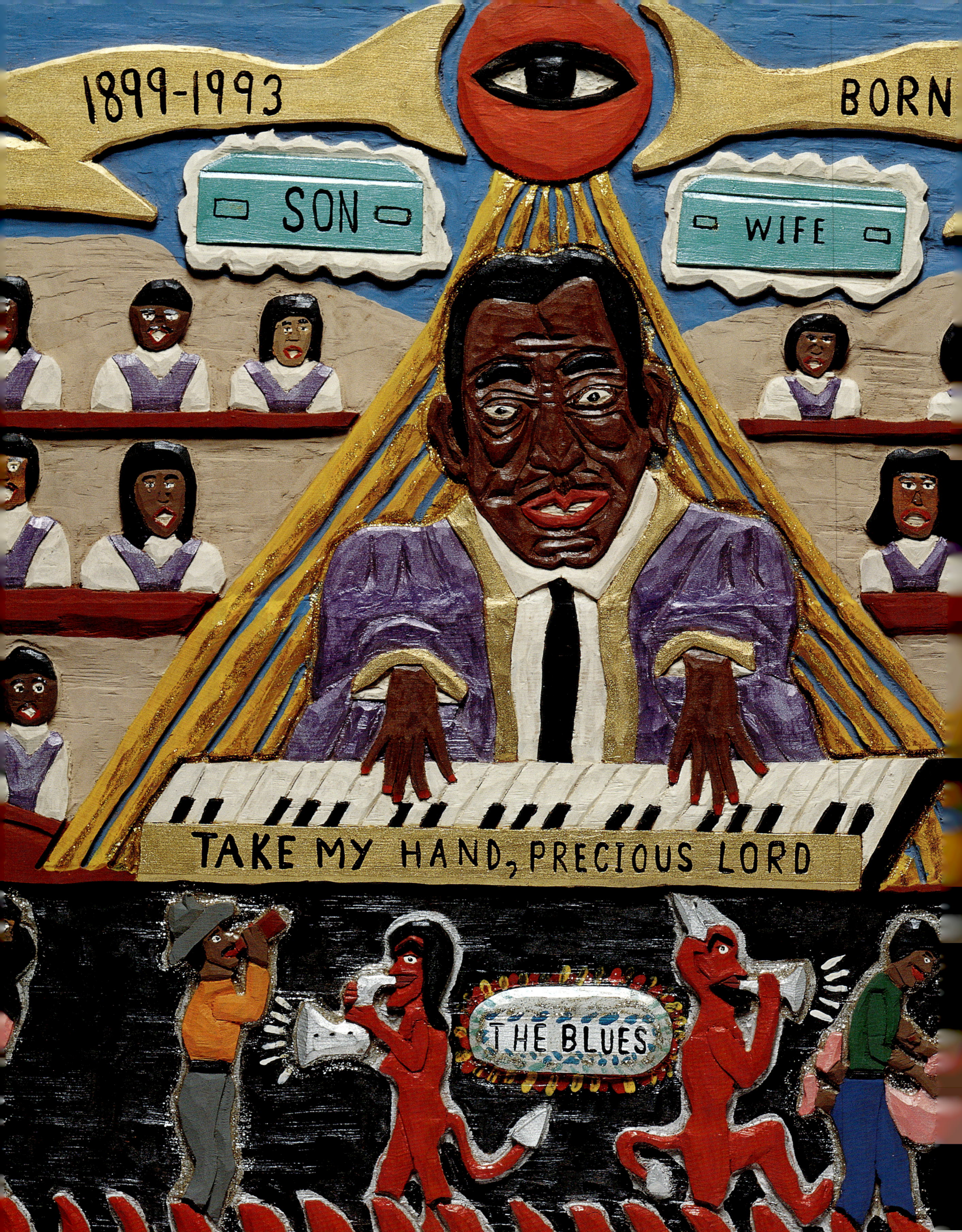
1899-1993
BORN
SON
WIFE
TAKE MY HAND, PRECIOUS LORD
THE BLUES

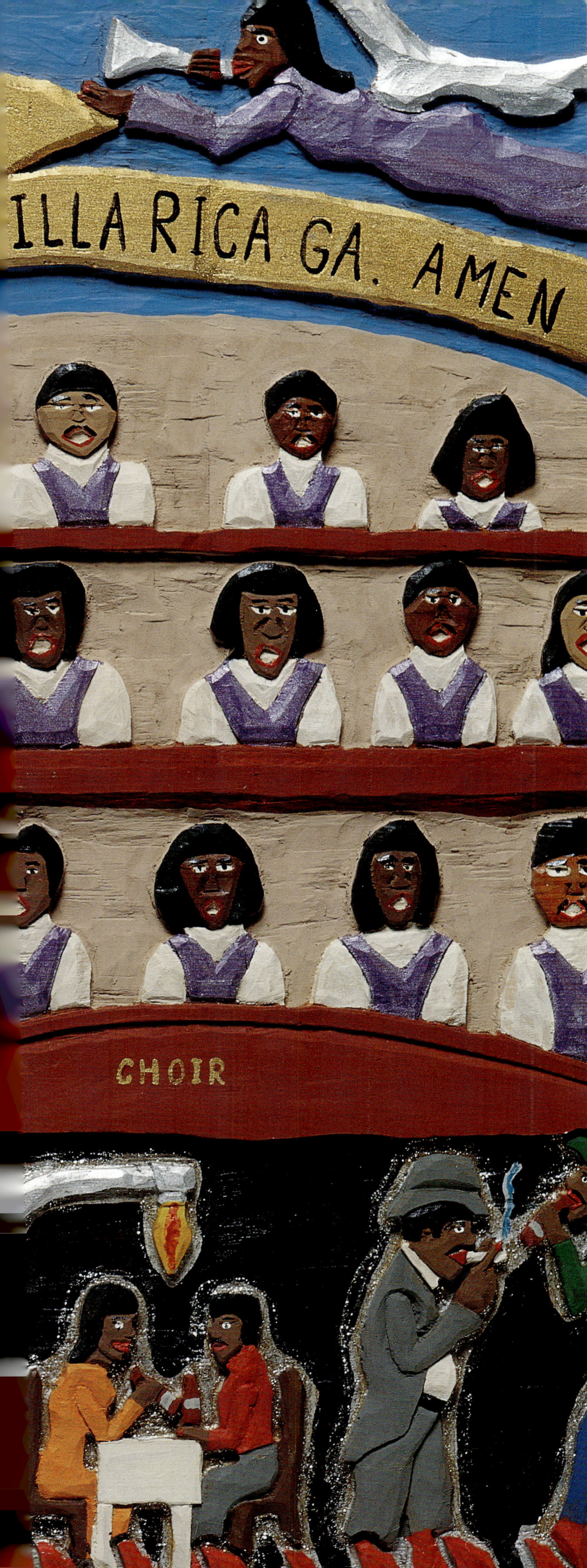

Catalogue

Leroy Almon, *Thomas Dorsey* (cat. 7, detail)

Cats. 1–2

William Adkins

Born 1932
Kansas City, Missouri

Addled Scratcher Fork, ca. 1995
Ballpoint pen on posterboard
22 × 28 inches
Acquired from Margaret Doan, 1995
1997.42

Diphiore Dthuiore Feather Gamble, ca. 1995
Ballpoint pen on posterboard, envelope, feather, cashier's checks, money order, and dollar bill
22 × 28 inches
Acquired from Margaret Doan, 1995
1997.43

William Adkins's elaborate ballpoint pen drawings on posterboard display a startling amalgamation of practicality, imagination, and wit. The formal appeal of his works may belie their utilitarian intent, for their creator proposes devices to relieve daily drudgery, assist with mundane tasks, or provide entertainment. Eugene W. Metcalf has noted that Adkins's inventions "play with and satirize the seemingly limitless and disconnected meanings available in the commodities we use."[1] Many of his gadgets, which bear such whimsical names as *Cottage Cheese Valentine Winged*, are intended to perform several functions. Adkins conceives these intricate designs as patent drawings for his inventions, many of which he has produced by using found materials. Each drawing carries on its reverse a certificate giving instructions and applications for the apparatus and sometimes a monetary value Adkins has assigned. The artist typically rolls his posterboard drawings into cylinders for storage and presentation, tucking inside any accompanying materials, such as the feather and documents now attached to the reverse of *Diphiore Dthuiore Feather Gamble*.

Adkins compiles the elements of his drawings to form bold structures of strange formal elegance. Directional lines, often obsessively repeated, combine with vectors and rows of text to create a sense of movement around the machines, whose uncertain intent bemuses the viewer.

Both of the Adkins drawings in the Hahn Collection are plans for gambling "sports," as their inventor calls his games. The *Addled Scratcher Fork* is to be built of forks, a metal bottle, heavy wire, a plastic bowl, string, a "wood round," and a bowl. The assembled device, powered by a motor scooter, would rest in a pocket of sand. The player bets on which set of forks strung in the "addle" (the wide arc at the top) will beat the "end cap" attached to the dowel running through the center of the contrivance.[2]

Diphiore Dthuiore Feather Gamble (pronounced "dithfor dither") is to be played by tossing a feather into the "toss bowl" (a mug-like container of wire) apparently by means of a propeller equipped with the fingers from a glove. The hand-drawn certificate on the reverse puns, "the certificate is for the handeycap of lost fingers." Adkins assigned a value of $18,800 to this game, as noted in the certificate, in which he also enumerated the materials required for its construction: red feather, glove fingers, plastic, hulled corn, propeller, and wire bowl. The artist's own explanation of the contraption was, "This is a little feather sport, win or lose."

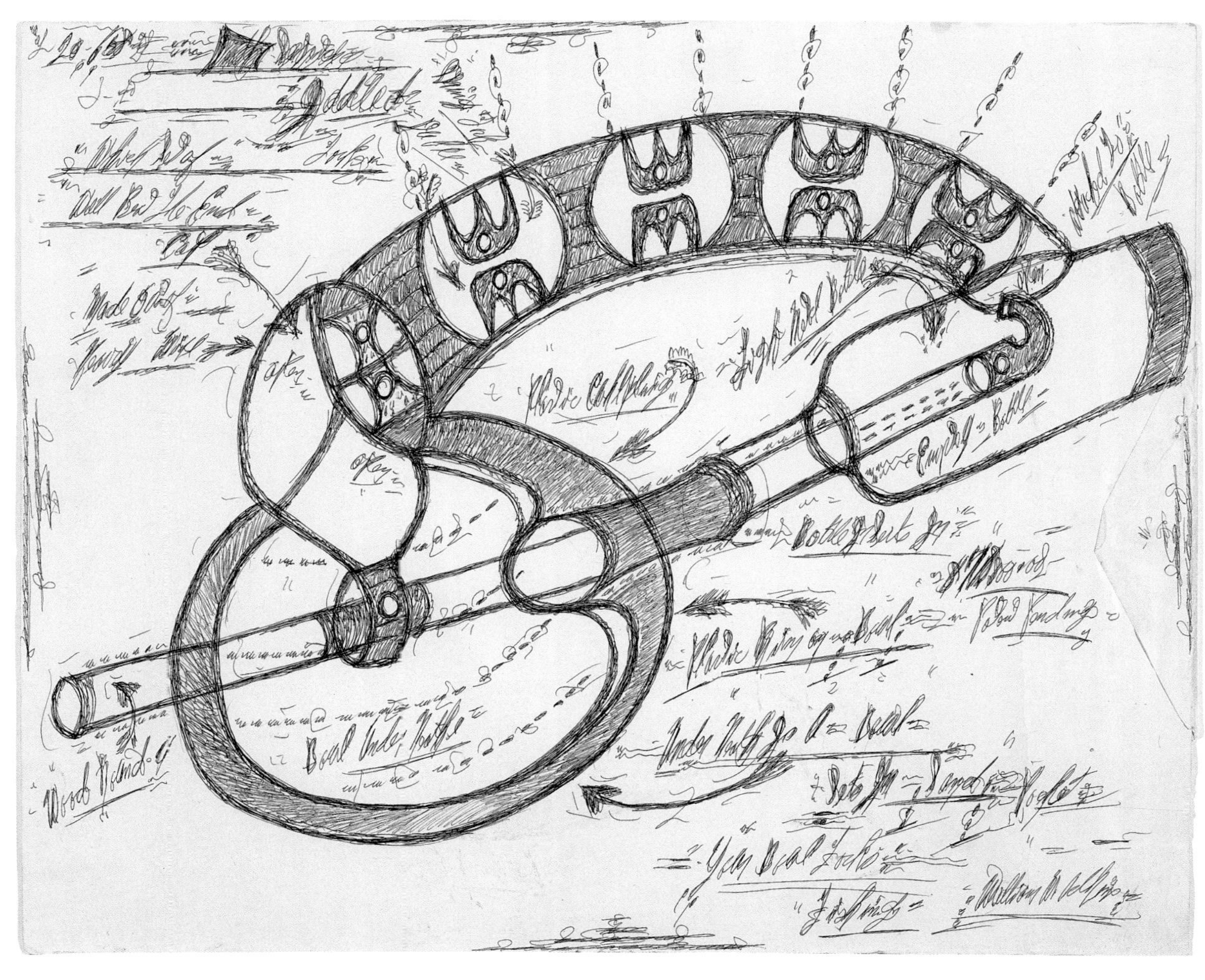

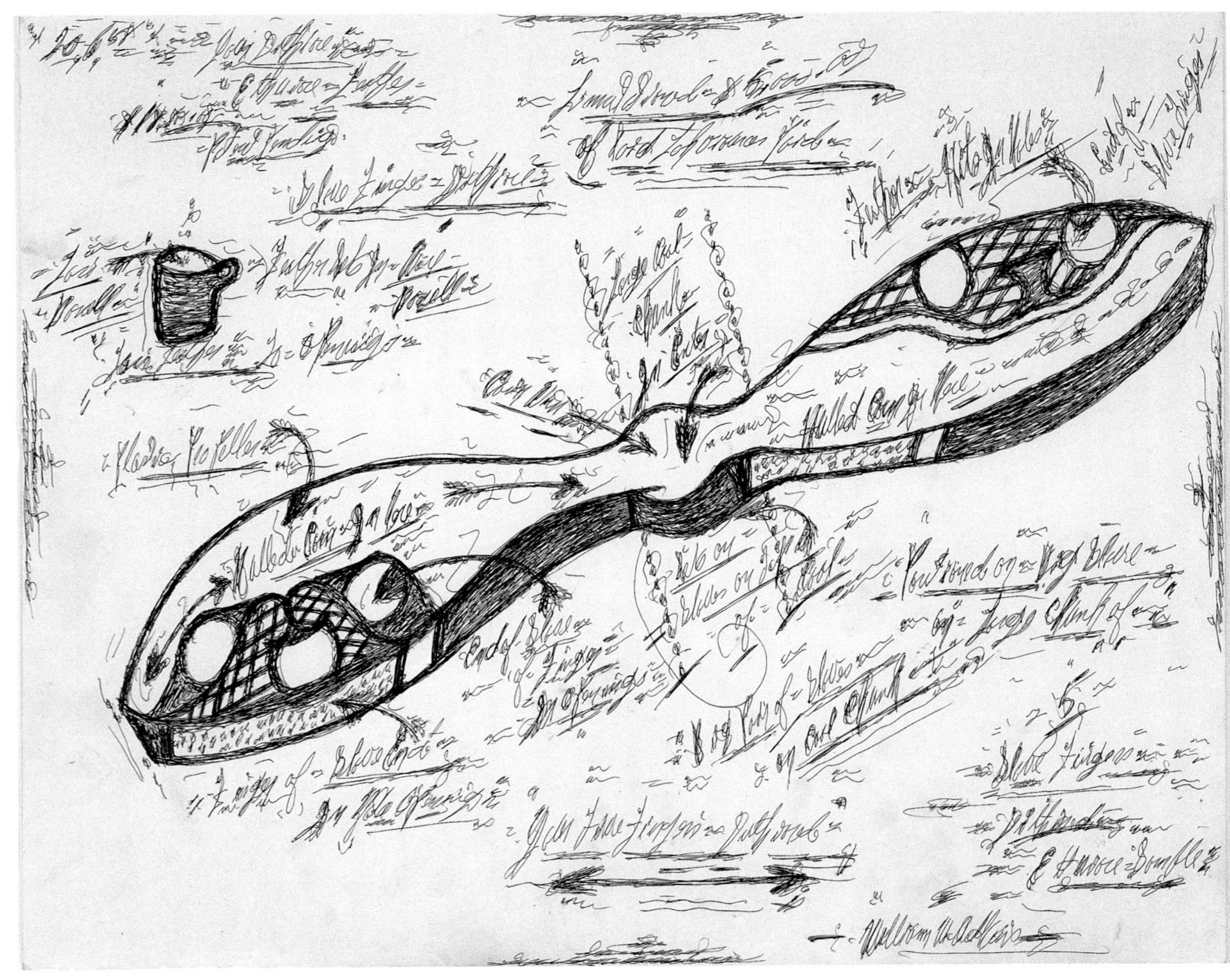

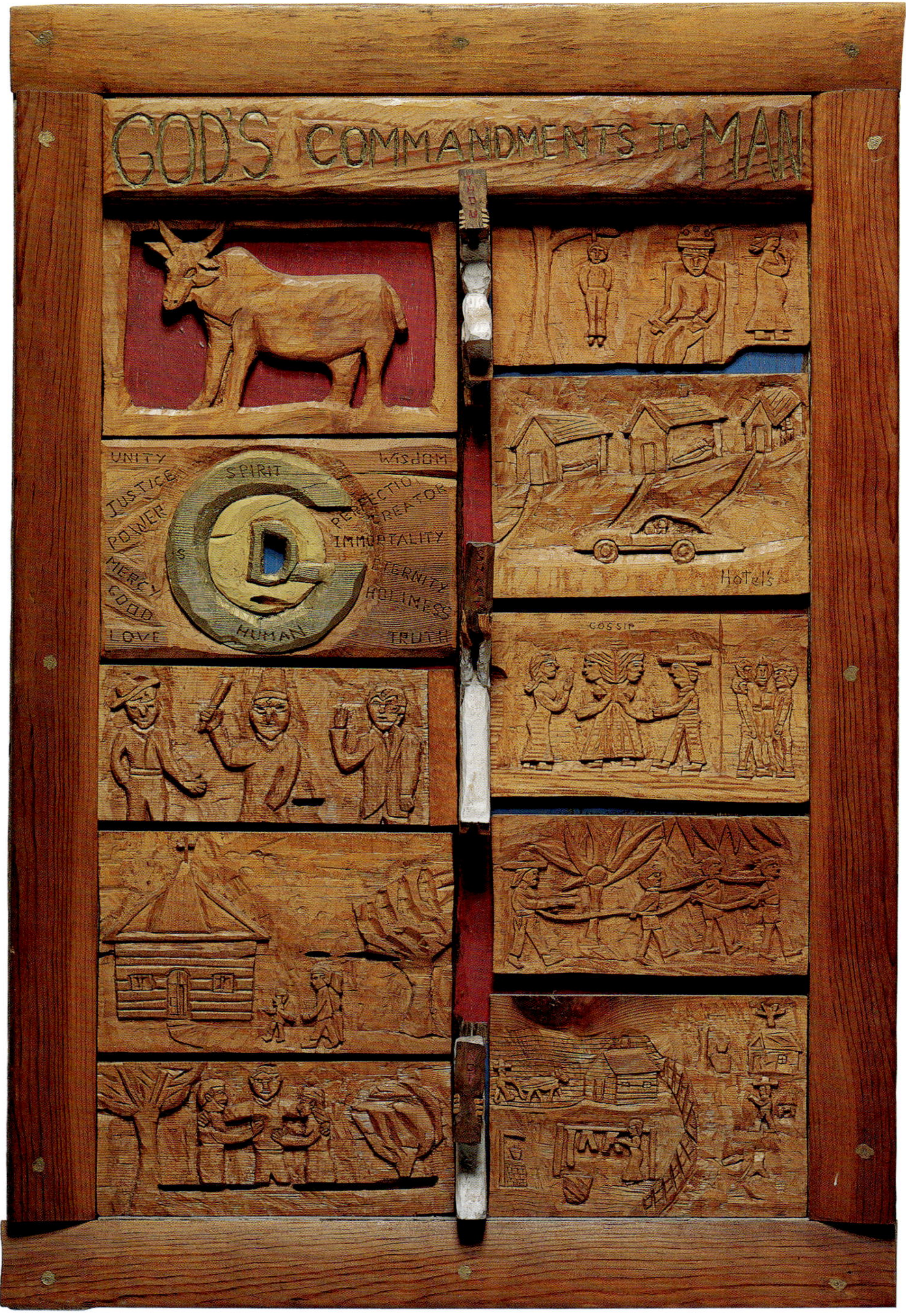

Cat. 3

Leroy Almon

1938–1997
Columbus, Ohio

God's Commandments to Man, 1980
Carved wood with paint and stain
33¼ × 23 × 3 inches
Acquired from the artist, 1991
1997.44

This carving was executed in Columbus, Ohio, while Leroy Almon was apprenticed to Elijah Pierce, who was then almost ninety years old.[1] Almon's friendship with the older artist made him want to learn to carve: "Elijah Pierce was a man of God who always demonstrated his love by actions. Elijah Pierce was my spiritual teacher. For one whole year I listened to him. I watched him. I believed him. I began to carve."[2] Pierce's influence is evident in the interest in narrative that pervades Almon's early works and in the segmentation of the pictorial space. Almon told Marshall Hahn that Pierce himself carved some of this work to illustrate the instructions he was giving his apprentice.

Almon's carving style is shallow, particularly on this piece. The sparing use of paint is unusual for this artist, whose works are more often brightly polychromed. Each of the Ten Commandments is represented by a discrete panel on which the precept is illustrated, in most cases, by a narrative scene. Down the middle runs a column bearing three white-robed figures who hold tablets saying "Thou," "Shalt," and "Not." In one, which seems to represent the first commandment ("Thou shalt have no other gods before me"), bright golden letters G-O-D in concentric overlay draw the eye toward the object of veneration. Eight of the panels portray the commandments using tableaux. They offer modern interpretations of the behavior in question, such as the lynching, judicial execution, and suggestion of abortion that exemplify "Thou shalt not kill" and the row of hotels that house adulterous couples. For Almon, scripture was a vital force capable of illuminating contemporary experience. As art critic Catherine Fox has pointed out, even his biblical carvings can "be seen as contemporary social parables."[3]

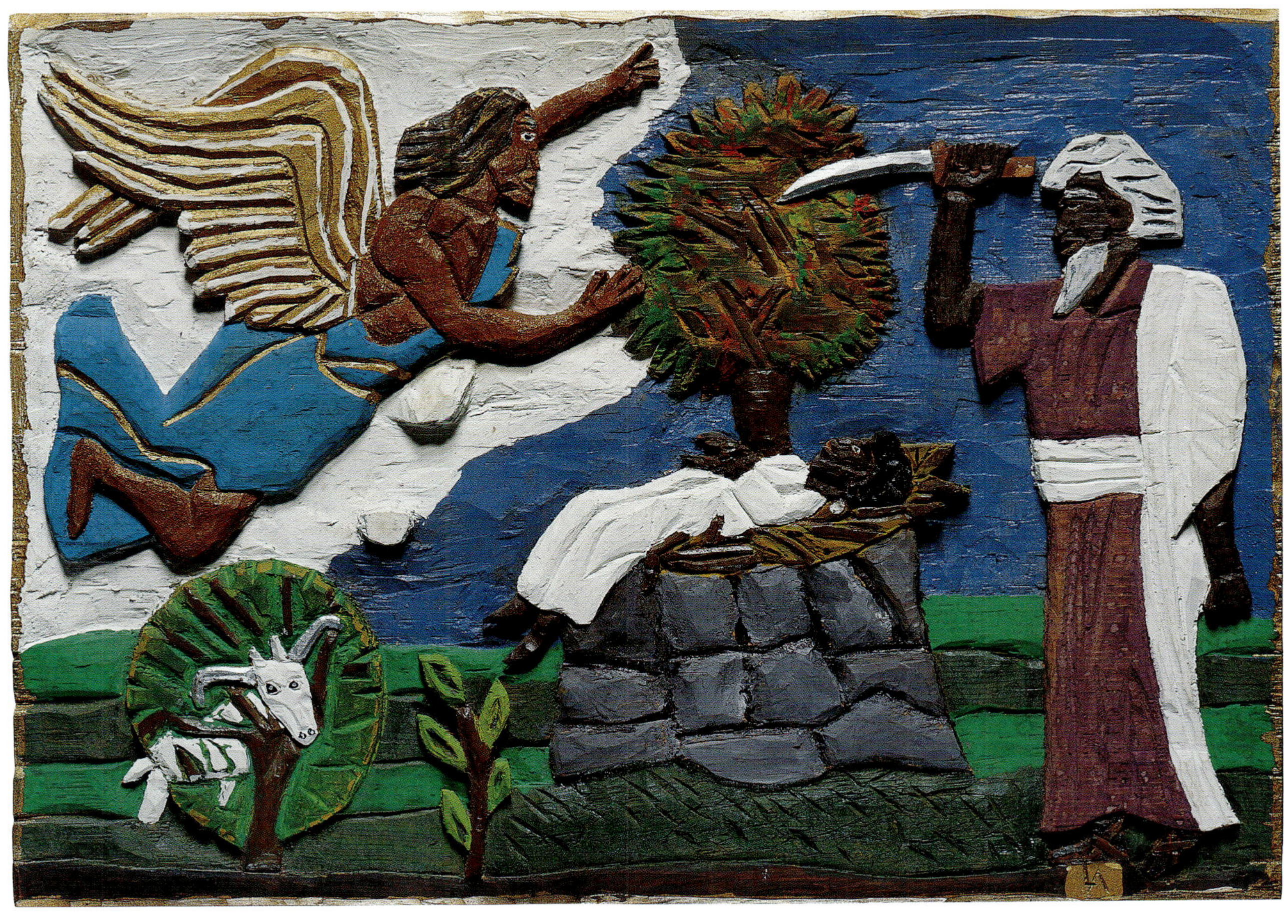

Cat. 4

Leroy Almon

1938–1997
Columbus, Ohio

The Sacrifice of Isaac, 1981
Carved wood with paint
11¼ × 16 × 1 inches
Acquired from William S. Arnett, 1994
1996.158

"Everything I do comes from the spirit world; it's spiritually motivated. That's why I give God all the glory. I've got thousands of pictures still in my head to do, so I just keep working," Almon told an interviewer in 1991.[1] He was not a painter of visions but of tales so familiar they had become part of him. Here the well-known story of Abraham's sacrifice of Isaac has a power that belies the simplicity of its presentation. As Abraham raises the knife to kill his beloved son, his arm is immobilized in the rush of wings and blinding light that heralds the angel's appearance. Isaac is almost an afterthought, lying limp on the stone altar, his legs loosely dangling. Meanwhile, the small ram who sticks his head through the bush appears to apprehend his own fate.

Almon would draw a scene on paper before transferring it to the wooden panel. "There's a lot of planning that goes into it before I start carving," he said. Using hand chisels and pocketknives, he executed his designs in soft woods such as basswood and cedar and then painted them with discount house paint. Despite escalating demand for his work, the artist maintained a high standard of craftsmanship in both conception and implementation. The consistency of his art bespeaks Almon's conviction that his talent was a sacred trust from God.

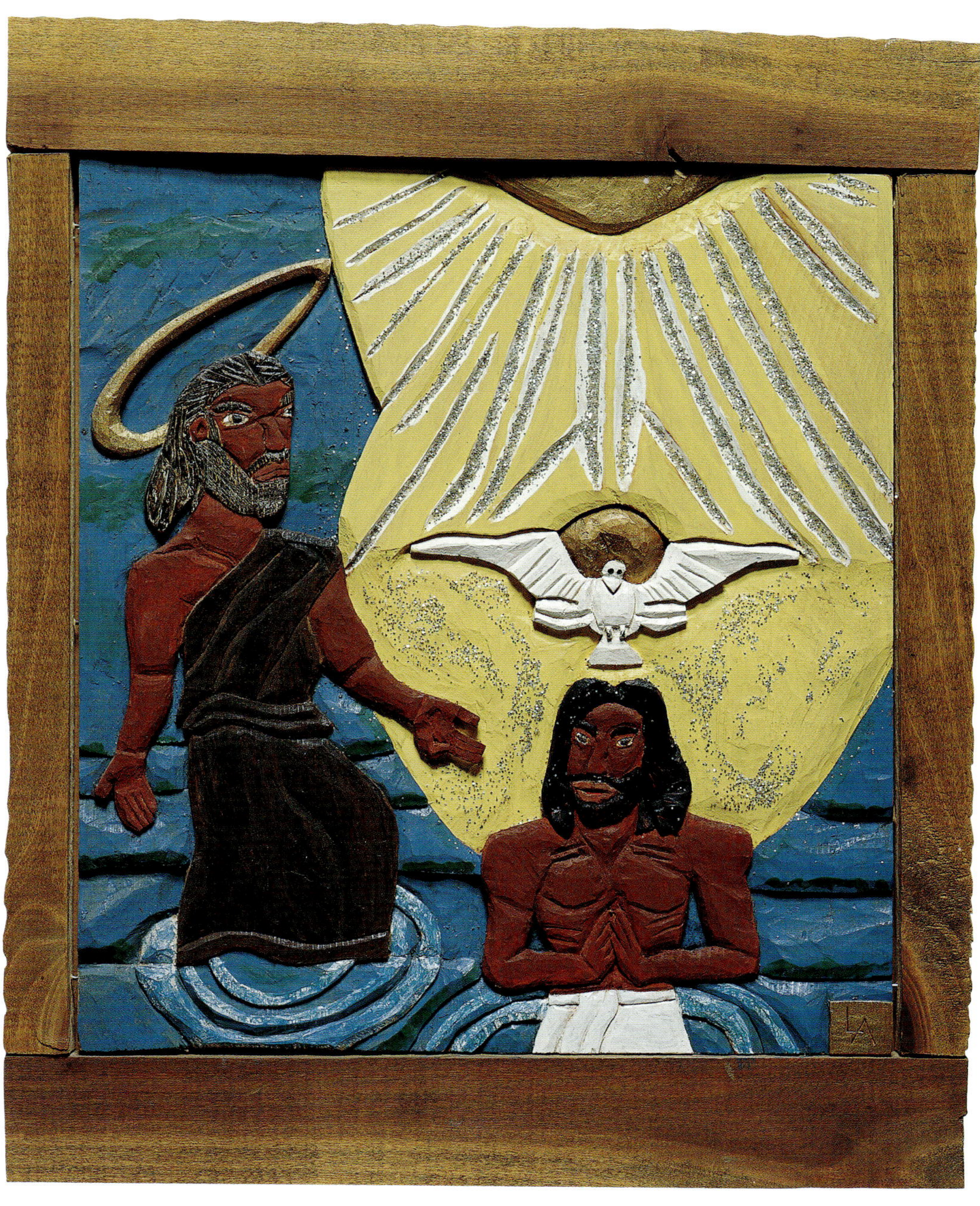

Cat. 5

Leroy Almon

1938–1997
Tallapoosa, Georgia

The Baptism of Jesus, 1983
Carved wood with paint
16 × 13¼ × 1 inches
Acquired from William S. Arnett, 1994
1996.155

A SELF-STYLED "FOLK ART PREACHER," Almon regarded his talent as a gift and the godly use of it as a duty, saying "I am only an anointed artist of God and I only create that which is put in my spirit by the Holy Ghost. Since my High Priest is Jesus Christ, all the praise, glory, and credit go to the Lord."[1]

In *The Baptism of Jesus* Almon presents the subject matter economically. He reduces his palette to six plain colors and his forms almost to their geometric foundation. Concentric circles form the halo and ripples of water while parallel lines mark the river. Rays of the spirit come from above with just enough irregularity to spare a shaft for John the Baptist. The scene's internal movement is stilled. The total effect is one of simple grandeur, its humanity augmented by John's quietly expressive gesture toward Christ.

Asked about his portrayal of biblical figures as blacks, Almon told an interviewer, "Everybody sees God as they are. The Bible says we're made in his image. I hold true with that."[2]

Cat. 6

Leroy Almon

1938–1997
Tallapoosa, Georgia

Slavery Time, 1990
Carved wood with paint
36 x 22⅝ x ¾ inches
Acquired from the artist, 1994
1999.95

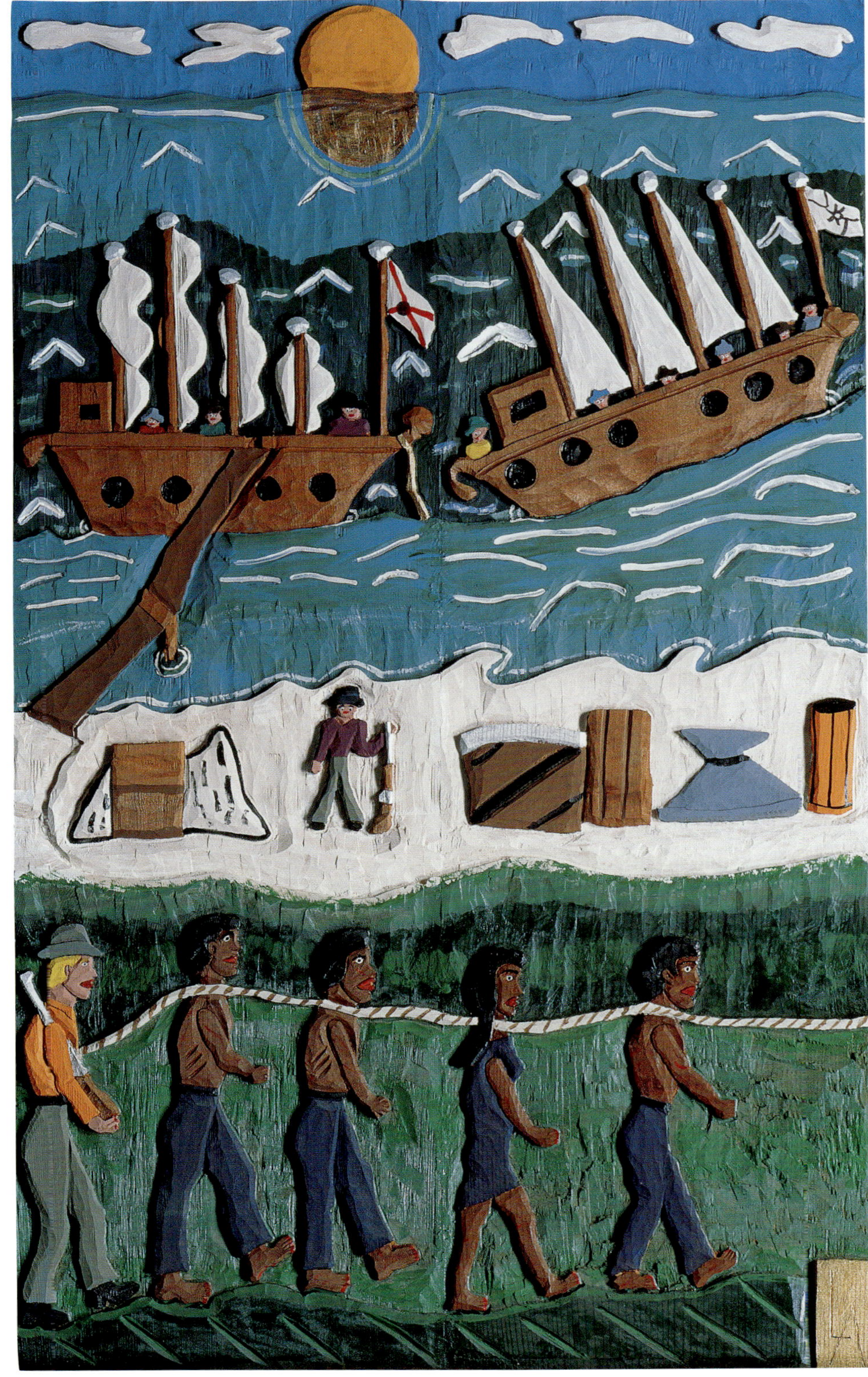

Both sacred and historical subject matter came naturally to Almon, who wished to communicate his belief in the power of religious salvation and self-reliance as antidotes to the destructive effects of racism on African Americans. Almon once said, "The American people have a bad habit of forgetting from whence they came."[1] Reminding them was a vital function of his artistic calling.

Although its crafting and composition seem to be all his own, Almon almost certainly took the title for this piece from his mentor Elijah Pierce. Between 1965 and 1973, Pierce created at least two reliefs titled *Slavery Time*, which are quite different in conception from Almon's. Both are composite designs showing various scenes from slave life and the period after Emancipation.

In Almon's carving, a pumpkin-colored sun sets into its coppery reflection above a scene whose soothing oceanic colors belie the grim events depicted below. Almon divided his single narrative field into a series of horizontal bands that function as registers, separating the heavens, ships at sea, shore, and slaves. The artist has left the location vague; it is not clear whether the episode takes place in Africa or the Americas. White faces peer over the sides of two sailing ships as enslaved Africans march in lockstep before an armed slave driver. Only the presence of a female slave among the group disrupts the feeling that this could be a twentieth-century chain gang. Almon was ever mindful of history's impact on the present, and he believed that the origins of some modern miseries lay in the dehumanizing horrors of slavery.

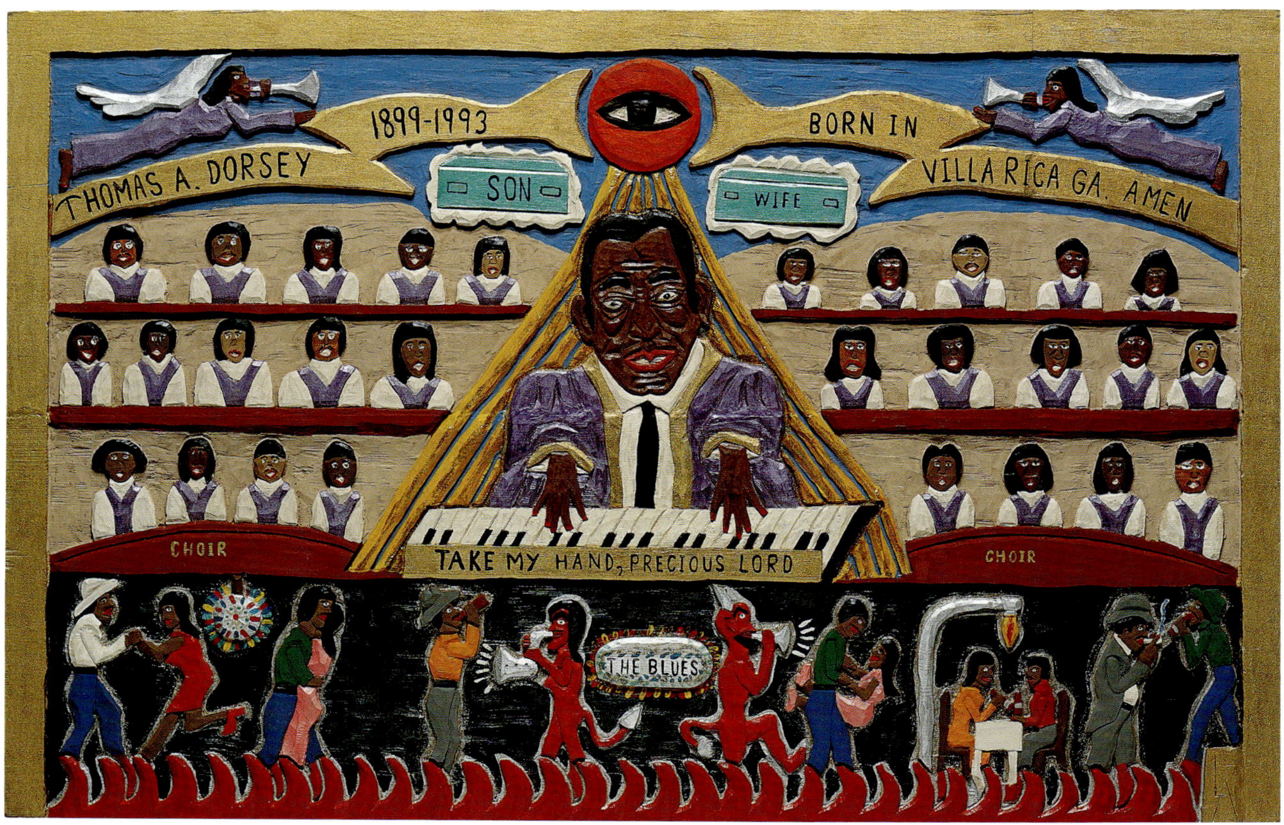

Cat. 7

Leroy Almon

1938–1997
Tallapoosa, Georgia

Thomas Dorsey, 1994
Carved wood with paint
27½ × 35⅝ × ¾ inches
Acquired from Thomas A. Dorsey Birthplace and Gospel Heritage Festival, Inc., 1994
1996.156

Known as the "Father of Gospel Music," Thomas Dorsey gave up a successful career as a blues composer and musician for a sacred vocation following the deaths of his wife and newborn child in 1932. Dorsey taught himself to play the piano by watching vaudeville pianists on Decatur Street in Atlanta, where his preacher father moved the family when Thomas was a child. By the time he was seventeen Dorsey had also taught himself to read music. After moving to Chicago in 1916, he performed with Ma Rainey and Tampa Red. During the late 1920s Dorsey vacillated between the blues that were bringing him fame and profit and the religious music he suspected was his true calling. Following the tragedies of 1932 a despondent Dorsey composed "Precious Lord, Take My Hand," a haunting plea for solace. He then broke with the blues entirely and devoted himself to spreading the word of God through music. Injecting the energy and rhythms of the blues into an already lively African American religious song tradition, Dorsey created a new musical form that would resonate far beyond the walls of the church. As Mahalia Jackson, one of his first soloists, remarked, "All this mess you hear calling itself soul ain't nothing but warmed over gospel."[1]

Almon has neatly encapsulated the critical events that prepared Dorsey to embrace sacred music. Horn-playing devils flank a garish silver sign announcing "The Blues," while sinners on the road to perdition dance, embrace, drink, and smoke in nightclubs and juke joints as the flames of Hell lick at their feet. Above the debauchery rises an orderly gospel choir, like the one Dorsey first organized in Chicago. From the eye of God at the top of the composition stream glittery rays that cloak the commanding figure of Dorsey. Near his head float the cloud-bedecked caskets of his young wife and infant son.

In purchasing this piece, Hahn helped fund the Thomas A. Dorsey Birthplace and Gospel Heritage Festival in Dorsey's hometown of Villa Rica, Georgia. This meticulously carved and painted work was commissioned to serve as the model for a larger monument to honor Dorsey.

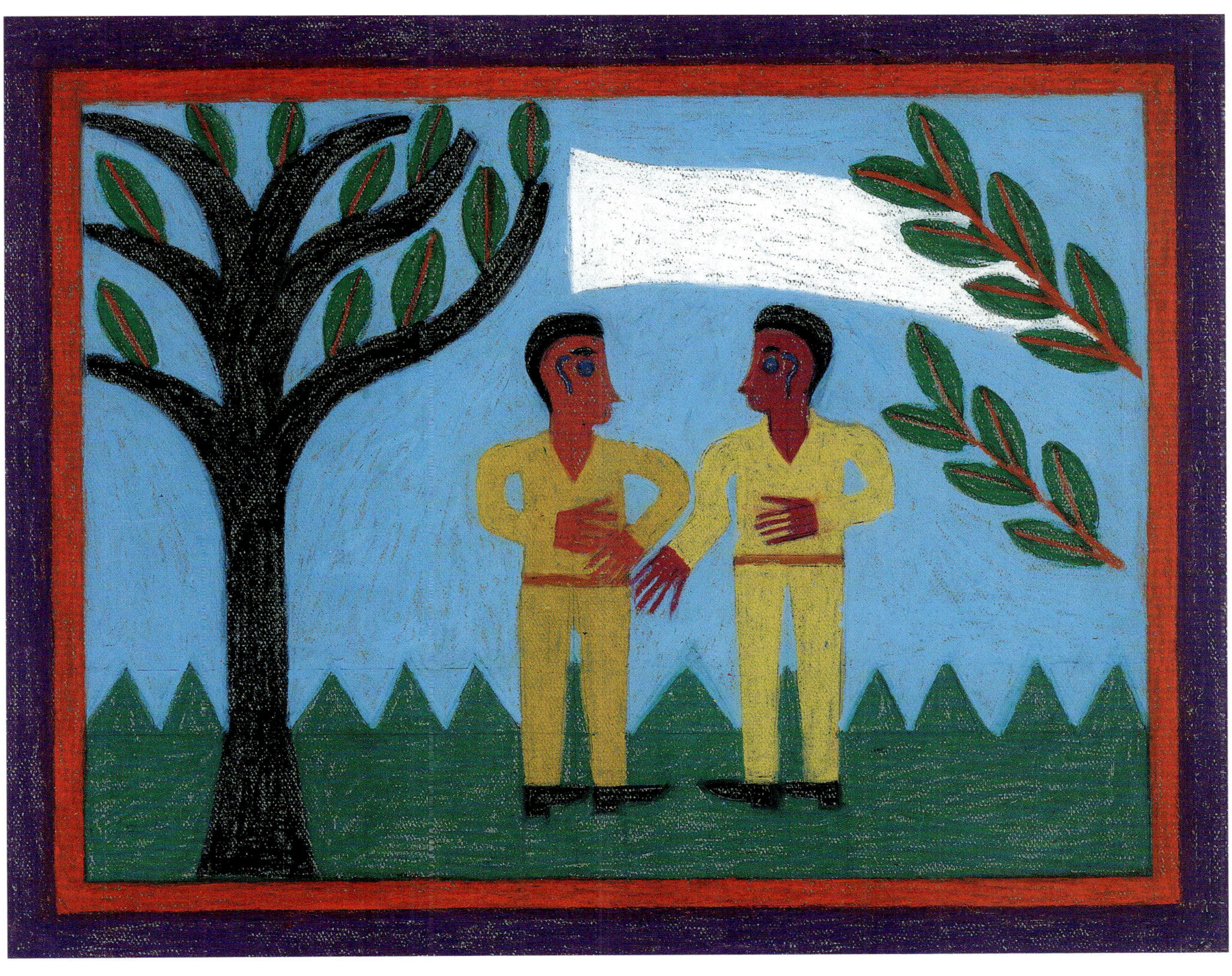

Cat. 8

Eddie Arning

ca. 1898–1993
Austin County, Texas

Untitled, 1969–1973
Oil pastel on paper
19¾ × 25¾ inches
Acquired from Ricco/Maresca Gallery, 1995
1996.159

Eddie Arning probably drew his inspiration for this work from a magazine illustration or other printed material, as was his custom. Periodicals and books were the primary connection between this artist and the world outside the nursing home in which he spent a decade making art. This work is typical of Arning. The heads and feet of the two figures are rendered in profile on perfectly frontal torsos; they have large eyes, concave noses, hook-like ears, and sleek hairlines. Stiff-fingered hands and the upward flowing branches and vermilion-veined leaves give the drawing an impression more suggestive of alertness than rigidity. Behind the men, spiky hills jut above the horizon like fence pickets. Perhaps the most intriguing element of this work is the angular cloud. Stark white against the robin's-egg-blue sky, this strange shape hovers like a canopy or a sheet billowing in the wind.

Arning's unusual palette is somewhat restricted in this work: the eggplant and vermilion of the borders and the details of leaves and faces render a cohesive and harmonious composition. He has also limited the human figures to oranges and golds that complement the blue sky. In doing so, this master colorist has made them pop out of the background, conveying a sense of depth while preserving the flatness of forms.

Cat. 9

David Butler

1898–1997
Patterson, Louisiana

Boat with Two Monkeys and a Squirrel, ca. 1984
Paint on metal
27¾ × 33¾ × 1½ inches
Acquired from Gasperi Gallery, 1993
1997.47

David Butler's art manifests his profound spirituality; he emphasized, "It's not magic" but the product of a God-given gift of dreaming: "I dream about things I gonna paint and then I do it. Dreams is what tells me what to do, but God gave me the gift."[1] In order to realize these dreams, Butler would first sketch a chalk design on a sheet of tin—preferably rusted because it "paints better"—then cut out the form and internal details with a meat cleaver or chisel and ball peen hammer.[2] He would puncture the tin with nails to create holes for attaching found baubles and bits of plastic or reflective surfaces. He would then coat the object with house paint, preferring strong unmixed primary and secondary hues, before attaching decorative odds and ends.

This whimsical concoction represents a boat carrying monkeys atop its mast and a squirrel on its prow. Intense, well-preserved colors invigorate a design already animated by ebullient curves and forceful diagonals, as the kaleidoscopic dots with which Butler often decorated his sculptures effervesce on the surface. The interplay of positive and negative space is highly sophisticated.

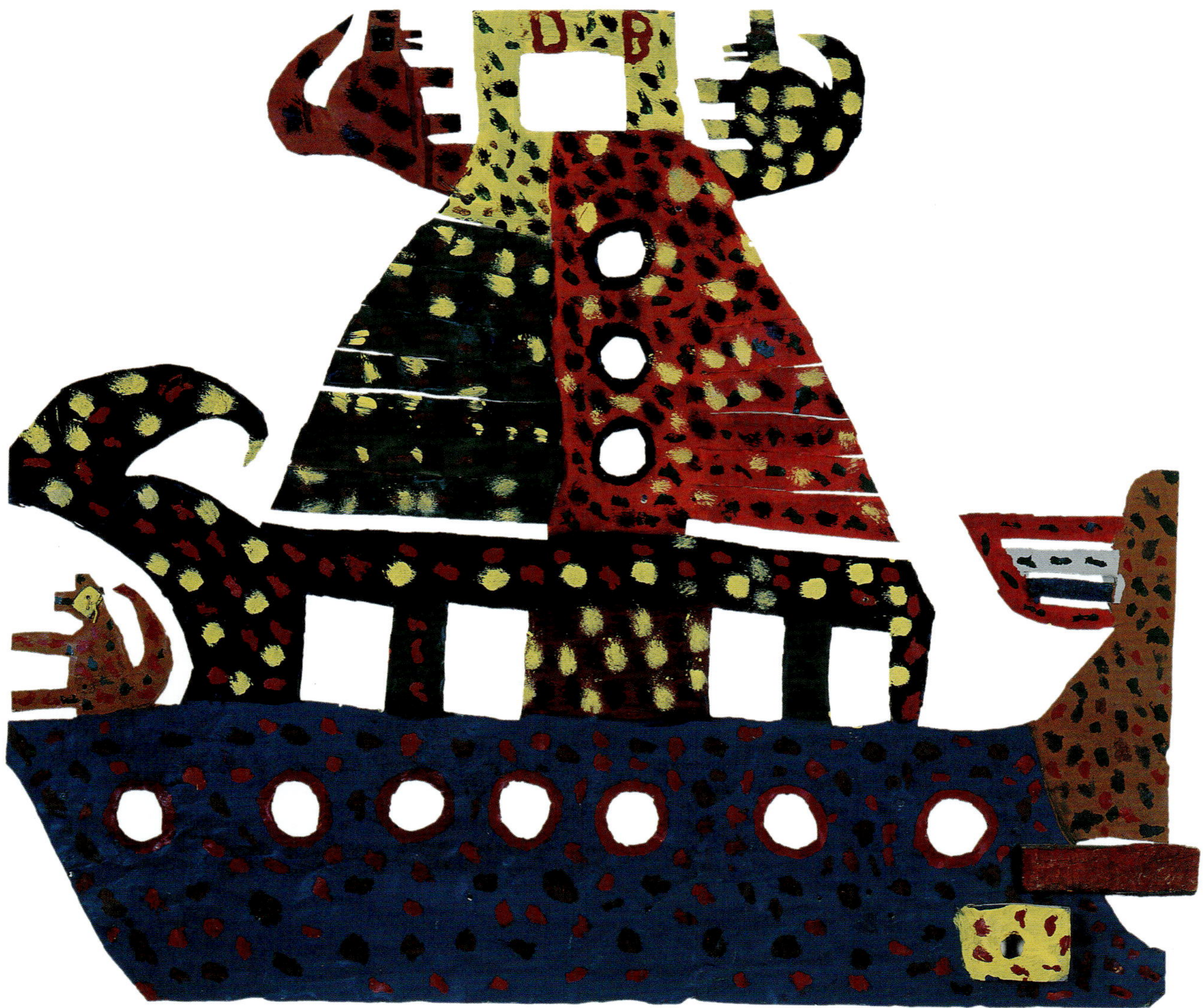

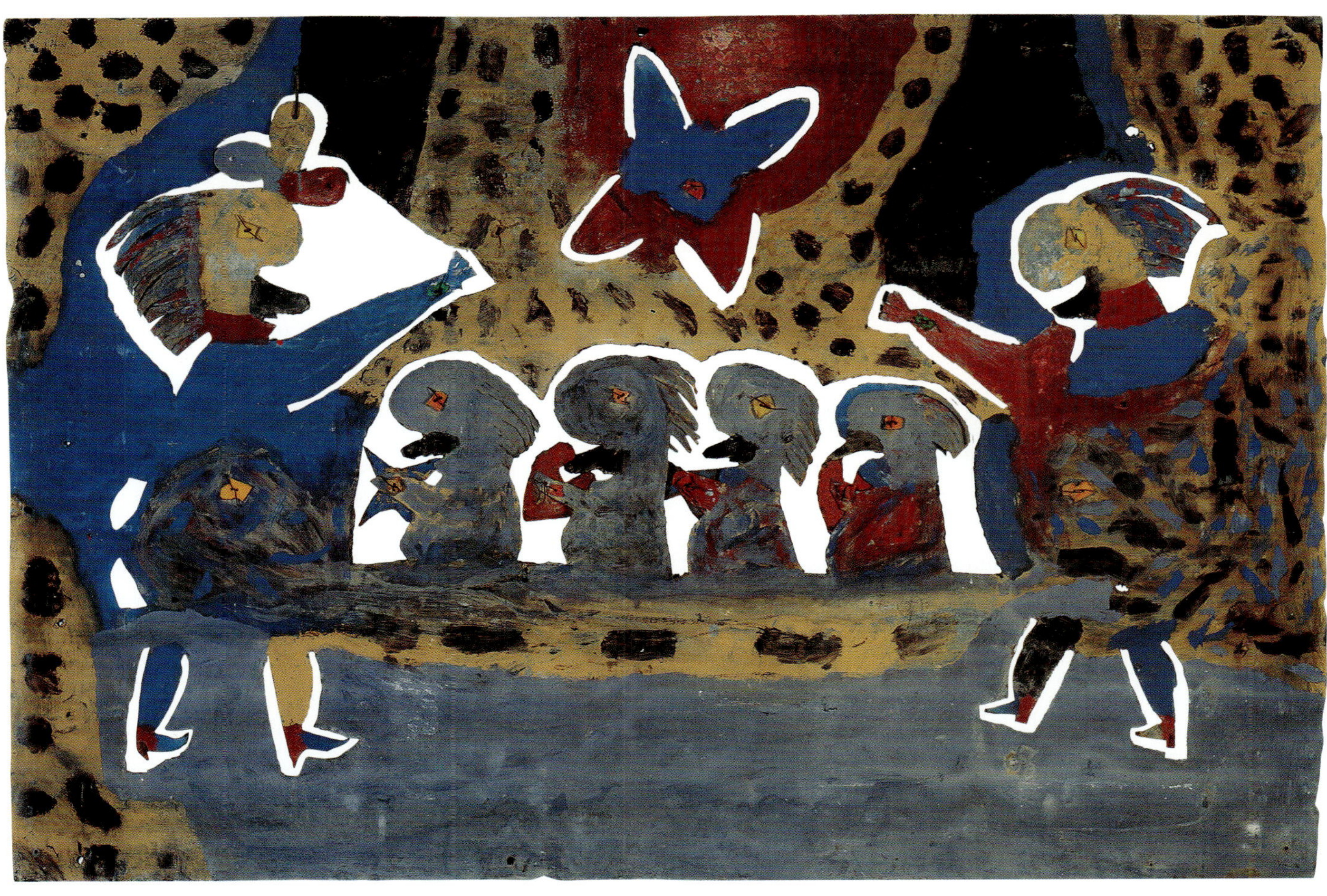

Cat. 10

David Butler

1898–1997
Patterson, Louisiana

The Last Supper, ca. 1984
Paint, plastic, and nails on metal
27¾ x 42½ inches
Acquired from William S. Arnett, 1994
1997.48

The son of a carpenter and a missionary, Butler inherited his father's aptitude for bricolage and his mother's spiritual energy. Combining these traits, he created an exuberant outdoor environment—a masterpiece that shielded this shy man from the world even as it brought him fame. Butler filled his small yard and the walls, doors, and windows of his house with whirligigs, birds, animals, and moving figures—to the delight of neighborhood children. He also found a way to carry his environment with him in the form of an elaborately decorated bicycle. Butler shared his creations enthusiastically and readily replaced the pieces he sold to admirers.

The Last Supper is a window screen the artist fabricated from perforated tin. Tom Patterson suspects the purpose of these objects may have been apotropaic, helping to shield Butler from pernicious forces after the death of his wife.[1] In any event, Butler enjoyed watching the changing light patterns thrown by these objects and found the privacy they created soothing.

The weathered condition of this piece, its colors subdued by oxidization, suggests a long life outdoors. Before a patterned background two large figures, one of whom represents Christ, flank a group of four smaller subjects, who represent the disciples, seated at a table. The disciples hold objects that might spin in a breeze. Butler formed the limbs and heads of the outer figures by cutting the tin to free them from the surrounding metal, increasing their unrestrained attitude. Eyes and belt buckles are small painted tin rectangles wired onto the main piece. The four-pointed star above the vessel appears often in Butler's work and is a common motif in Haitian and African art.

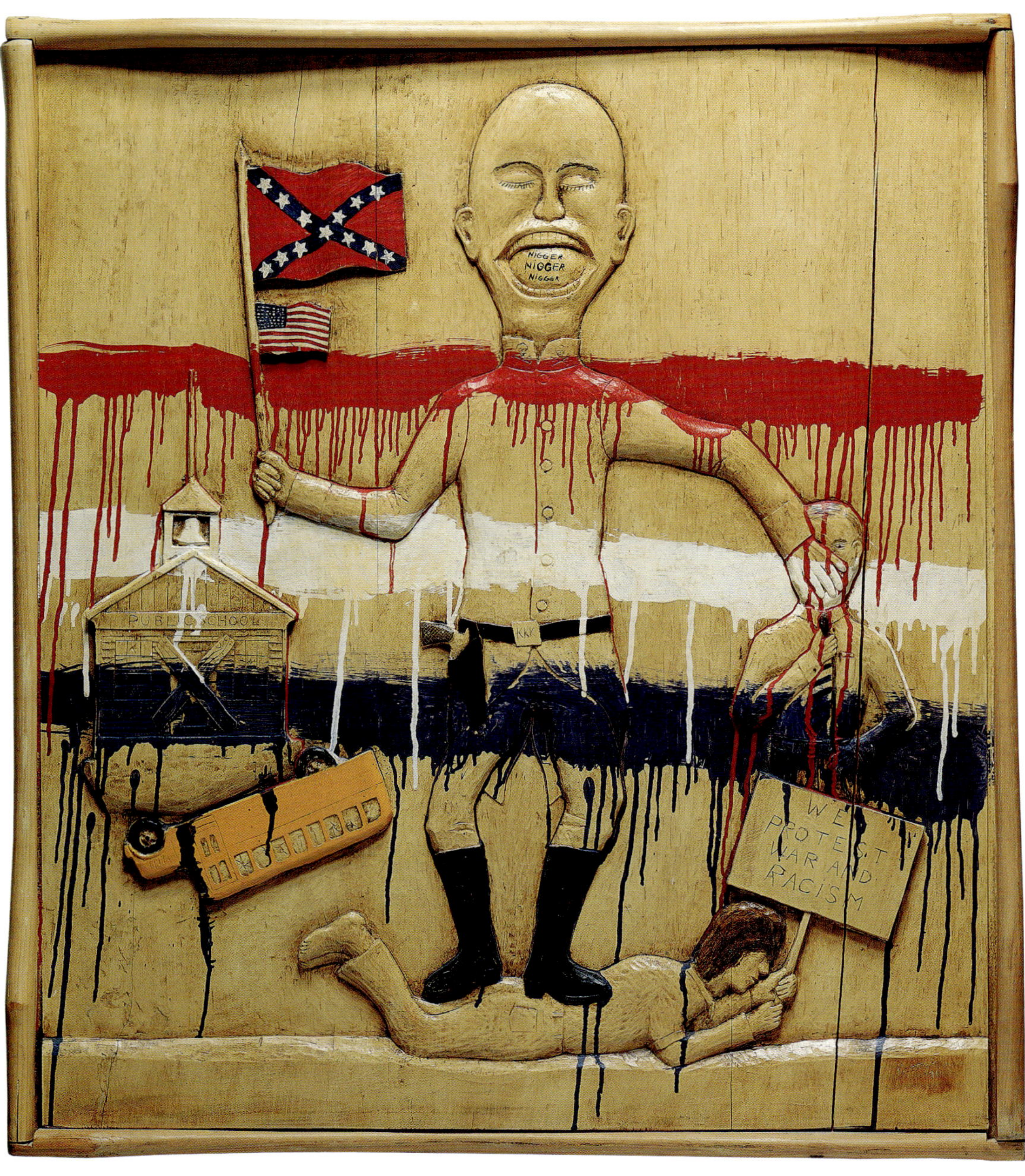

Cat. 11

Ned Cartledge

Born 1916
Atlanta, Georgia

The Flag Waver, 1970
Carved wood with paint
36¾ × 33½ × 2½ inches
Acquired from the artist, 1995
1996.33

The Flag Waver is the earliest known example of Ned Cartledge's relief carving, the medium for which he is primarily recognized today. This painted wood carving, which the artist considers one of his strongest pieces, expresses his dismay over the Southern racial disturbances of the 1960s and 1970s. Although the overpowering central figure can be read as a generic bigot, it resembles former Georgia governor Lester Maddox, famous for his refusal to serve blacks at his Pickrick restaurant. An overturned school bus and boarded-up public school below this figure decry the plight of education in the face of segregationist fanaticism. The flag waver, mouthing the words "Nigger, Nigger, Nigger," holds a staff on which a large Confederate flag tops a tiny U.S. flag. As he stands on the back of a protester, the extremist claps his hand over the mouth of a journalist. Three horizontal streaks dripping red, white, and blue overlay the image, reinforcing the chromatic similarity of the flags. Only the flags are untouched by the weeping colors. A broad ruby line severs the racist's head from his body.

Cartledge framed the picture in axe handles, the time-honored weapon of mobs. Maddox sold such "Pickrick Toothpicks" to like-minded customers during his highly publicized effort to maintain an all-white clientele.

Cat. 12

Ned Cartledge

Born 1916
Atlanta, Georgia

Don't Hide Your Light Under a Bushel, 1986
Carved wood with paint
20⅜ x 23½ x 1 inches
Acquired from the artist, 1991
1996.32

CARTLEDGE OFTEN SAYS that he is not inspired but provoked into producing his disputatious wood carvings. Inspired by the passage from the Sermon on the Mount ("Let your light shine before men")[1] and provoked by the hesitancy of a Pennsylvania friend to display his artistic talent, Cartledge created this work. His friend, the secretary of Cartledge's World War II battalion association, drew what Cartledge considered "amazing pictures of famous people" but refused to show them because of a bad experience with a gallery.[2] Cartledge accused him of hiding his light under a bushel and has inscribed the back of this panel: "Modesty is for those without talent."

As abstract as it is narrative, this work is uncharacteristic of Cartledge in that it does not incorporate text, relying instead on a visual metaphor to convey its point. An "interesting looking" bushel basket Cartledge found in his yard served as the model for this piece, in which flattened perspective combines with stunning textural rendering to produce an object of great visual sophistication. Cartledge points out that he "even carved in the staples that held the basket together." The sharply rendered basket seems to hover above the ground, lifted by the light upwelling beneath it.

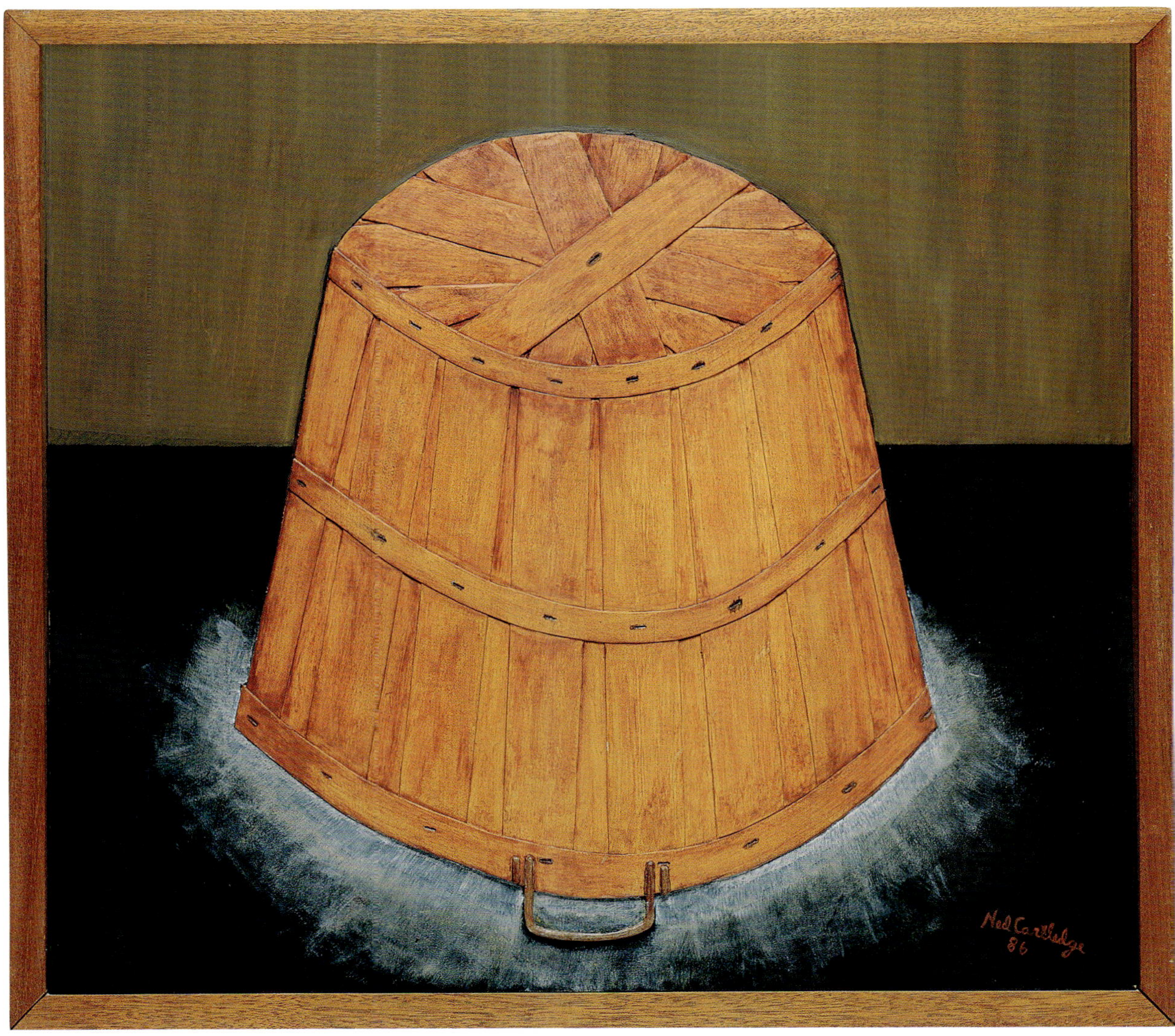

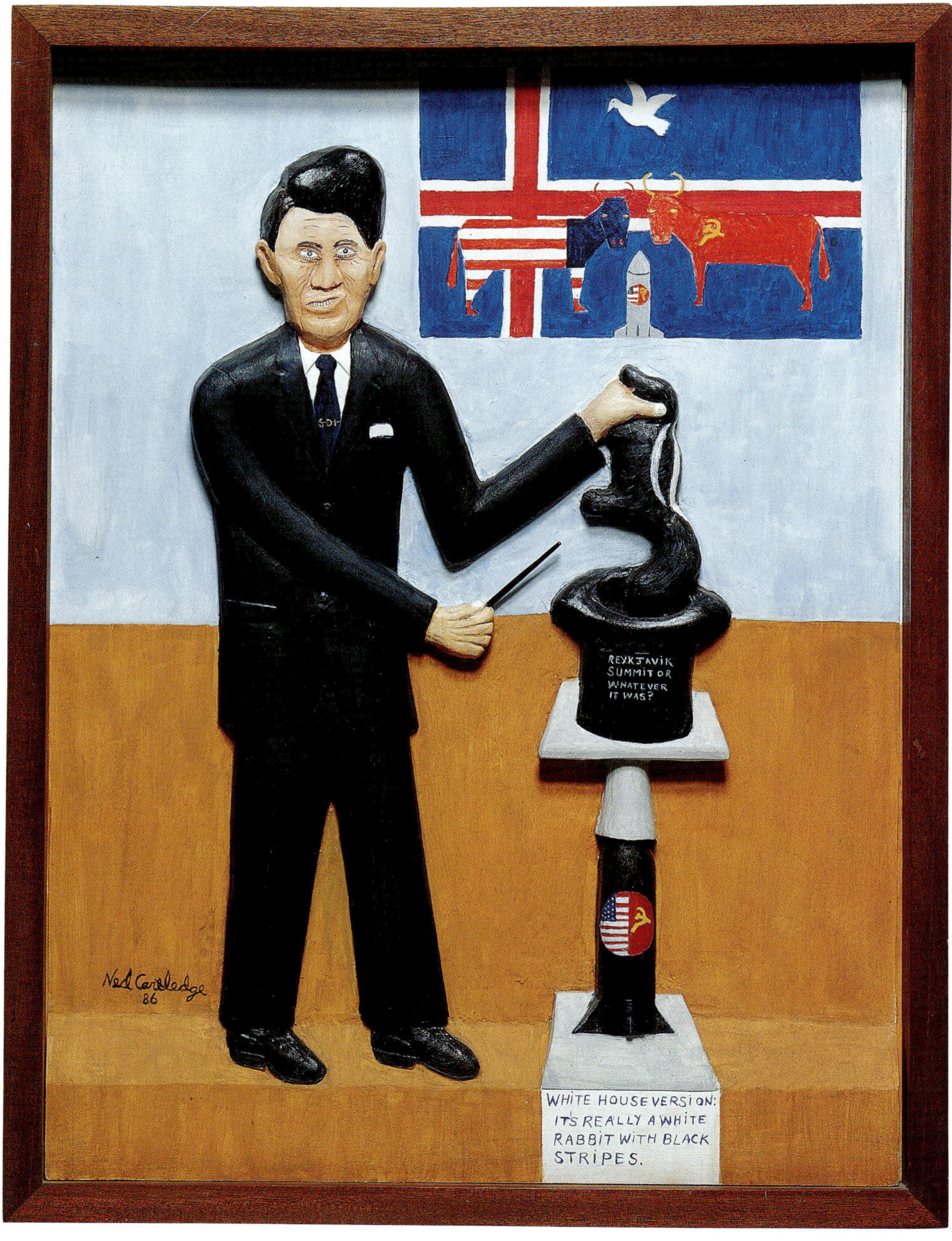

Cat. 13

Ned Cartledge

Born 1916
Atlanta, Georgia

The Reykjavik Rabbit, 1986
Carved wood with paint
22¾ x 17¾ x 1⅝ inches
Acquired from the artist, 1995
1996.165

"My work is not done to display my carving or painting skills which at best are mediocre, but to make comments on situations which I consider to be important or relevant," says Cartledge.[1] This emphasis on commentary may be seen in his depiction of the October 1986 meeting between Mikhail Gorbachev and Ronald Reagan in Reykjavik, Iceland. The fact that the meeting was not billed as a summit—because the two heads of state did not want to raise public expectations of progress toward nuclear disarmament—prompted the inscription "Reykjavik summit or whatever it was?" on the hat.

The dove of peace flies over two bulls representing the United States and the Soviet Union. Below their heads rests a missile emblazoned with the combined flags of both countries, indicating little difference between the military might of the two superpowers. Another rocket forms the base of a small table on which rests a magician's hat from which Ronald Reagan, wearing a tie inscribed "SDI," pulls a skunk.[2] According to Cartledge, "Reagan, regarded as such a magician, got skunked at the meeting" because Gorbachev was so much better informed.[3] Cartledge claims a great admiration for Gorbachev's courage in pursuing more conciliatory relations between the two superpowers.

Cat. 14

Ned Cartledge

Born 1916
Atlanta, Georgia

Fundamentalist Preacher Negotiating with a Black Hoer, 1989
Carved wood with paint
20½ × 27½ × 1½ inches
Acquired from the artist, 1995
1997.49

THE ARTIST APPROACHED THIS PIECE with a feeling for classical symmetry, bifurcating the scene between nature and architecture. "My work is always symmetrical," Cartledge has said. "Even my house is, though that's not why I bought it."[1] Bold colors and lucid geometric shapes in straightforward relationships create a precisely ordered world where everyone's role, from man of God to tiller of the soil, appears carefully prescribed.

Knowing that the hearer would associate the title with then-current news reports of Louisiana televangelist Jimmy Swaggart's escapade with a white prostitute, Cartledge was inspired to create this work by the play of homonyms. While the image may suggest an encounter charged with moral turpitude—in which the outcome of the negotiations would have nothing to do with agriculture—the artist claims that this was not his intention. Instead, recalling country churches of his youth that kept small cotton patches to supplement their incomes, he transformed the scandalous antics of televangelists into an innocent exchange between an itinerant field-worker and a country pastor whose plot needs cultivation. Though it makes a deft comment on an economic system in which "white folks usually get black folks to do their menial work,"[2] the scene does not imply the stinging criticism of televangelism contained in Cartledge's 1985 *Church of the Gullible*.[3] As the artist points out above his signature, "Things aren't always like they sound."

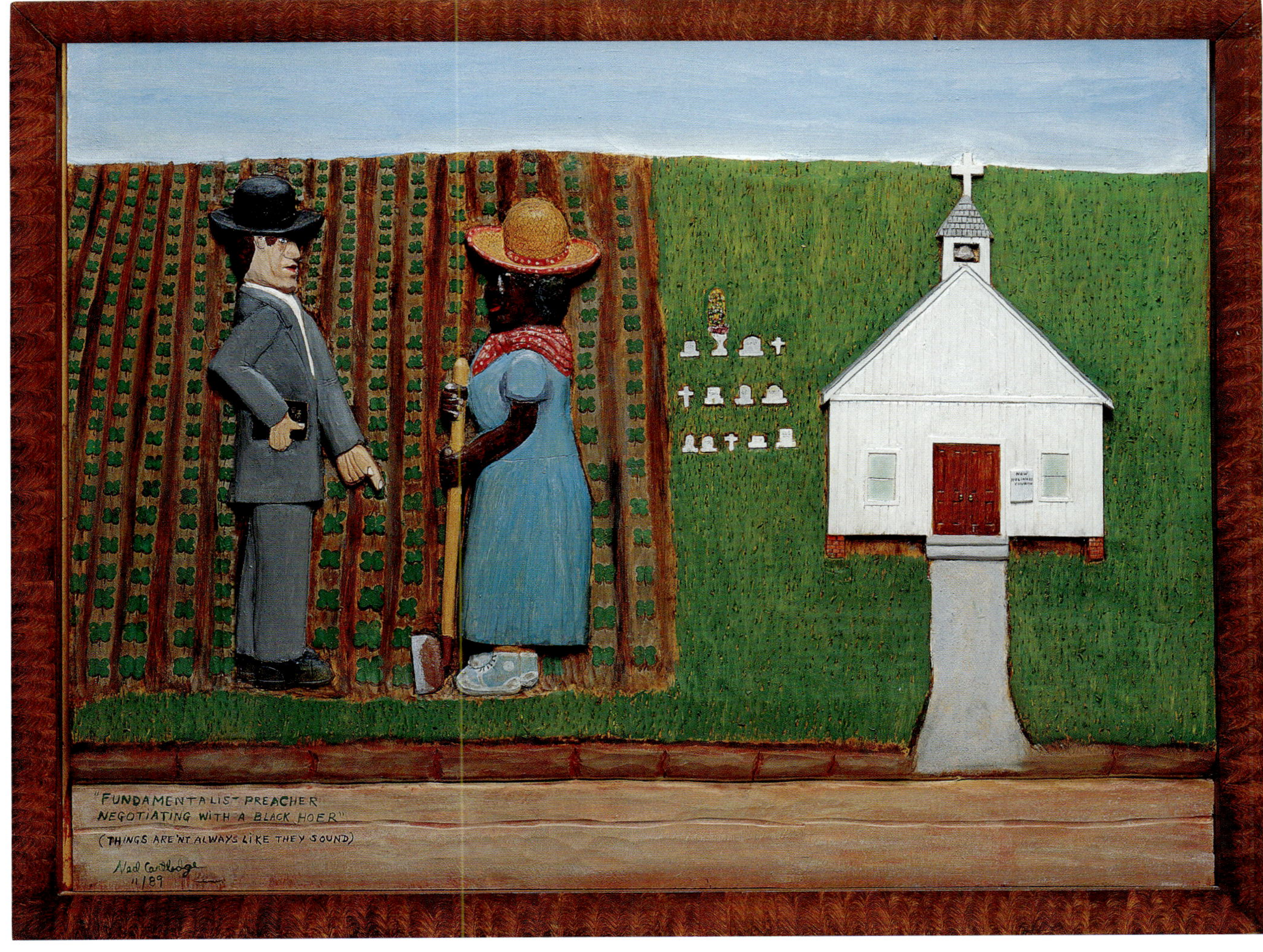

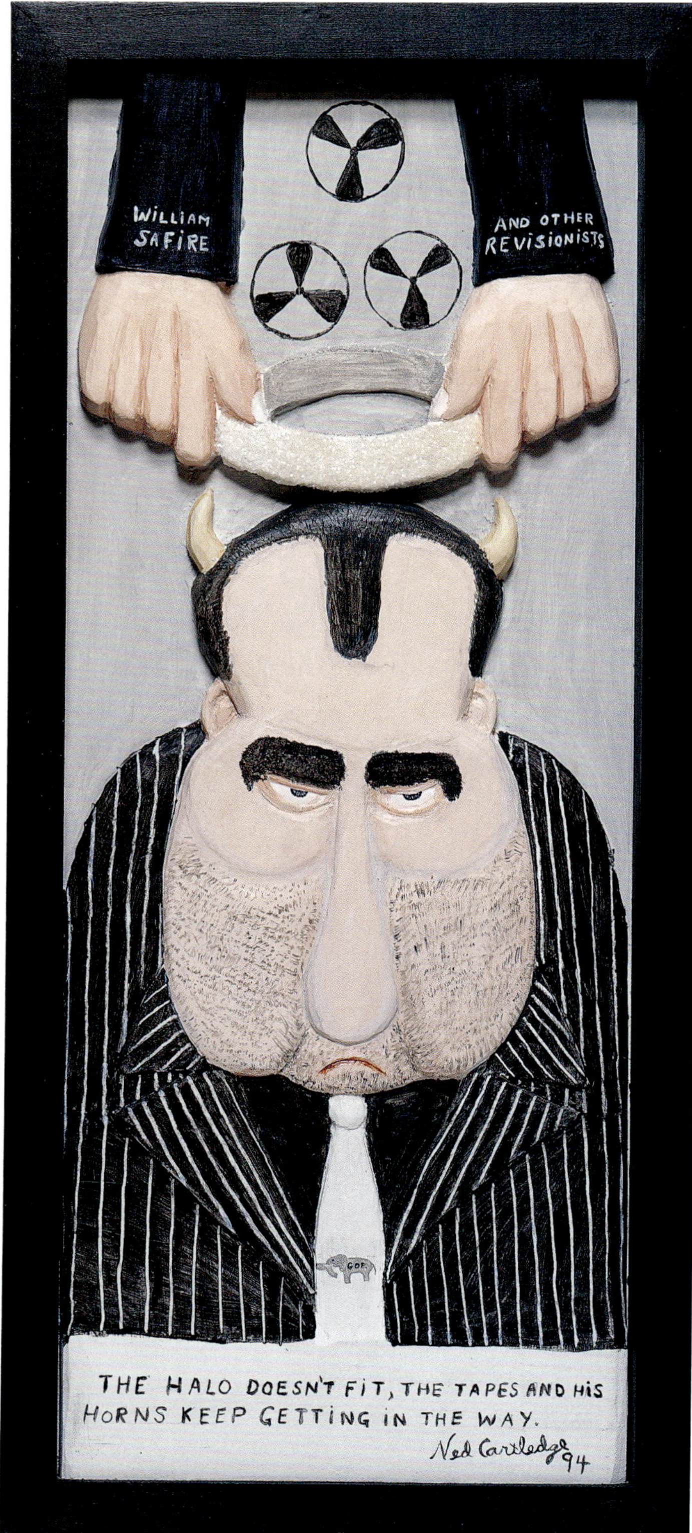

Cat. 15

Ned Cartledge

Born 1916
Atlanta, Georgia

Nixon, 1994
Carved basswood with acrylic paint
27½ x 12½ x 1¾ inches
Acquired from the artist, 1995
1996.163

Annoyed by the effort in the early 1990s to rehabilitate the reputation of former president Richard M. Nixon, Cartledge created this demonstration of simple physics: two solid bodies cannot occupy the same place at the same time. Across the bottom is the legend "The halo doesn't fit, the tapes and his horns keep getting in the way," and the anointing arms are identified as "William Safire and other revisionists." Convinced that those who would canonize Nixon were indulging in revisionist history, the artist responded with this assertion of Nixon's bad character and the evidence of erased tapes. Along with his trademark five o'clock shadow, Nixon wears a pinstriped suit and white tie, looking like a Prohibition-era Chicago gangster. His tie tack is the GOP elephant.

Cat. 16

Raymond Coins

1904–1998
Westfield, North Carolina

Valley of the Dry Bones, 1986
Carved steatite
17 × 19 × 1⅝ inches
Acquired from Berman Gallery, 1993
1997.50

Raymond Coins believed in personal guidance from God, often manifested through dreams. Visited by visions from youth until middle age, Coins incurred the anger of fellow members of the Rock House Primitive Baptist Church in the 1930s, when he revealed the warnings his dreams contained about a potentially divisive church leader. After the furor died, he took care in deciding with whom to share his visions. The dreams and their aftermath left an imprint on his memory; much later in life he began to carve them in bas-reliefs like this work.

Coins once told Tom Patterson of a dream in which he and the preacher of the Rock House Primitive Baptist Church encountered a field full of skeletons roused by the sound of gospel music emanating from a nearby house.[1] Coins must have found parallels between local church issues and the predicament of the Israelites during the Babylonian captivity, for this dream, illustrated in *Valley of the Dry Bones,* is a variation on the vision of Ezekiel that was set to music in two spirituals titled "Dry Bones."[2] In the biblical story—regarded as a promise of the reunification of the Israelites in Jerusalem—God instructs Ezekiel to prophesy to the scattered bones. As he preaches, the bones reassemble themselves, grow flesh, draw breath, and become an army of the Lord.

In Coins's work, two upright figures, representing the artist and the pastor of his church, stand near a small house. They are surmounted by a nearly identical pair. Into a protrusion on the right of the stone are carved the smaller supine figures of the skeletons (which look remarkably like the living men). Coins has cleverly adapted his composition to suit the shape of the stone, whose subtle low-relief carving is barely visible without a strong raking light.

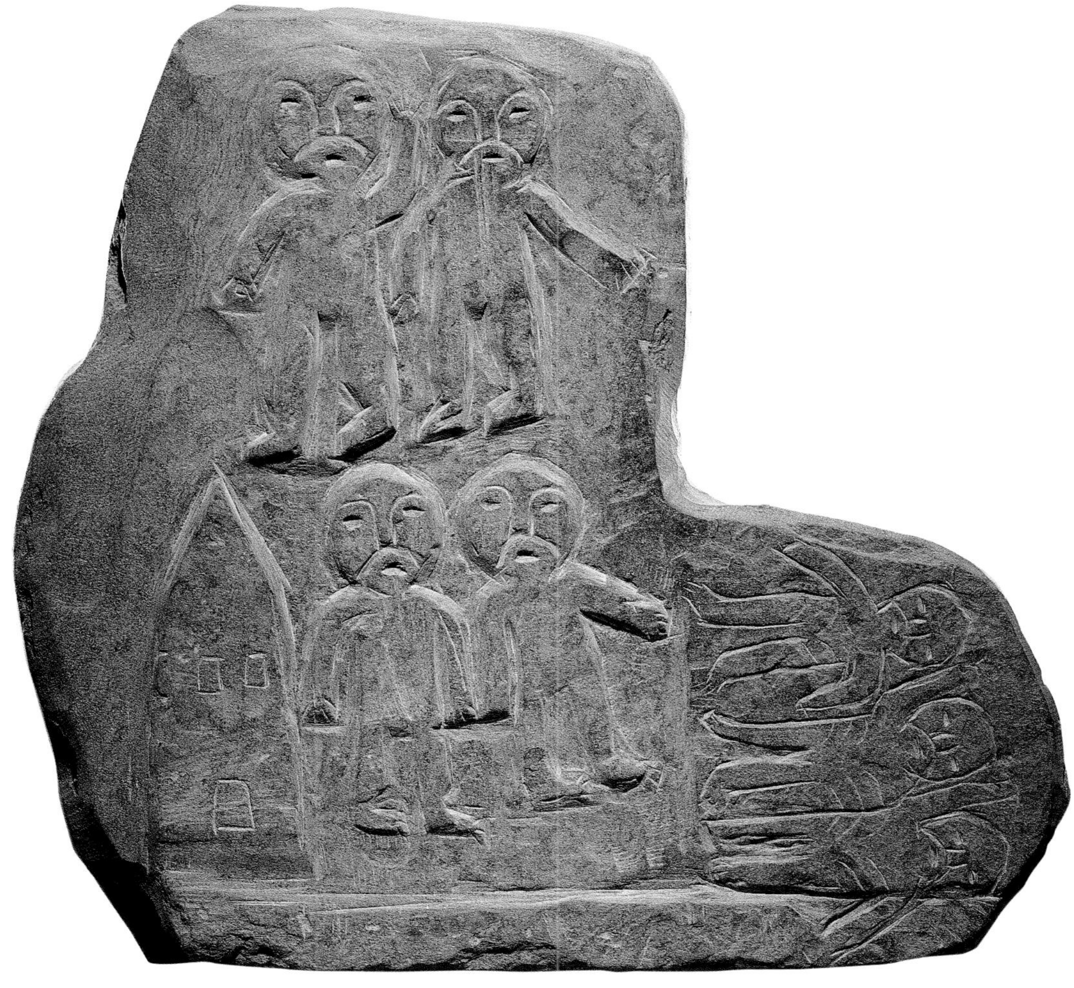

Cat. 17

Raymond Coins

1904–1998
Westfield, North Carolina

Best Friends, ca. 1988
Carved steatite
17⅞ x 13¾ x 3 inches
Acquired from Berman Gallery, 1993
1997.51

The subject of this rare secular stone relief by Coins is the New Farmer's Warehouse in Mt. Airy, North Carolina. In addition to farming tobacco, Coins worked as a floor manager at this warehouse during twenty-five or thirty tobacco auction seasons. During a series of interviews in 1984 and 1985, he recalled, "I guess I lost [money] ever' year in the warehouse. I'd work one year an' say, 'Well, I'm not goin' to do this no more!' But everybody'd get after me, an' I was right back. So I worked in the warehouse an' I farmed too. That'd throw me to sell my 'bacca late. Bacca'd go down [in price] some at the last of the market. I still don't think I gained anything by workin'."[1]

Coins derived this scene from a 1939 newspaper photograph of himself and his friend Harvey Lench that may have been taken at the warehouse.[2] In the photograph, the two straw-hatted men sit cross-legged before a pallet containing a towering pile of tobacco. Lench, on the left, holds a match to a tobacco leaf he has just rolled while Coins twists a leaf in his lap. Here the heap of tobacco is represented by the hexagonal shape between them, covered with hatchings that indicate the bound stems. Curving above it is a line of indecipherable writing that folklorist Roger Manley believes may represent the argot of the auctioneer's call.[3]

Coins carved his reliefs in the soft local steatite commonly called soapstone. The artist explained his working method: "I got a rock saw, but I ain't got the right blade. I got a sander. I chisel the rock with a little ol' axe, I wore it out, about; it's got a broke handle. I can turn the rock up this way an' that way, an' see where to make [cuts]. . . . I check the rock, an' pick out what I want out of it. I can jus' about see the picture in there. Then take the chisel an' axe cut it down, then sand it."[4]

Cat. 18

Raymond Coins

1904–1998
Westfield, North Carolina

Untitled, ca. 1988
Wood
36 x 30 x 20 inches
Acquired from Charles Locke, 1994
1996.166

When Coins began carving to relieve the boredom of retirement in 1968, he fabricated Indian stone artifacts like those found around his farm. From these he moved on to small human figures he called "doll babies," and from these to animal figures suggested by the shapes of the rocks he found. When Coins began to carve wood, he approached it the same way, conceiving the final form from the natural appearance of the tree he intended to use.

With its toothless mouth and tiny ear bumps, this sculpture of a dog is typical of Coins's austere wood carvings. Stiff legs with toes nicked into the ends jut from improbable sites on the torso, their locations determined by the tree's growth pattern. Coins's dog is trim, with a slender tuck-up and a stubby tail. A few pronounced tool marks are visible on the otherwise sleek surface.

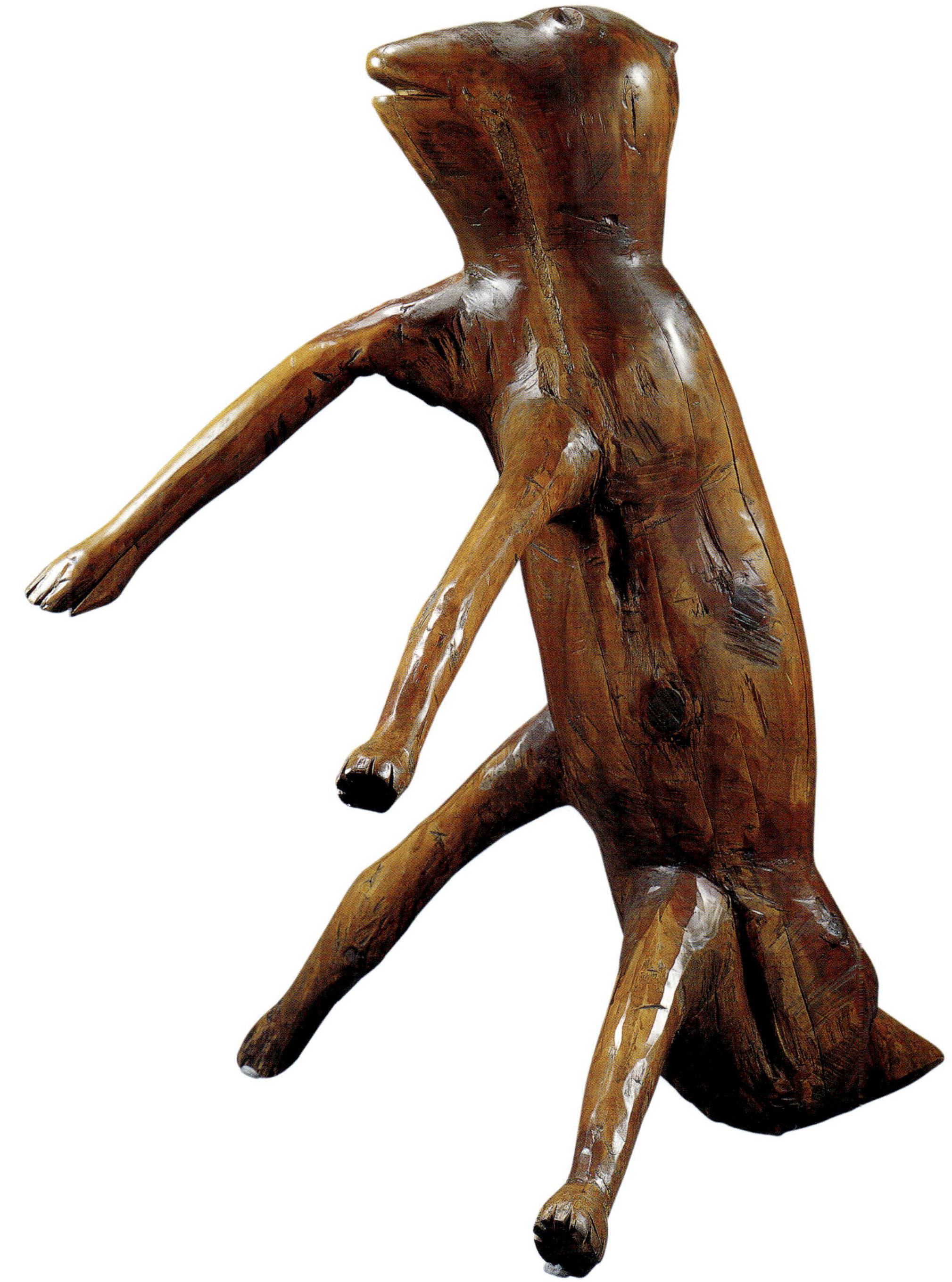

Cat. 19

Henry Darger

1892–1973
Chicago, Illinois

40 at Jenny Richee Facing attack by blengiglomeneans who mistake them for little Glandelinians because they wore gray unforms [sic], *the only way to save save* [sic] *themselves is to undress & hide the Glandelinian uniforms* [Recto], 1910–1972

Long after Cromer Andren Jack Evans and Vivian girls mistaken for girl scouts by Abbieannan soldiers and held prisoners [Verso 1], 1910–1972

At Frances Atlanta a second Glandelinian rascal captured and forced to respect Vivian girl princesses [Verso 2], 1910–1972

At Frances Atlanta/The result of the persuit/though they escaped 2 are injured Angelina Aronburg and Jennie Turmer with them [Verso 3], 1910–1972

Watercolor, pencil, and ink on paper
18¾ x 69¾ inches
Acquired from Ricco/Maresca Gallery, 1995
1997.52a & b

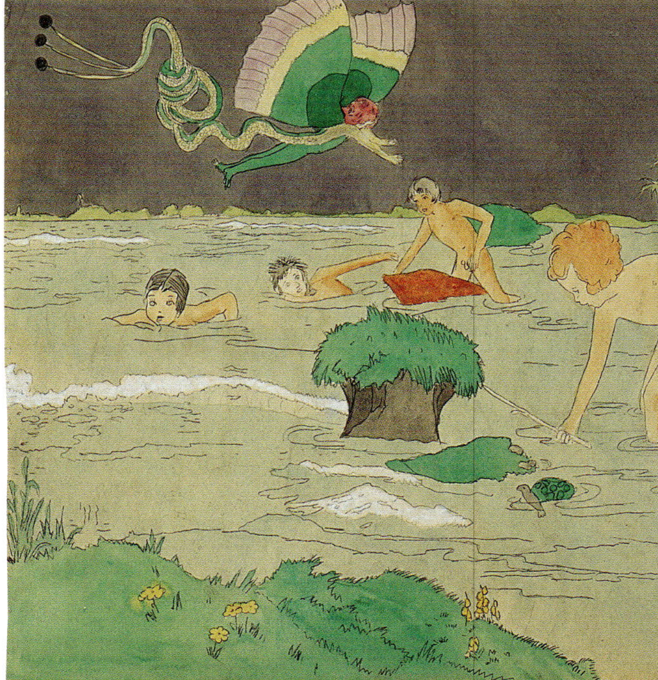

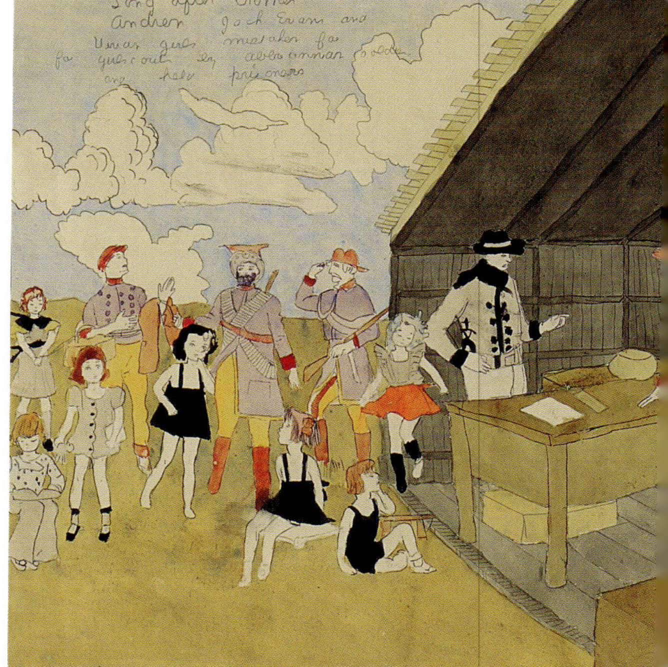

In a 15,145-page typescript that he began around 1909, Henry Darger invented a world of ineffable beauty and unspeakable horror, which he later illustrated with more than 250 double-sided watercolors. Overflowing with menace and violent detail, *The Story of the Vivian Girls, in what is Known as the Realms of the Unreal, of the Glandeco-Angelinian War Storm, Caused by the Child Slave Rebellion* is an archetypal tale of good versus evil. It recounts the wars between the citizens of various nations on a distant planet, including the malevolent Glandelinians, who enslave children, and their enemies, the Christian Abbieannians. The story's heroines are the seven blonde Vivian sisters, Abbieannian princesses who ultimately lead their nation to triumph.

Adept at arranging intricate compositions, Darger was also an imaginative and subtle colorist whose delicate hues unify his complex designs. During the last third of his life Darger created a stock of over two hundred figures, enlarged through photo-processing. He traced these shapes onto his works and often integrated them with collage elements. Darger's narrative and drawings demonstrate a fascination with the details of physical suffering. They are filled with scenes of appalling brutality into which he threw his young heroines and from which he always delivered them—although their child-slave companions were often sacrificed to Glandelinian blood lust.

Darger illustrated *The Realms of the Unreal* long after he had written it, and the pictures do not always depict specific incidents from the book. While the episode portrayed on the long horizontal sheet titled *40 at Jenny Richee* . . . is not drawn from the manuscript, it does relate to events described there. Jenny Richee is a place mentioned more often than any other in *The Realms of the Unreal* and the locale of many of its illustrations.

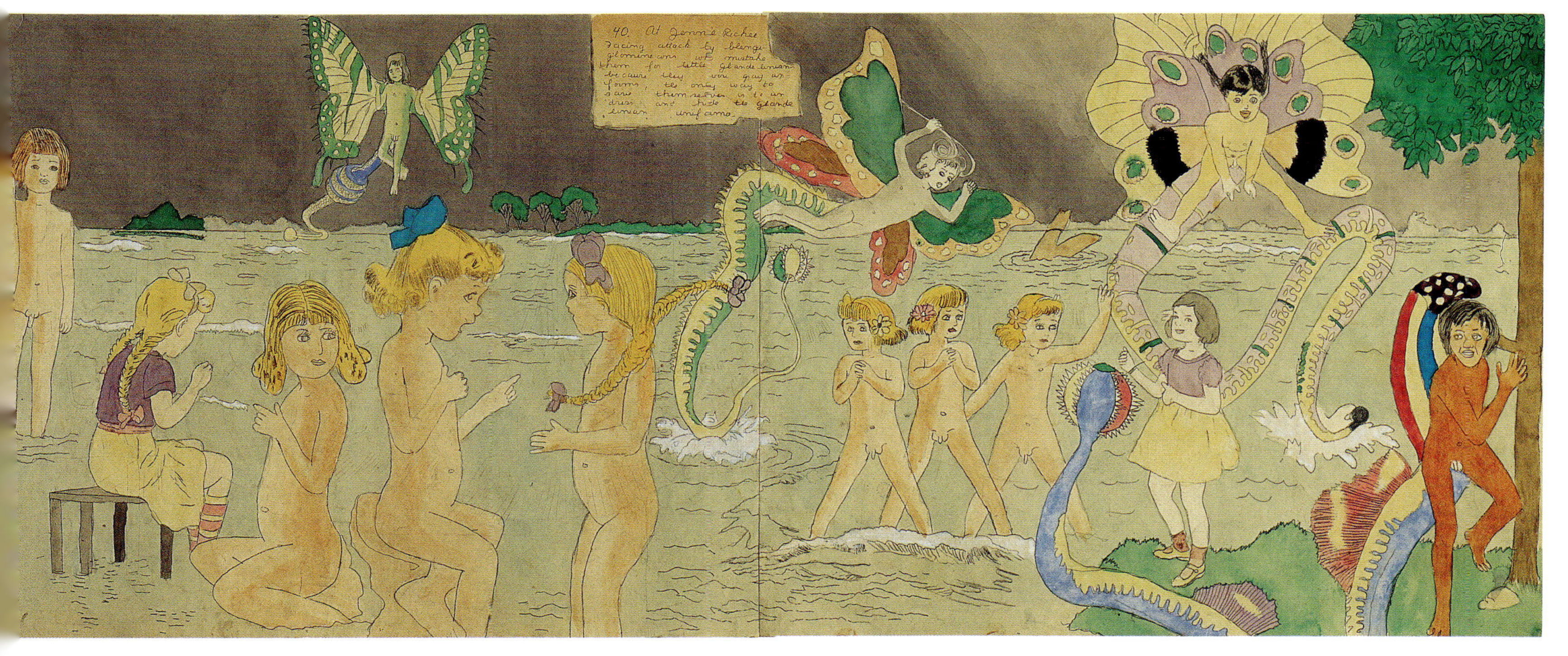
40. At Jennie Richee
Facing attack by blengins
whom mistake
them for little Glandelinian
because they are
forms, the only way to
save themselves is to un
dress and hide the Glande
linian uniforms

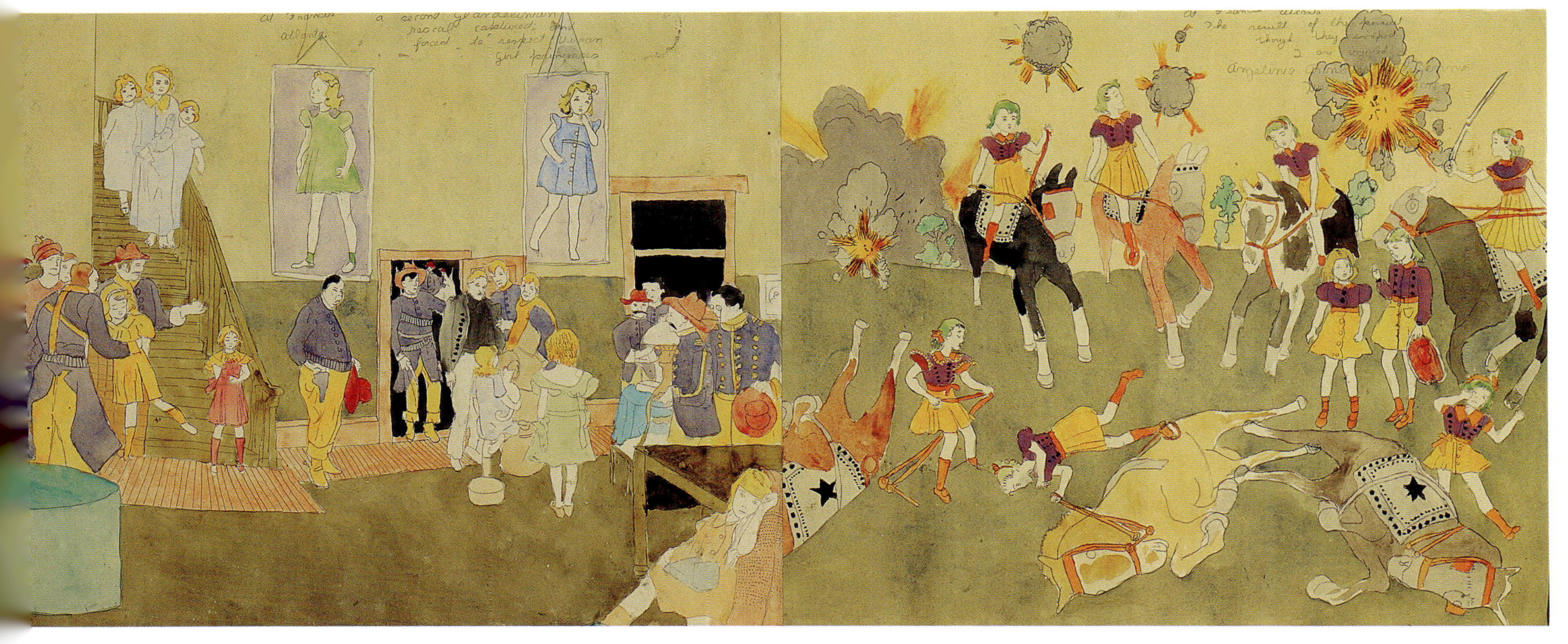

Blengiglomeneans (Blengins for short) are enormous flying dragons who protect the Vivian girls and despise Glandelinians for their cruelty to children. The Vivian girls sometimes disguise themselves, wearing gray and black Glandelinian uniforms when on reconnaissance missions. This time the trick has backfired, putting the girls in danger from their own allies—and giving Darger an opportunity to undress them. (Darger often portrayed his young subjects nude, usually with male genitals.) The one Vivian sister who wears purple and yellow (the Christian colors) is not at risk. The children stand amid the waters of a flood so great that the land sinks beneath its weight. One of the principal disasters in *The Realms of the Unreal,* the flood has been caused by the Glandelinians blowing up dams. The sky behind them is blackened by vast fires that burn the high ground.

The three scenes on the reverse depict episodes all found in the unbound seventh volume of *The Realms of the Unreal,* demonstrating that Darger created his illustrations in a somewhat systematic way.[1] Details such as time of day and number of participants sometimes differ between text and illustrations.

The left verso picture depicts an event following the catastrophic battle of Cromer Andrean. Darger's humor emerges as Violet Vivian and her guardian, General Jack Evans, are once again endangered by their Glandelinian disguises. The Vivian sister and one of the story's greatest heroes become victims of their own ruse when friendly Christian forces led by Sargent Henry Darger mistake them for the villains. The following excerpt from *The Realms of the Unreal* describes their arrest:

> There was a rush and they were surrounded. Violet being seized roughly by two soldiers while two more dragged Evans to his knees, and as he shook them loose with his strong arms he was set upon by a dozen and held fast.
>
> "I've got a monster, Sargent." cried one of the men.
> "Hold still you wriggling worm." cried another.
> "Spies from the Glandelinian camp, Sargent Darger, that is certain." said another voice, "Don't take them prisoners, shoot them where they are."[2]

The central verso picture is set in the headquarters of the Christians at Frances Atlanta, site of one of the most important battles of the war. A Glandelinian intruder has been caught after a noisy fight with Jack Evans. Purple-and-yellow-uniformed Christian generals mill about before portraits of the Vivian princesses, who emerge in person on the stairs. "Seven little white robed figures at this moment appeared, they being Violet and her sisters, the little girls having been aroused also by the shot and the confusion of the struggle. . . ."

The right verso picture also depicts an incident from the Battle of Frances Atlanta. Amid exploding bombs, the Vivian sisters flee on gray and black saddled horses stolen from the Glandelinians. Angelinia Aronburg and Jenny Turmer, important friends of the princesses, are hurt when their horses fall:

> BANG.
>
> A high explosive burst right near them, and the horses Violet and her sisters were riding sank to the ground mangled and bleeding the little girls being caught under the horses but not injured severely though the little girls were badly scratched by flying fragments. . . .

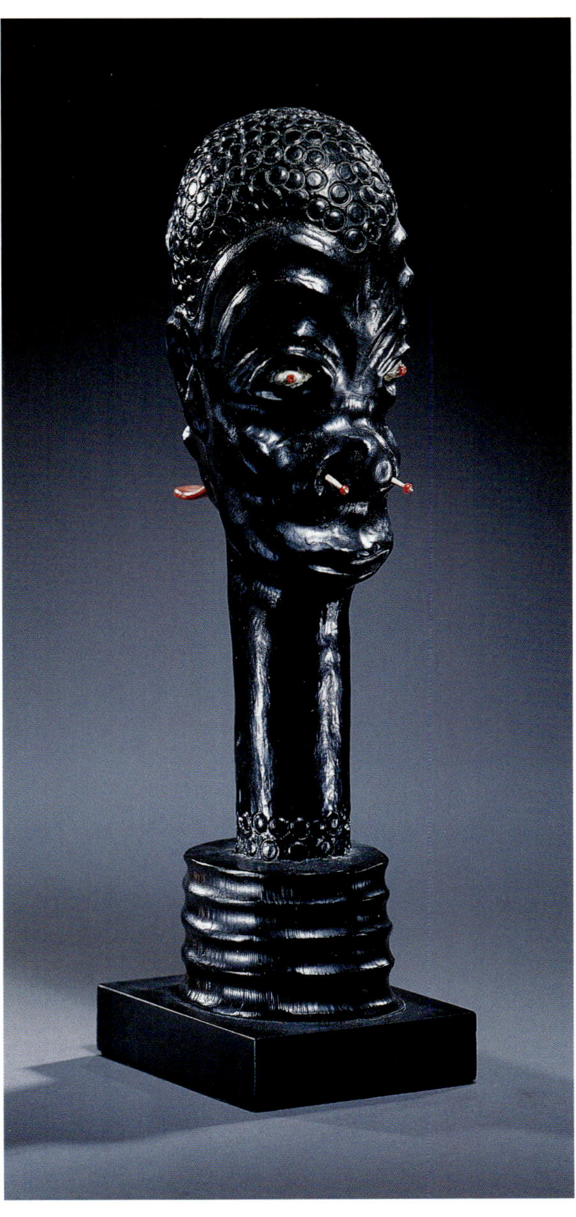

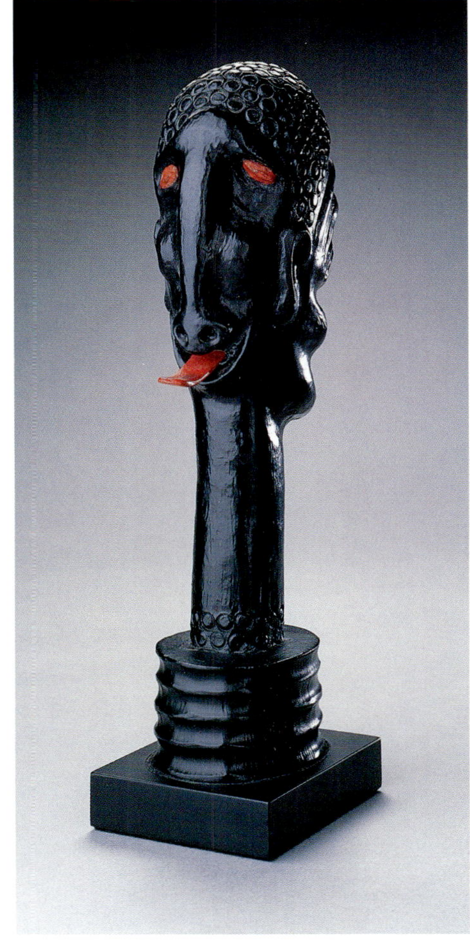

Cat. 20

Ulysses Davis

1914–1990
Savannah, Georgia

Untitled, 1970s
Carved wood with paint, glass beads, and toothpicks
13½ × 3⅝ × 4⅜ inches
Acquired from Knoke Galleries of Atlanta, 1993
1996.31

Although Ulysses Davis read library books about African history and often sculpted African-themed objects, he denied his work was influenced by African art, saying, "things just come to me."[1] Nevertheless, it is impossible to scrutinize this carving without conjecturing some debt to African sculptural forms, since it bears affinities with objects from both the West Guinea Coast and Zaire. Even so, Davis has made this form his own. From the nostrils of one of its faces project red beads impaled on toothpicks; from the mouth of the other protrudes a rigid, impudent scarlet tongue. Bulging white-painted eyes blaze through pupils made from red glass beads, an example of the shiny "twinklets" Davis loved to collect and use in his work.[2]

Various kinds of repetition establish a strong sense of rhythm in the piece. In addition to the sequence of neck rings, the eyebrows are repeated in radiating curves up to the hairline. Rows of circles—probably created with a handmade stamp of the sort Davis used to decorate both his sculptures and the woodwork of his barber shop in Savannah—represent tightly curled hair and decorate the base of the neck.

For the more than two hundred carved wood figures, furniture pieces, and reliefs he created during his lifetime, Davis used shipyard lumber, pieces donated by his friends, or wood he bought at lumberyards. He never made preliminary drawings or models, but reduced the mass with a hatchet before refining the form with a chisel. To add textural details he sometimes used tools of his barbering trade, such as the blade of his hair clippers. Very different from the series of sculptures generally regarded as Davis's masterpiece—dignified individual busts of forty-one presidents carved in mahogany (except Buchanan, in pecan)—this intriguing head provides a glimpse of the formal variety that Davis produced.[3]

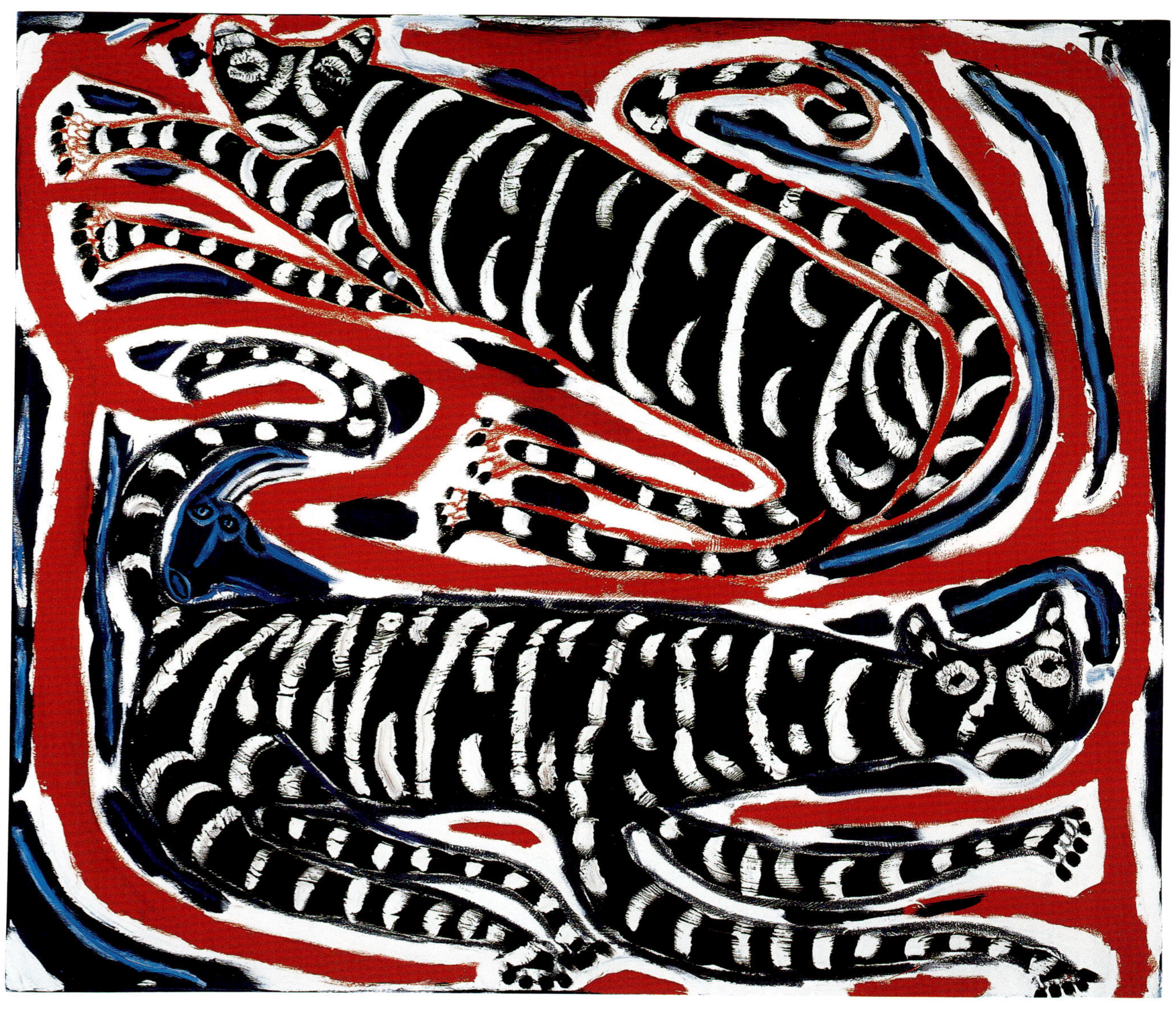

Cat. 21

Thornton Dial

Born 1928
Bessemer, Alabama

Smooth-Going Cats and the Hard-Headed Goat, 1990
Oil on canvas
65⅞ × 78 inches
Acquired from William S. Arnett, 1994
1997.61

This painting was created during a brief period when Thornton Dial experimented with artists' oil colors without incorporating found objects. Disliking the technique, he soon returned to his practice of painting assembled pieces with enamel. *Smooth-Going Cats and the Hard-Headed Goat* employs the red, white, and blue indicative of the United States, Dial's constant frame of reference "because that's all I know, the things that come into the United States."[1] Symbolic colors and undulating curves integrate the figures and unify the composition.

If this painting is a technical departure for Dial, it is by no means an iconographic one, as it combines two of his most familiar symbols: tiger and goat. Two large cats writhe across the canvas, while, between them, a blue goat pushes its head out. The goat represents hard-headedness for Dial: "Plenty of peoples is hard-headed, like the goat. That goes for all peoples being hard-headed and not paying attention to things." But the interpretive process is never stagnant for Dial; meaning is always unfolding. He recently elaborated, "Some people's hard-headed, some of them trying to teach you something. Some peoples will listen, some won't. And the cat has to keep working. The cat has to pay attention to everything, just like you." The goat may also represent the perseverance required to succeed in a hostile environment, as Dial has indicated in earlier discussions of this symbol: the "hard-headed goat . . . will go anywhere, to the top of the mountain where the other animals are afraid."[2]

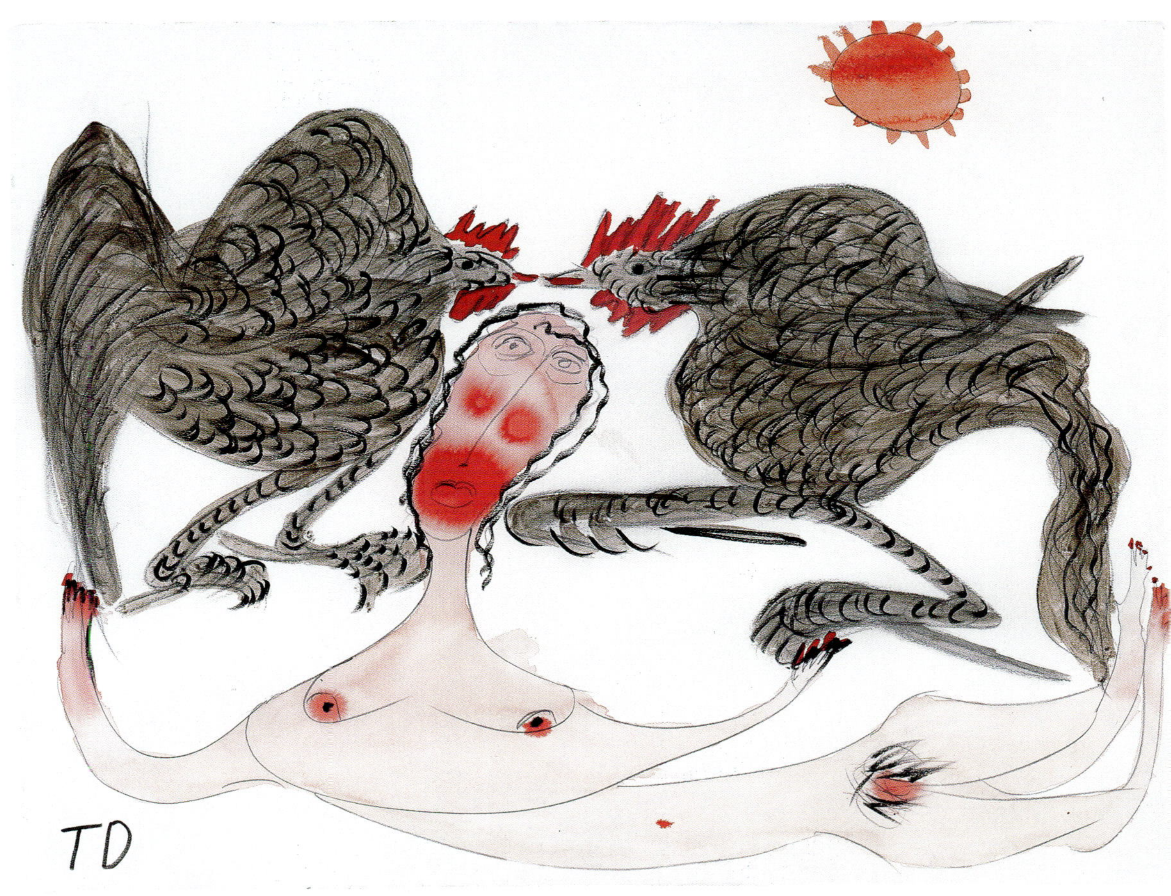

Cat. 22

Thornton Dial

Born 1928
Bessemer, Alabama

Rooster Picture, 1991
Pencil, watercolor, and oil pastel on paper
22¼ × 30 inches
Acquired from William S. Arnett, 1994
1997.62

In Dial's work, animals symbolize both the natural world and human traits, often simultaneously. He uses roosters and women to explicate relationships between the sexes. In this drawing, two roosters face off over the head of a woman whose sexual attributes are emphasized by the bleeding of scarlet paint applied wet-on-wet, a technique that mimics the uncontrolled nature of sexuality. Dial has often observed roosters around barnyards "fighting in the yard, they always fighting over womens. Mens is fighting the same way as roosters; we're all the same."[1] Dial's sinuous line creates a woman's body that is less an object for delectation than a sensuous suggestion of the importance of women in the world.

As is often the case with Dial's work, meanings proliferate. The artist says the piece is also about "fighting for your rights," a common theme in his work. The bird is also a metaphor for life itself, "flying all the time for something," suggesting the tenacity and intensity of the vital force.

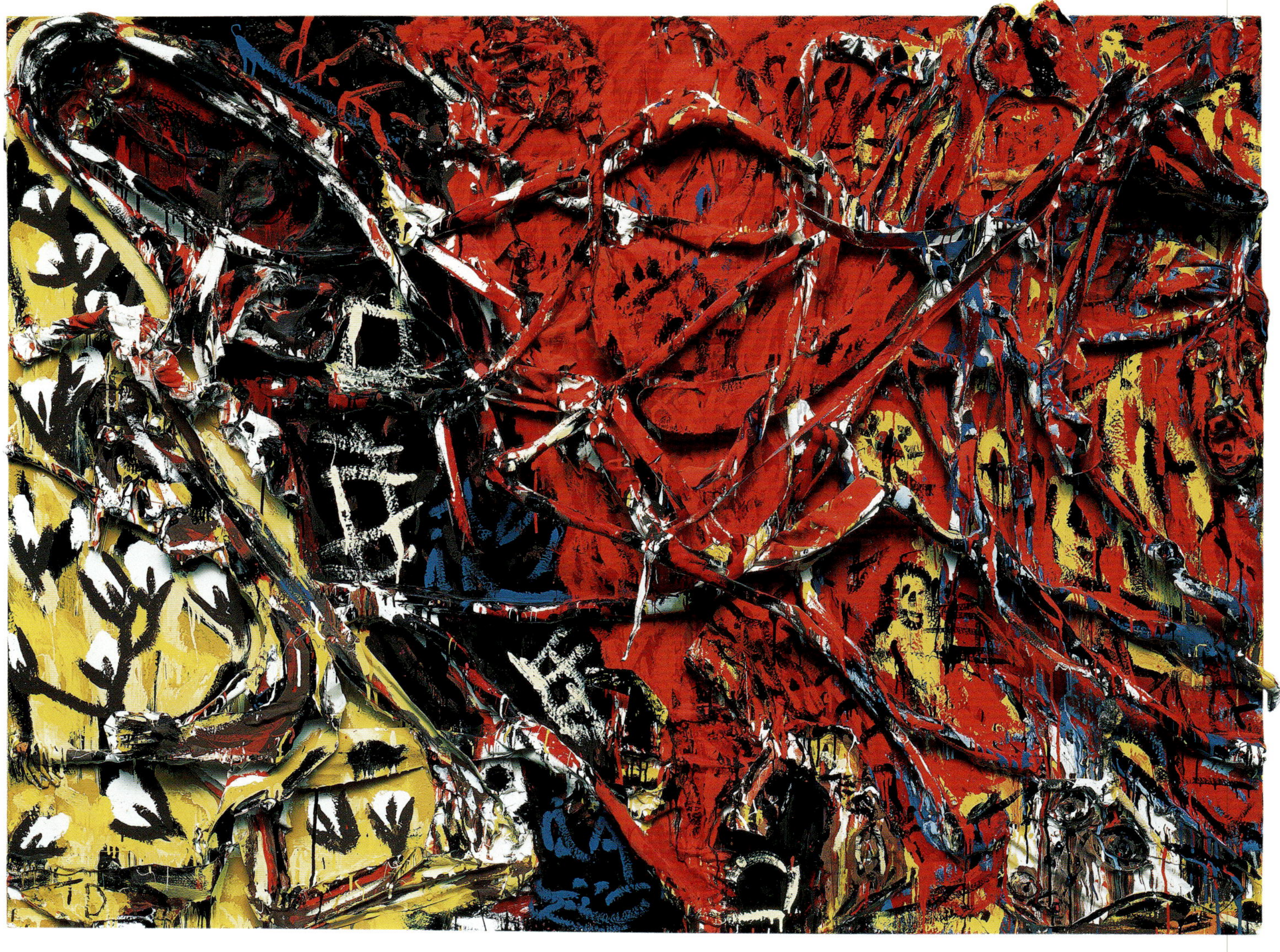

Cat. 23

Thornton Dial

Born 1928
Bessemer, Alabama

Heading for the Higher Paying Jobs, 1992
Enamel and oil paints, cloth, tin, wood, and industrial sealing compound on canvas, mounted on wood
64½ × 90 × 9 inches
Acquired from William S. Arnett, 1994
1997.55

The evolution depicted in *Heading for the Higher Paying Jobs* illustrates Dial's view of history: "More things moving now than were ever moving in the history of life."[1] This mixed-media canvas portrays the migration of Southern African American workers from the cotton fields of slavery and sharecropping to more remunerative industrial labor. On the left, the Southern sun bakes the ground where a brown field hand picks cotton. Above, an open-mouthed mask struggles out of a dark coal vein from whose bottom peers the face of an observant tiger. Next, the broad, ruddy streak of an iron mine gives way to the blaze of a steel furnace that illuminates faces—some flatly painted and some built up into the viewer's space. Dial's painting also reveals the darker side of progress. The vine that constitutes the overseer's whip writhes from the cotton field through the mines into the steel mill, suggesting that the wage earner can still suffer the sting of an unfeeling economy. Hints of industrial accidents suggest persistent struggles, and farm animals symbolize embattled nature as they look back nostalgically before succumbing to the flames of material progress.

The importance of struggle in annealing the spirit is evident here. As Dial says, "It takes fire to harden the material. It takes beating to harden the material. That's life." The variety of materials encased and stiffened by enamels brushed, dripped, and drizzled on the thick surface illustrates the artist's conviction of the interdependency of things and people in this world. "We need it all. Same people, same materials, same iron, everything."

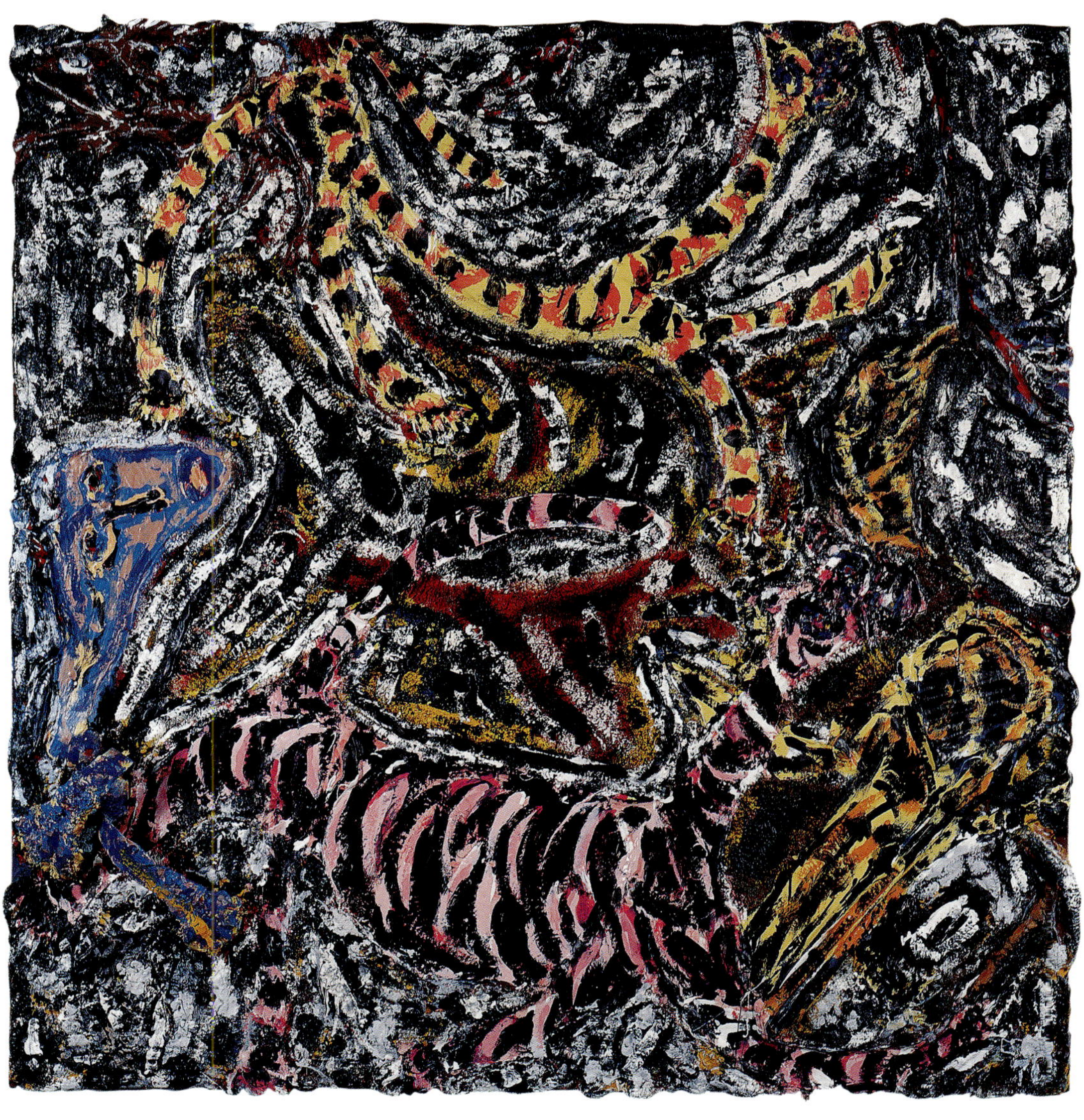

Cat. 24

Thornton Dial

Born 1928
Bessemer, Alabama

Proud Cats Made to Climb, 1992
Paint, metal, carpet, and rope on canvas and wood
64⅞ x 65⅛ x 6½ inches
Acquired from Ricco/Maresca Gallery, 1994
1997.60

Dial frequently employs the tiger to denote a person (often but not always African American) battling to prevail in the wilderness of American society. "Any time you get a cat, put him out there with nothing, he's going to survive just like you are. So he will kill, catch things. We do the same things. We fight for these things. Fighting for freedom, fighting for anything."[1]

Partially rendered creatures peer out of the swirling tumult of the work's surface. Smooth surfaces of painted metal embedded in rough carpet echo the plight of smooth-going cats in a turbulent world. Blood-red smears on the carpet and the top tiger's underbelly suggest a ferocious conflict with a blue creature whose outstretched claws are tipped with the same crimson hue. If the blue-faced creature relies on violent means to stay atop the heap, however, the cats' clean claws imply that tigers do not persevere merely by shedding blood but by maintaining their dignity in the face of the onslaught. As Dial points out, "Pride is important."

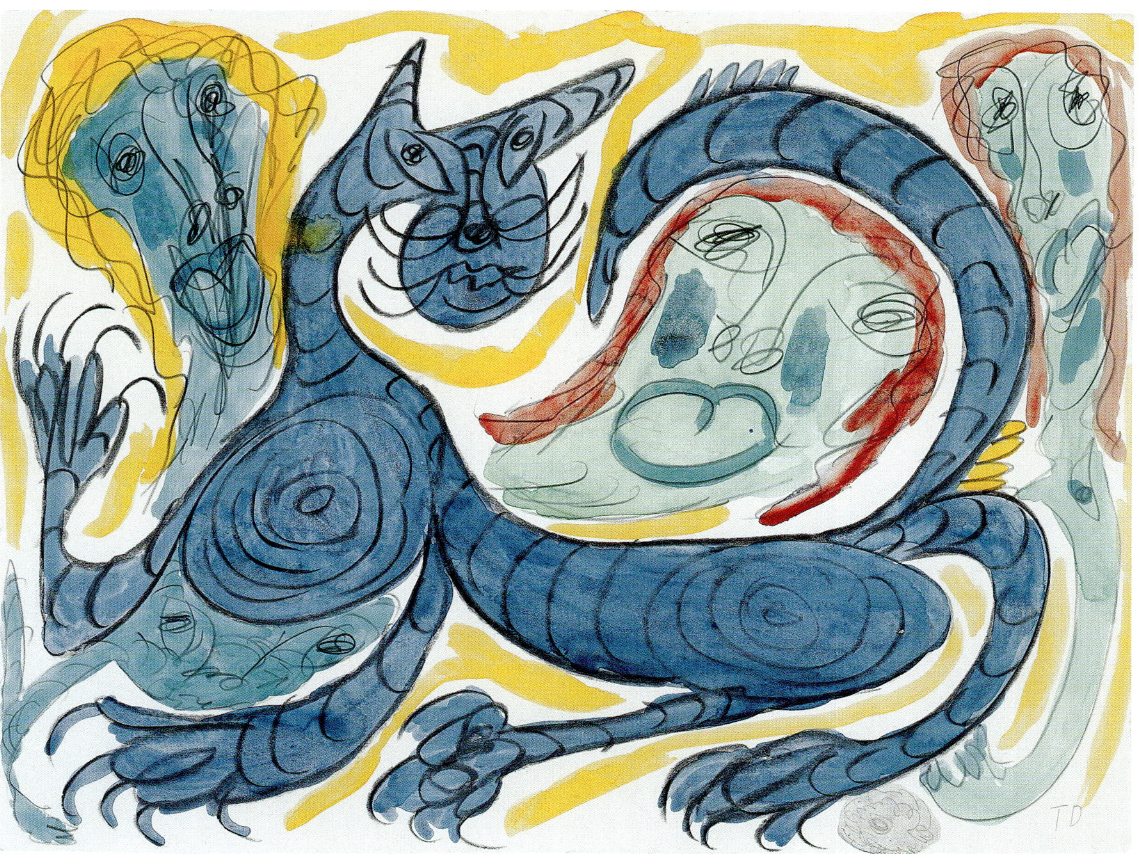

Cat. 25

Thornton Dial

Born 1928
Bessemer, Alabama

Invention of the Chainsaw, 1994
Pencil and watercolor on paper
22 × 30 inches
Acquired from William S. Arnett, 1994
1996.170

According to William Arnett, this drawing is part of a series dealing with the transformation of timber into paper. For Dial, that metamorphosis contains a vital moral element, since paper furnishes the raw material for books, which educate the poor and give them opportunities to climb up through the jungle of society.[1] In this exposition of the transcendent possibilities of natural materials, we see Dial's concern with the human stewardship of terrestrial gifts. "These are things we've found in the world, things we're going to leave in the world, so we got all that we can work for life to go on."[2]

Dial's "chainsaw" is also a "change-saw." Using woodworking as a metaphor for life, and punning "chain" and "change," Dial's reference to power tools suggests strategies for molding some of life's inevitable changes. Intertwined with and guarded by women, the tiger in this image shows off fearsome claws with a sly smile.

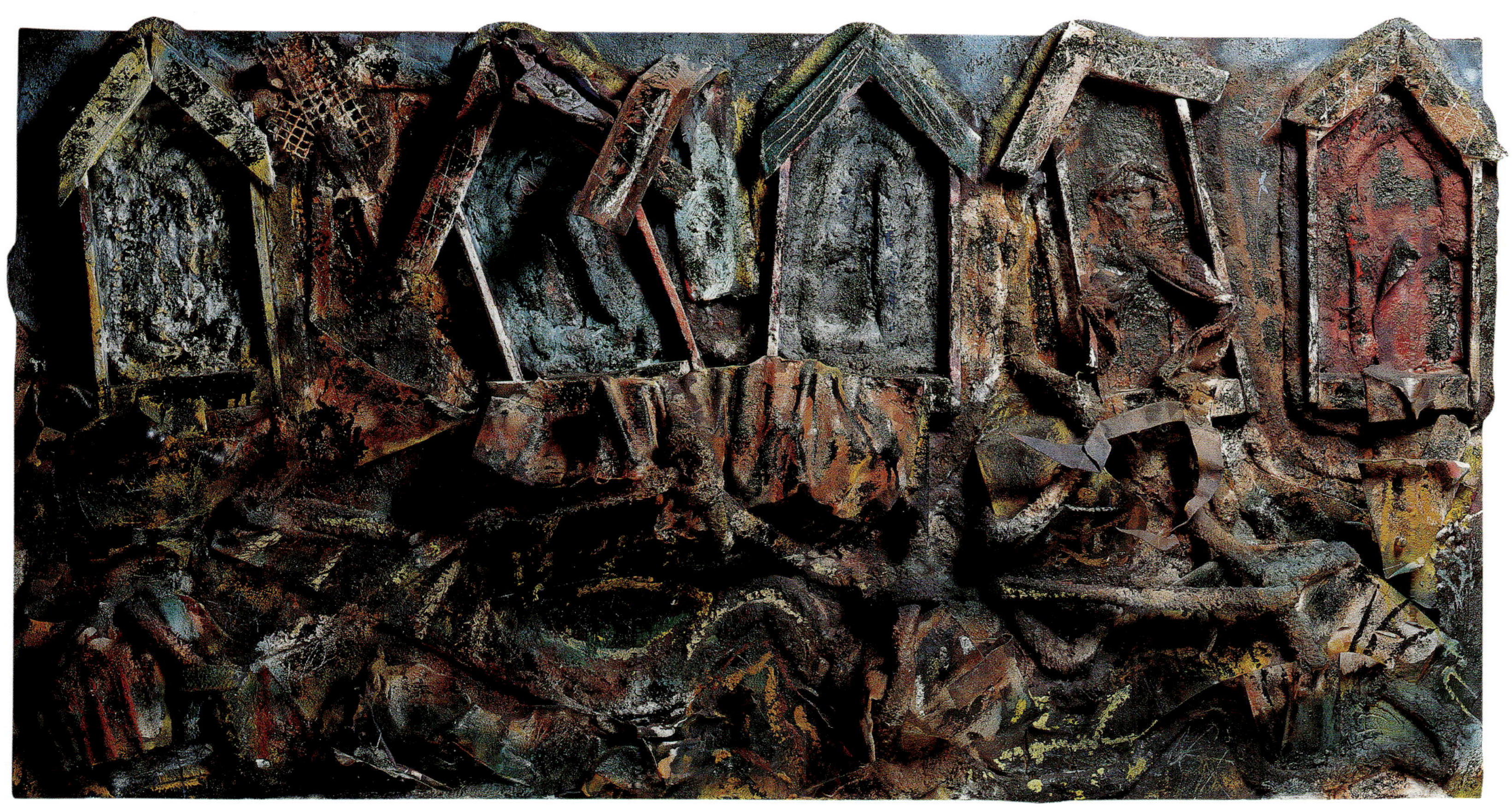

Cat. 26

Thornton Dial

Born 1928
Bessemer, Alabama

Old Projects, 1994
Paint, cloth, nails, wood, and tin on canvas and wood
32½ x 62 x 9 inches
Acquired from William S. Arnett, 1994
1996.171

Dial has worked at many trades. As factory worker, farmer, painter, carpenter, pipe fitter, fisherman, café owner, and home builder, he has honed his talents laboring in the community of Pipe Shop, Alabama. To these ventures he has brought not only the same spirit of enterprise and invention that marks his art-making but also a sense of the importance of industry in building a life or a character. The interdependence of life and work, "the idea of life, and what goes into a house," infuses *Old Projects*, whose inspiration came "just from things that I've known and have been around, you know? All around Bessemer and Birmingham I have worked, been around places like that, helped build them. Any time you help build a thing you become part of it."[1]

Contrived from disparate materials, the rough surface of *Old Projects* seems aged, crusty, and smoky. Dial's self-assurance as a colorist is displayed in the way soft, clear pastels work in and against earthy, somber tones. In some places Dial has scratched into the painted surface, leaving raw-looking scars. Scraps of wood, wire, cloth, and strips of metal and fabric imbue the surface with an astonishing depth, in which the shapes of hand tools and hints of figures are glimpsed. "Everything that we pick up means something to us. So these are things that come from sawmills and the things that we do work with in the United States. The stuff in it is the meaning of the piece. . . . And there's another thing you can't do with nothin': you ain't gon' carry nothin' away from here."

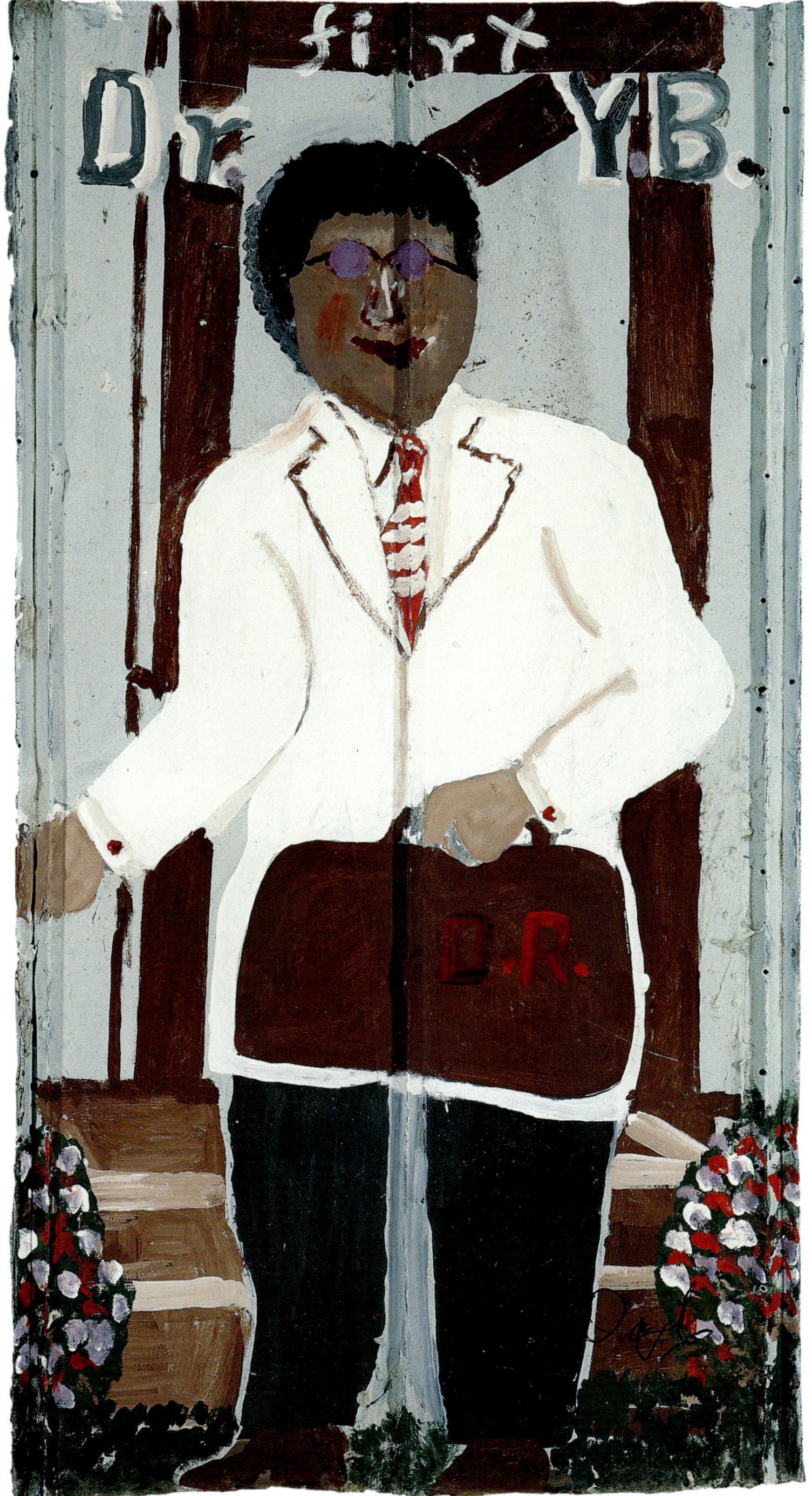

Cat. 27

Sam Doyle

1906–1985
St. Helena Island, South Carolina

First Doctor Y.B., 1970–1985
House paint on roofing tin
48⅛ x 25⅜ inches
Acquired from William S. Arnett, 1994
1997.63

This portrait of Dr. York W. Bailey was one of the ever-changing throng that crowded Sam Doyle's yard on St. Helena Island in the 1970s and early 1980s. His environment, which he named the Nationwide St. Helena Out Door Art Gallery, included pictures of local people and prominent Americans. As Lynne Spriggs has pointed out, "The artist was inviting members of the community to look at the paintings in his yard as they might look through an old photo album, reminding them of their common history and encouraging them to recognize and admire their individual places within that history."[1]

In his self-appointed role as local historian, Doyle created a "First Blacks" series commemorating the achievements of African Americans on St. Helena as they began to assume positions and acquire skills previously reserved for whites. Subjects who were members of his own family included his grandmother, Lucinda Ladson, a former slave whom Doyle depicted as St. Helena's first black midwife, and his brother James, who was the first black truck driver on the island.

Dr. Bailey was born at Cedar Grove Plantation on St. Helena in 1881. After attending Penn School, he earned his medical degree at Howard University in Washington, D.C., returning to St. Helena in 1906, where he remained until his death at ninety years of age. He served his community not only as the doctor, but as deacon, treasurer, and advisor for Brick Baptist Church. A gentle confidence seems to flow from the smiling physician as he stands facing the viewer, his medical bag gripped lightly in his left hand.

Cat. 28

Sam Doyle

1906–1985
St. Helena Island, South Carolina

John Chisolem, St. Helena's First Embalmer,
1970–1985
House paint on roofing tin
57 × 25¼ inches
Acquired from William S. Arnett, 1994
1996.29

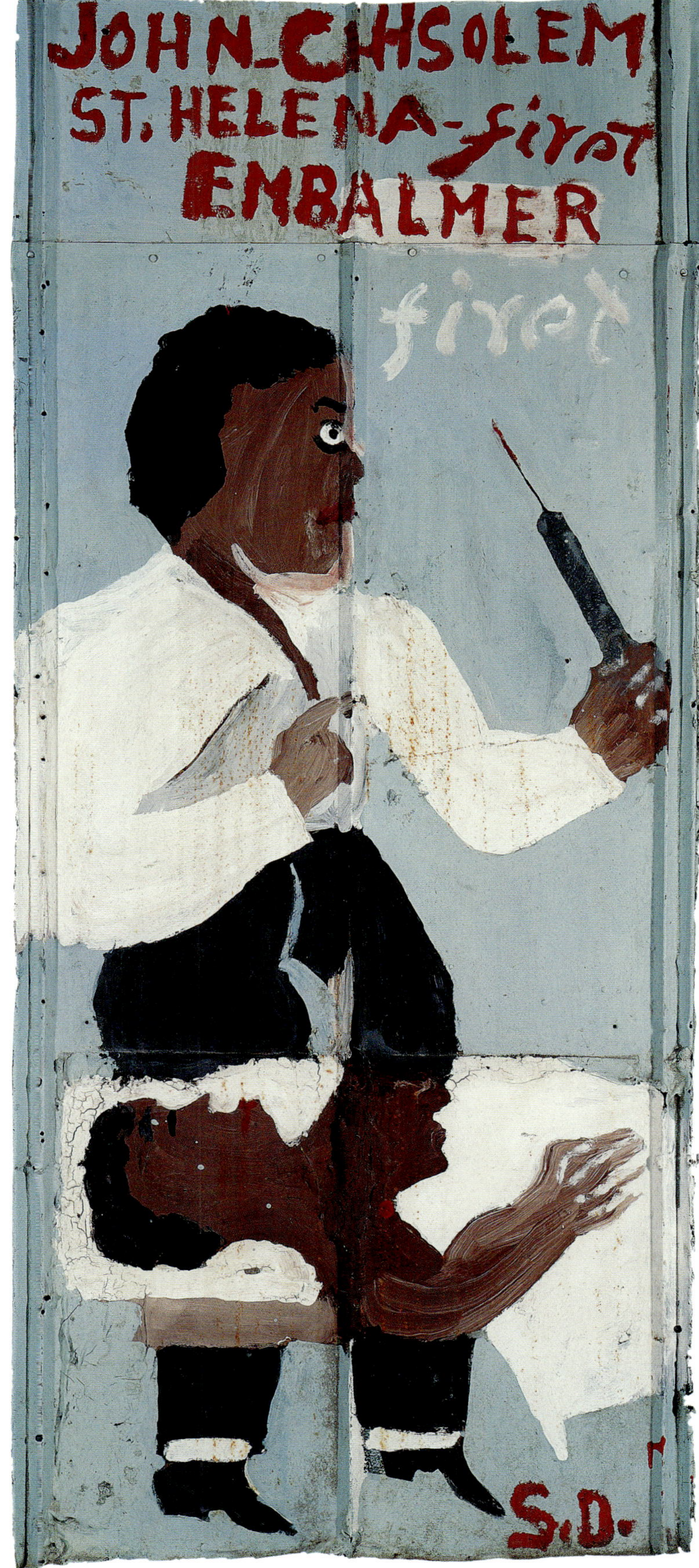

Isolated from the mainland, the inhabitants of the sea islands of the southern United States developed an idiosyncratic way of life that blends elements of African and European customs and languages. This Gullah culture, which preserves remainders of African speech, music, visual arts, and religion, persists into the twenty-first century on islands such as St. Helena. Among the African retentions is the special significance of death rites to the community, which parallels that found in many regions of Africa. William S. Pollitzer compares the importance of the funeral in sea island communities to its role in African communities, noting the survival of particular African burial customs among the Gullah.[1]

A painting from Doyle's "First Blacks" series, this portrait commemorates a member of the Chisolm family, who have taken care of burials on St. Helena and nearby Beaufort for generations and still do today. David Chisolm was the island's first black undertaker. Although he was not an embalmer, he provided a more dignified burial with his horse and cart than the family members of the deceased could. His brother Joe was the first to use a hearse rather than a wagon to transport bodies. John Chisolm—portrayed here—was David's nephew, and the first African American on St. Helena to practice embalming. Doyle recalled watching as a small boy while Chisolm embalmed his brother.[2]

The lines of the arms of both characters reinforce the flow of the composition as we follow Chisolm's gaze to the tip of the embalming needle, an instrument which seems to have made little impact on young Doyle: "I didn't understand what he was doing. It was all just natural fun to me. I didn't think anything of it."[3]

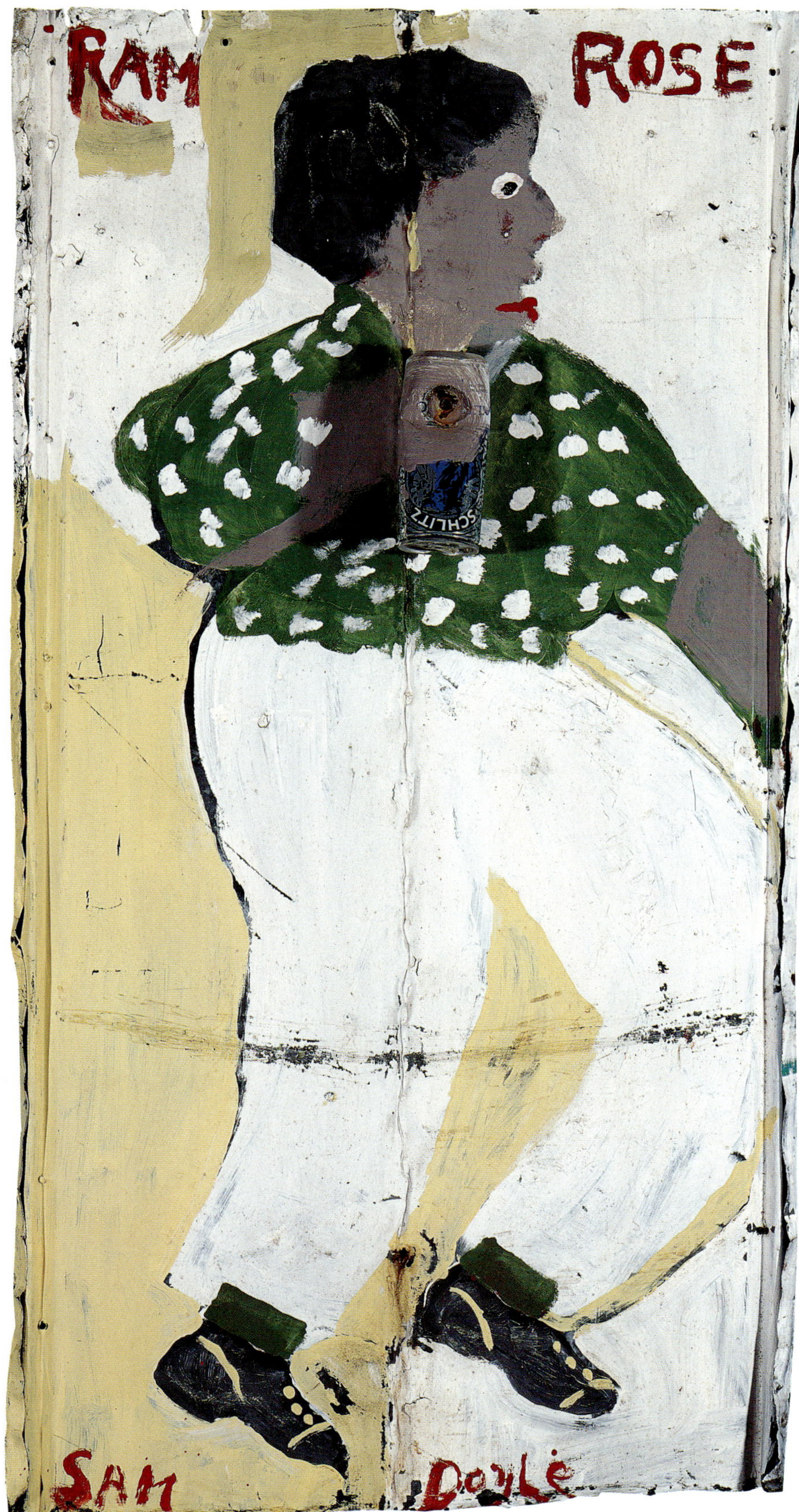

Cat. 29

Sam Doyle

1906–1985
St. Helena Island, South Carolina

Rambling Rose, 1970–1985
House paint and beer can on roofing tin
48 x 25½ inches
Acquired from William S. Arnett, 1994
1997.65

As Doyle's art became popular, he filled the gaps in his yard with new versions of pieces purchased by collectors. In most cases, he settled on a standard form of representation for each portrait, which he would repeat in subsequent iterations. But in his depictions of Rambling Rose or Island Beauty, he continually varied the pose of this St. Helena resident known for her wanderlust.[1] In this rendering, Rose's propensity to gallivant can be seen in her left leg, about to step off the edge of the painting. Doyle often communicated personality traits through poses. He also mounted his pictures of Rose so that she turned in the breeze. He regularly represented her wearing white pants and a polka-dotted shirt, usually green and white, and he often attached a beer can to his paintings of this character who, he said, was never seen without a beer. As Lynne Spriggs has written, Doyle's portraits often suggest both an individual and a type, so that Rambling Rose represents both the woman he knew personally and restless women in general.[2]

Rambling Rose may have acquired her nickname from the title of a 1962 song performed by Nat King Cole,[3] who was also painted by Doyle. Doyle enjoyed popular music and listened to it regularly while he painted outside. He painted many portraits of musicians, and several of his paintings bear the same titles as popular songs or spirituals.

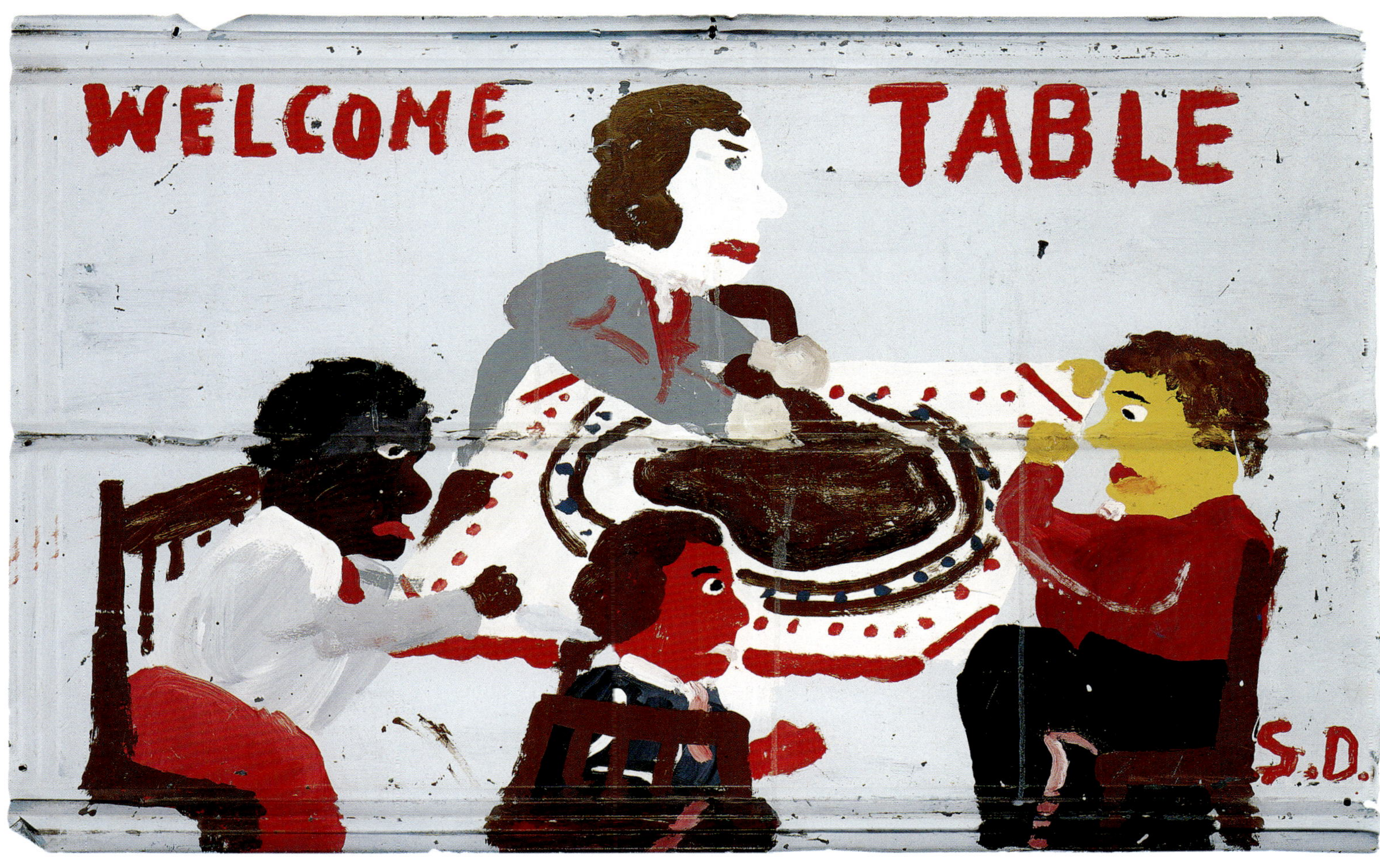

Cat. 30

Sam Doyle

1906–1985
St. Helena Island, South Carolina

Welcome Table, 1970–1985
House paint on roofing tin
26¼ × 43½ inches
Acquired from Robert Reeves, 1993
1996.174

Notwithstanding the many images he created of neighbors who practiced unconventional sexual behaviors, Doyle was a religious man and a regular churchgoer. A spiritual, "We're Gonna Sit at the Welcome Table,"[1] which includes the line "All kinds of people around that table, gonna sit at the welcome table one of these days," may have been Doyle's primary source for this apparent icon of racial harmony. Doyle has prepared a laden platter around which sit four men, red and yellow, black and white, seeming to exemplify the song's promise.

Lynne Spriggs also suggests that this image, which appears above a portrait of Martin Luther King Jr. in one Doyle work,[2] may refer to the eloquence of the Civil Rights leader, who declared in 1963, "I have a dream that one day on the red hills of Georgia, sons of former slaves and sons of former slave-owners will be able to sit down together at the table of brotherhood." In the High's version, the diners appear to be scowling. Doyle could be suggesting that changing attitudes to bring different races to the same table requires hard work.

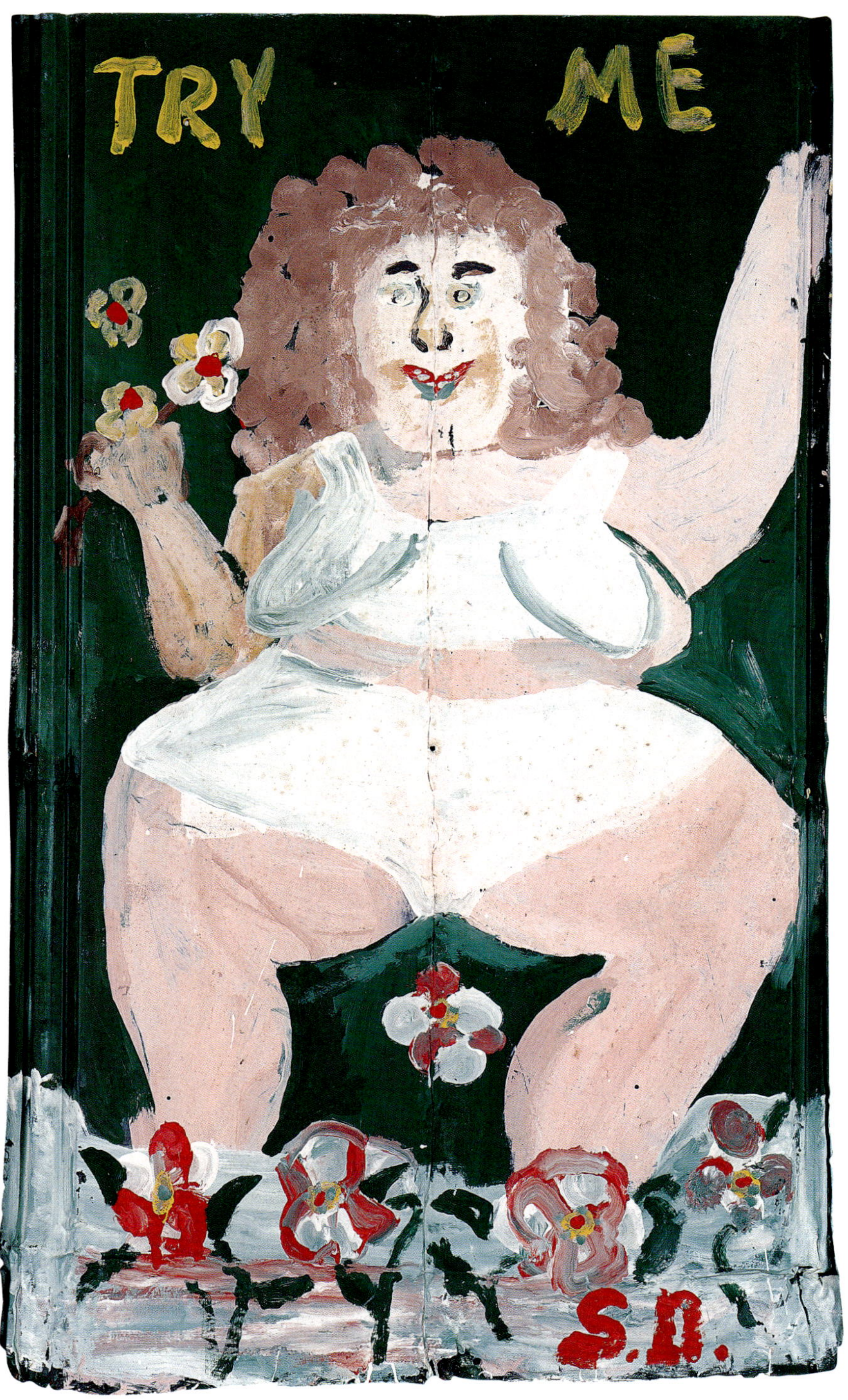

Cats. 31–32

Sam Doyle

1906–1985
St. Helena Island, South Carolina

Try Me, ca. 1981
House paint on roofing tin
41⅞ x 26⅝ inches
Acquired from William S. Arnett, 1994
1997.67

Frip, St. Helena's Best, 1970–1985
House paint on roofing tin
43⅛ x 52 inches
Acquired from William S. Arnett, 1994
1997.66

Although his body of work included nationally recognized figures, Doyle lavished painterly attention on people he knew. Using his favorite materials—roofing tin and sturdy enamel house paint—he worked for the edification of his neighbors, who recognized themselves in his vivid portrayals. Doyle painted a series of voluptuous women with suggestive names, including this depiction of a woman who visited him regularly and later said, "He never saw me like that, but he sure had a good imagination."[1] The painting's title may have been inspired by James Brown's plaintive 1959 rhythm and blues hit "Try Me."

The subject of *Frip, St. Helena's Best* likely lived and worked on property once claimed by the Fripps, the first white slave-owners to settle on St. Helena. In an example of the humorous double entendre often found in Doyle's paintings, it appears that Fripp's sexual member grows into the beam of his plow, perhaps suggesting a visual pun on this productive farmer's renowned aptitude for planting seeds.

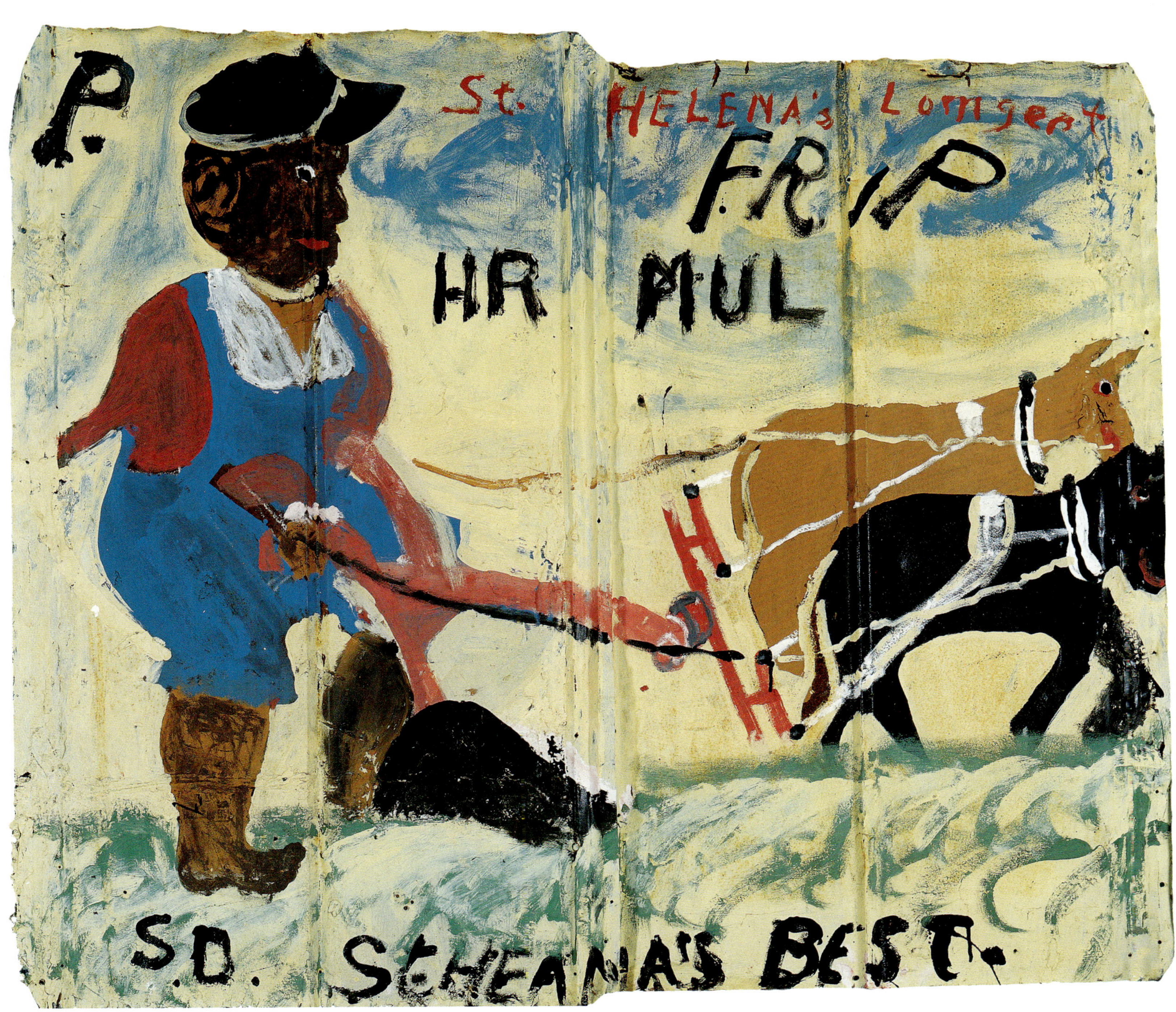
P.
St. HELENA's Longest
FRIP
HR MUL
S.D. StHEANA'S BEST.

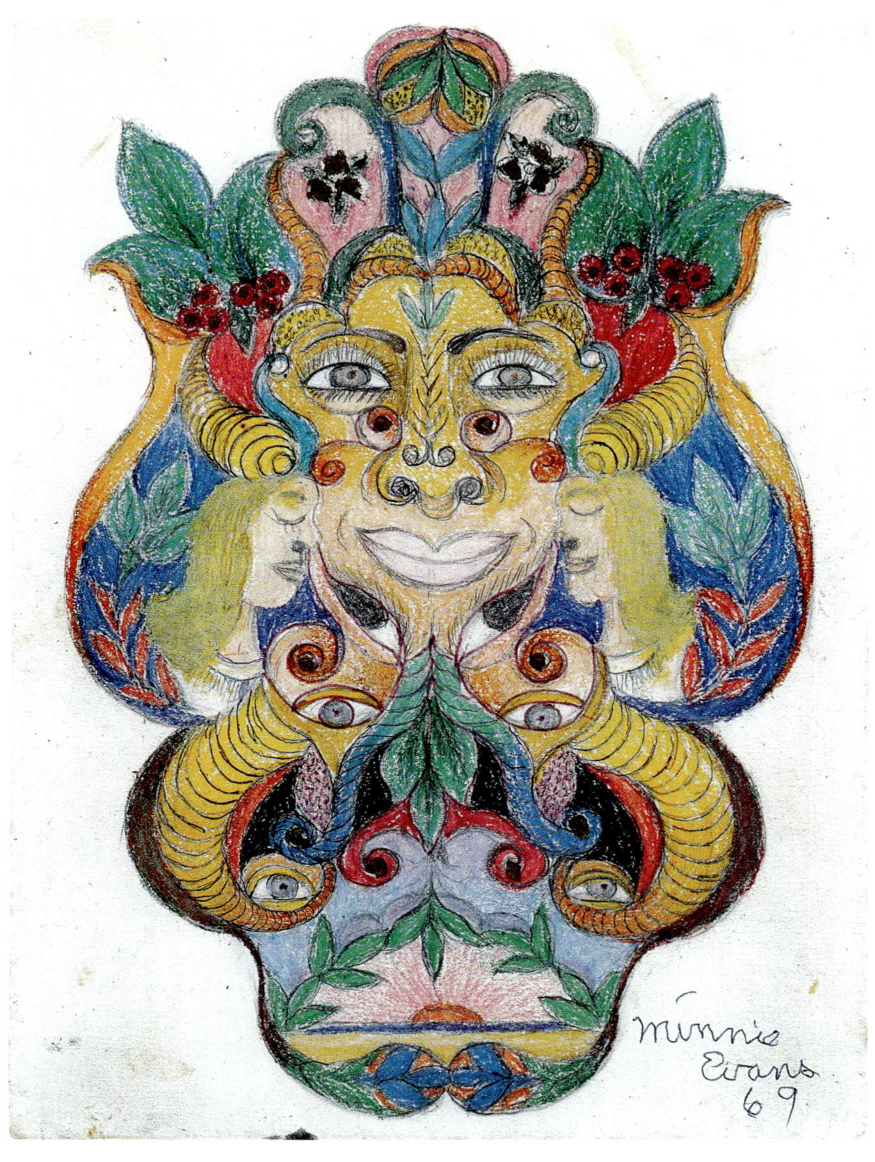

Cats. 33–34

Minnie Evans

1892–1987
Wrightsville Beach, North Carolina

Untitled (Three Faces Surmounting Landscape), 1963
Crayon and pencil on paper
11⅞ × 9⅛ inches
Acquired from Modern Primitive Gallery, 1994
1997.68

Untitled (Face Surrounded by Foliage), ca. 1963
Crayon, pen, and pencil on paper
11⅞ × 8¾ inches
Acquired from Modern Primitive Gallery, 1994
1997.69

To exaggerate the visionary aspect of Minnie Evans's drawings is impossible, for they were inspired by the dreams and visions that came to her night and day. The aesthetic results seem to have surprised even the artist. "Something told me to draw or die," she once said. "It was shown to me what I should do. . . . When I get through with them [the paintings] I have to look at them like everybody else. They are just as strange to me as they are to anybody else."[1]

In richly detailed drawings brightly colored with wax crayons, Evans layered worlds of nature and spirit, plant and animal, human and divine in symmetrical compositions of swirling intricacy. Her spring of imagery was steadily replenished by the flowers and foliage of Airlie Gardens on the Pembroke Estate near Wilmington, North Carolina, where she was gatekeeper for twenty-seven years.

A central visage forms the focus of many of her drawings, including both of these. Their mask-like flamboyance hints at Carnival, which, with Evans's Trinidadian ancestry, may underlie the frequent comparisons of her designs with those from the Caribbean, where her great-grandmother was born. In one, the jewel-like colors of foliage and mysterious biomorphic forms enshrine the unattended central figure. In the other, ruby, amethyst, and sapphire give way to soft pastels; the central face is flanked by two blonde creatures, who may be angels, and eyes that manifest an omnipresent God appear in pairs above a fanciful landscape in the first flush of morning. Both possess the lush exuberance and curvilinear line that make Evans's works sing.

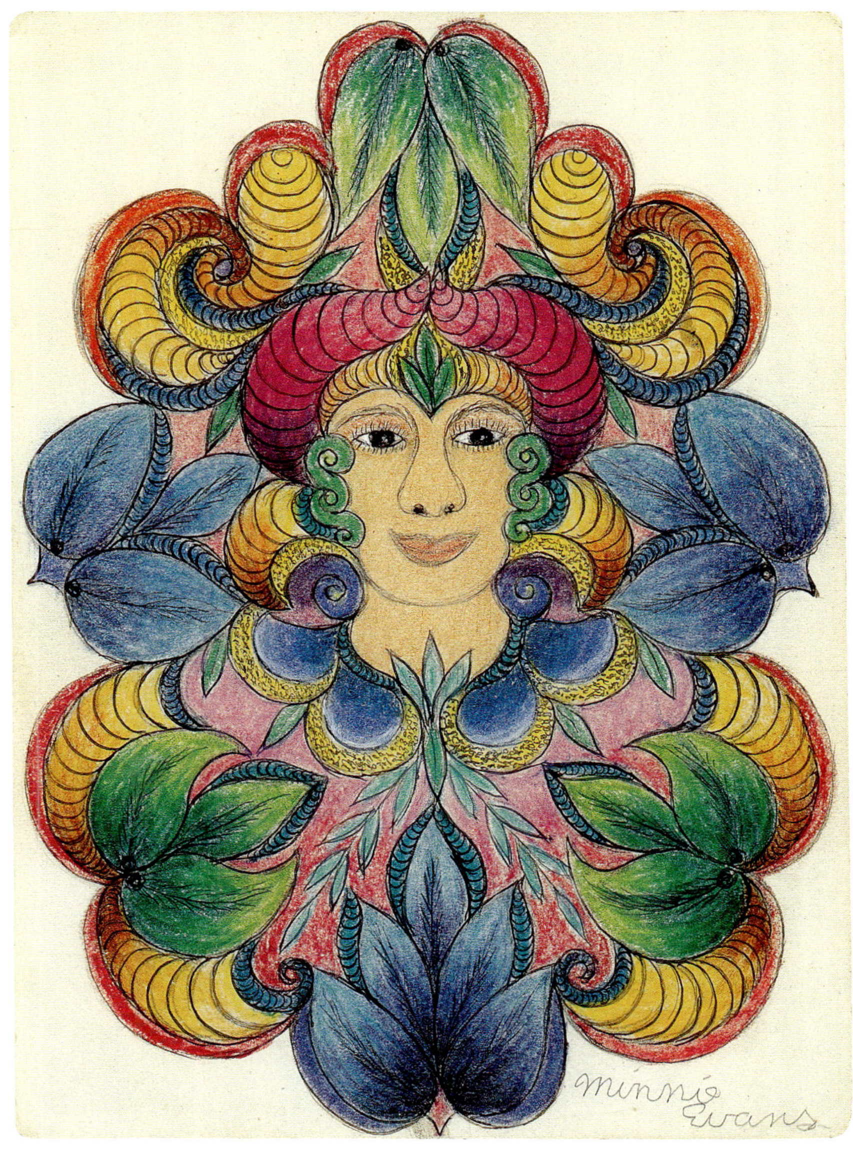

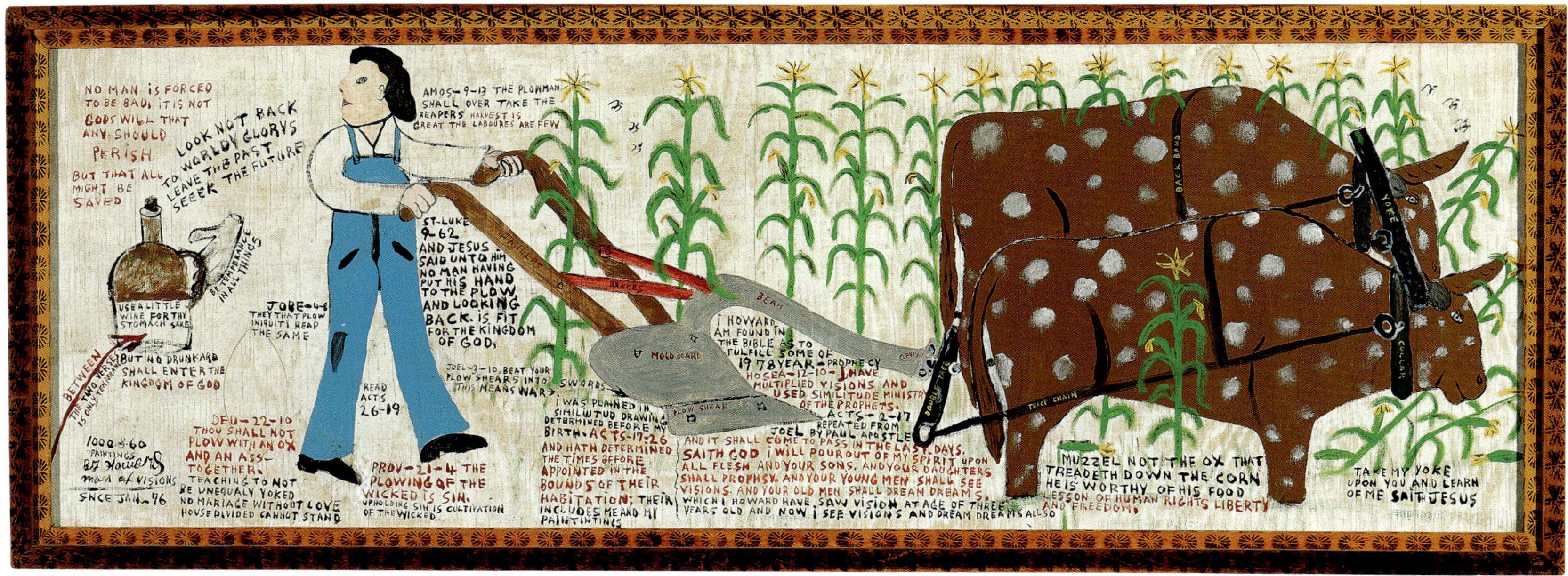

Cat. 35

Howard Finster

Born 1915
Pennville, Georgia

Take My Yoke Upon You and Learn of Me Saith Jesus,
#1,060, 1977–1978
Paint on board with embossed wood
17½ × 48¼ inches
Acquired from Charles Locke, 1993
1997.74

The weathered condition of this painting attests to its lengthy time on the side of the office building in Howard Finster's northeast Georgia environment, Paradise Garden. Painted during Finster's second year of production, its design is relatively open behind the inscriptions, unlike the tight control and detailed stylization found in many of his other works.

As the plowman looks backward toward a little brown jug, his oxen tread down rows of tasseling corn. Between farmer and plow appears a verse from the Gospel of Luke (9:62): "And Jesus said unto him no man having put his hand to the plow and looking back is fit for the kingdom of God." Finster filled virtually every available inch of this work with scripture and pious messages about salvation, temperance, and plowing. He also speaks of his destiny, confirmed by visions, to spread the word of God through illustrative teachings: "I Howard am found in the Bible as to fulfill some of 1978 year-prophesy/Hosea-12-10 I have multiplied visions and used similitude ministry of the prophets."[1]

Finster's expansive commentary exemplifies a Southern fascination with the written word.[2] In addition to incorporating excerpts from and references to Deuteronomy, Job, Hosea, Joel, Amos, Luke, and Acts of the Apostles, Finster labeled each part of the plow and sprinkled in his own aphorisms. For the artist, who began writing articles for local newspapers when he was a young man and published a book of inspirational poems in 1934, the permanence of a painted message offers advantages over the spoken sermon. "Now when I write a message, that message not goin' away with the wind. And the people not gonna forget it from one service to another. And that's why I'm in folk art. I'm preachin' in thousands of homes alayin' here on my bed."[3]

Cat. 36

Howard Finster

Born 1915
Pennville, Georgia

In My Father's House Are Many Mansions, #4,392, 1985
Plexiglas, plastic, beads, toys, and sequins
18 × 14⅝ × 9 inches
Acquired from Berman Gallery, 1993
1997.72

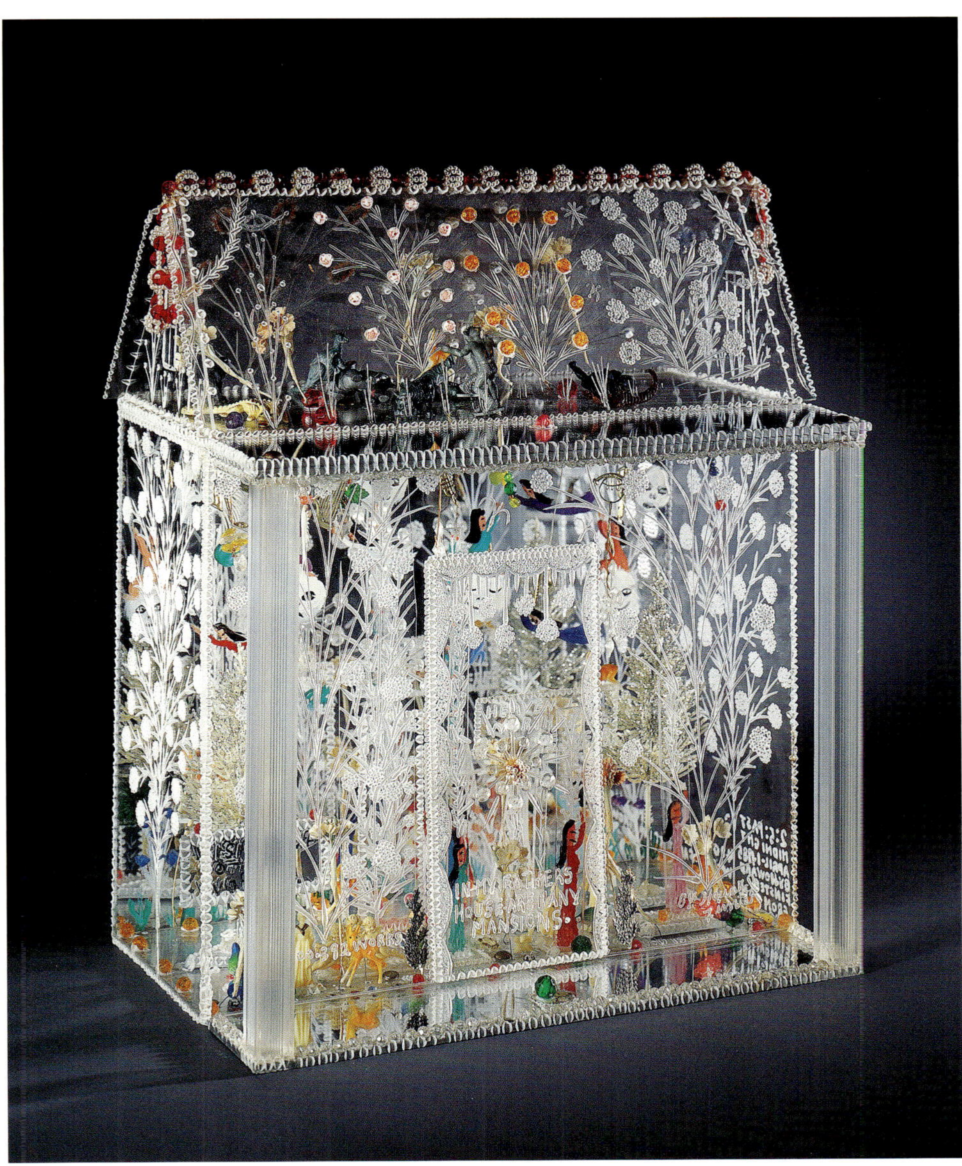

Finster has been constructing mansions for decades. "You walk into God's house, and it's so big you see the fireplace ever so big, and the mantel may be fifty foot up there, and you see other mansions inside of the living room of it. Houses in houses. Like this place here would just be a little corner in some room."[1] After he began painting, "a feeling to do that, to make dimensional things" impelled him to devise a series of plastic and glass representations of Paradise. "I put a whole lot of stuff in there," he declared, using the found materials he has been collecting since 1945.

The crystalline beauty of Finster's Heaven is realized in clear and mirrored layers replete with silver and punctuated with flashes of brilliant hue. An open portico recalls the Greek Revival style of the classic Southern mansion. The mirrored top, bottom, and back walls multiply the contents of the box and the space within it. Finster burned simple, delicate decorations into the clear acrylic partitions with a wood-burning tool, frilling edges and marking doors and windows. Beneath the peaked roof, crowned with plastic rubies and seed pearls, coexists an assortment of plastic toy creatures: a warrior wearing a horned helmet and another from some science fiction world, an alligator, a jaguar, a kangaroo with her joey, a fawn, a gorilla, a hippopotamus, a rhinoceros, a lizard, and an elephant whose ears are painted pink. Below them, the interior is decorated with plastic beads, tiny bunches of fabric flowers, and silver paper holly. Plastic jewels and sequins are strewn on the floor. Strings of jewels and gold musical instruments hang from the ceiling above deer, blue and green birds, and garland-bearing putti. On the mirror that forms the back wall, bright-robed angels with long dark hair soar between or perch on clouds with painted faces. In the midst of this multitude reposes a miniscule nativity with shepherds, sheep, and wise men. Hanging midway back, a sign reads, "Heaven is worth it all/Meet me there." On the floor near the front is a notice that "God is Love."

Finster has often worked reflective surfaces into his creations. He embedded mirrors into an interior archway in the first concrete block home he built, placed them inside the light shaft at the center of the World's Folk Art Church in Paradise Garden (which might be regarded as the ultimate Finster mansion), and attached them to suncatchers he hung in the Garden. The spatial play of reflected light allows him to highlight the limitlessness of the spiritual world. "You can put up to five dimensions" in his mirrored boxes, he says. The artist signed this work in three places, suggesting his pride in this dazzling conception, about which he said, "That's the beautifullest thing I ever made."

Cat. 37

Howard Finster

Born 1915
Pennville, Georgia

George Washington, #6,903, 1987
Paint on board
48 × 48 inches
Acquired from Charles Locke, 1994
1997.71

Finster's first painting was a 1976 portrait of George Washington, copied from a dollar bill when he received his calling to "paint sacred art." Doubting his ability, Finster knew he needed to put this command to an immediate trial. "And right then it come to me: 'I'll just take a dollar bill outta my billfold, I'll tape it to a piece o' plywood, and I'll go out in fronta my bicycle shop, and I'll draw George Washington on a piece o' paper from his picture on that dollar bill. I'll let myself know right now that I can't do it. So that's what I done, 'cept I found out immediately I *could* do it. . . . And I just started off paintin' right there. I started drawin' George Washington on the streets out there 'round my house, and drawin' big sun rays out on the street with ol' scrap paint colors people'd give me, all different colors. And I been paintin' ever since."[1] He has created countless representations of George Washington, portraying him in various poses and at many ages. For example, a large portrait of the first president adorned the front of Finster's studio at Paradise Garden, and at the request of Allen Jabbour, Folklife Center Director at the Library of Congress, he painted Washington for the Library.

In this portrait of a young Washington, the president's head seems to materialize amid a cluster of terrestrial "Mansions of Honor," which reflect Finster's fascination with architecture.[2] Behind them, angels interspersed with stars and carefully modeled planets create a foulard-like design against a deep blue sky. Within the dense patterning of the painting's lower portion appear religious statements, dogs, deer, and graceful figures reaching to pluck bright fruit from brilliantly leaved trees. The proliferation of detail blends Washington's torso into the background and renders him at once spiritual and physical, his massive face rising amid the throng.

For Finster, Washington was not only the first president of the United States, but a man of God who lived by the Ten Commandments.[3] The artist feels a mystical connection to the patriot: "I had a vision of George Washington. . . . Some people who are gone on mean more to me than the people who are living now because their imagination was more designed on my line. They're a little deeper embedded in my brain cells. I get to dwelling on them because they have more to dwell on."[4] But Finster's Washington is also a figure of loss who displays the painter's nostalgia for a potent kind of integrity he believes the modern world has forgotten: "We've come a long way from his trail. I don't know that we've had many presidents of his measure since."[5] This artist—who has portrayed many U.S. presidents and figures of popular culture—feels he bears a responsibility to share his historical interpretations. "I make the marks that I was sent here to make. I'm writing a history that I was supposed to write. . . . I honor our former leaders and founders by drawing them and trying to keep their memories living and by remembering their great works, their life stories, and their wisdoms."[6]

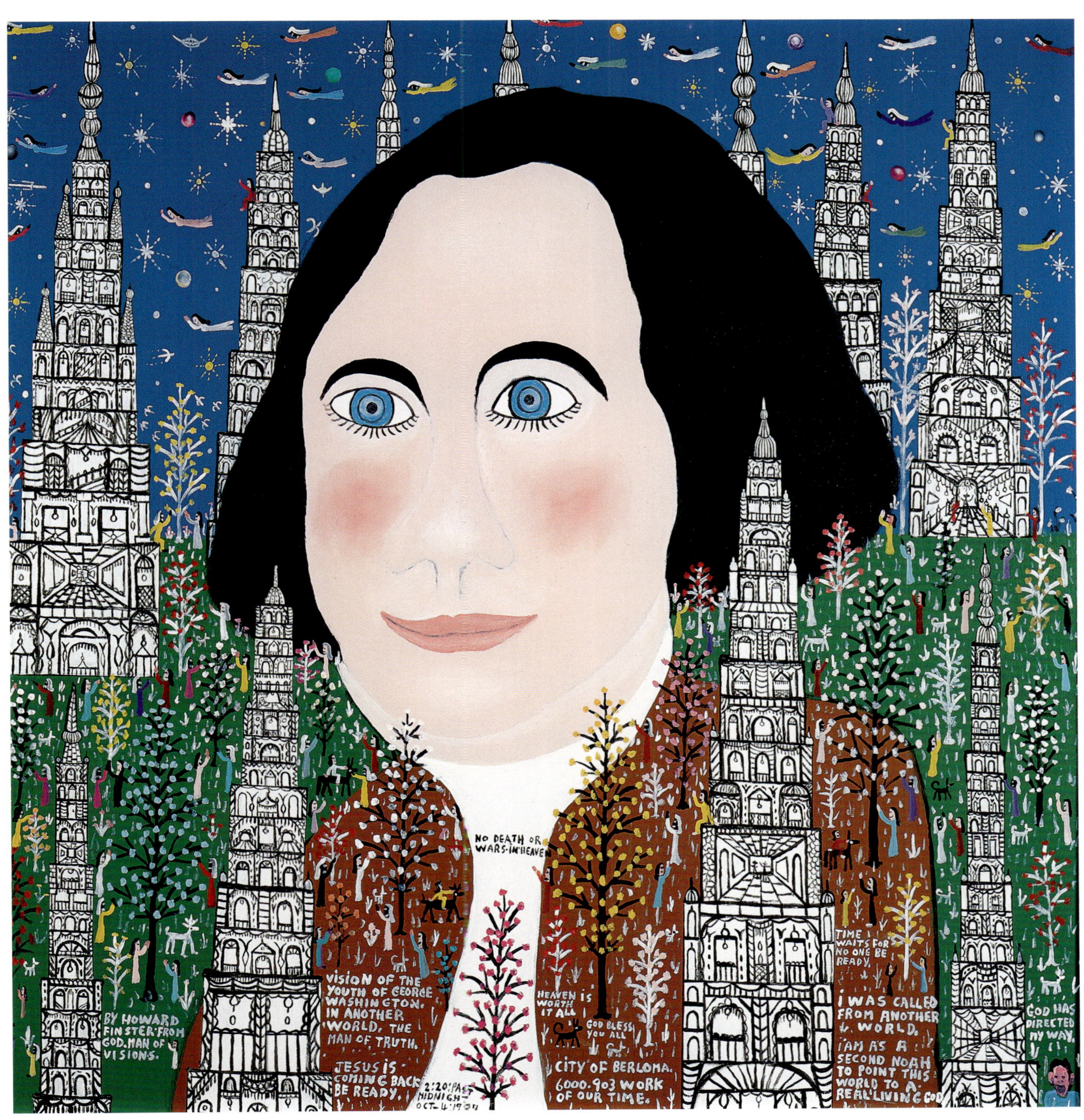
NO DEATH OR WARS-IN HEAVEN
BY HOWARD FINSTER-FROM GOD. MAN OF VISIONS.
VISION OF THE YOUTH OF GEORGE WASHINGTON. IN ANOTHER WORLD. THE MAN OF TRUTH.
JESUS IS COMING BACK BE READY.
2:20 PAST MIDNIGHT OCT-4-1994
HEAVEN IS WORTH IT ALL
GOD BLESS YOU ALL
CITY OF BERLOMA.
6000.903 WORK OF OUR TIME.
TIME WAITS FOR NO ONE BE READY.
I WAS CALLED FROM ANOTHER WORLD.
I AM AS A SECOND NOAH TO POINT THIS WORLD TO A REAL LIVING GOD
GOD HAS DIRECTED MY WAY.

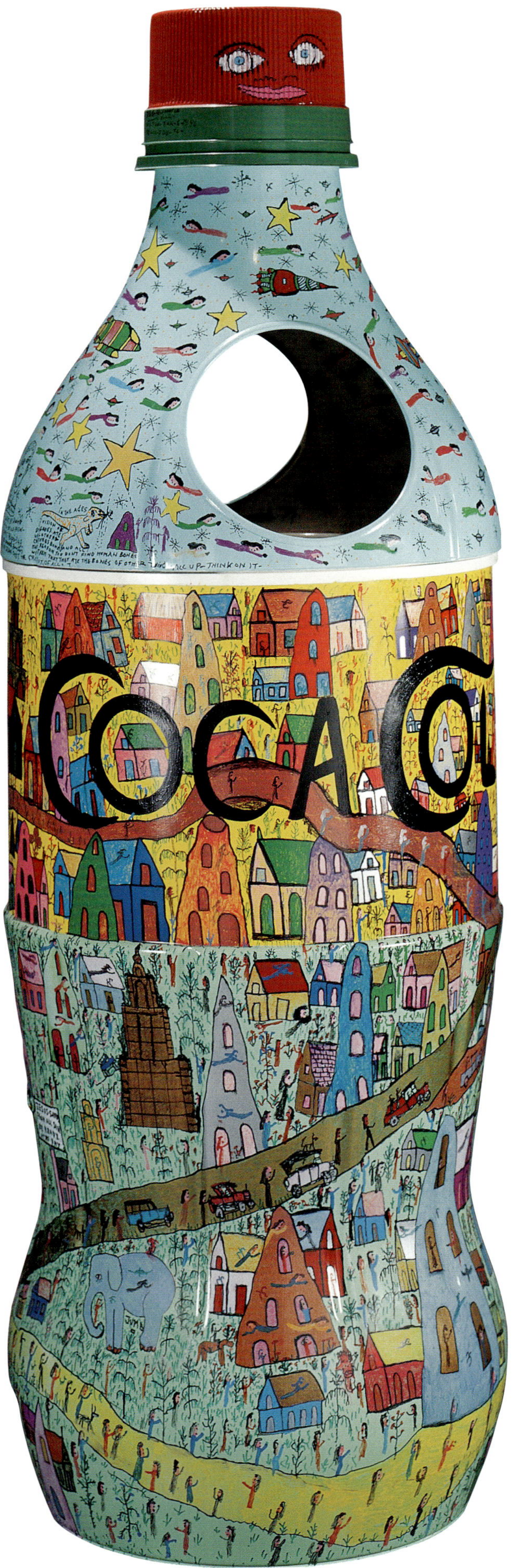

Cat. 38

Howard Finster

Born 1915
Summerville, Georgia

Coca-Cola Bottle, #38,348, 1995
Paint on prefabricated plastic bottle
65½ × 22 × 22 inches
Acquired from the artist, 1996
1996.175

This outsized Coca-Cola bottle belongs to a family of images depicting Finster's favorite drink. Finster has also embellished Coca-Cola advertising materials, and he used discarded Coke bottles filled with marbles to construct the walls of the pump house at his northeast Georgia environment, Paradise Garden.

In contrast to other Coke bottles—which primarily bear testimony to Finster's love of the soft drink—the subjects on the Hahn Collection bottle are diverse. Finster divided the composition into three registers corresponding to the bottle's structural divisions, unifying the top and bottom portions by painting their backgrounds the same color. Around the upper section circles a host of Finster's familiar multihued angels accompanied by stars and spaceships in silver and bright tones. Inside, angels and birds share the celestial sphere with the cow who jumped over the moon. Paths leading around and up the bottle toward Heaven weave together the lower sections, which are dedicated to earthly realms. The cars that share the roadways with people and animals symbolize the danger of worldly thrills; as Finster has pointed out, we "won't need no cars and blood on the highway" in the kingdom of Heaven.[1] Images of placards commemorate a "big tent revival" and Finster's leadership of several Baptist churches during the 1940s, while messages such as "Jesus saves from all sin/Be ready at his day" evoke the devotional signposts that once proliferated along rural highways throughout the South.

Commissioned by Marshall Hahn and painted on a plastic container provided by former Coca-Cola Company executive Douglas Ivester, this is the second of three huge bottles the artist obtained from the corporation. In 1989 the soft drink manufacturer gave him a 13-foot, 350-pound hollow plastic replica, which he covered in portraits and messages. Merging his religious convictions, his love of the beverage, and his confidence in the godly principles of former Coca-Cola Company chairman Robert Woodruff, he inscribed this evocation of Hell's horrors beside the face of Coca-Cola formulator Dr. John S. Pemberton: "All across the world I find Coca-Cola except in one place. In a vision I went to Planet Hell one night and there was not one Coca-Cola there. Not even one empty Coke bottle there in Hell. Man if you like Coke as good as I do you better stay out of Hell. Robert Woodruff never will send Coke to Hell. Stay out."[2] The Coca-Cola Company, which is headquartered in Atlanta, repaid the compliment by commissioning a third giant three-dimensional Coca-Cola bottle from Finster to represent the United States in the Coca-Cola Olympic Salute to Folk Art held during the 1996 Olympic Games in Atlanta.

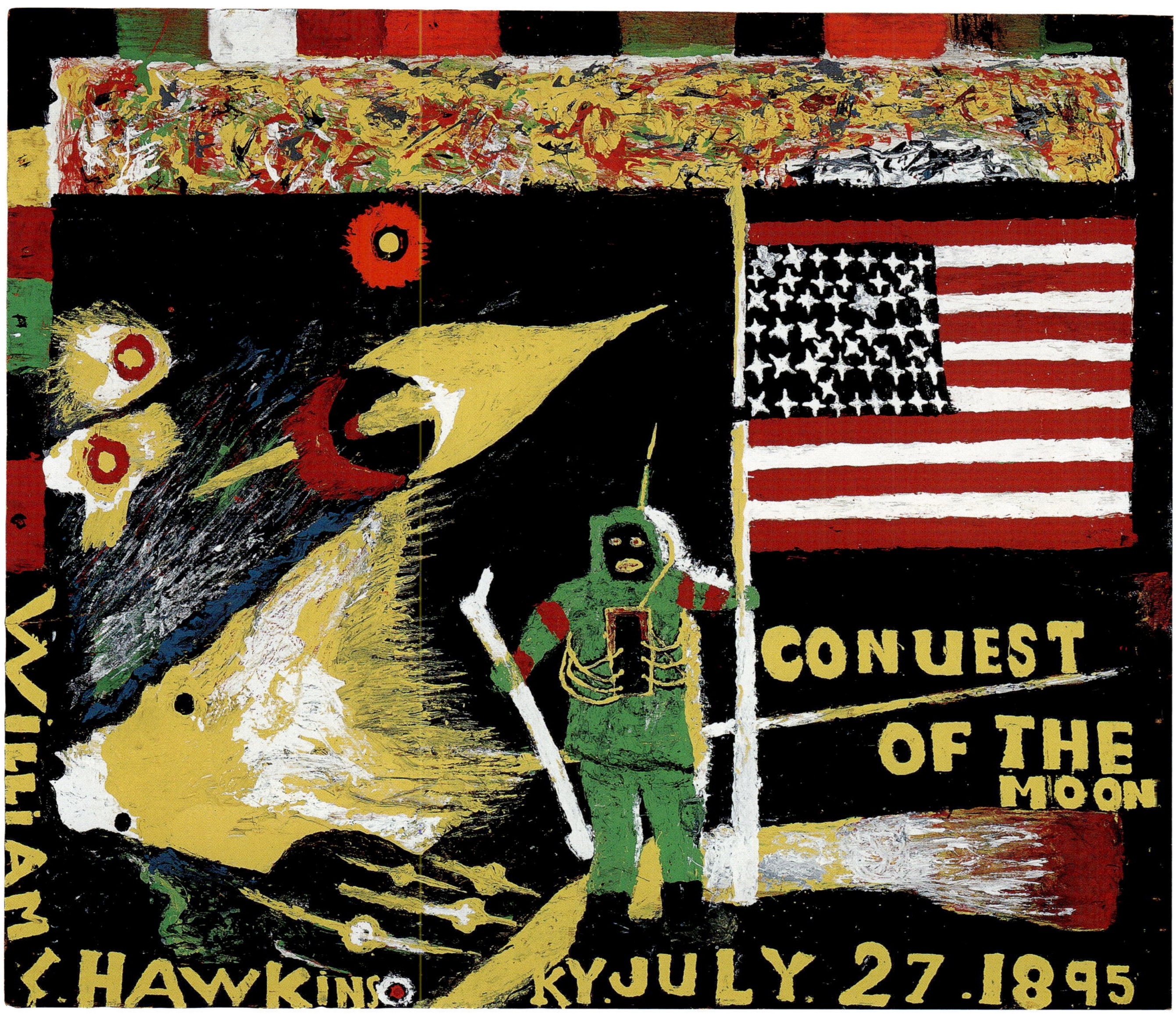

Cat. 39

William Hawkins

1895–1990
Columbus, Ohio

Con[q]uest of the Moon #1, 1984
Enamel paint on Masonite
48 x 56⅛ inches
Acquired from Ricco/Maresca Gallery, 1995
1996.27

The earlier of at least two treatments of the subject, this painting of the first moon landing—with its sophisticated composition, fantastic colors, and virtuoso brushwork—is regarded as one of William Hawkins's greatest achievements. Behind the small astronaut in his audacious green space suit, the black infinity of the cosmos erupts in a riot of explosions and rockets as if the universe itself were hailing—or protesting—the achievement of humankind. Hawkins's furious brushwork energizes the scene and dances near the top of this image in a decorative band that recalls stitch-work samplers. Casting the astronaut as a black man implies a critique of American twentieth-century history as it affirms this event as a "giant leap" for all humankind.

Never one to bow to convention, Hawkins took liberties with the design of the American flag. His version has the regulation thirteen stripes, but only forty-eight irregular stars rather than the fifty that were in place during the Apollo mission.

In contradiction to the once-popular notion that self-taught artists create outside the influence of popular culture, Hawkins collected images from magazines and books to use as inspirations for his works. Although he often borrowed entire scenes for his paintings, Eugene Metcalf and Joanne Cubbs believe that this painting is a composite of several images from popular periodicals.[1]

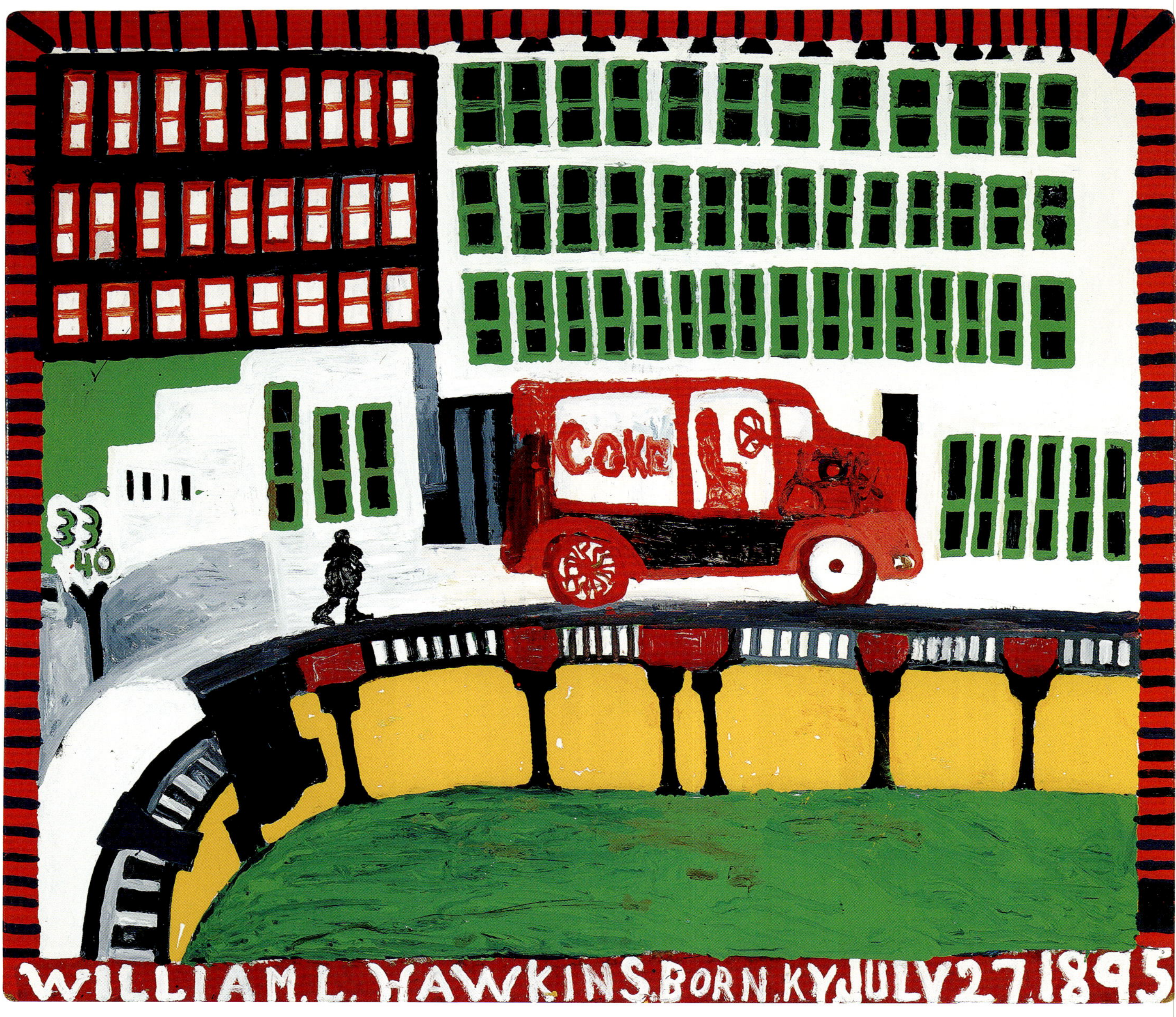

Cat. 40

William Hawkins

1895–1990
Columbus, Ohio

State Office Building #2, 1985
Enamel paint on board
46 × 55 inches
Acquired from Ricco/Maresca Gallery, 1994
1997.82

That Hawkins found architecture, especially that of grand and important buildings, visually stimulating is evident in the many treatments of Columbus, Ohio, landmarks he produced during the 1980s. Except for a brief period of military service during World War II, Hawkins never left his adopted city after he arrived there in 1916. He became an integral part of his community, claiming to have fathered thirty-two children there, and many people depended on him for support. A well-known figure in his neighborhood, he became a community leader, albeit a nonpolitical one.[1]

Hawkins grew up watching his grandmother make quilts, and he seems to have translated the color patterning and design dynamism of that art form into paintings such as *State Office Building #2*, with its limited but vibrant palette and abstract treatment of the structure's fenestration. In contrast to the still façade, the roadway sweeps up from the lower left corner. It is uncertain whether the Coca-Cola delivery truck that occupies the center of the composition was taken from the original source or whether Hawkins added it himself, to contrast with the solidity and permanence of the buildings or to commemorate his own former profession as a delivery truck driver.

Cats. 41–43

William Hawkins

1895–1990
Columbus, Ohio

Tyrannosaurus #1, 1987
Enamel paint on board
56½ × 48 inches
Acquired from Ricco/Maresca Gallery, 1994
1997.86

Tyrannosaurus Rex, 1988
Pencil on paper
14 × 11 inches
Acquired from Ricco/Maresca Gallery, 1995
1997.85

Stegosaurus, 1988
Pencil on paper
14 × 11 inches
Acquired from Ricco/Maresca Gallery, 1995
1997.83

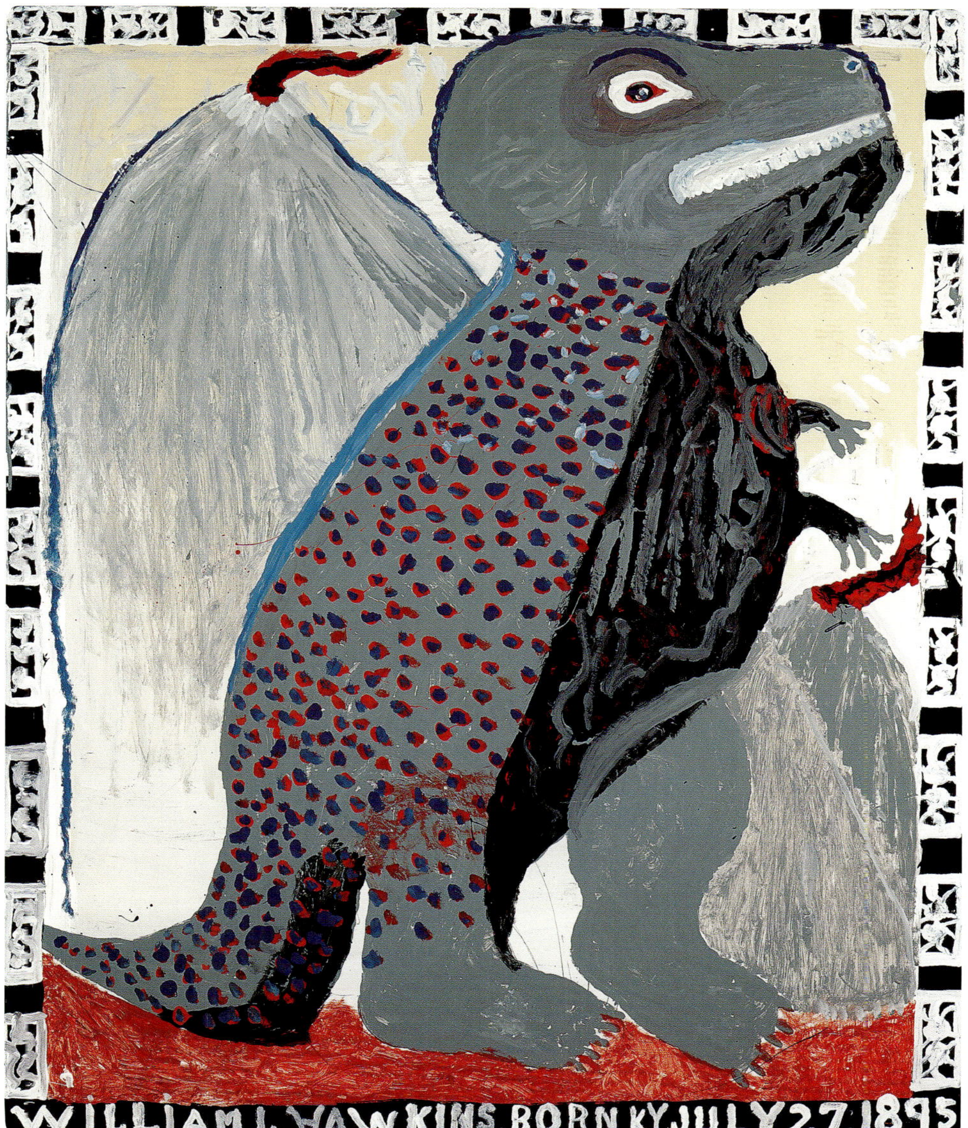

In *Tyrannosaurus #1*, Hawkins mimicked the texture of reptilian skin in the impasto and dappled color of the dinosaur's back. His fierce eye, emphasized by its position at the center of a cluster of concentric forms, blazes with the same fiery red that spews from the volcanoes. The tyrannosaurus lumbers across fresh red earth, newly forged from iron-laden lava. Behind it, volcanoes rise, outlined—a treatment unusual for Hawkins, and one he probably borrowed from his source, a slender children's reader called *Dinosaur Time*.[1] The border of this painting is also exceptional, with curious spidery forms enclosed in rectangular cells.

In addition to his paintings, Hawkins made many pencil drawings. Almost identical in composition, and probably drawn from the same source, *Tyrannosaurus Rex* appears to be a study for *Tyrannosaurus #1*, though the drawing was created a year later than the painting. A rough sketch, devoid of background or shading, it throbs with the vitality typical of Hawkins's work.

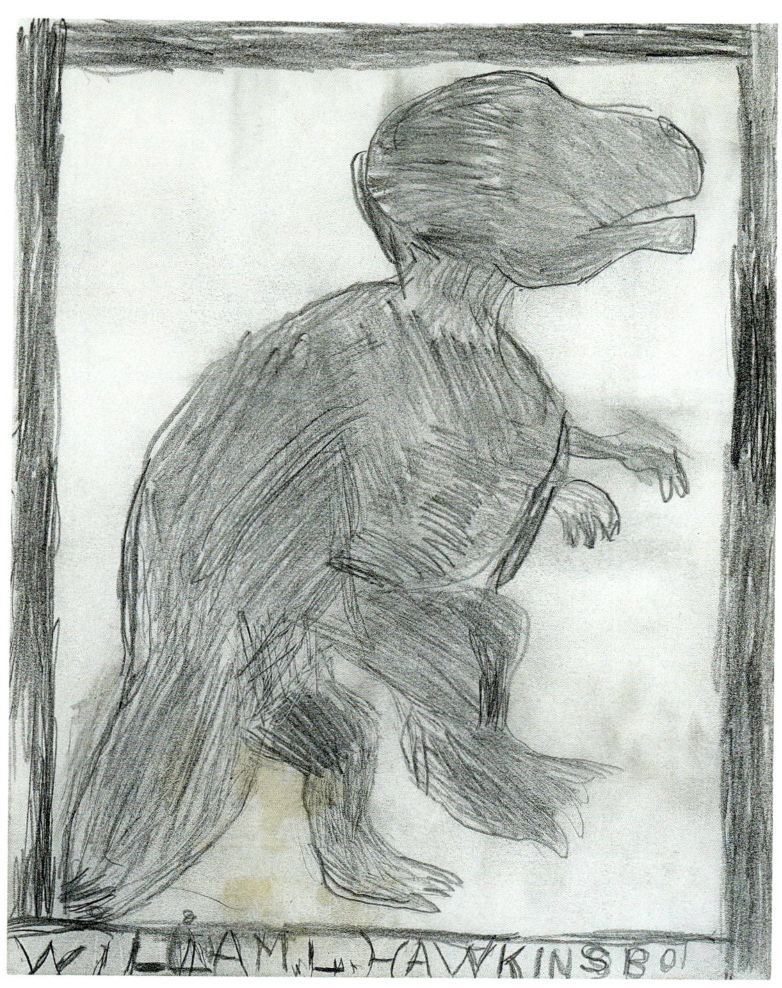

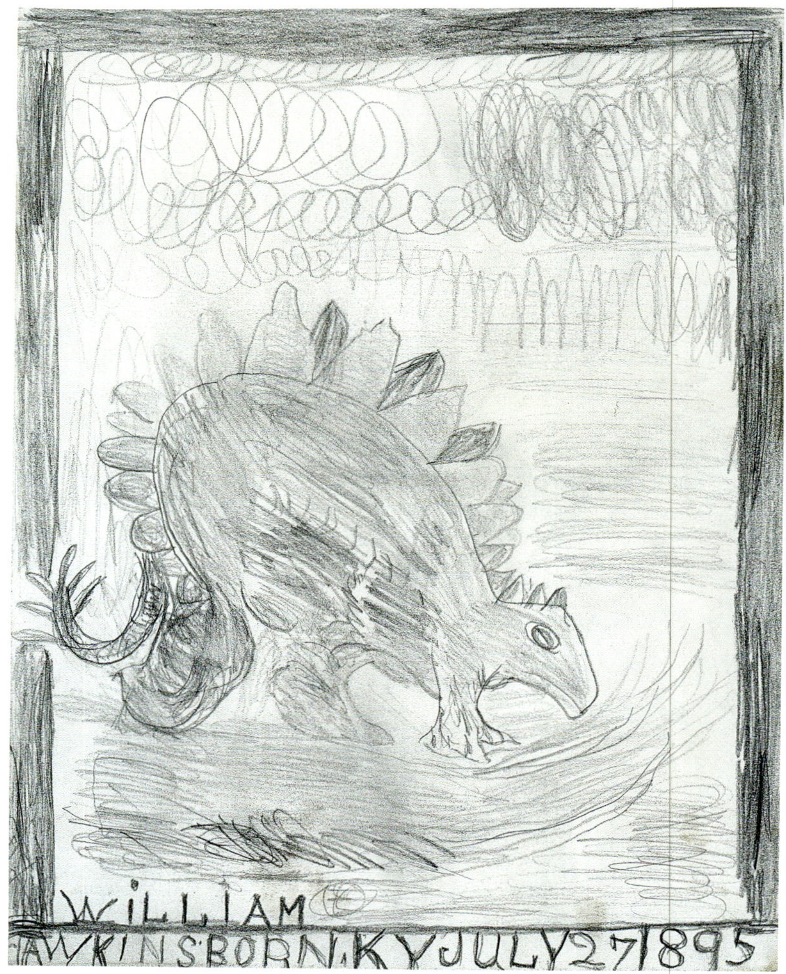

Like *Tyrannosaurus Rex, Stegosaurus* is not an elaborate drawing. As was his custom, Hawkins made no attempt to shade the form for the illusion of volume, although gradations of light and dark add interest to the surface. He roughly pencilled in the background, filling in the top of the sky with lazy, looping strokes. Despite the casual approach this seems to imply, the line is sure and formal rhythms thrive, seen in the brief alternation of dark and light plates across the top of the spine and the repetition of curves in the tail and back legs. The tail's extension into the drawing's border emphasizes not the size of the creature but the motion of the appendage. Hawkins re-created this work from *Dinosaur Time* as well, eliminating the original's setting but retaining the circular form of rippling water around the reptile's forefoot.

Hawkins associated prehistoric creatures with the familiar animals of his rural youth, referring to them as "hogs," "lizards," or "snakes."[2] Frank Maresca believes Hawkins's paintings of single dinosaurs are "undoubtedly autobiographical."[3] Hawkins may have viewed the t. rex, a vigorous predator, as an apt symbol for his own personal and artistic prowess, of which he was proud.

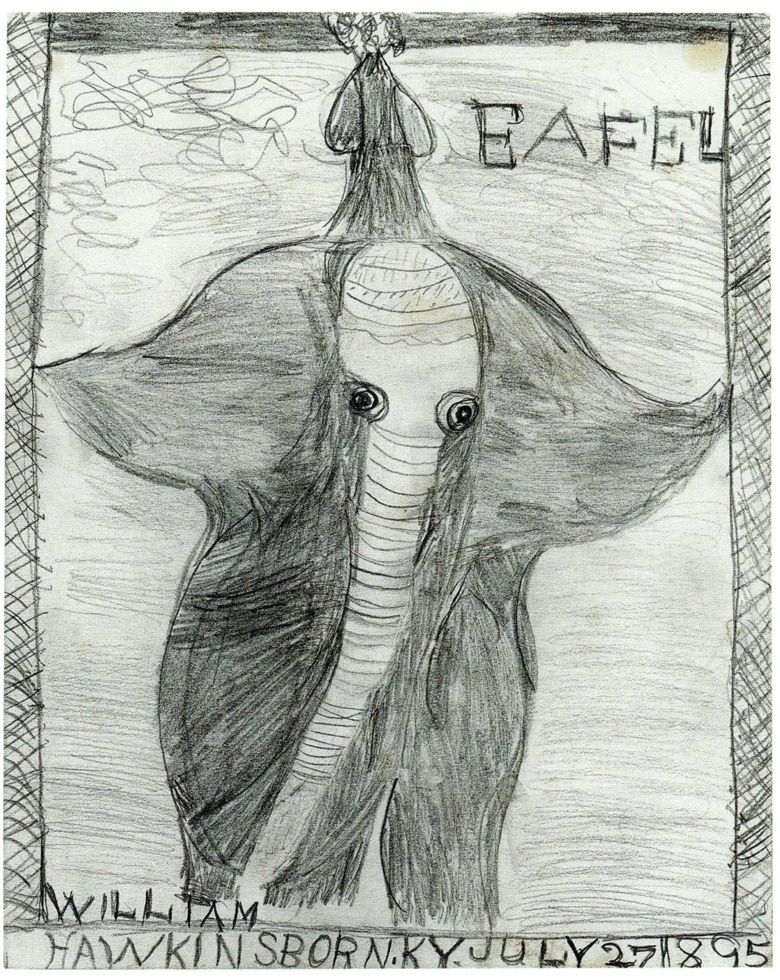

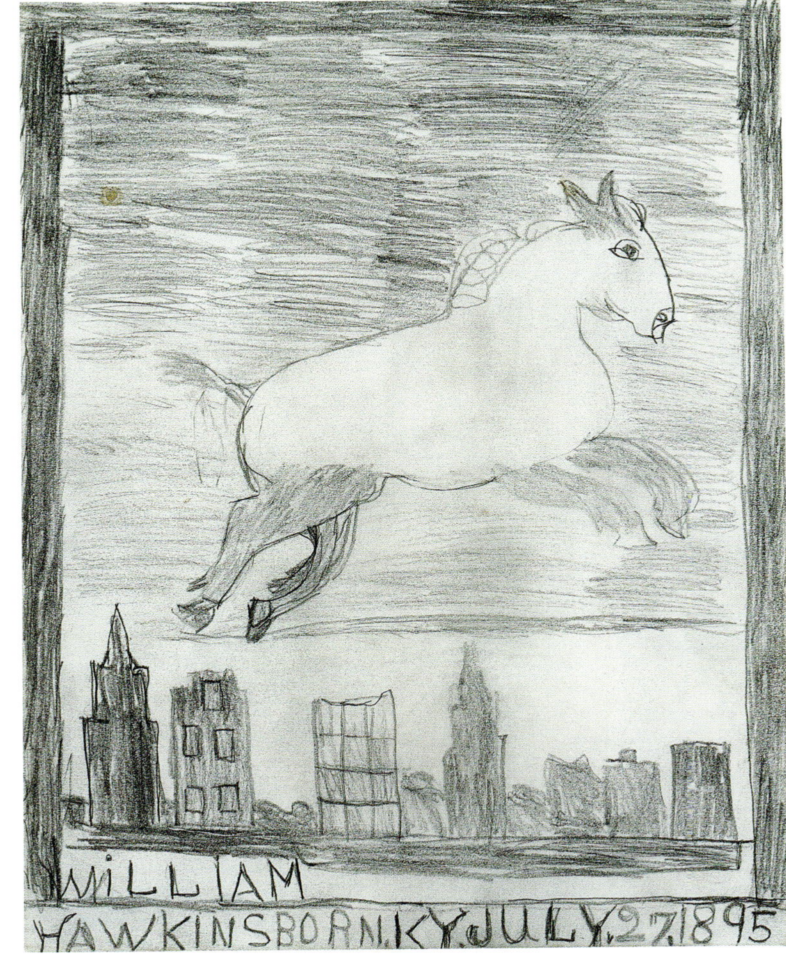

Cats. 44–45

William Hawkins

1895–1990
Columbus, Ohio

Elephant and Rider (Eafel), 1988
Pencil on paper
14 × 11 inches
Acquired from Ricco/Maresca Gallery, 1995
1997.78

Flying Horse, 1988
Pencil on paper
14 × 11 inches
Acquired from Ricco/Maresca Gallery, 1995
1997.79

HAWKINS'S PENCIL DRAWINGS display the energy of an artist who knew what he wanted to say and how he wanted to say it. Horses and elephants were two of his favorite subjects, embodying characteristics Hawkins valued in himself, such as hard work, perseverance, and fruitfulness.[1]

In *Elephant and Rider (Eafel)*, the pachyderm's colossal back thrusts a small human figure, schematic but exotically garbed, into the drawing's top border, a device Hawkins sometimes employed to emphasize great size. The animal's upswept ears brush the sides of the pencilled frame and impart an almost buoyant aspect to the massive creature. Bulging eyes, rendered in concentric circles, peer from the ridged trunk, the texture of which is suggested by parallel lines.

In *Flying Horse*, a wingless horse soars across a dark-shaded night sky and seems to be supported on a streak of stratus cloud hovering over the city. Hawkins seldom shaded forms to depict depth, but rather to add variety to the surface of the work. Distance is conveyed through scale alone, without the assistance of aerial perspective or overlapping forms.

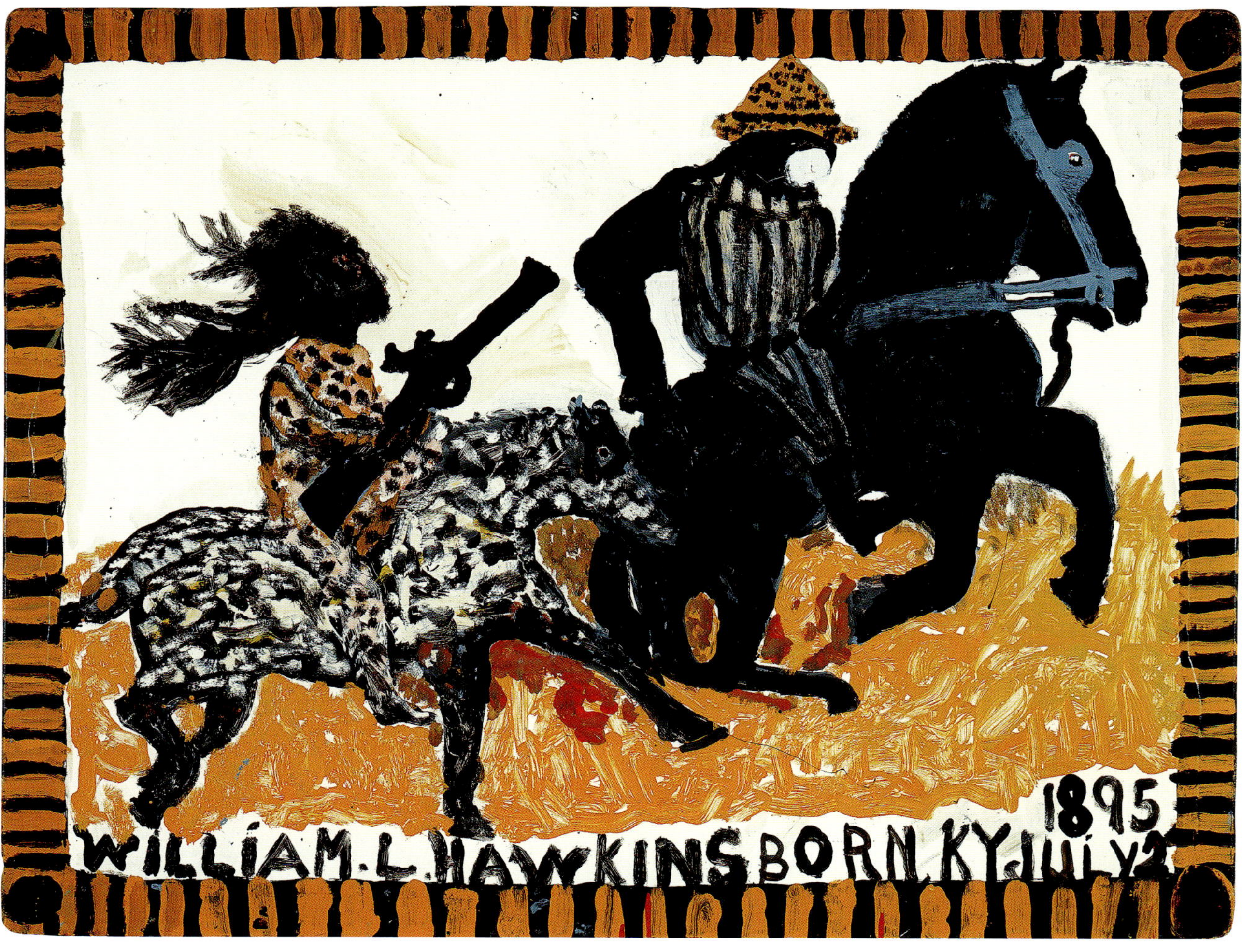

Cat. 46

William Hawkins

1895–1990
Columbus, Ohio

Indian Chasing White Man, 1988
Enamel paint on board
36 × 48 inches
Acquired from Ricco/Maresca Gallery, 1995
1997.80

Hawkins grew up on his grandparents' farm in eastern Kentucky and taught himself to draw by copying pictures from calendars and horse auction announcements. The effects of this bucolic upbringing stayed with him throughout his adult life in the bustling city of Columbus, Ohio. Animals were a favorite subject of the drawings and paintings he produced during a prolific last decade until his death at ninety-four. Hawkins was captivated by America's Old West, a fascination that may have stemmed from pride in his own mixed racial roots: black, white, and Native American.[1] These two themes are united in the artist's representation of a mounted chase.

Hawkins referred to his photographic and illustrated source materials as his "research." He would hunt through the suitcase in which he kept them until he found a resonant image; then he would paint or (as he said) "improve" it.[2] On several occasions his inspiration came from *The Golden Book of America,* a collection of stories from U.S. history for young people. In 1985 and 1987, Hawkins interpreted *Buffalo Hunter,* an image from that book, in paintings and drawings. *Indian Chasing White Man* seems inspired by other paintings of the Old West reproduced in that volume.[3]

Hawkins's appreciation of equine anatomy is apparent in this work, as it is in his many other portrayals of horses (see cat. 45). *Indian Chasing White Man* surges with movement. The Indian's hair flies; the legs of his mount thrust forward; his legs blur into the flank of the horse, dappled as they both are. At the same time, a quiet mystery pervades the scene, largely because of the shadowy vagueness of its principals' faces.

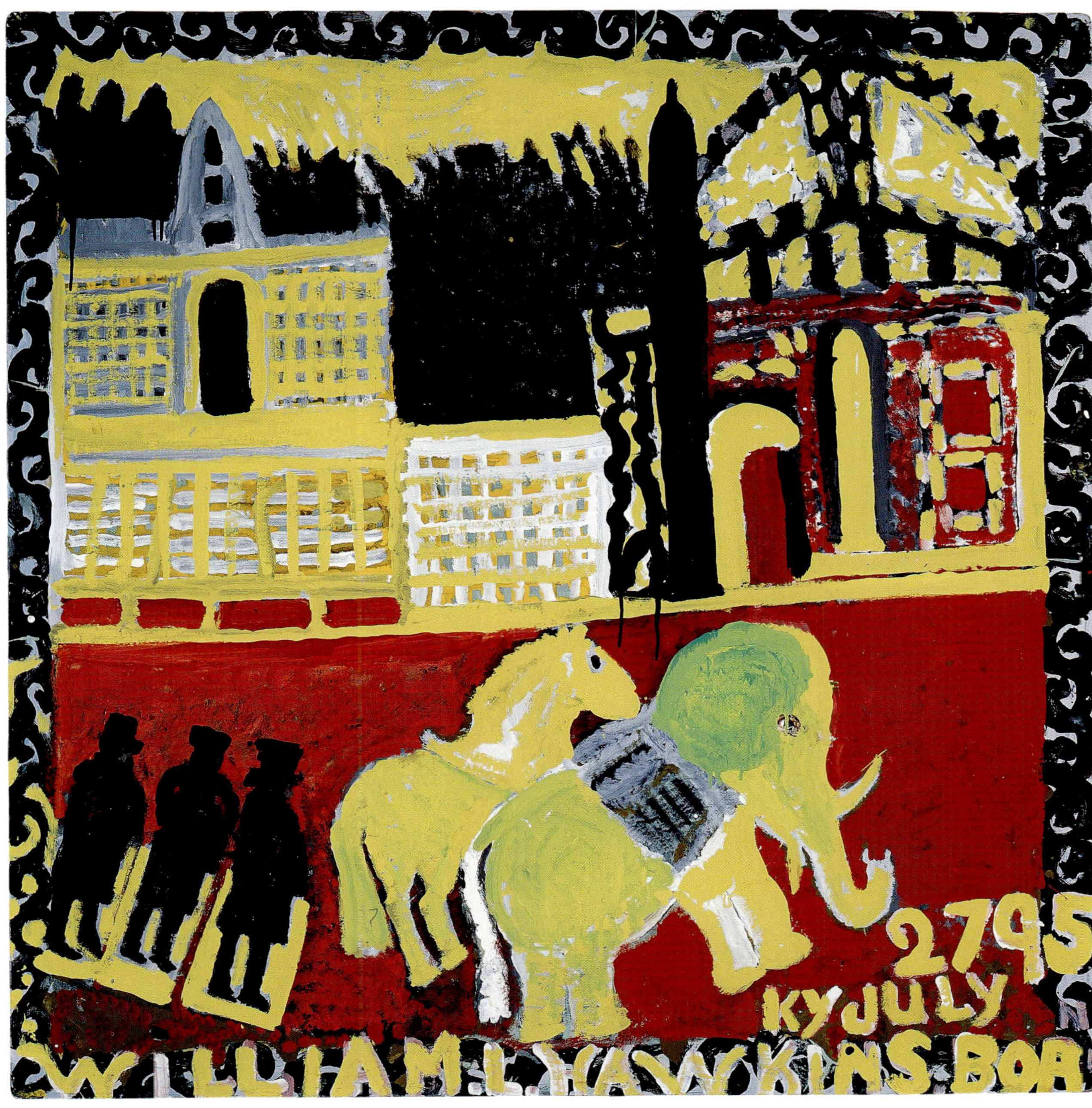

Cat. 47

William Hawkins

1895–1990
Columbus, Ohio

Indian Courtyard, 1988
Enamel paint on board
48 × 48 inches
Acquired from Ricco/Maresca Gallery, 1994
1997.81

William Hawkins painted several pictures of India, whose grand architecture and exotic beasts must have appealed to him. He also painted elephants and horses and may have felt that he shared their salient traits: fertility, dedication, and the will to work hard.[1]

Rich red, lime green, and lemon yellow shimmer against black details in this painting. The upper-right quadrant contains an energetic passage of decorative brushwork, while the buildings on the left are simplified into chromatic grids with dynamic patterning that Hawkins may have derived from his grandmother's quiltmaking.

Hawkins incorporated his signature, birth date, and home state into the edges of each painting, making his borders another ubiquitous design element. Here the border takes the form of elaborate black on gray scrollwork appropriate to the exotic scene.

Cat. 48

William Hawkins

1895–1990
Columbus, Ohio

Tiger and Bear, 1989
Enamel paint, paper, duct tape, and sand on board
42 × 48 inches
Acquired from Ricco/Maresca Gallery, 1994
1997.84

Control and disorder collide in Hawkins's collage-painting *Tiger and Bear*, in which a rail protects her grassy nest beneath a roaring tiger and a snarling bear. The quiet bird contrasts with the animals Hawkins usually portrayed: enormous, fierce creatures like these combatants, whom he regarded as alter egos, engaged in a daily struggle to survive.

Although the animals' battle dominates the scene visually, humankind dominates it psychologically, as Joanne Cubbs and Eugene Metcalf have noted. The tiger's image, taken from a carnival or circus poster, is that of a captive beast, and the photographs of a man and a monkey scaling a palm tree came from travel brochures.[1] Terraced farmland, marked by man's endeavor, occupies two fragments of an aerial photograph. At the edge of the composition, torn in two and glued awry, is a photo of a large specimen tree in a manicured lawn.

Hawkins presents divergent types of fearsomeness in his bloody-clawed opponents. He renders terror tangible in his use of the crisp, detailed lithograph of the tiger—razor-edged teeth and fangs all too clear—and amorphous terror in the nebulous bear, the sort of inchoate monster that arises from fog, fire, or dreams, the more terrible for its indistinctness.

Hawkins first incorporated collaged elements into his paintings in 1986.[2] In addition to speeding up production of pictures—and picture-making was always a money-making endeavor for Hawkins—adopting mass media images in their familiar forms provided an immediate connection with his audience.[3] The artist integrated these illustrations into his composition, extending them with paint onto the ground and sometimes working the background color over their edges. He finished the composition with a lively border of black overlaid with robust white scrollwork.

While the tiger is attached to the board with duct tape, the bear is built up above the support using a technique Hawkins developed to create a fur-like texture for his animals, mixing cornmeal or (as in this case) sand with paint. Hawkins called his use of such three-dimensional effects "puffing up" a painting.[4] The bear's eyes began as elements in a magazine photograph. Hawkins blended them into the animal's head with black paint. Recognizable as human eyes, they produce an eerie effect—they seem to provide this indefinite monster with an almost human soul.

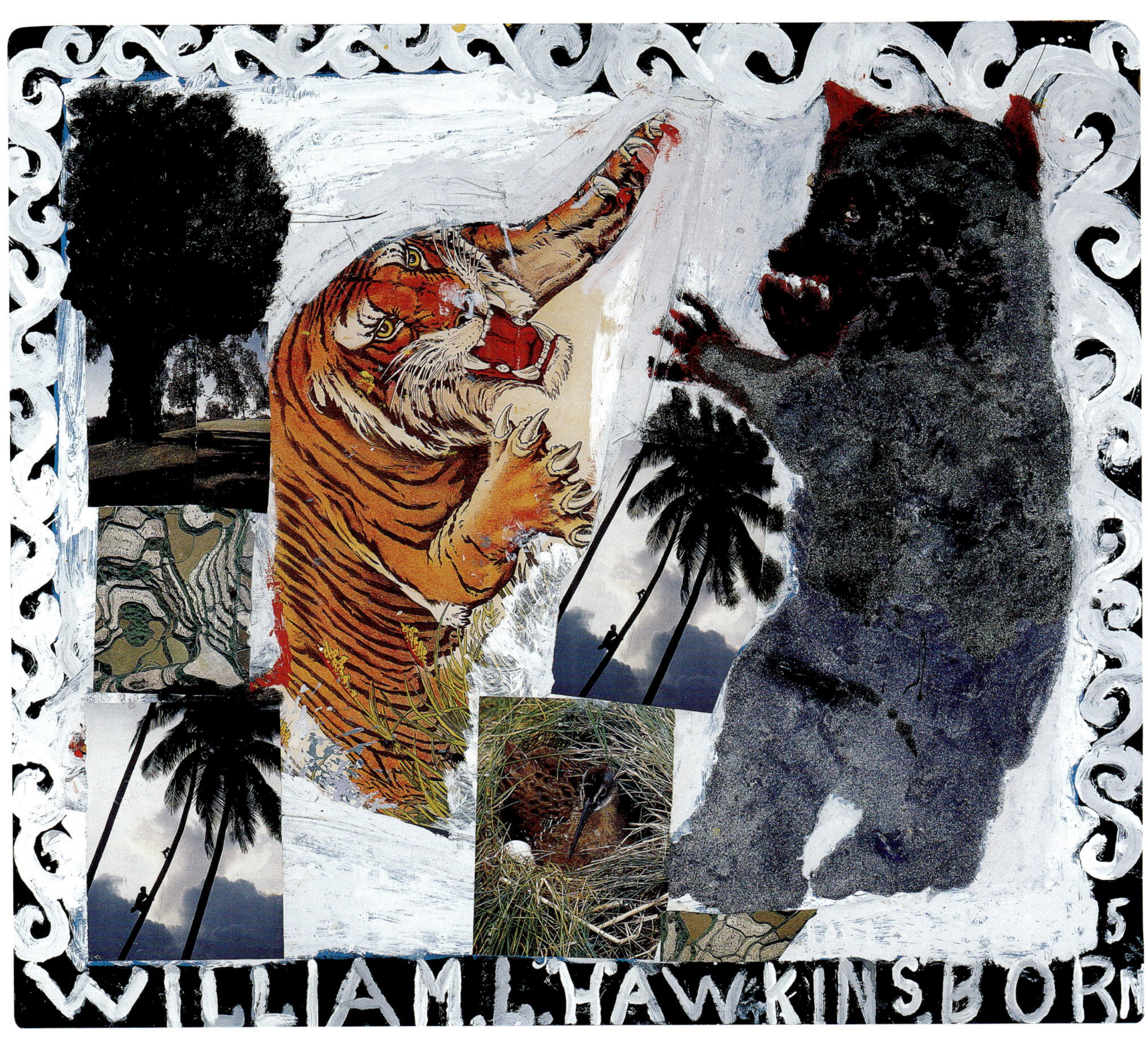
5
WILLIAM.L.HAWKINSBORN

Cat. 49

Lonnie Holley

Born 1950
Birmingham, Alabama

Blown Out Black Mama's Belly, 1994
Rubber, cloth, and wire coat hanger
84 x 22 x 4 inches
Acquired from William S. Arnett, 1996
1996.40

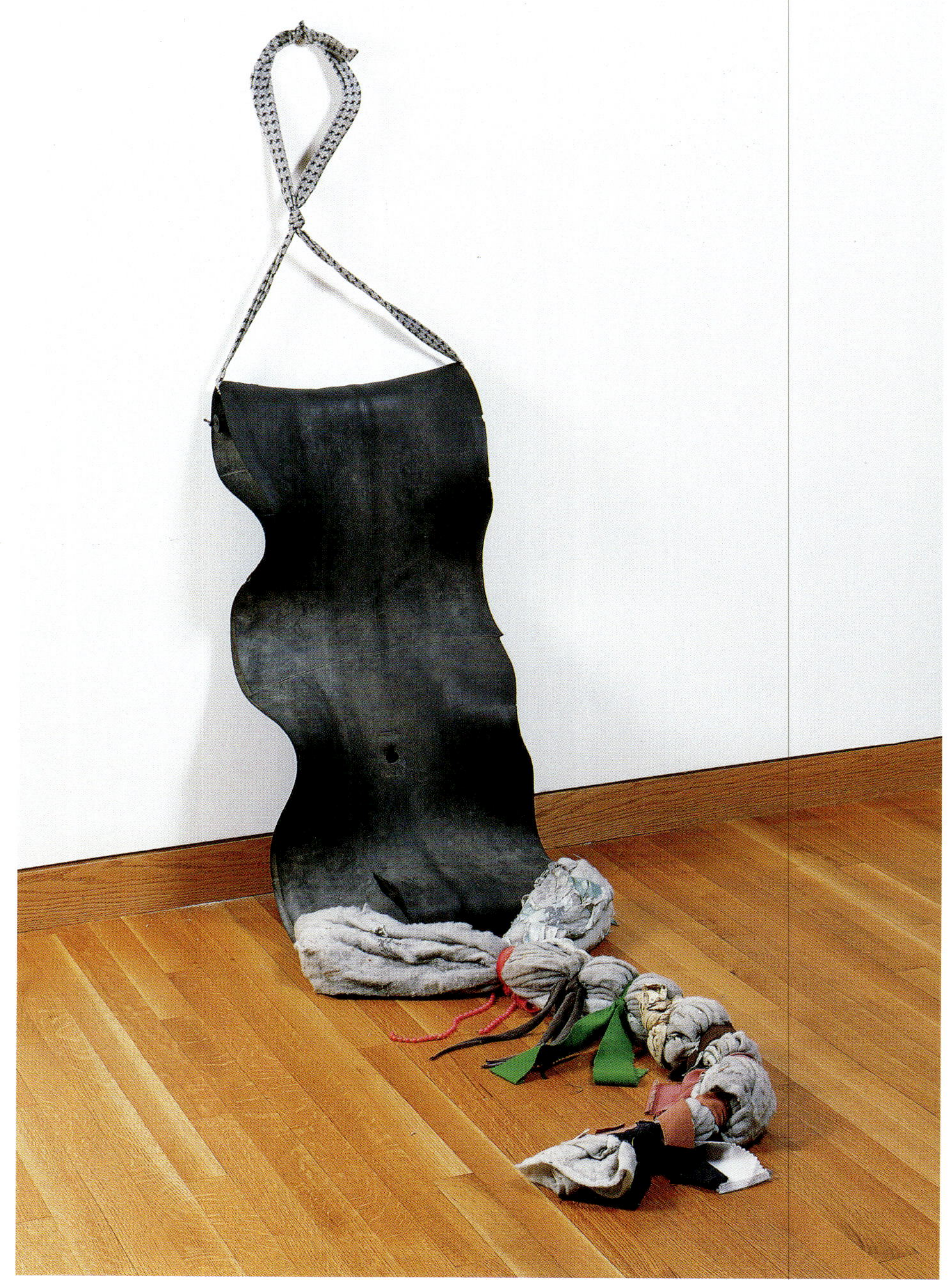

Lonnie Holley describes his process of making art out of other people's castoffs as "transforming, but also with a purpose and a meaning."[1] That purpose is often to honor the lives and sacrifices of those who have gone before. "I don't want to get too far from the honoring," he says. This assemblage of stretched inner tube and scraps of cloth is Holley's tribute to his mother.

According to Holley, Dorothy Mae Holley Crawford bore many children before her death in 1986. The ligatures on the lower portion of the piece represent the tied off umbilical cords of this long series of children and, by extension, the children of the world. Holley's amazement at the somatic stress of bearing and nurturing so many children pervades his homage. "This was did with the inner piece of rubber that goes inside your big old transfer truck tire, and it shows how the belly had been stretched and deformed and brought back in place. . . . That's a lot of re-growing inside of you . . . and you know a woman that actually shedded that much of herself, that's a lot of making of human flesh!" Such evidence of physical wear is connected to a fecundity—both physical and psychic—that lies at the root of Holley's aesthetic. "Peoples have been looking for life to come out of the womb. Why can't it come out of the thought of man and woman just as well as out of the body of man and woman?"

The recycled materials in Holley's assemblages suggest their previous uses. A necktie supports the structure while recalling its human wearer. Years of hauling products across the continent left a patina of age and use on the dirty rubber inner tube. The umbilical of shredded stuffing spreads out on the ground like a chaise longue left to weather, and the fabric ties remind the viewer of discarded clothing. Holley's juxtaposition of these accreted meanings urges the viewer to think about the relationship of past and present, the duality of matter and spirit, and the cycle of life and death. In so doing, Holley's art "kinda invites the mind. It invites the mind to say 'Let's care. Where we wouldn't care, let's care.'"

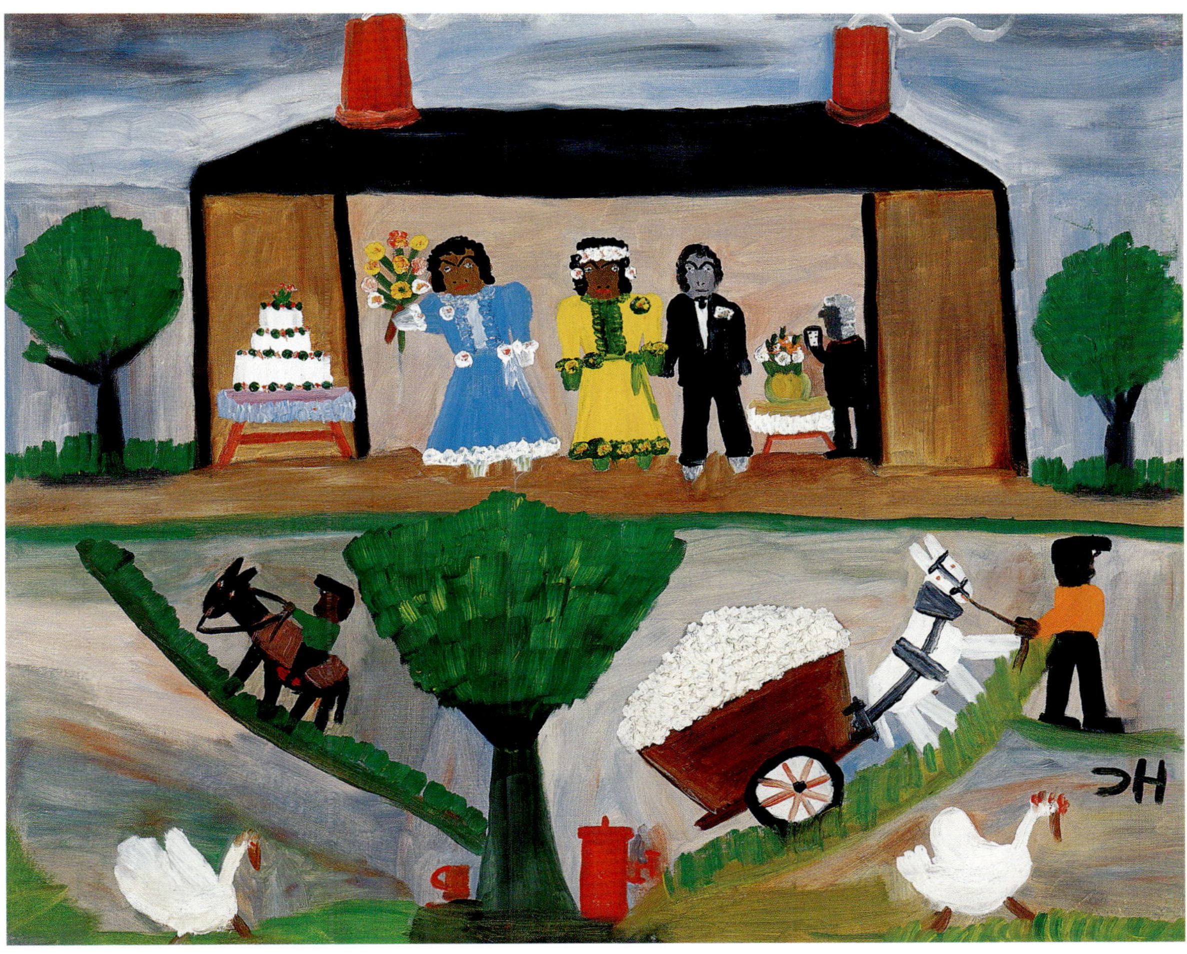

Cat. 50

Clementine Hunter

ca. 1886–1988
Melrose, Louisiana

The Wedding, 1960
Oil on canvas
21⅜ x 27½ inches
Acquired from Americas Folk Heritage Gallery, 1991
1996.176

Despite the toil and poverty in her life, Clementine Hunter painted exuberant memories of the daily proceedings at Melrose Plantation, where she spent more than eighty years. She said she re-created whatever came into her head. Depicting work, worship, and revelry, Hunter fashioned lighthearted scenes—except when she portrayed the Crucifixion or the commotion of the local juke joint on Saturday nights—peopled with African American plantation servants and farmhands. Using vivid colors and flat forms, Hunter painted (or "marked," as she said) her pictures with a grace and ardor that she credited to her creator: "God gave me the power. Sometimes I try to quit painting. I can't. I can't."[1]

Bisecting this scene of a plantation wedding, the artist layered the mundane and the sacred. Farmhands labor in the cotton fields below while the nuptials take place in the upper register. Except for the groom, whose newly acquired conjugal status may give him more standing, the men in the painting are smaller than the women, as Hunter's men usually are. At the bottom of the picture are two goosters, Hunter's imaginary hybrid bird that combines the best of a goose and a rooster.

Hunter signed the painting in her characteristic manner. After using an ordinary "C" for some years, she reversed the letter to differentiate her signature from that of her employer, Cammie Henry, who also painted.

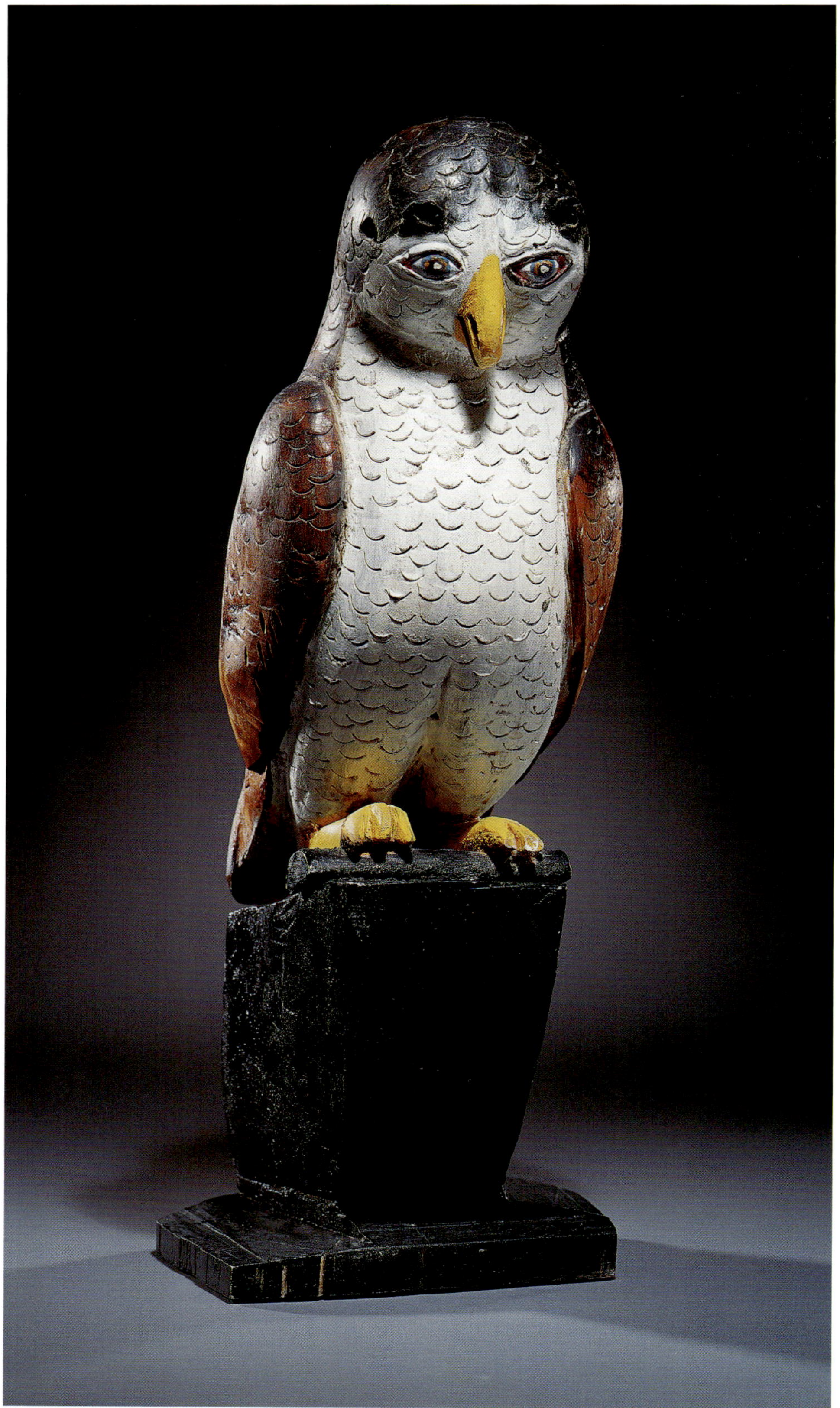

Cat. 51

S. L. Jones

1901–1997
Hinton, West Virginia

Owl, 1988
Carved wood with enamel paint
18 x 6½ x 6½ inches
Acquired from Mrs. S. L. Jones, ca. 1996
1997.88

In his youth, S. L. Jones loved to hunt, especially at night, when he could hear owls hooting. Well versed in the woodland lore of Appalachia, he knew that an answering cry would signal the advent of rough weather. During these hunts he whittled small figures of animals while he waited for his dog to scent game.[1] Many years later, after he had retired from the Chesapeake and Ohio railroad, his wife's death left Jones lonely, with too much time on his hands. He began creating carvings of animals like those he had whittled in his youth, and he continued to produce animals, in wood and on paper, throughout his art-making career.

Jones carved this sagacious owl for his second wife. With close attention to detail, he drilled small ear holes beside the eyes and cut delicate nostrils into the precisely realized beak. He represented the feathers of the back and breast with hundreds of crescent-shaped gouges. Staring with shallow-set, bloodshot, humanoid blue eyes, the owl seems to smile as if pleased with its intellect. The bird's feet rest lightly on its heavy perch.

Jones worked with readily available woods he knew well, such as poplar, black walnut, or maple. He blocked out his pieces with a chainsaw before refining the forms with chisels and rasps. Finally, he added finishing details with a knife before coloring each design with house paints or stains.

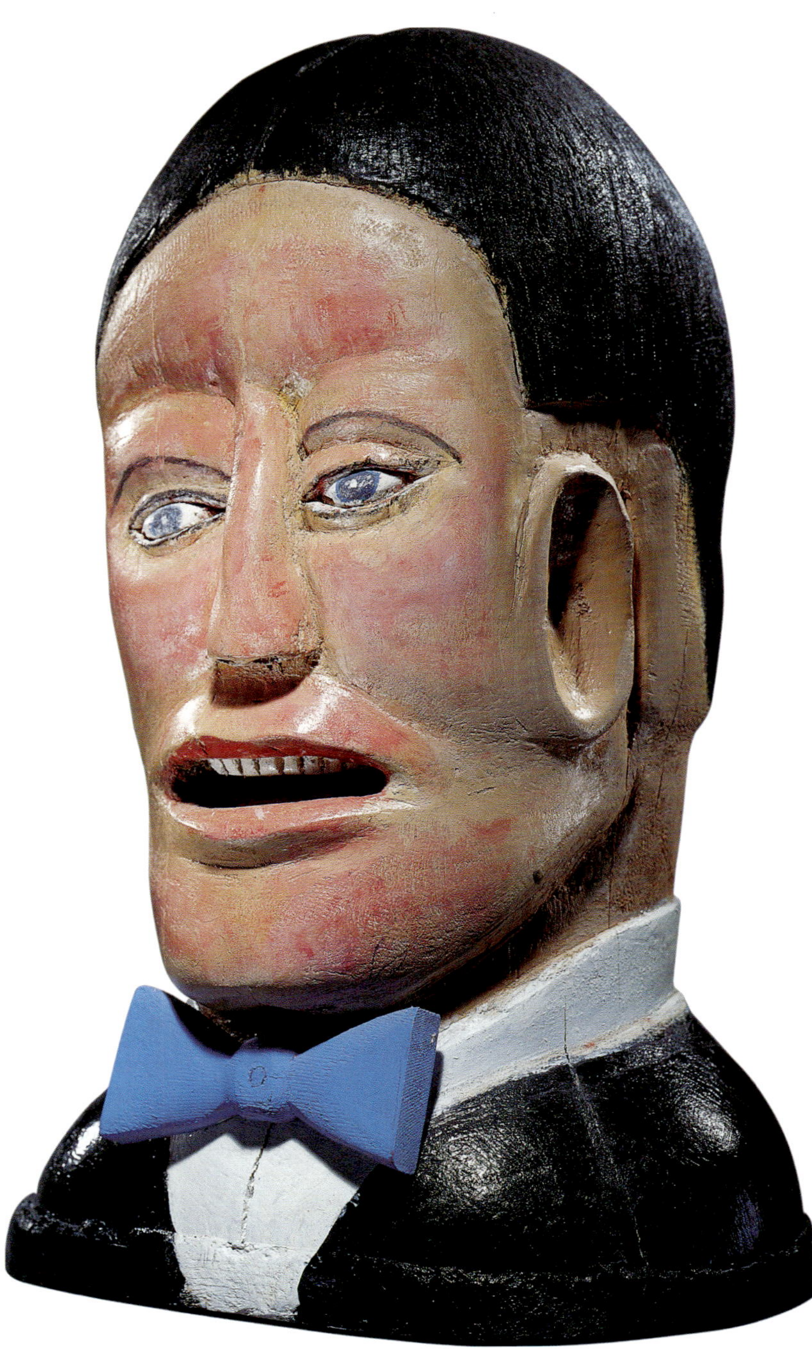

Cat. 52

S. L. Jones

1901–1997
Hinton, West Virginia

Untitled, 1990
Carved wood with enamel paint
18¼ × 11½ × 9¼ inches
Acquired from Dean Jensen Gallery, 1994
1997.89

Jones first carved small figures of people and animals, but the scale of his creations grew with his carving skills until, by the mid-1970s, he was producing oversized pieces like this bust of a man. Jones displays concern with defining details: the hole drilled in the middle of the flat, shell-like ear; the incised line around the hairline and through the part; and the grooves that delineate teeth in the open mouth. Except for the deeply carved mouth, the relief is low: both nose and ears are long, straight, and quite flat. The blue eyes have enormous black pupils enlivened by a central spot of white. Jones's trademark bow tie, carved separately, is nailed onto a crisp white collar.

This bust is reminiscent of a carnival statue and at first glance appears to be all geniality. But carnival is a world turned on its head, where everyday experiences become bizarre and bigger than life. With its intense, skewed gaze, exaggerated size, and imposing mass, this seemingly benign character suggests a similar twist on the commonplace.

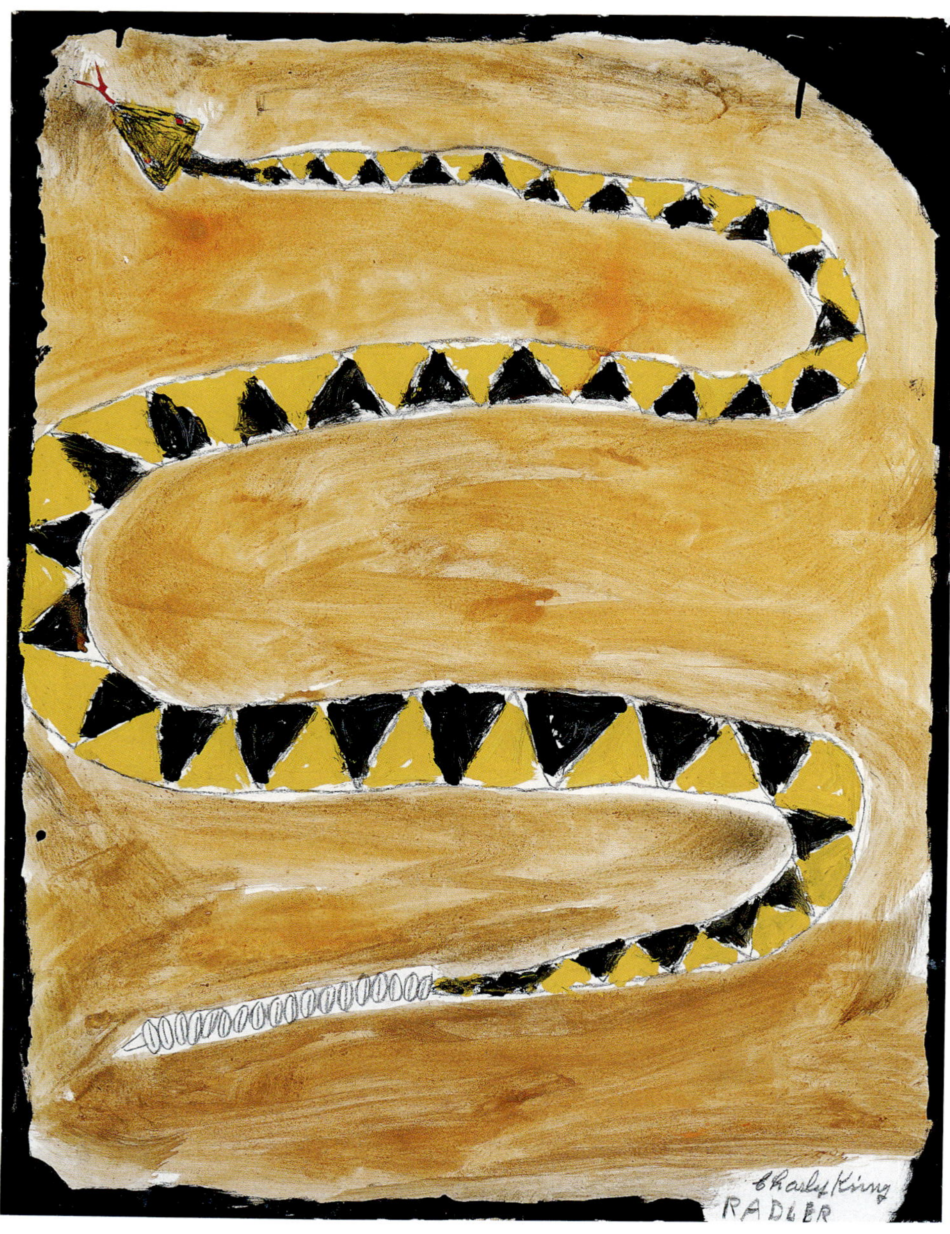

Cat. 53

Charley Kinney

1906–1991
Lewis County, Kentucky

Radler, mid-1970s–1991
Paint and crayon on paper
28½ x 22⅜ inches
Acquired from Charles Locke, 1993
1997.90

Charley Kinney's three major themes were the mountain life of Kentucky, spiritual motifs, and animals—ranging from everyday barnyard species to exotic jungle creatures. *Radler* may refer to the world of spirits. If it is an avatar of Satan, the rattler connects this painting to a large group of Kinney's works. Like the tempter, who often appears in the guise of the ordinary, this snake is familiar but deadly. Among the commonplace perils Kinney recognized were women: "I don't want to get hooked up to some woman that'd try to change my ways."[1] Thus, in Kinney's personal iconography, the snake may also express his distrust of women, which he openly voiced in a painting of another rattlesnake labeled "Femal."[2]

As the serpent's body undulates, it crowds the left border of the picture, producing a tension that calls to mind the threat of the rattle. The top border plays subtly with and against the curves of the rattlesnake's body while, more dramatically, the diamond-back pattern echoes the form of the snake's triangular head. *Radler* exemplifies the free brushwork and black painted borders typical of Kinney's paintings.

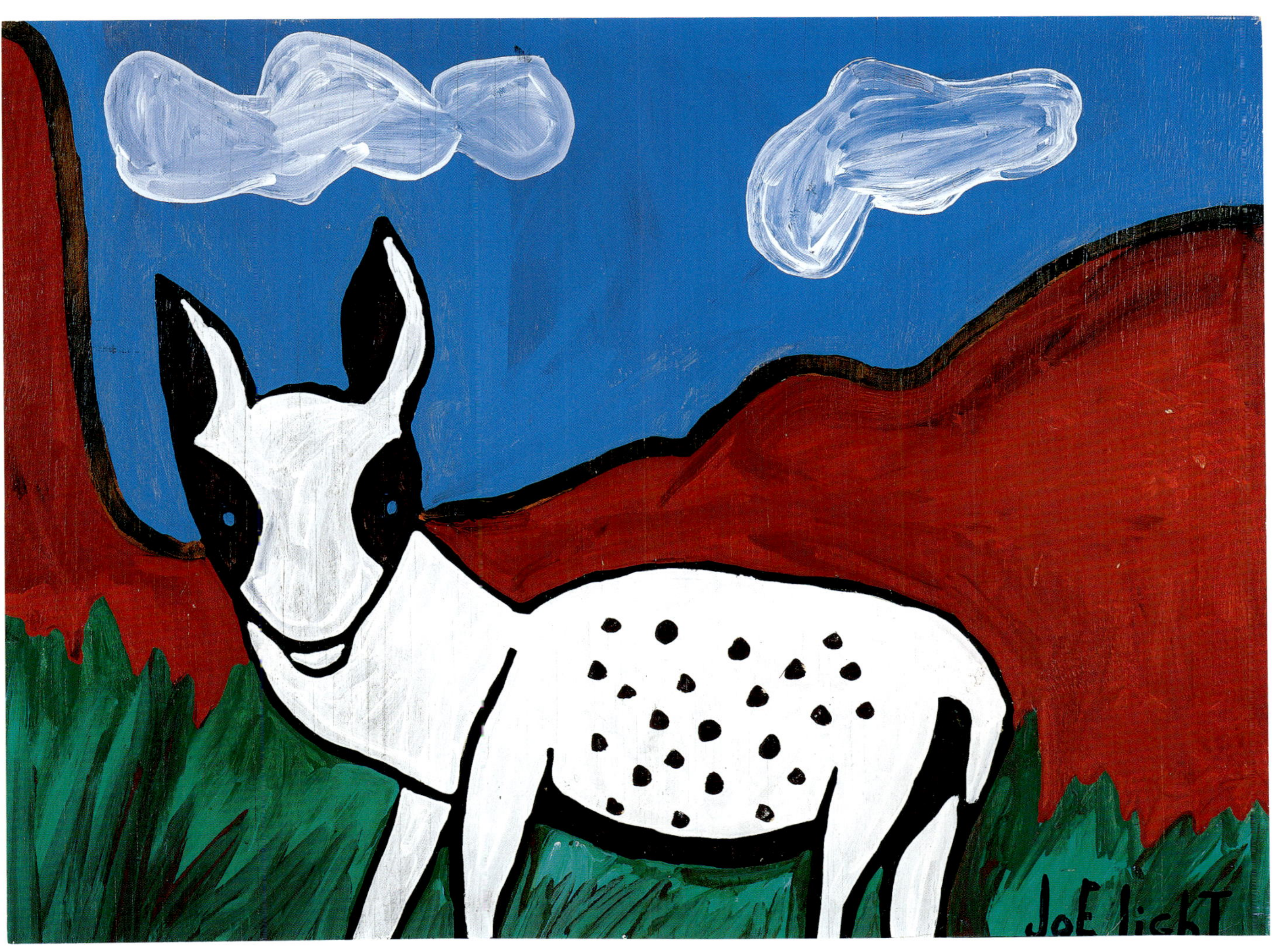

Cat. 54

Joe Light

Born 1934
Memphis, Tennessee

Untitled, 1985–1992
Paint on plywood
35 × 47¾ inches
Acquired from Charles Locke, 1992
1997.92

Joe Light has been deeply concerned about social problems since his conversion to Judaism while serving a prison sentence in the 1960s. He counsels his neighbors on these problems through his art. In the signs he has hand-lettered since 1975, Light urges better behavior on those who pass his Memphis home, and in bold paintings he conveys his views about the spiritual value of mundane things. Demonstrating a vivid sense of design, his spare compositions magnify their subjects, which are usually taken from nature. Neither shadows nor shading impede the force of Light's heavily outlined forms and broad fields of bright, pure colors. As Gary J. Schwindler has noted, Light uses monumental size and radical simplification of composition to intensify the commonplace into something strange and significant.[1]

Certain characters have such symbolic significance for Light that he paints them repeatedly. Particular animals, fish, and flowers hold special places in the taxonomy of Light's religious ecology. "All animals mean something to me, but some are special," says the artist, according to whom the creature in the Hahn Collection painting is probably a goat.[2] Although the goat is not among the most significant of Light's personal symbols, it does have biblical associations for the artist, who puts his own idiosyncratic spin on Judaism's traditional dietary laws. He regards scavenging animals as the natural cleaners of the earth and their sacrifice to the human stomach as a cause of current environmental problems. Nevertheless, Light considers the stimulus for this image to have been more artistic than religious, saying it arose primarily from "a feeling I wanted to just paint something."

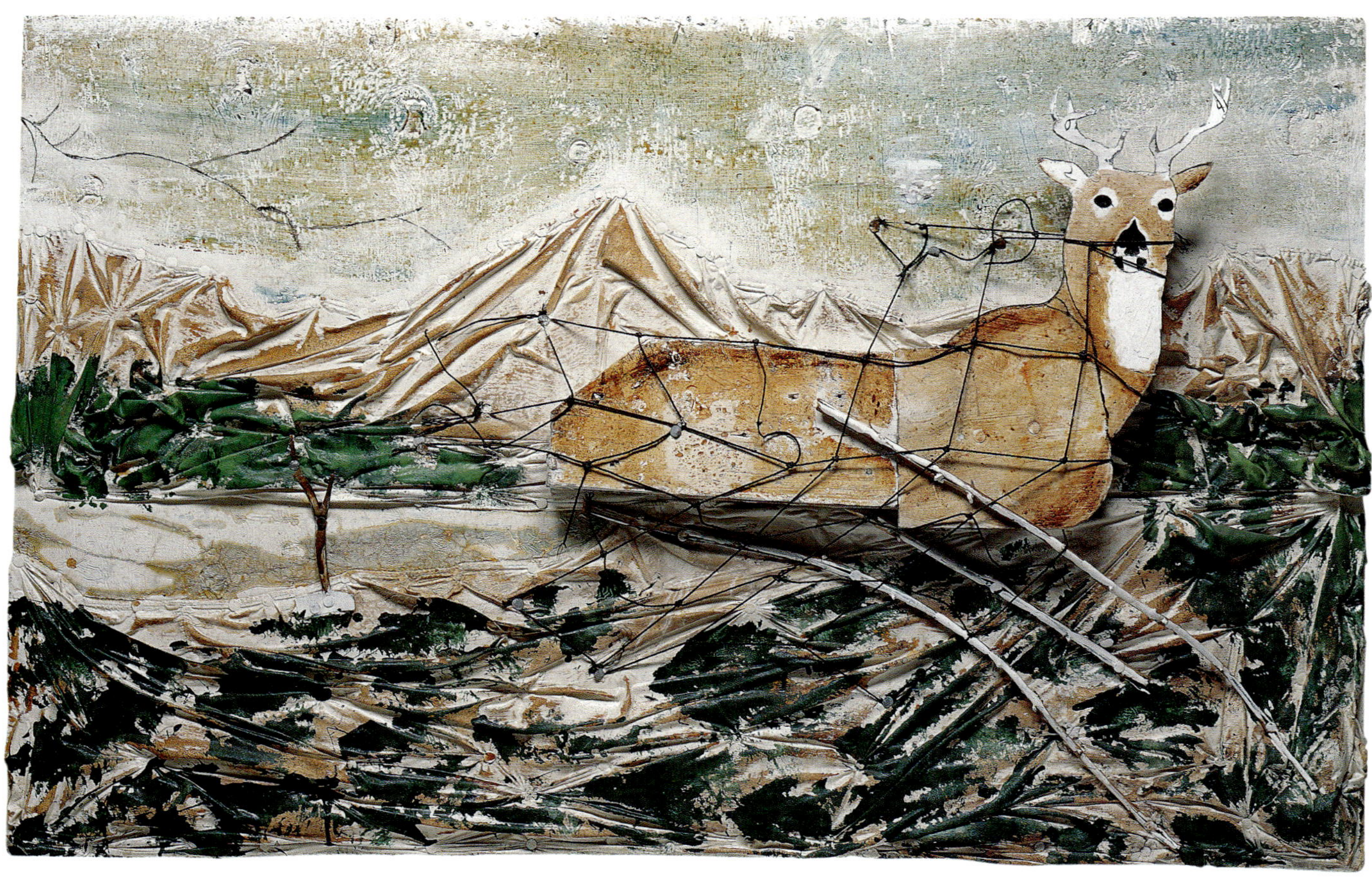

Cat. 55

Ronald Lockett

1965–1998
Bessemer, Alabama

Traps, ca. 1991
Paint, fabric, wood, metal, and netting on plywood
30 × 48 × 3 inches
Acquired from William S. Arnett, 1994
1997.93

Traps is the first piece in a series Ronald Lockett called "Instinct for Survival." The works in this series depict deer caught in fences or netting. The animal served as a symbol for Lockett's brother David, who was one of the first Americans captured in the Gulf War.[1]

From the dainty legs of the deer to the creased, stiffened fabric of the landscape, texture reinforces the symbolism of the work. Real netting binds the buck, a beautifully realized animal form. Before being attached to the panel, the front half of the stag was painstakingly cut from tin and nailed to the found wooden block that forms its hindquarters. Attached to the body with unsettling abruptness are legs made of fragile sticks. The use of snipped tin links this work to a vernacular tradition of cutting metal; tin snips were used by farmers all over the South to construct outbuildings. Several well-known self-taught artists, including David Butler and Thornton Dial, adapted this material to art-making.

Cat. 56

Ronald Lockett

1965–1998
Bessemer, Alabama

Cover of Night, ca. 1992
Paint, chicken wire, nails, photograph, and cellophane on plywood
47⅞ x 40⅛ inches
Acquired from William S. Arnett, 1994
1997.94

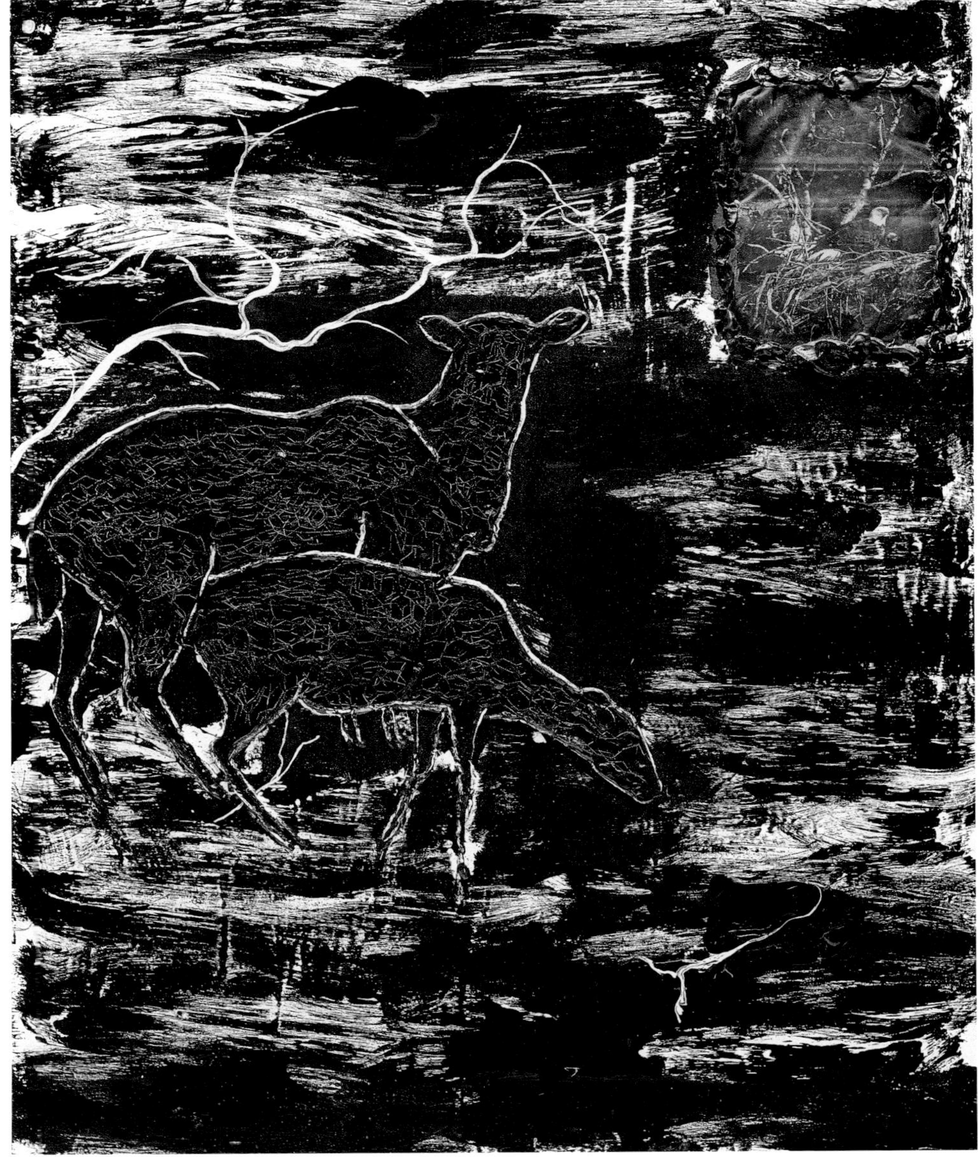

Art historian Paul Arnett describes Lockett's approach to his subject matter as "making folk tales with animals."[1] The artist was raised among relatives who remembered the African American and Native American folklore of the Deep South. Early in his career, Lockett chose the deer as his primary alter ego, regarding it as a creature of gentle demeanor, apt to be preyed on by fiercer animals. At ten or twelve years old, he was drawing deer and buffalo on the outside walls of houses, and his iconography remained constant until his death.

Lockett's painting displays extraordinary sensitivity to nuances of line. He typically worked slowly, deliberately, and somewhat sporadically, perpetually fascinated by the techniques of others and circumspect about his own. Viewing an Anselm Kiefer collage at a collector's home prompted Lockett to experiment with ways to work photographs into his paintings. He began incorporating windows into the upper parts of his work, sometimes adding a smaller painting and sometimes cutting an opening in the support and inserting a picture. Although Lockett's window symbol always represents a shift in time or consciousness, its specific meanings vary. It could signify death or the afterlife, the Garden of Eden, images of the divine, or a shift in time. The precise meaning of the windowed eagle feeding its young is unknown, but coupled with the doe and smaller deer below, it may reinforce the idea of nurturing.

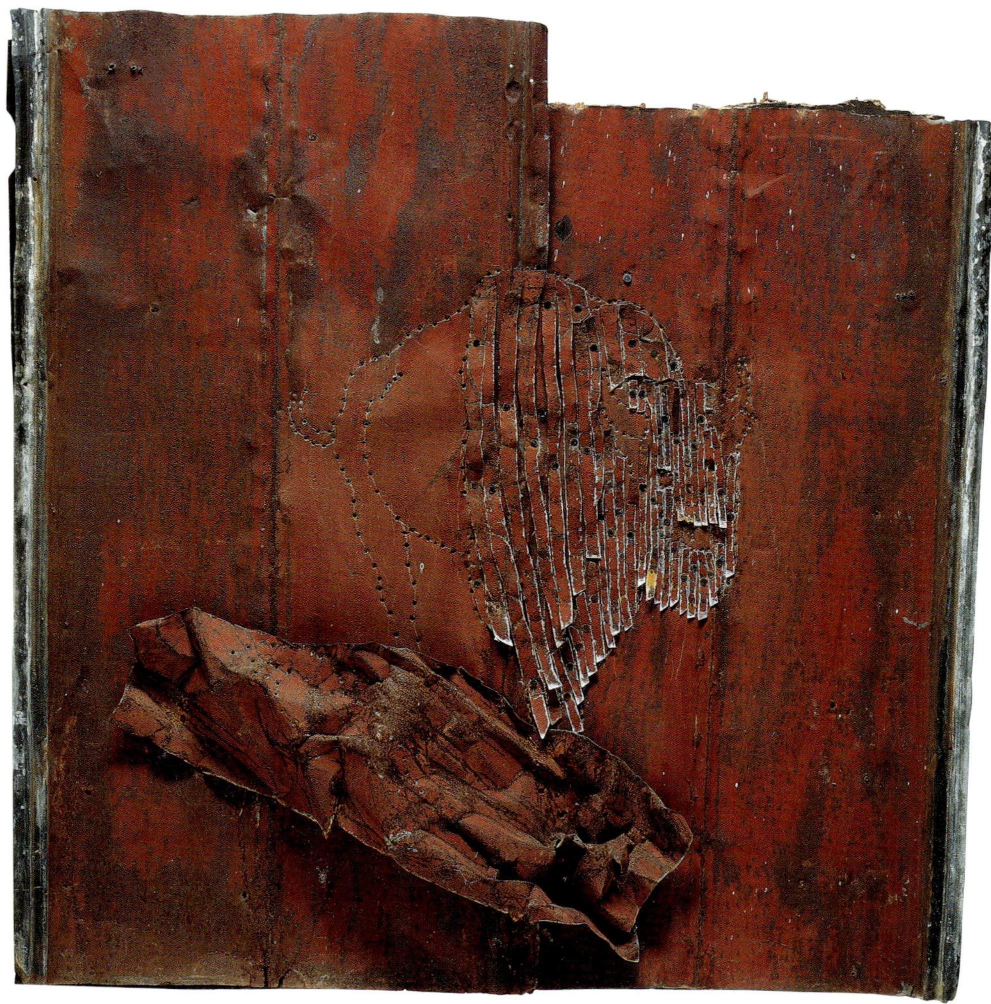

Cat. 57

Ronald Lockett

1965–1998
Bessemer, Alabama

Facing Extinction, ca. 1994
Welder's chalk (?) on metal mounted on wood
49⅜ × 47⅝ × 3½ inches
Acquired from William S. Arnett, 1994
1996.179

THE SHEET OF METAL is painted an ancient, mottled red. The paint rusts and flakes, revealing bare gray metal and a florescence of corrosion around holes made by nails and use. Out of this background flickers the form of a buffalo, its hindquarters elegantly rendered in chalk, its shaggy forequarters built up from ribbons of the same red metal. The whitened ends of these strips give the buffalo a grizzled appearance. Outlines of haunches, horns, and nose resonate with the staccato of nail holes punched along the chalk lines. The animal stands on a piece of crumpled tin as if on rocky ground.

Lockett's tin pieces have to do with death and remembrance. Much of his early work concerns genocide, especially the decimation of Native American populations, whose cultures he admired and probably learned about from television documentaries, according to Paul Arnett. (Television may also have influenced the look of *Facing Extinction*, Arnett believes, pointing out the similarity between this ghostly figure and the afterimage of the freshly switched-off tube.) Lockett may have heard his cousin Thornton Dial talk about his own Native American maternal grandparents. In this case, he memorialized both the buffalo and their Native American hunters, who were nearly eliminated by the advance of white settlers.[1]

Lockett received the tin he used in his buffalo series from Dial, who had painted it decades before, when it shrouded a barn he owned. Lockett explained the genesis of his tin sculptures to William Arnett: in an Atlanta collector's home, he saw a tin horse by Deborah Butterfield and a Holocaust-related work by Jewish artist Christian Boltanski. Lockett said he sympathized with the pain in the old metal of Butterfield's piece and the subject matter of Boltanski's. Lockett was haunted by the feeling that he was a member of a doomed generation of black men.[2] Educator Vincent Harding has observed that the perforations in Lockett's bison tin reliefs—which look like bullet holes—link the series to the artist's anxiety about the plight of young black men.[3]

Cat. 58

Sister Gertrude Morgan

1900–1980
New Orleans, Louisiana

Jesus Is My Air Plane, ca. 1970
Watercolor, ballpoint pen, and pencil on paper with heavy thread and safety pin
17 × 4 × 4 inches
Acquired from Fleisher/Ollman Gallery, 2000
2000.10

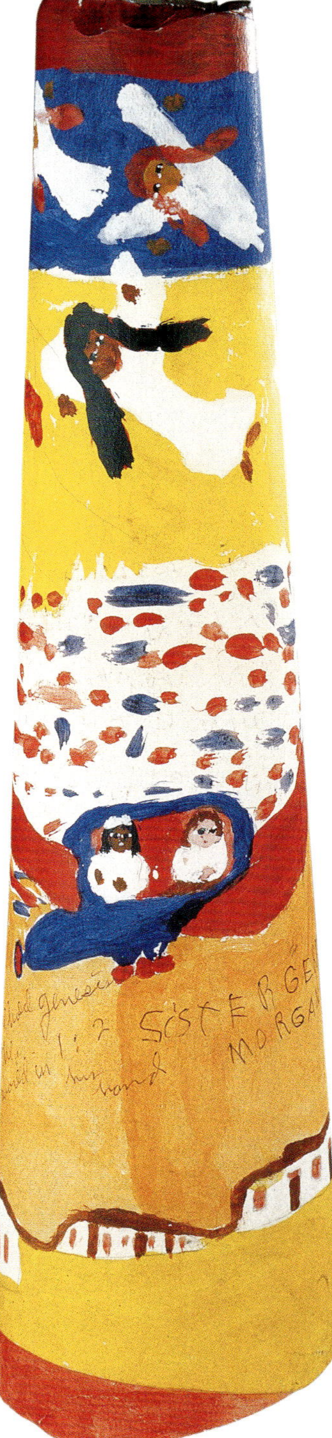

Sister Gertrude Morgan was called to preach in her thirties and devoted the rest of her life to ministering to needy children and evangelizing. In the mid-1950s, she received a message from God telling her that she was destined to be the bride of Christ. From that time on, she wore only white clothing. Through her ecstatic and often apocalyptic art she produced visual aids to reinforce her message of salvation.

Morgan used this paper megaphone to sing and chant her gospel message from a kiosk at the New Orleans Jazz and Heritage Festival. Rolled into a loose cone stitched together with heavy thread and safety-pinned for good measure, the paper is painted with a wide swath of orange and vivid primary colors interrupted by white and black. Flying over the buildings below, Sister Gertrude sits beside Jesus in the cockpit of a small airplane. Above them, angels soar around the apex of the cone.

Morgan customarily intermingled writing with images in her paintings. Just below the plane is penned "he hold the world in his hands," as well as a reference to Genesis 1:2. Wrapping around the megaphone just above the plane is a thick band of pencilled script interspersed with spots of red and blue. Enough of the faded lettering remains to see that it spells out a variant of one of the artist's own poems: "Jesus is my air/Plane, you hold/the world in your hand, you/Guide me through the land/ Jesus is my air Plane I/say Jesus is my air/Plane We're striving for/That Promised land. Come/On, Join our Band let's make/it in that Kingdom land."[1]

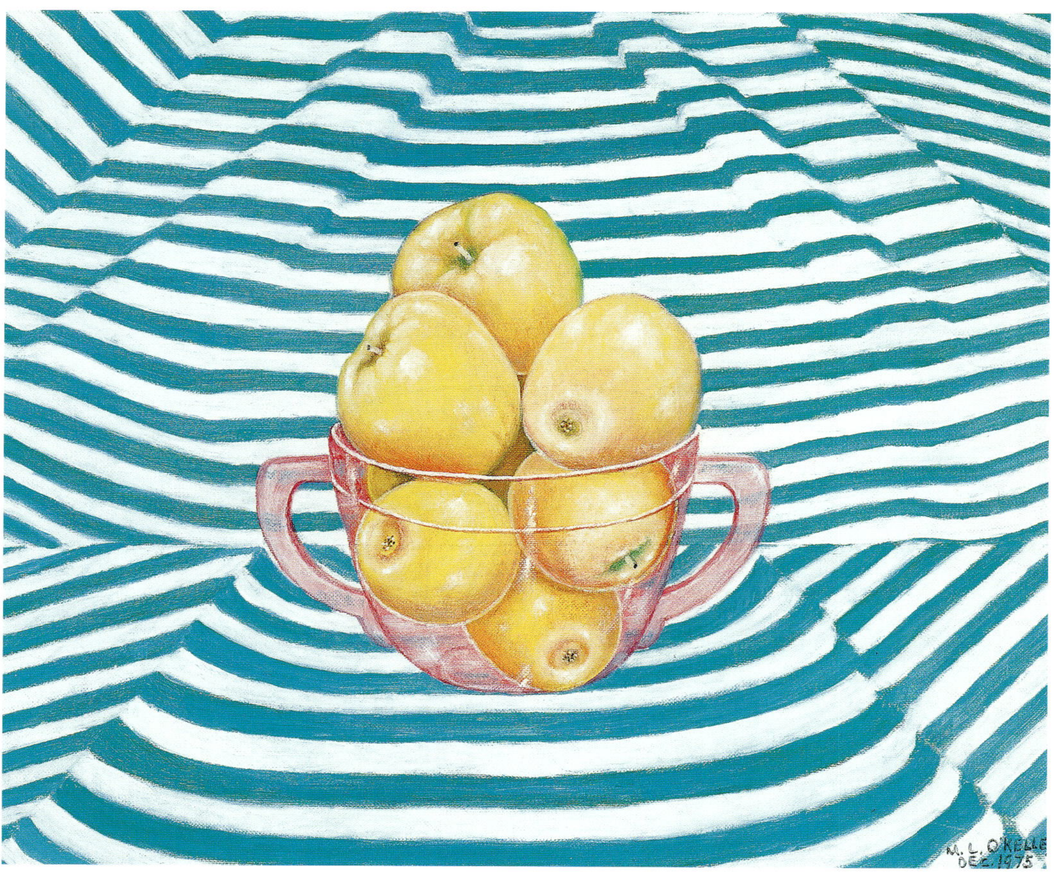

Cat. 59

Mattie Lou O'Kelley

1908–1997
Maysville, Georgia

Untitled, 1975
Oil on canvas
15¼ × 19¼ inches
Acquired from the artist, 1990
1997.99

In Mattie Lou O'Kelley's untitled still life, golden apples nestle in a pink glass bowl set on a billowing striped tablecloth. Her use of clean, crisp colors conveys the essence of warm, bright summer sunshine.

The painting is deceptively simple. Set squarely in the middle of the composition, the transparent bowl is perfectly frontal, its handles extended outward. Evenly shifting the triad of primary colors, O'Kelley has used a balanced group of green-blue, violet-red, and orange-yellow of equal saturation with touches of orange-red. The subtly colored and shaded apples, each barely haloed in light, demonstrate O'Kelley's accomplished draftsmanship. The folds of the cloth are carefully arranged in almost perfect symmetry, but slight variations in the pattern provide visual interest and the stripes create an almost hypnotic rhythm. In fact, the spatial relationship between bowl and tabletop cannot be resolved—the bowl hovers above an impossible object.

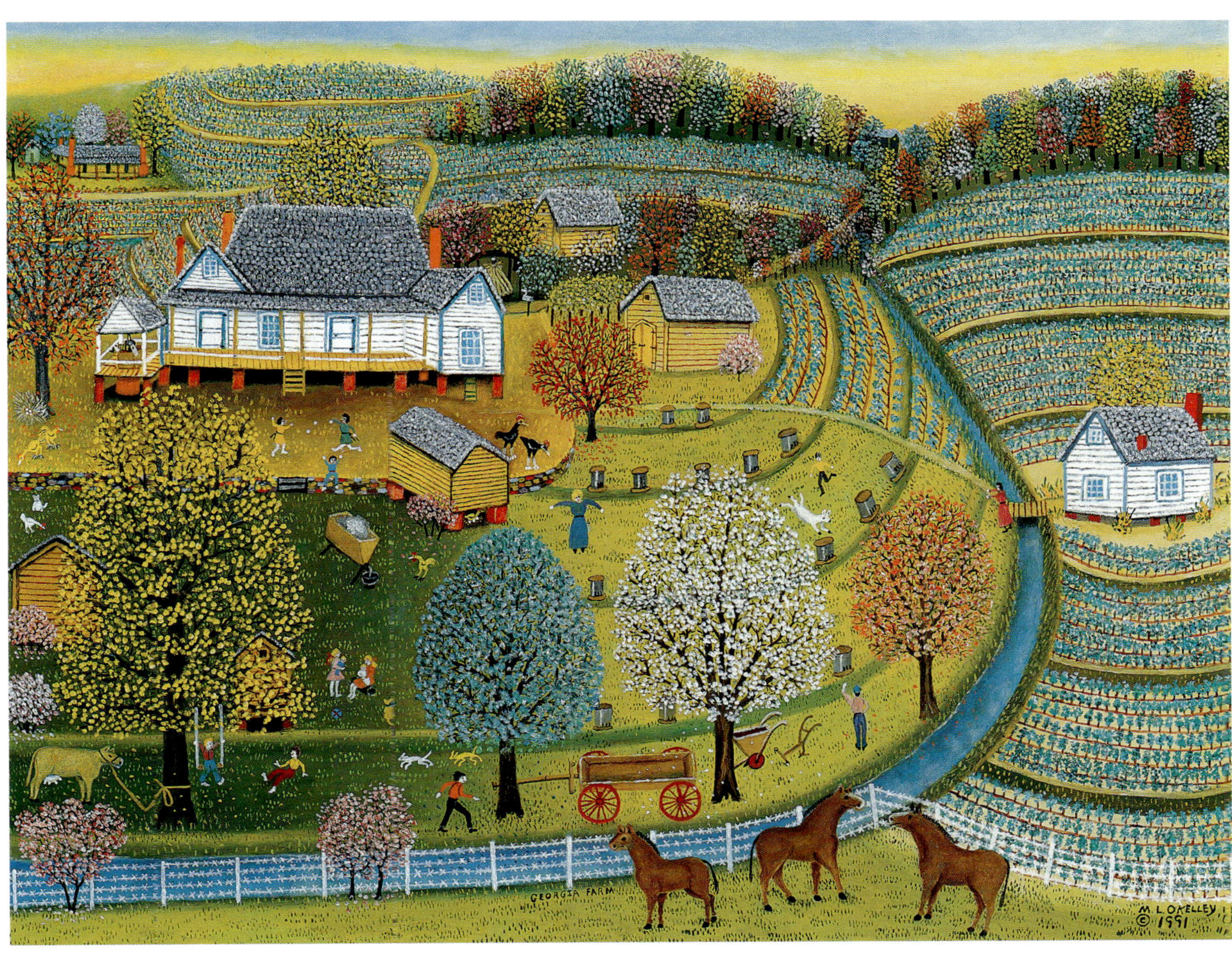

Cat. 60

Mattie Lou O'Kelley

1908–1997
Decatur, Georgia

Georgia Farm, 1991
Acrylic on canvas
23⅜ × 31⅜ inches
Acquired from the artist, 1991
1996.184

O'Kelley is best known as a memory painter. "An exquisite recorder of time and place," as Robert Bishop described her,[1] she painted embellished recollections of her childhood on her parents' hill farm in north Georgia. She began to pick cotton, the family's cash crop, at age six. As she grew older, she made quilts, tended livestock, and canned vegetables.

Simple joys fill this image. Abundance and fertility reign on this prosperous farm, from the rows of neatly planted vegetables to the nest with four eggs tucked under an orange-leafed tree. A hen roosts beneath an outbuilding, and at least seven children play. Something of the peaceable kingdom lingers here: a cat sits placidly by while a chicken pecks fearlessly a few feet away.

O'Kelley painted large scenes such as this by applying small dabs of color to the canvas. The resulting texture is reminiscent of needlework, especially in areas of repetitive patterning, such as the ranks of turquoise crops in buff fields. She distorts perspective so that space is flattened, creating remarkable planar arrangements of color and design. Scale is altered as well—chickens are bigger than the children playing in front of them. Perhaps the most personal element of O'Kelley's paintings is their idiosyncratic color, particularly the fantastically colored trees for which she is well known. In *Georgia Farm*, plants wear leaves of every conceivable candied tint. Even the more naturalistic hues are immoderately vivid.

O'Kelley painted with her canvas lying flat on a table. To reach the top, she would move to the other side of the table and paint upside down. "I start in with the main things first, just sketchin', then I work in the little stuff. I usually put the sky first, workin' around the edge. My hand shakes just a little bit so it's easier that way."[2]

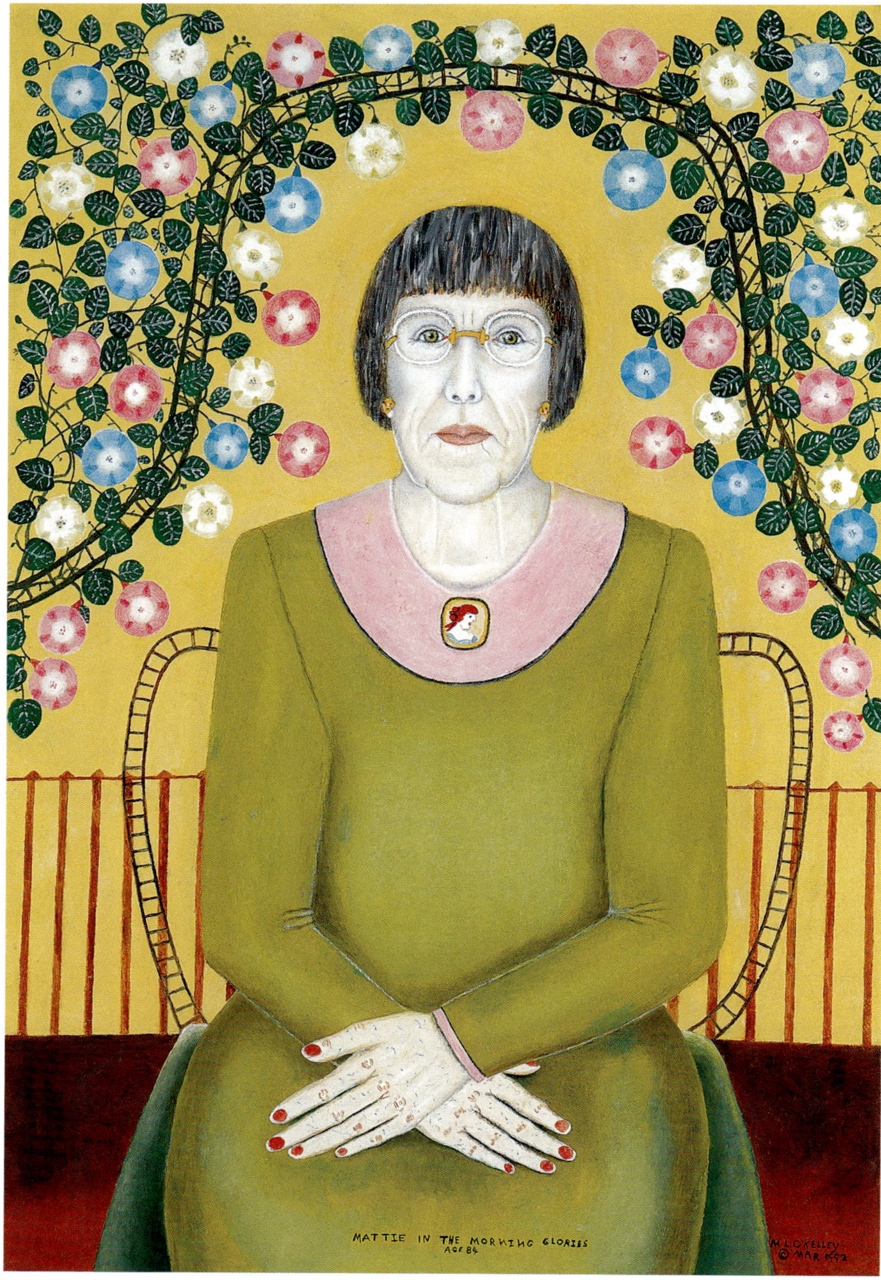

Cat. 61

Mattie Lou O'Kelley

1908–1997
Decatur, Georgia

Mattie in the Morning Glories, 1992
Oil on canvas
39⅛ × 27⅜ inches
Acquired from the artist, 1992
1996.30

THIS IS THE LATER of two self-portraits O'Kelley painted for Marshall Hahn. In it, the eighty-four-year-old artist wears a cameo pin Hahn brought her from Italy, characteristically enriching its colors from the pale tones of the original jewel.

In contrast to the bright but harmonious tints in which she rendered the blossoms of the arbor above her, she clothed herself in sour-apple green and its complement, pink, and set herself against a lemon yellow background. Assisted by the geometric simplification of the rigid body—reminiscent of limner paintings—the trio of astringent hues disrupts what might otherwise be a cloying scene.

The artist's hands bear the marks of a lifetime of hard work. Although O'Kelley complained that her hands looked ugly—in life and in the portrait—this artist, who regularly sweetened her childhood memories as she interpreted them on canvas, chose here to paint her hands as they were. Her one concession to vanity seems to have been adorning her nails with bright red polish to match her ruby lipstick.

Morning glories had a special significance for O'Kelley. They grew wild around her tiny house in Maysville, Georgia ("just for me," she said),[1] and she often painted them in baskets brimming with floral splendor. "Sometimes I wish I had all the morning glories I ever painted and gave a morning glory show in dead of the winter," she wrote.[2]

Cat. 62

John Perates

ca. 1895–1970
Portland, Maine

St. Peter and St. Paul, 1940s
Carved wood with paint
73⅞ × 39 × 5⅛ inches
Acquired from Keny Galleries, 1998
1998.40

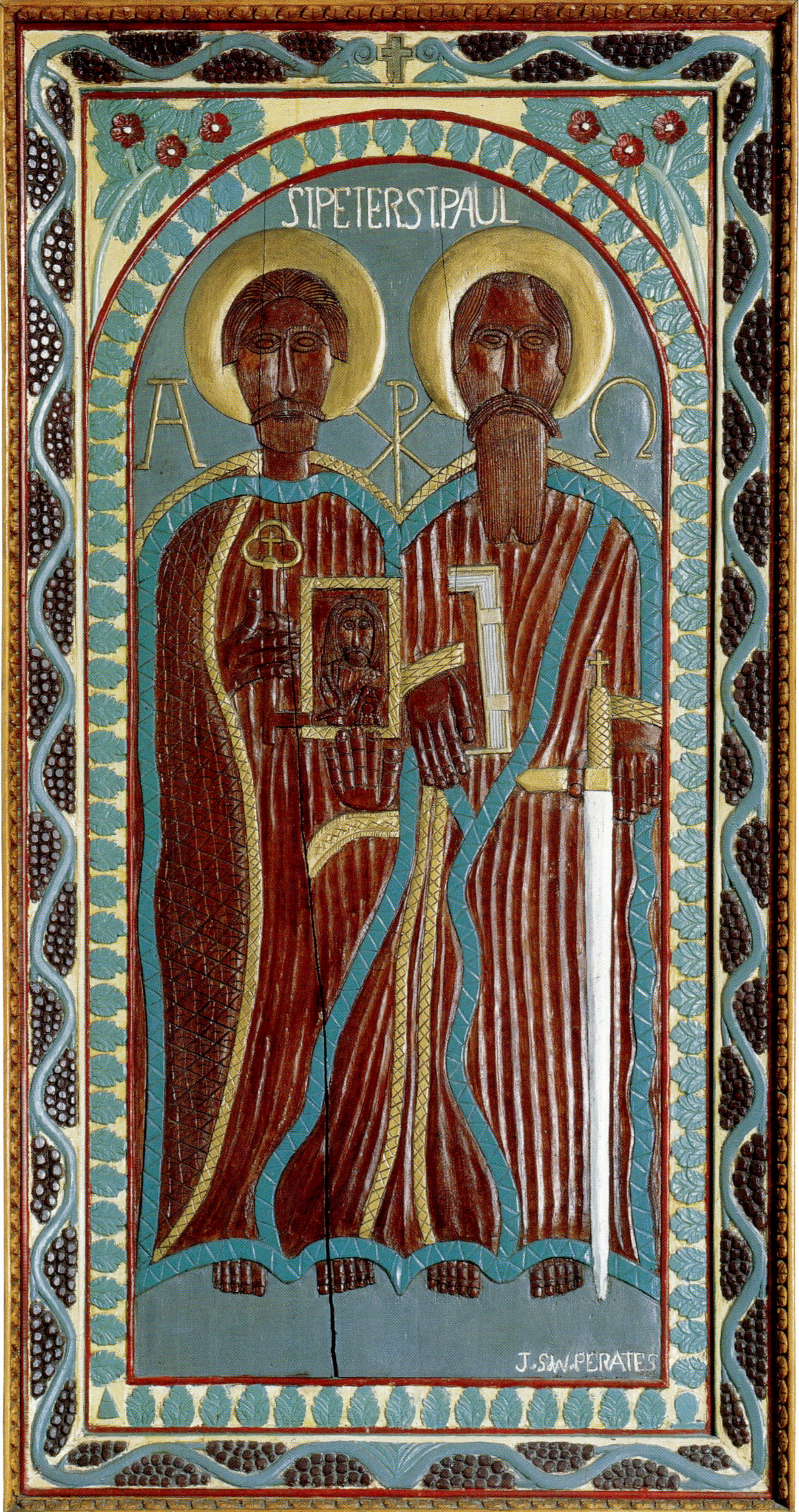

Three rich vegetal borders surround John Perates's representation of St. Peter and St. Paul. The outermost consists of an unpainted frame depicting leaves nestled within leaves. Inside, bunches of purple grapes hang from an undulating teal vine. On the innermost border, acanthus leaves of a soft sea-green rest on pale yellow. These subtle colors harmonize the patterning of the borders and prepare the eye for the tracery and proliferation of low-relief ornamentation adorning the main figures. Zigzags, cross-hatchings, and gold trim bedeck the chitons of the two apostles, and lozenges proliferate on Peter's himation. Meticulous striations bring texture and order to hair and beards and surround the eyes of the saints with radiant eyelashes. Identical treatment of the men's robes and similar carving techniques on their faces unite them visually.

Perates was trained as a woodcarver by his grandfather in Greece before he immigrated to Maine, where he became a cabinetmaker. As World War II approached he began the religious carving for which his faith, birthplace, and profession had prepared him: to carve a series of panels depicting the life of Christ, the composers of the New Testament, and the earliest church fathers. Perates derived his style from the tradition of Byzantine icon painting that he had known since childhood. In the established manner, St. Peter holds in his right hand the key to the kingdom of God and in his left an icon of Christ Pantocrator (Ruler of All). St. Paul grasps the sword of his martyrdom, while his book of epistles disappears into the folds of his robe.

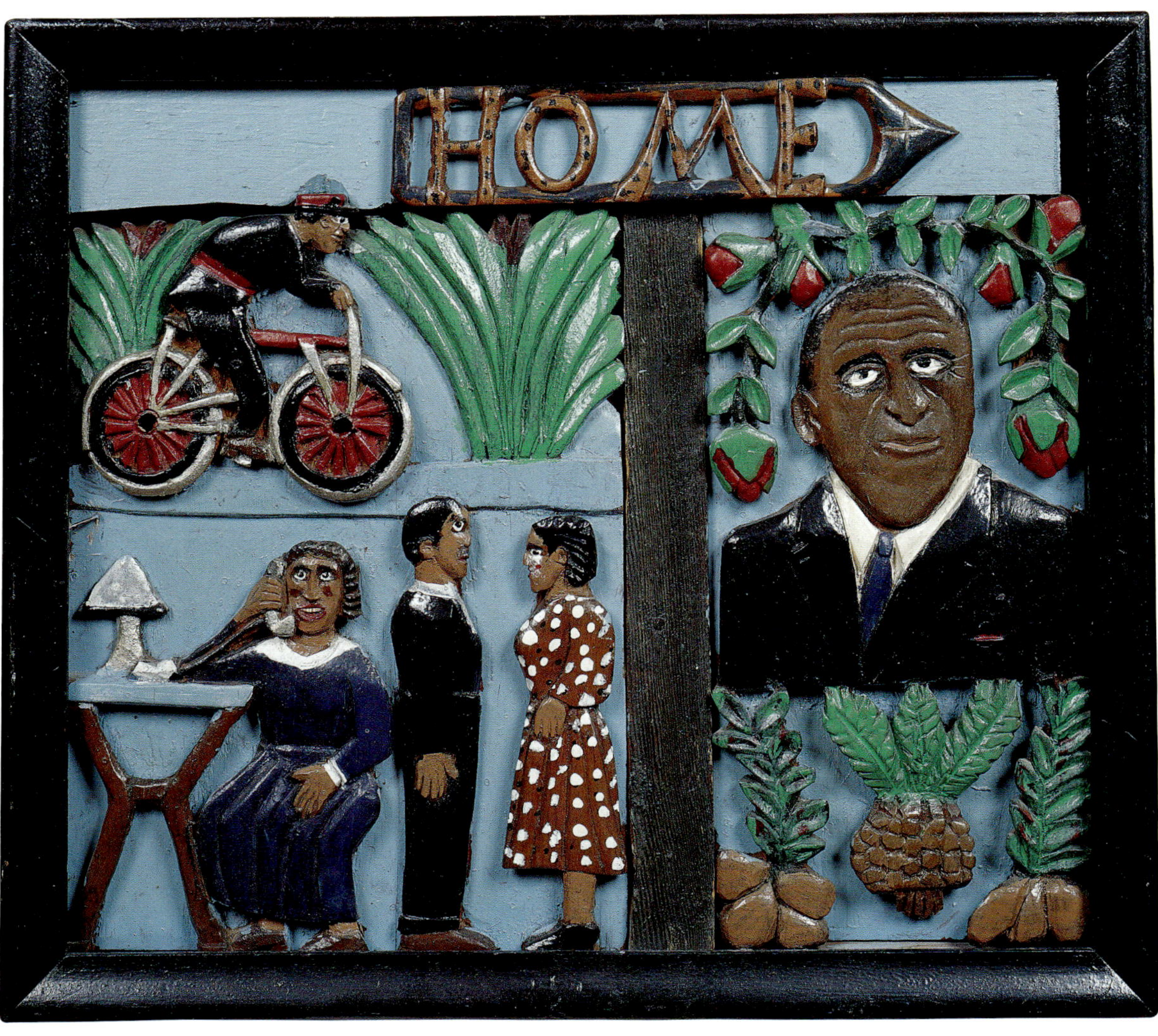

Cat. 63

Elijah Pierce

1892–1984
Columbus, Ohio

Three Ways to Send a Message: Telephone, Telegram, Tell-a-Woman, ca. 1941
Carved wood with paint
15½ x 18 x 1½ inches
Acquired from Keny Galleries, 1998
1998.80

THREE WAYS TO SEND A MESSAGE: *Telephone, Telegram, Tell-a-Woman* displays the adept carving and assured, complex design Elijah Pierce achieved at the height of his artistic powers. The relief is deeply cut, but the overall effect is of a fairly flat pictorial space polychromed in soothing colors.

The left panel of the composition illustrates a misogynistic old joke about the relative effectiveness of common methods of communication. A telegraph deliveryman speeds down a road. Below him, a woman talks on the telephone and a couple talk in person. Pierce considered gossip a noteworthy vice; he dealt with it more than once in his art.[1] The right panel contains a portrait of African American scientist and professor George Washington Carver haloed by boughs laden with fruit like the persimmons that grew at his boyhood home.[2] Carver's bust surmounts a display of sweet potatoes and peanuts, subjects of some of his most productive agricultural investigations. Across the top panel the word "Home" is enigmatically carved.

The relationship between text, tableaux, and portrait is unclear. A shift from self-evident to more subtle moral messages is seen in other multipaneled Pierce works, such as *Pearl Harbor and the African Queen*.[3] In *Three Ways to Send a Message*, Pierce juxtaposes the communications of daily life with the transmission of knowledge, encompassing information's public, private, helpful, and harmful aspects.

Cat. 64

Elijah Pierce

1892–1984
Columbus, Ohio

Christ and Lady, 1968
Carved wood with paint and glitter
21½ x 16½ x 1¼ inches
Acquired from Keny Galleries, 1994
1997.102

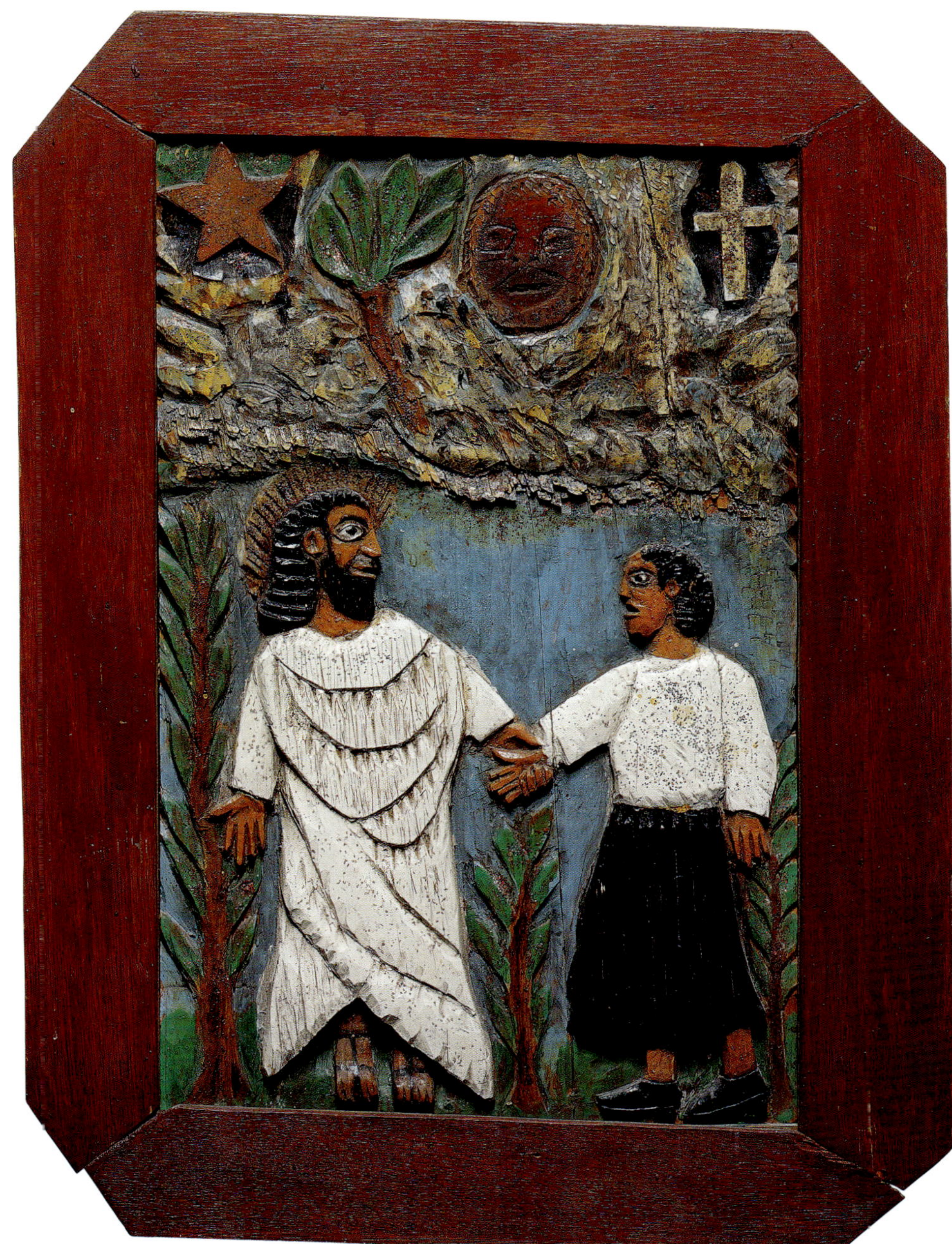

PIERCE BELIEVED that God led him to preach through his carvings. "I usually pray over a piece of wood before I ever put a knife into it," Pierce said. "I'm depending on Him for my inspiration and He gives it to me."[1]

Pierce derived many early images from cartoons and popular media. The simplification and immediacy of those sources appear in this relief of Jesus clasping a woman's hand. Her twentieth-century garb suggests that the scene may represent Christ offering spiritual guidance to a modern woman; however, the items arranged across the top of the picture suggest that it may have been inspired by a biblical passage. Above the figures shine four symbols for Christ, who is referred to in the scriptures as the morning star, the tree of life, and the sun of righteousness.[2] All but the cross, signifier of Jesus' resurrection, appear in the final chapter of Revelation, which describes the new Paradise. In addition, that chapter promises the faithful that they will see the Savior face-to-face, as the woman does here. The deep hue of Pierce's sun may illustrate Revelation 22:5, which declares that the sun's light will be unnecessary because God illuminates Paradise.[3]

Proficiently carved and tidily painted, this piece includes finely executed details such as Christ's sandals and the tiny ears of both figures. Pierce fashioned the sun from a knot in the panel. The carving technique conveys a sense of spontaneity and interest in texture. Top and bottom sections—perhaps Heaven and Earth—are separated by a band of fringed wood. Swirling blues and yellows embellish the deeply grooved surface of the top section. Glitter glistens on the surface, suggesting the radiance of Paradise.

Pierce began each work by drawing a detailed image, sometimes tracing or copying his mass media sources. He carved soft woods, usually pine, with a pocketknife and chisel, then sanded and painted the surface in bright paints before finishing the piece with varnish or shellac and occasionally a sprinkling of glitter.

Cat. 65

Martin Ramirez

ca. 1895–ca. 1963
Auburn, California

Inmaculada, 1950s
Crayon, pencil, watercolor, and collaged papers
92 × 45 inches
Acquired from Phyllis Kind Gallery, 1999
1999.93

While hospitalized as schizophrenic for over thirty years, Martin Ramirez never spoke, but he created a body of powerful artworks built around a group of personal icons, including a Madonna figure he depicted many times. Although she is one of Ramirez's favorite images, little has been written about her importance in the artist's body of work.

Ramirez spent his early years in the western Mexico state of Jalisco, where he probably saw Roman Catholic icons, locally carved figures, and regional interpretations of European religious symbols. Appearing on *retablos* behind altars across Mexico is the *Virgin Inmaculada*, or Virgin of the Immaculate Conception, which presents the Madonna as the woman clothed with the sun described in the twelfth chapter of Revelation.[1] She often appears crowned with stars, standing on the moon, with a serpent beneath her feet. In addition to such conventional paintings, Ramirez would have seen *santos* carved in the indigenous style, including, possibly, figures of the Virgin clothed in the region's traditional attire.[2]

The central figure in *Inmaculada* is dressed in Indian clothing from the *huaraches* on her feet to her *huipil*, or handmade shirt of traditional design. On her shirt are agricultural motifs handed down from pre-conquest days. Her crown bears parabolic cave symbols—also seen in pre-Columbian designs—while its spikes are tipped with round blue stars or celestial orbs. She stands on a globe like the moon of the traditional *Inmaculada*, and beneath her feet is a snake. The snake, a traditional form of Satan, is charged with consequence. It is master of the underworld—locus of death, but to the Meso-American also a place of magic and regeneration.[3]

Ramirez's mastery of space and patterning is unmistakable. Areas shrink and swell through the use of repetitive line and rhythmic arcs. The curved forms below the figures' feet appear at once convex—as shells—and concave—as caverns. Striations in the women's garments cascade from neckline to waist to hem. Energy flows up and out from the hands, cuffs, and crown of the larger figure. The pottery traditions of Jalisco, handed down from pre-Columbian days, may have provided Ramirez with a model for the fine linear patterning of his drawings as well as his use of the deer and dancer imagery that appear in many other works.[4]

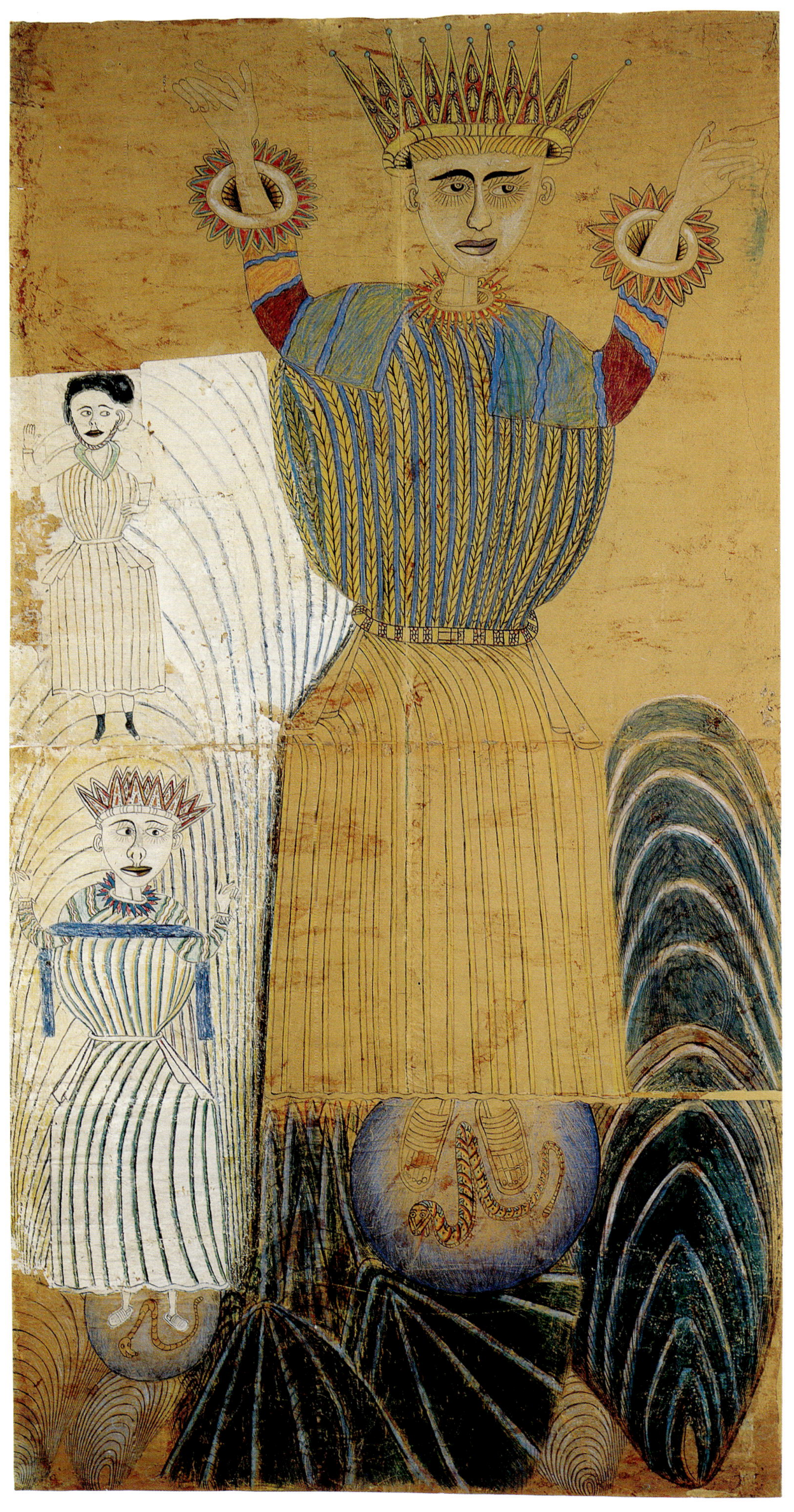

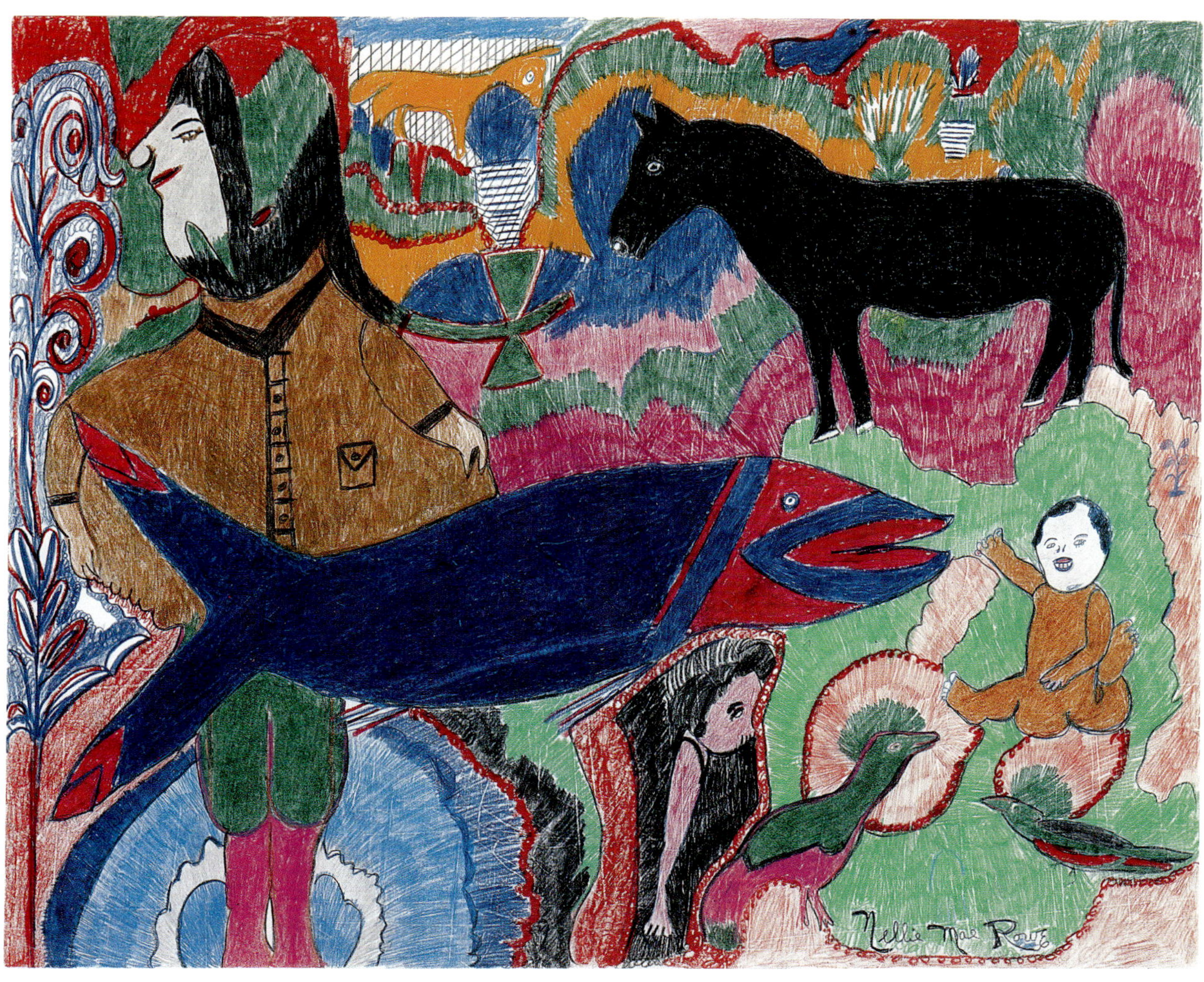

Cats. 66–68

Nellie Mae Rowe

1900–1982
Vinings, Georgia

Red and Blue Fish, ca. 1979
Crayon and pencil on paper
19 × 24 inches
Acquired from Charles Locke, 1994
1997.107

Woman in Orange and Red, ca. 1979
Crayon and pencil on paper
19 × 24 inches
Acquired from Charles Locke, 1994
1997.108

Happy Days, 1981
Crayon and pencil on paper
18 × 24 inches
Acquired from Charles Locke, 1994
1997.105

Upon the death of her husband, Nellie Mae Rowe's passion to create erupted in various media, including gloriously tinted drawings. Rowe's palette ranged from ecstatic brilliance to the elegant subtlety of *Happy Days*. The texture of her crayon strokes covered a similarly varied scope, with heavily encrusted color abutting feathery light passages, as in *Red and Blue Fish*.

Rowe often drew portraits or pictures of everyday life, historical events, and childhood memories. She explained some works to her patrons and titled others. But for many drawings she provided no clue to unravel the skeins knitted by her fecund imaginings. Her improvisational creative processes assured that compositions and objects within them were protean. "I draw what's on my mind," she said. "If I'm going to draw a tree, I wouldn't know what kind it's going to be until I get started. Then it may turn out to be different from what I started it to be."[1] Her friend and dealer Judith Alexander recalled that Rowe would sometimes seem irritated when pressed to identify an element of her drawings and respond, "It is what it is."[2] Rowe's drawings constituted a form of worship: "I try to draw because He is wonderful to me. I just have to keep drawing until He says, 'Well done, Nellie, you have been faithful.' Then I will know that I have finished my work."[3]

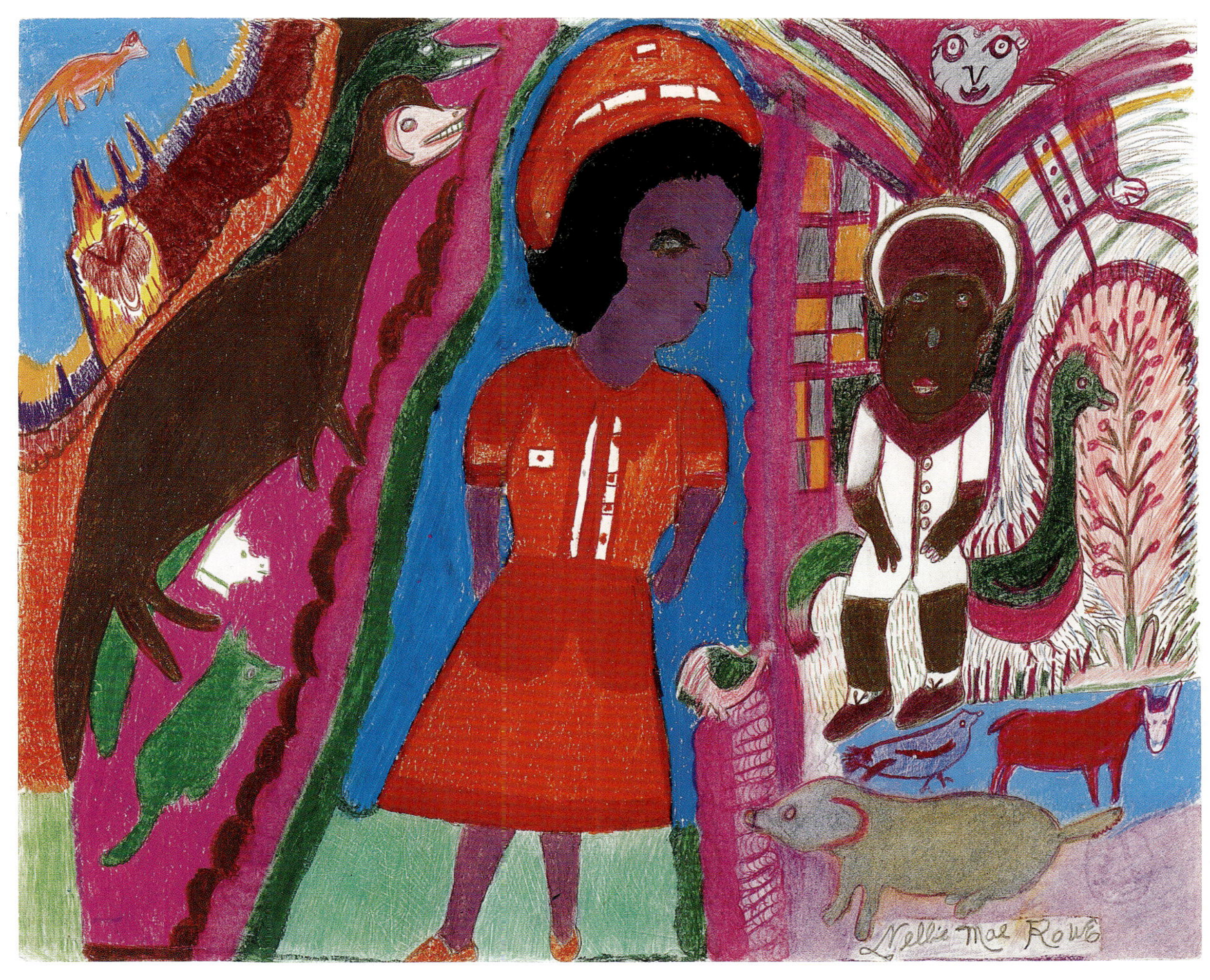
Nellie Mae Rowe

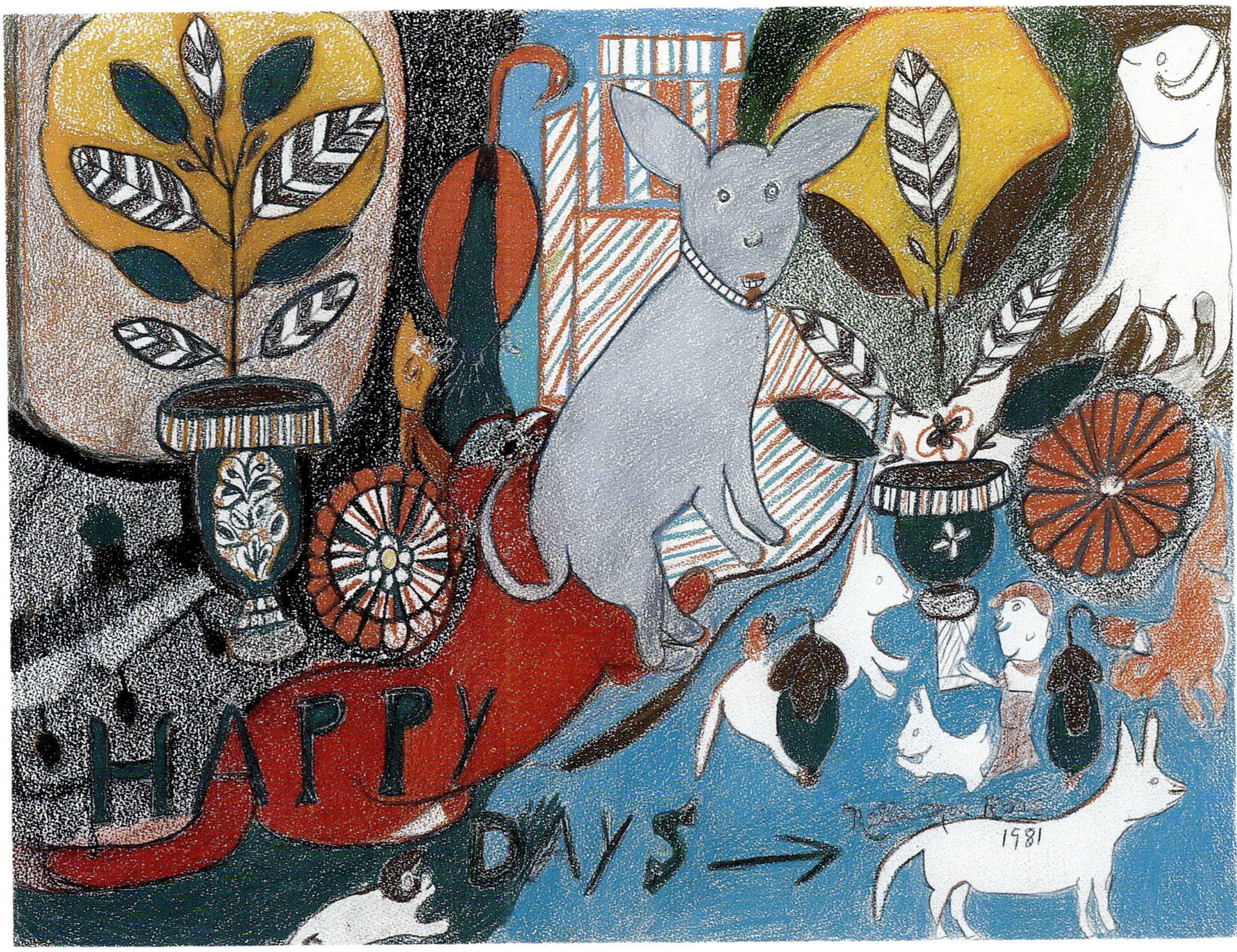
HAPPY
DAYS
1981

Cat. 69

Mary Shelley

Born 1950
Ithaca, New York

Cow and Daffodil Buds, 1988
Carved wood with paint
21½ x 23 x 1½ inches
Acquired from Charles Locke, 1993
1999.97

Mary Shelley was playing with her reputation as a carver of cows when she combined a bovine with a magnified image of daffodil buds. "Affectionate, sweet, and a bit klutzy,"[1] cows are familiar beasts to Shelley, whose grandparents owned a dairy farm and whose mother studied animal husbandry in college. A symbol that "doesn't bore me," the cow has proven potent and flexible as employed by Shelley, conveying different themes and representing various aspects of her shifting concerns and experiences. Recalling the placidity of cows waiting to be fed or milked, she contrasts their quiet expectation with the anxiety of the artist awaiting the occasional sustenance of nourishing praise. Shelley admires the patience and immediacy cows exemplify. "Getting through the arduous work of carving," Shelley says, requires "focusing on the moment." In some of her works, cows have stood in for the domesticated woman. Underlying the layers of personal meaning in this piece may be a faint resonance of political comment: in the late 1970s, as the Equal Rights Amendment faced probable defeat in the U.S. Senate, Shelley vowed to continue carving cows until women received the same constitutional protections as men.

Working from photographs, Shelley usually produces groups of eight or nine thematically related pieces. This group was inspired by photos of flowers she took using a newly acquired close-up lens. An artist who enjoys the formal nuances of size and scale, she indulged herself by reveling in the carved details of this whimsical juxtaposition in which the solidity of sharply rendered forms contrasts with the dream-like implausibility of distorted dimensions. Arcing across the sky, a yellow band returns the viewer's gaze to the cow and daffodils by counteracting the diagonal movement of the carving strokes and the upward thrust of the scene's many verticals. The flat gold-leafed inner frame is a remainder of Shelley's former career as a signpainter: the inner frames of her later pieces are carved as well as leafed.

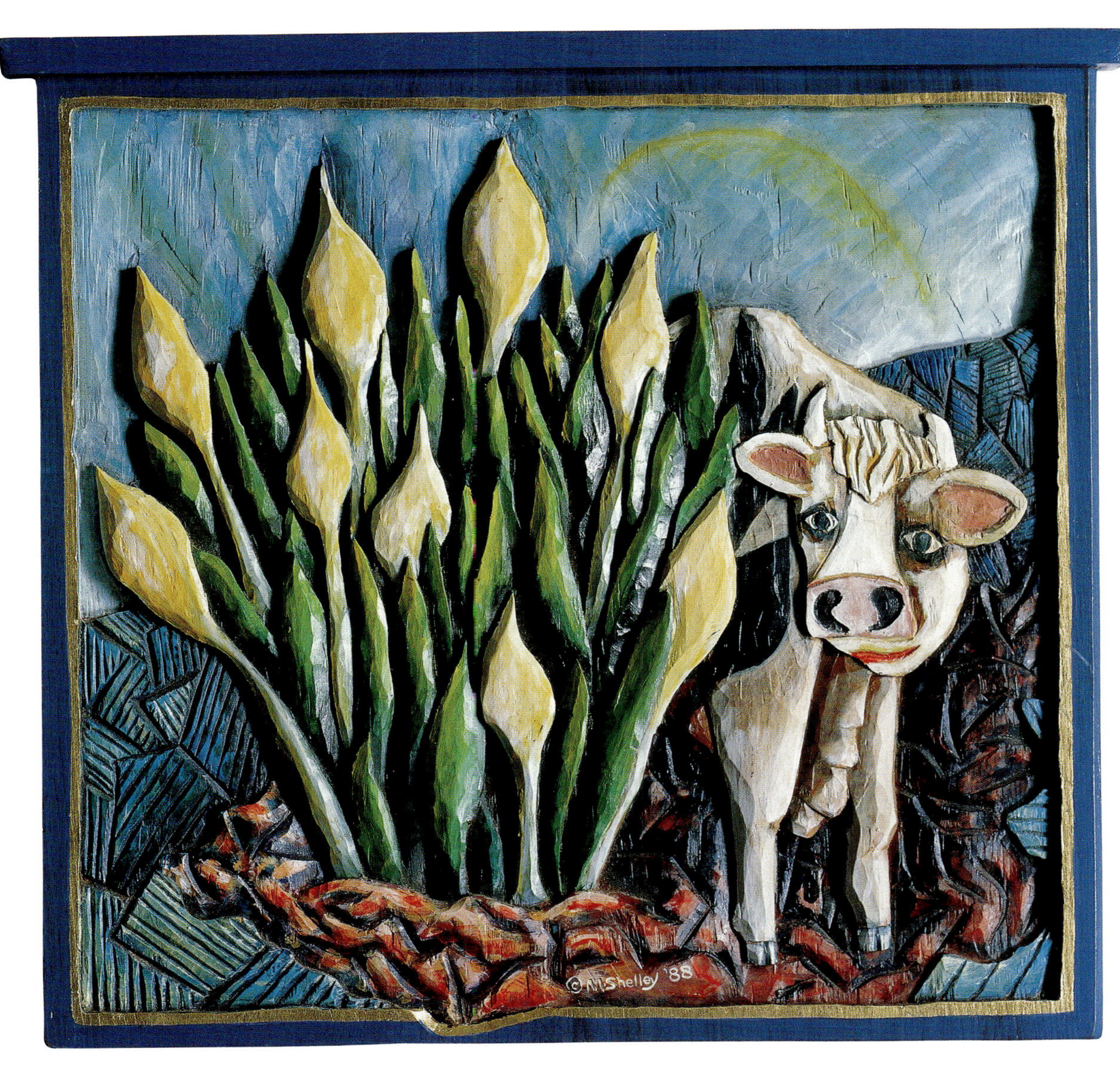
©M.Shelley '88

Cat. 70

Herbert Singleton

Born 1945
New Orleans, Louisiana

Hallelujah Door, 1993
Carved wooden door with enamel paint
115¼ × 48¾ × 1¾ inches
Acquired from Barrister's Gallery, 1994
1996.185

Herbert Singleton turns found wood into records of life in the New Orleans neighborhood of Algiers, illustrating the resilience needed to survive in this dangerous environment. Robert Knott finds the community a double-edged sword for Singleton, creating an array of personal problems while inspiring his art.[1] "The way I see it, I'm between good and evil. You got to endure to the end. That's the name of the game," Singleton has said.[2]

Singleton most frequently carves detailed scenes on discarded planks and doors. His most common themes are street life, the oppression of blacks, biblical stories, and the New Orleans jazz funeral. With consummate narrative skill, Singleton depicts a jazz funeral on the *Hallelujah Door*.

Across the top rail, mourners follow a casket carried by pallbearers. Interwoven among those figures are the words "Glad you dead you old rascal you," from a 1929 song by New Orleans jazzman Sam Theard. In the lyrics, a cuckolded speaker rants against the adulterous visitor who has stolen the favors of his wife, announcing, "I'll be glad when you dead, you rascal, you!"

The three pairs of door panels display events of the death rites. The lower pair depicts the body lying in state at the funeral parlor, hands clasped and head on a small pillow, and a female mourner dressed entirely in white. The central pair of panels displays a gravedigger and the above-ground burial vault typically used in New Orleans. Singleton's dealer Andy Antippas believes the artist may be making a political point here, comparing the decent burials given those who can afford them with the grim alternative: interment in a potter's field, where the corpses float out of the earth during floods.[3] In the top panels, black angels and a black St. Peter welcome the soul to his eternal home.

Across the bottom rail, the word Hallelujah appears in large letters, signaling the moment when the body has passed over and the soul is saved. The exclamation expresses the joyful turning point between the sorrowful funeral procession and the celebratory return from the cemetery. Up the center stile strut the musicians, playing their instruments. On the outer stiles and central rails three second-line dancers wave bright handkerchiefs while four hold aloft umbrellas, whose presence distinguishes both the New Orleans jazz funeral and the funerals of some African communities. "Buck jumpers" cavort on the central rails. The bodies of the second-line dancers, offset across the breadth of the door, provide a visual analogy to jazz syncopation.

At the bottom of the right stile a woman in a red dress flouts convention, signifying the disappearance of traditional values in the community. Singleton has said, "In former times you would never see someone dressed in red in a funeral procession, because it shows disrespect to the dead."[4]

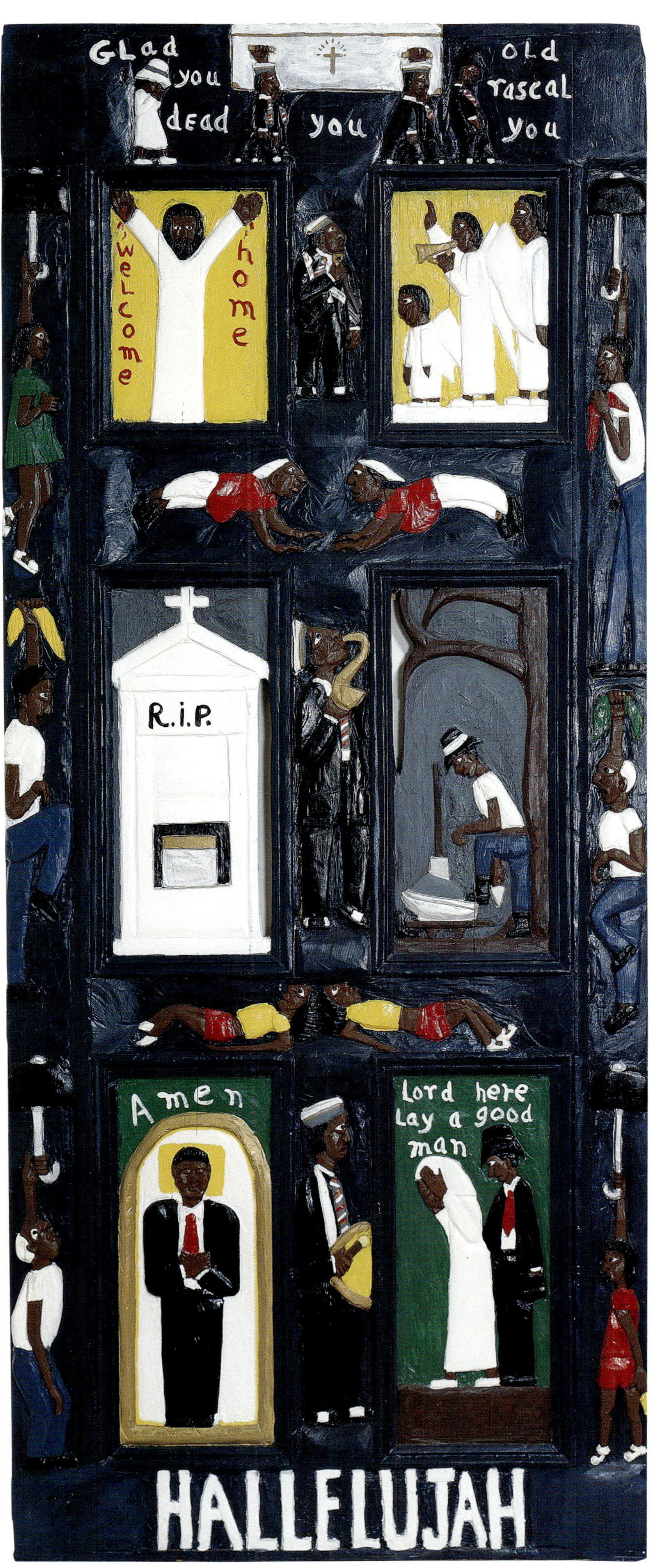

Glad you dead you
old rascal you
welcome home
R.I.P.
Amen
lord here lay a good man
HALLELUJAH

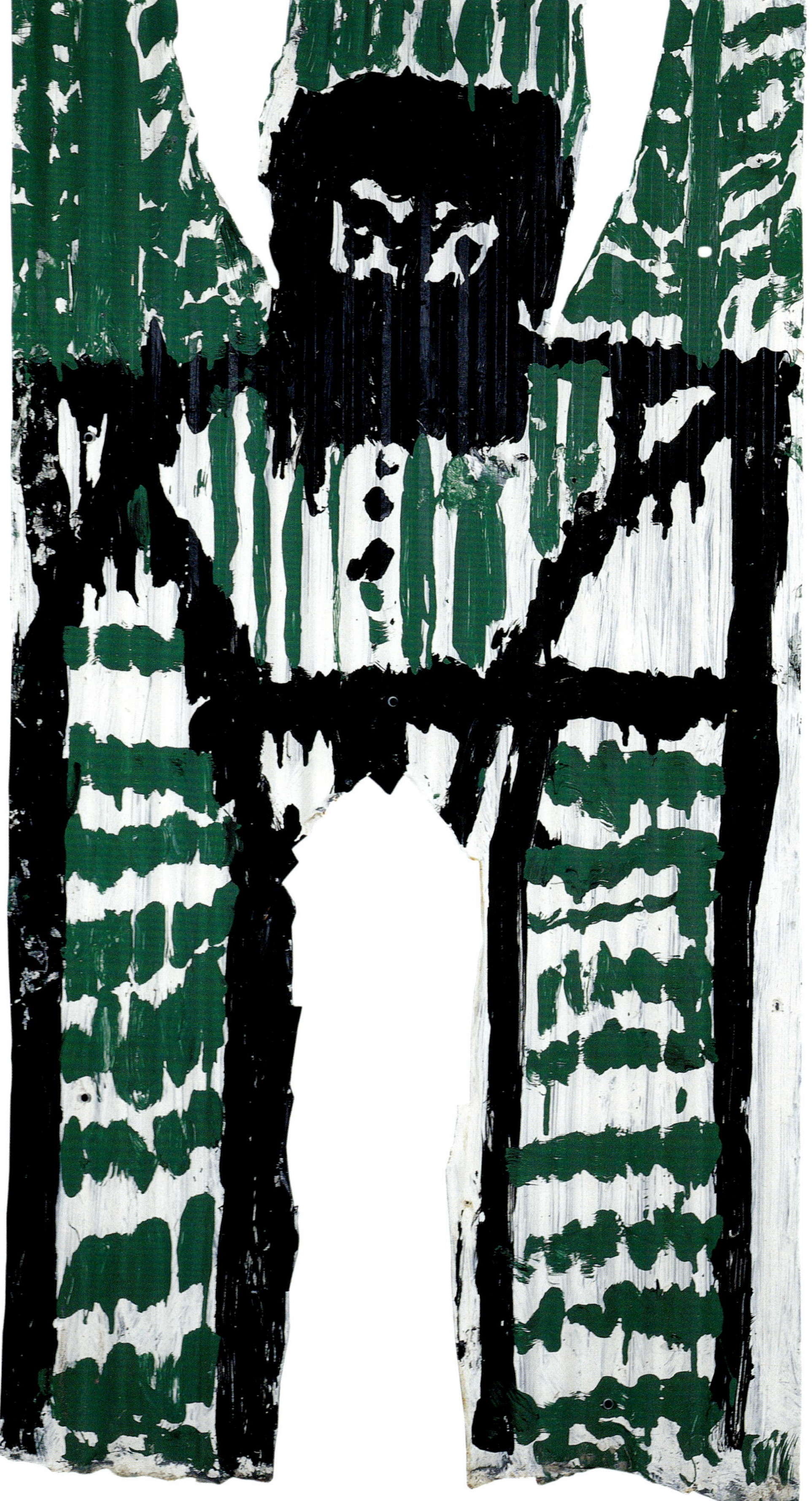

Cat. 71

Mary T. Smith

1904–1995
Hazelhurst, Mississippi

Untitled, 1980–1986
Paint on corrugated metal
49⅛ x 27 inches
Acquired from William S. Arnett, 1994
1996.187

Around 1980, Mary T. Smith began lining the fence surrounding her one-acre yard with representations of people and animals painted on corrugated metal and wood. After filling the fence, she moved on to her house, the doghouse, and her son's garage. She did it, she said, to decorate the yard and to glorify God. Located on a Mississippi highway, it soon became one of the best-known self-taught environments in the South. "I just be making pictures all the time. I put 'em up everywhere. People pass by in their car and they honk. They come look an' see my pictures," she said in 1983.[1]

Smith painted portraits of local people, herself, and spirits, often solitary and always frontal. She also painted members of her enormous menagerie of dogs, and occasionally other animals. The earliest figures, some over seven feet tall, have separate arms and legs attached with wire or nails.

The power of her early creations comes from their raw simplicity. Heavily outlined and created with only two or three unmixed colors, they frequently take the form of busts, much like the talking heads of television commentators. Her paintings often include phrases, such as "Hoo Hi Theh," "I was in a rake [wreck] the Lord was for me," or "Candy is what I want." This example depicts a man standing before a forest. Displayed near the highway, it may have reminded Smith of the changes she had seen in the countryside during her long life in rural Mississippi. Smith hacked the roofing material into a rough "W" shape with an axe, as the jagged edges testify. Rust on the support has bled through the paint, recalling the panel's original location in Smith's stunning chorus of outdoor celebrants.

Cat. 72

Mary T. Smith

1904–1995
Hazelhurst, Mississippi

Untitled, ca. 1986
Enamel paint on chipboard
48 x 27⅜ inches
Acquired from William S. Arnett, 1994
1997.109

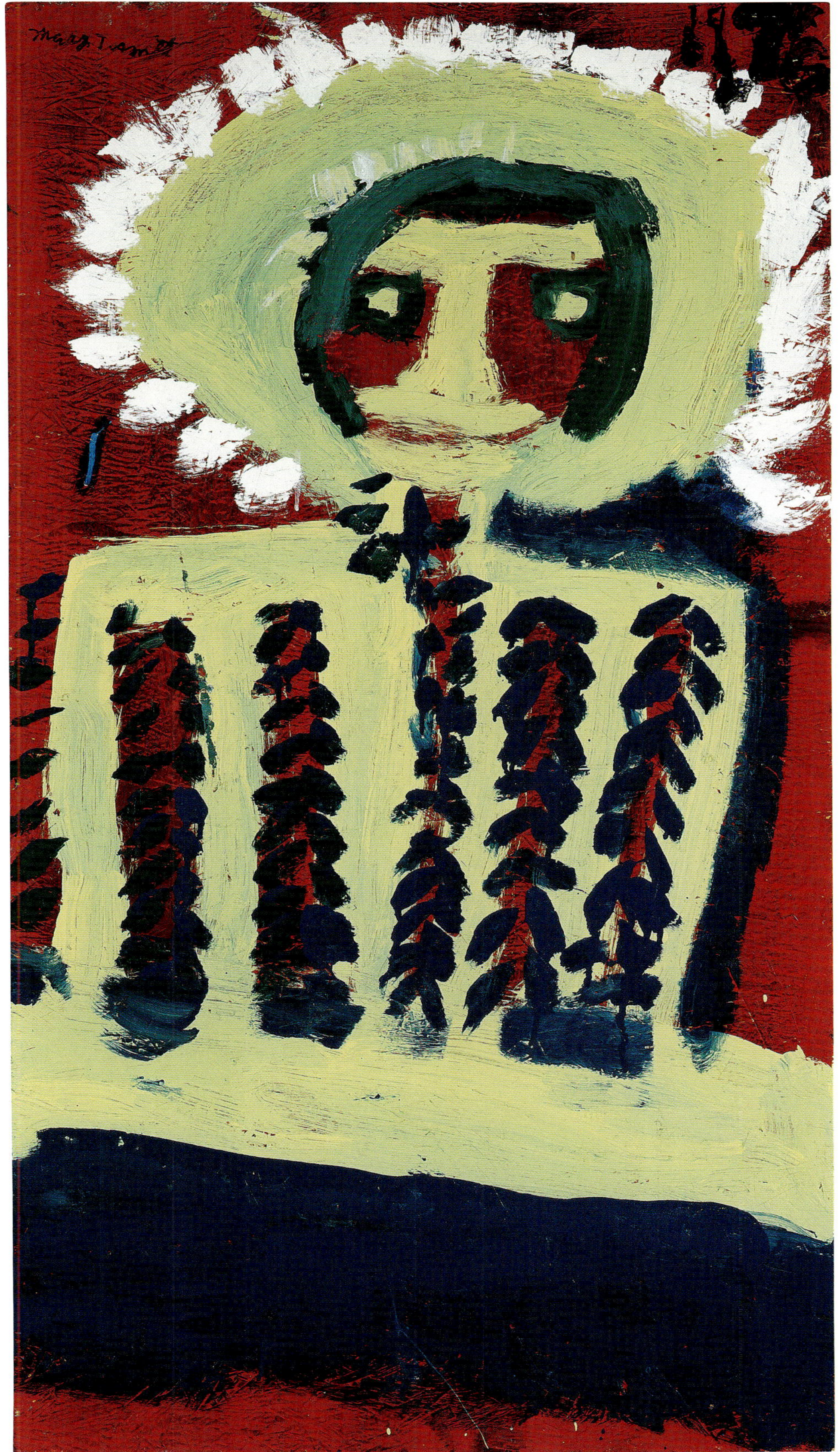

This painting owes its expressionistic energy and immediacy to Smith's quick and forceful brushwork. The thickly applied tertiary colors of chartreuse and dark teal are unusual for this artist, who normally used white, black, or both plus pure unmixed primary and secondary colors. Smith composed a perfectly flat figure, its only depth coming from the layered paint. Her arrangement of simple geometric shapes for the body is similar to the early painted metal pieces that adorned her yard. The subject's square torso and shoulders, stacked like building blocks, rise from a base of two broad areas of flat color. On this rectangle sits a simple circle—the imposing head—which radiates a white halo. The rich treatment of the head echoes the many Smith figures that wear elaborate hairdos or headdresses.

Although the date appears to read 1976—which would make this one of her earliest known works—stylistically this piece is much more closely related to Smith's later paintings, such as *The Great-Grandmother Me* of 1987 with its slashing dots of color,[1] and it is painted on the kind of regular, smooth-edged support more typical of the works she created after 1984. According to William Arnett, this may be a self-portrait.[2]

Although Smith was not a painter of Bible scenes, religious feeling pervades her art. "Look here," she said in 1983, pointing to the inscription on one of her works: "'The Lord is good. I know the Lord.' I paint pictures for the Lord."[3]

Cat. 73

Mose Tolliver

Born ca. 1920
Montgomery, Alabama

Self-Portrait of Me, 1987
House paint on plywood
24 × 23¾ inches
Acquired from William S. Arnett, 1994
1997.110

In startling contrast to Mose Tolliver's vigorous erotic scenes and peaceful nature motifs, some of his more grotesque self-portraits display distorted perspective, fierce mouths, and glaring eyes. Usually busts rather than the full-length figures Tolliver later adopted, they may be identified with the artist—despite their fantastic effect—by a cap of grizzled hair. This head's abstracted vertical red and yellow eyes resonate with similarly tinted nostrils over a monstrous toothy mouth. The neckless head is screwed onto a humped blue shoulder while the bottom of the pea green face is twisted in profile away from the frontal forehead. Tolliver's subjects typically fill the entire picture, but here the head presses aggressively against the frame while the asymmetrical composition further disquiets the viewer.

Although Tolliver painted this panel in the late 1980s, it is based on one of his earlier designs, in which he represented only the head because "I didn't know how to make the legs right on them then."[1] William Arnett has said that this series of self-portraits was inspired by the classically styled profile on a plaque that hung on the artist's bedroom wall.[2] After painting several variations on the subject, Tolliver identified the works in the series as self-portraits. When asked recently why he drew the features in such a distorted manner, Tolliver spoke of his desire to make these portraits different from his others, adding, "That's the way I wanted them."

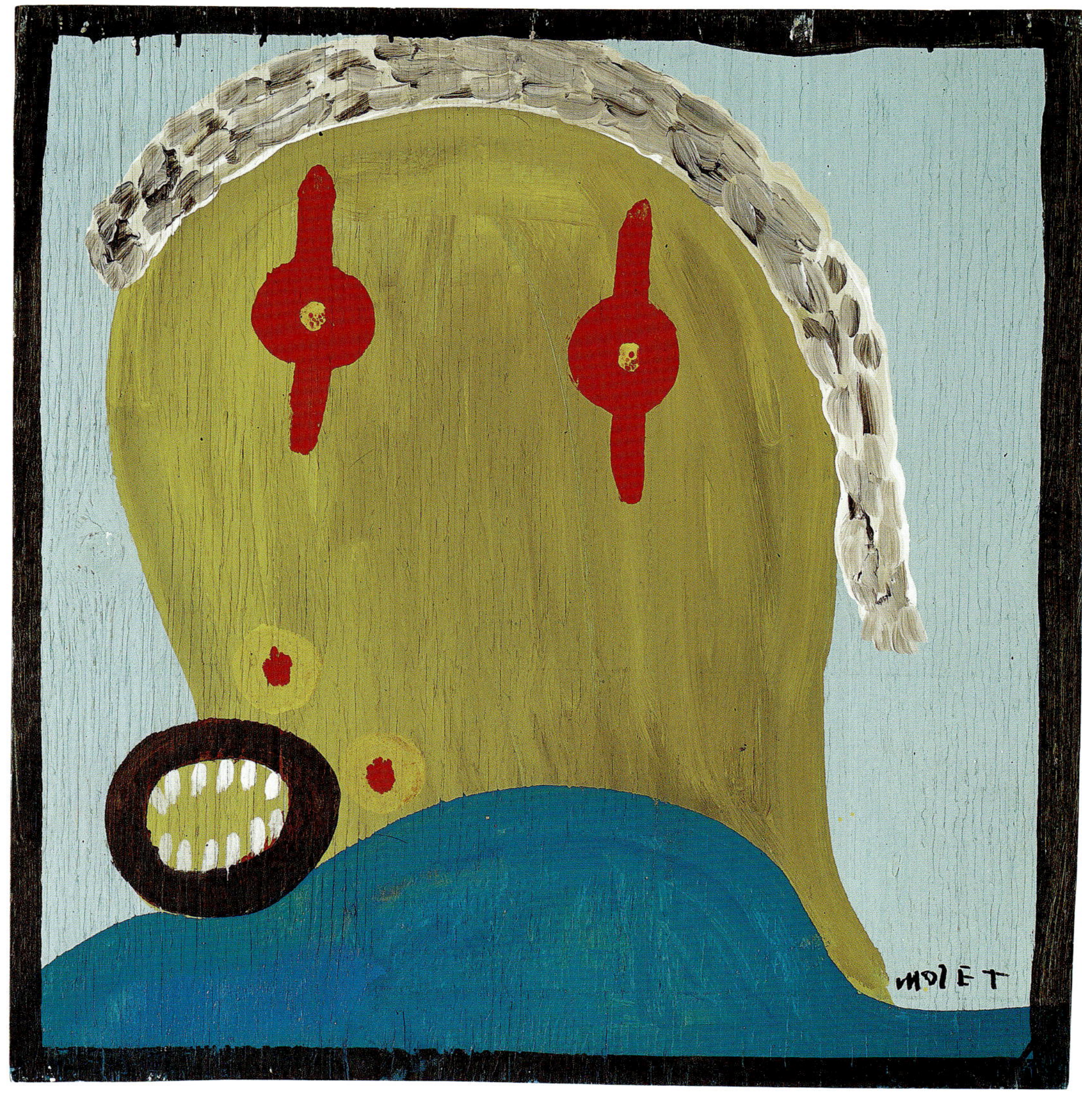

Cat. 74

Mose Tolliver

Born ca. 1920
Montgomery, Alabama

Self-Portrait of Me on Crutches, 1987
House paint on wood paneling
33 × 18½ inches
Acquired from William S. Arnett, 1994
1996.192

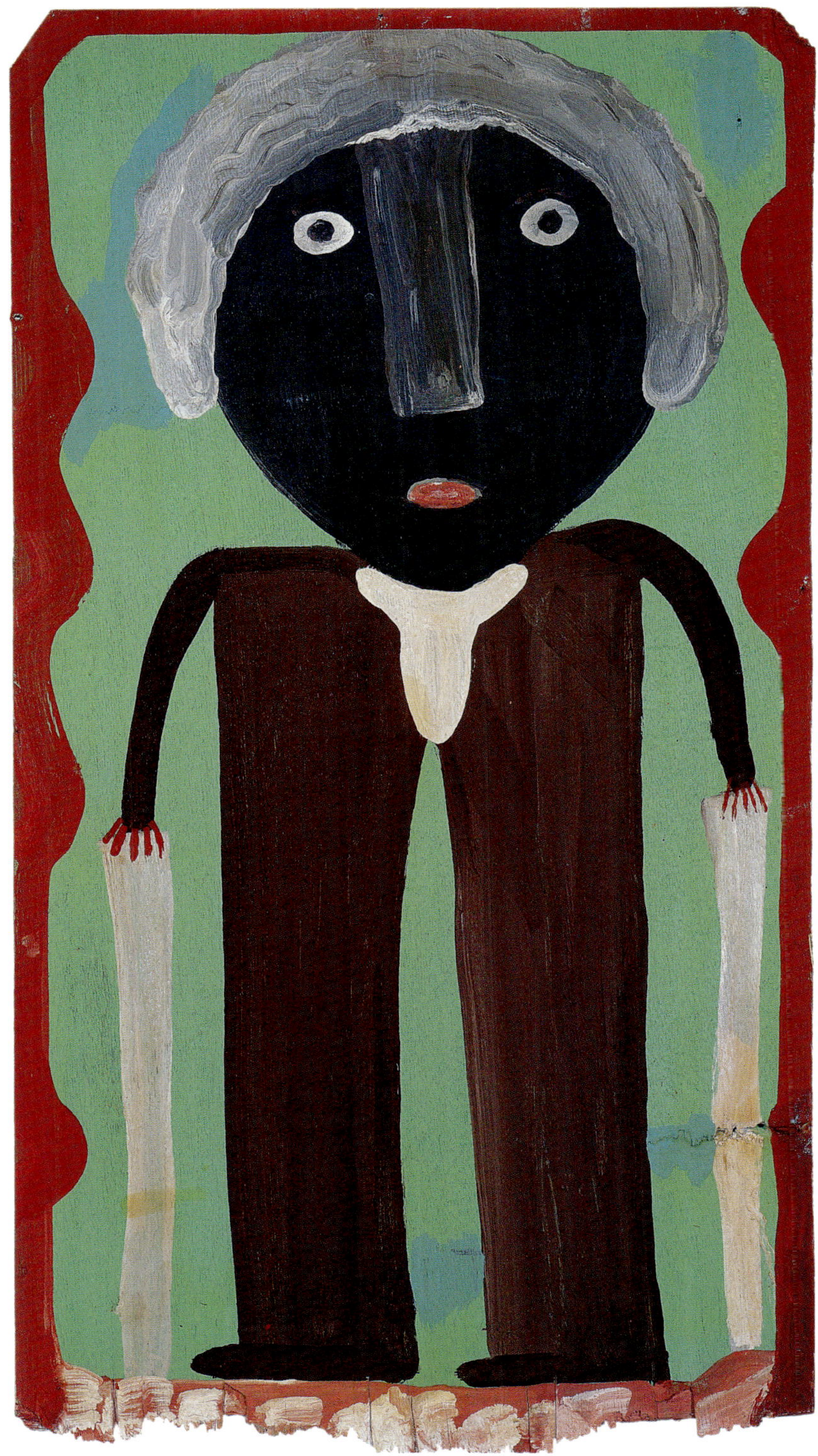

One of an ongoing series of self-portraits whose inspiration can be traced to a Bill Traylor drawing,[1] this painting stands in stark contrast to *Self-Portrait of Me* (cat. 73). Usually full-length figures, the works in this series are symmetrical and stable, their subjects recognizably human. Centered and frontal, the imposing image completely fills the composition. Arms spring out of a stable rectangular body only to be arrested by the upward thrust of crutches. The necktie directs attention back to the face, which confronts the viewer directly. The artist's own bristle of gray hair, elliptical face, oval mouth, and almond eyes complete the likeness. Tolliver says he "made this one like an old man" although he makes other images of himself "all kinda way."[2]

The palette of red, green, brown, and black is more life-like than that of *Self-Portrait of Me*. The greens and reds are vibrant rather than unsettling, giving the subject of this work a more serene quality. Tolliver typically combines a painterly approach with a linear style, his hard edges tempered by expressive brushwork. The border has been elaborated, possibly to work in stray touches of paint, and patches of pink have transformed the saw-ravaged bottom edge into a decorative element.

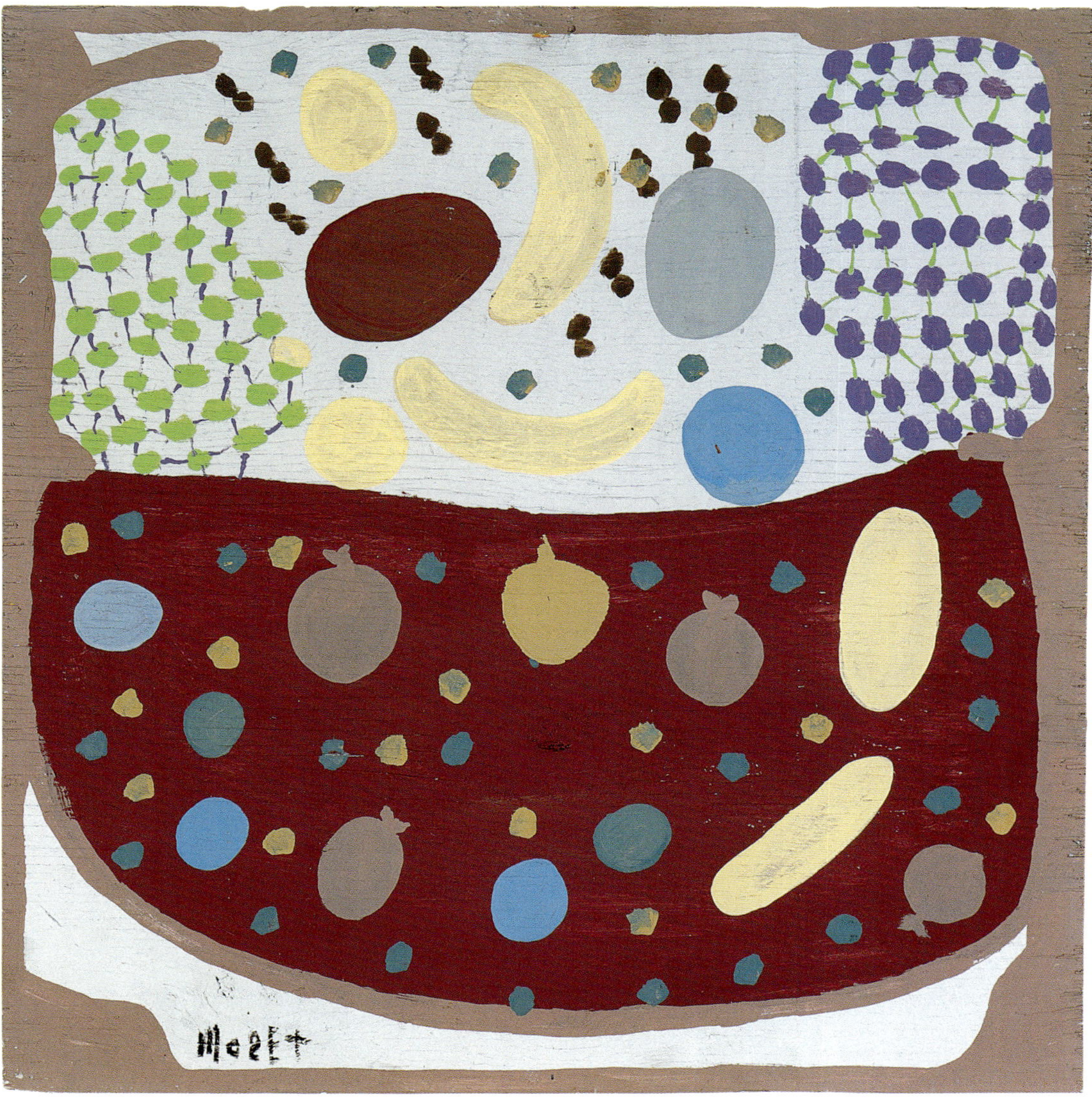

Cat. 75

Mose Tolliver

Born ca. 1920
Montgomery, Alabama

Chinese Fruit Basket, ca. 1987
House paint on wood
$23\frac{7}{8} \times 24\frac{1}{4}$ inches
Acquired from William S. Arnett, 1994
1999.99

In this ebullient painting, bunches of grapes form a flanking network containing the bananas, apples, and pears that effervesce from the container. Tolliver chose a palette of cool pastels to offset the exuberance of his flying fruit, while whimsical colors reinforce a feeling of fantasy. The artist plays with the border or painted frame of this piece, extending it into and across the image so that it becomes a design element, integral to the composition.

The fruit basket paintings mark the late stage in a formal process through which Tolliver maintained the purpose and form of a container but changed its nature. His baskets themselves began as images of boats, metamorphosed into watermelons, and then became fruit bowls with the boat-watermelon-bowl shape remaining constant. William Arnett compares this process to the game of "Gossip" in which a whispered message is transformed as it moves further from its source.[1]

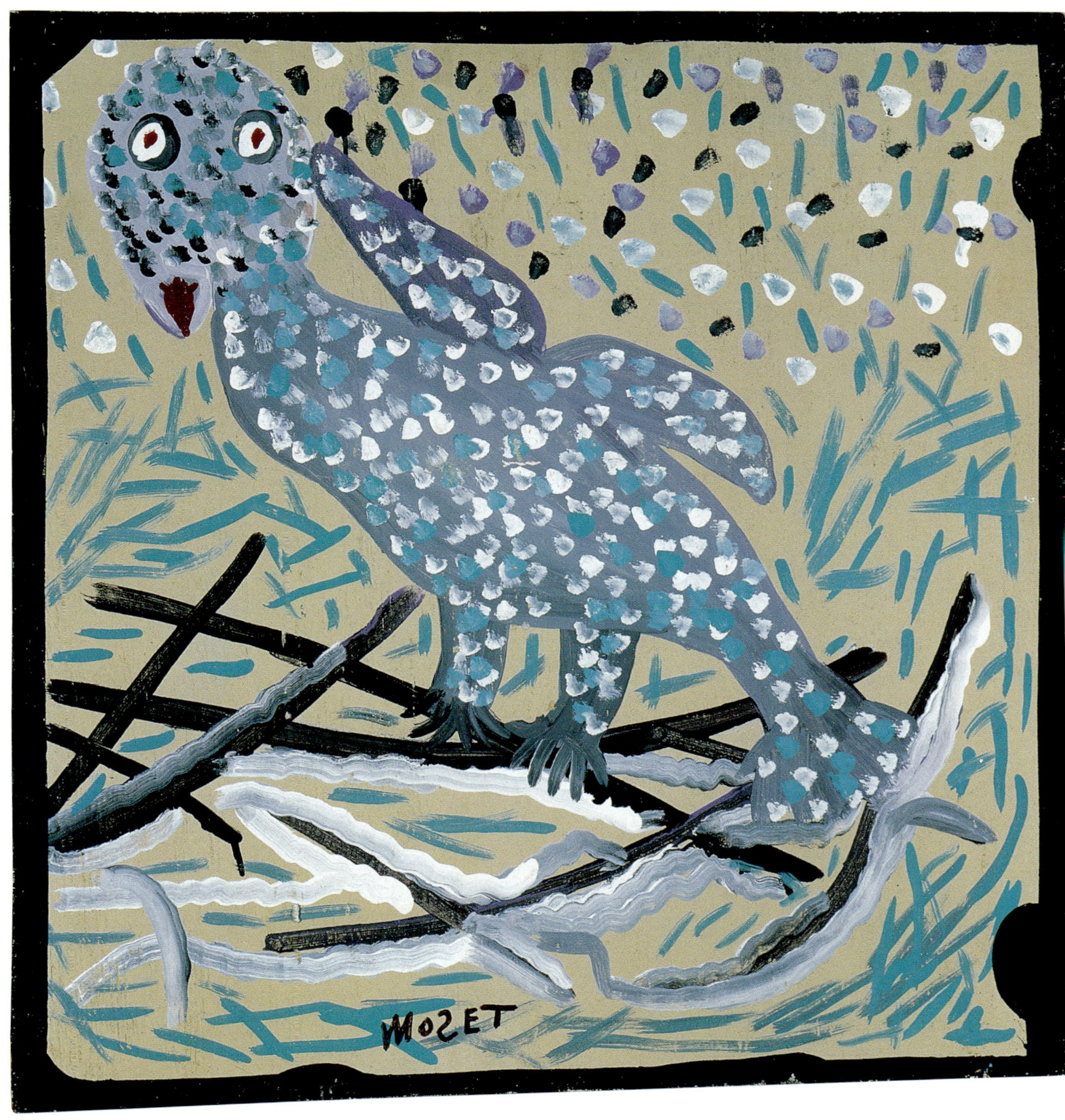

Cat. 76

Mose Tolliver

Born ca. 1920
Montgomery, Alabama

Hootin' Owl, ca. 1987
House paint on wood
27¼ × 26½ inches
Acquired from William S. Arnett, 1994
1999.100

Like early sign or limner painters, Tolliver often takes commissions, sometimes creating dozens of paintings of the same subject. Many of his most famous images have evolved from renditions of everyday things or pictures people have brought him to reproduce. More visual than visionary, Tolliver first creates his idiosyncratic version of an object or picture and then alters it in subsequent variations. The later paintings become increasingly simple and abstract as he moves farther from his source, copying his own copies. This elaborate depiction of an owl was reproduced from a series Tolliver painted in the 1980s, which was in turn almost certainly derived from an image, perhaps from a book, that he was commissioned to copy.[1]

In Tolliver's rendition of the owl, allover patterning couples the bird with the background. The subtle and sophisticated palette for which the painter is known is evident here as he punctuates lilac, aqua, and white with accents of burgundy and black. A gentle beige background further softens and unites the elements of this celebration of color and form.

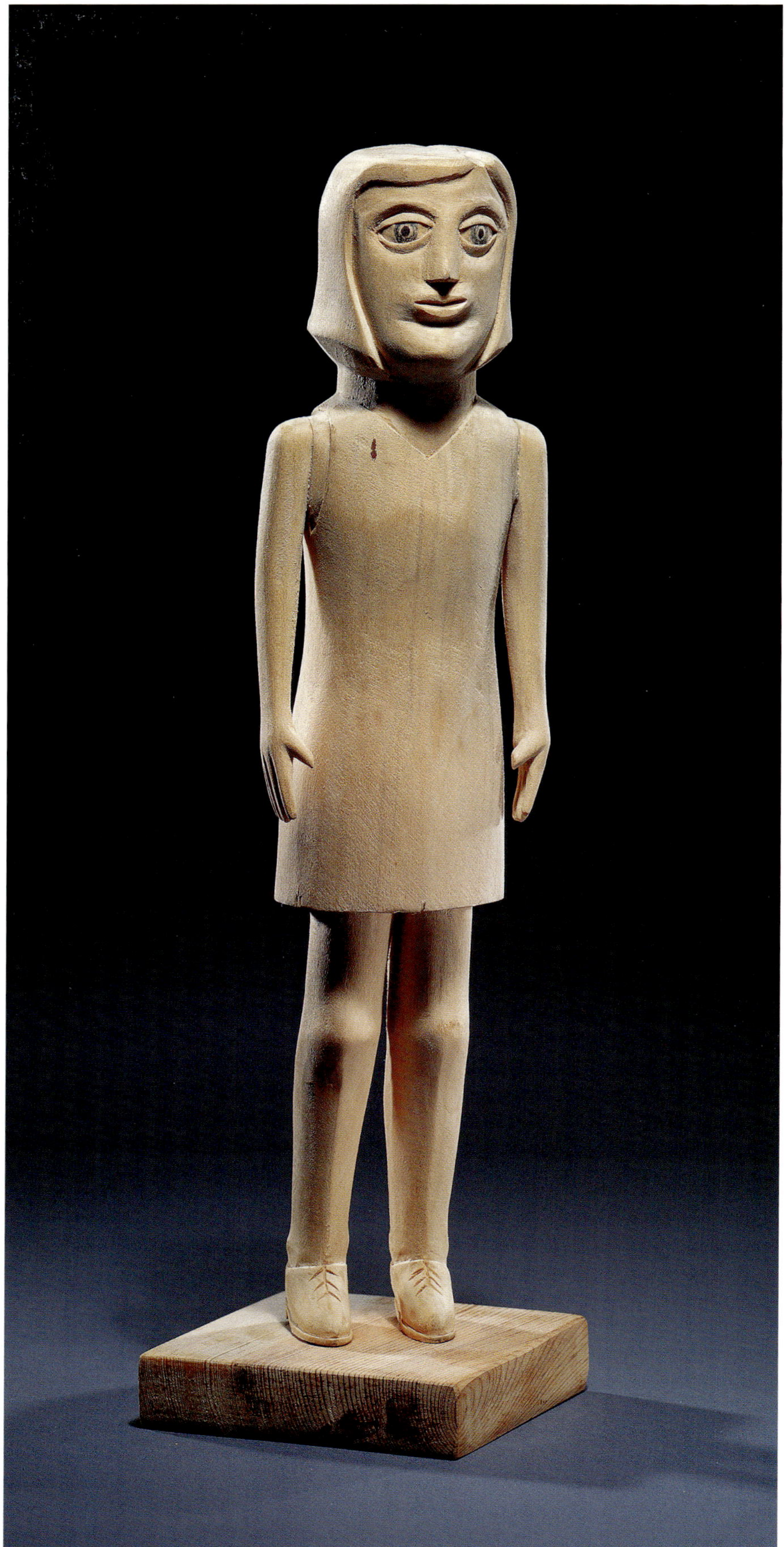

Cats. 77–78

Edgar Tolson

1904–1984
Campton, Kentucky

Untitled, 1977
Carved wood with pencil and ink
12½ × 3½ × 3⅝ inches
Acquired from Charles Locke, 1993
1997.111

Untitled, late 1970s
Carved wood with pencil and ink
12½ × 4⅞ × 4⅞ inches
Acquired from Charles Locke, 1993
1997.112

Edgar Tolson's work reflects the folk carving traditions of the Appalachian culture that nurtured it as well as the forces of the larger art market. Although he carved canes, animals, solitary human figures, and stories from the Bible, he also carved such contemporary characters as hippies and political figures, the caged unicorn from the Metropolitan Museum's famous tapestry, and at least one portrait of a patron's pet.

The two figures of women shown here display the rigid poses and stylized, staring faces common to Tolson's carvings. Their stiff arms, which were separately carved and glued on, terminate in graceful, delicately carved hands. Both have jutting chins, aquiline noses, and shallow eyes whose irises were colored with pencil, the pupils with dark ink. Despite the reductive nature of the forms, small details differentiate the two figures. Cat. 77 is slimmer and more delicate, wearing a wistful expression in her large gray eyes, her mouth slightly askew. Cat. 78 wears a placid, compliant expression, and it is her eyes that are askew. The revealing neckline of her short-sleeved dress provides a glimpse of how comfortable this former preacher seems to have been creating sexually suggestive imagery of the sort he made explicit in his earlier Fall of Man series.

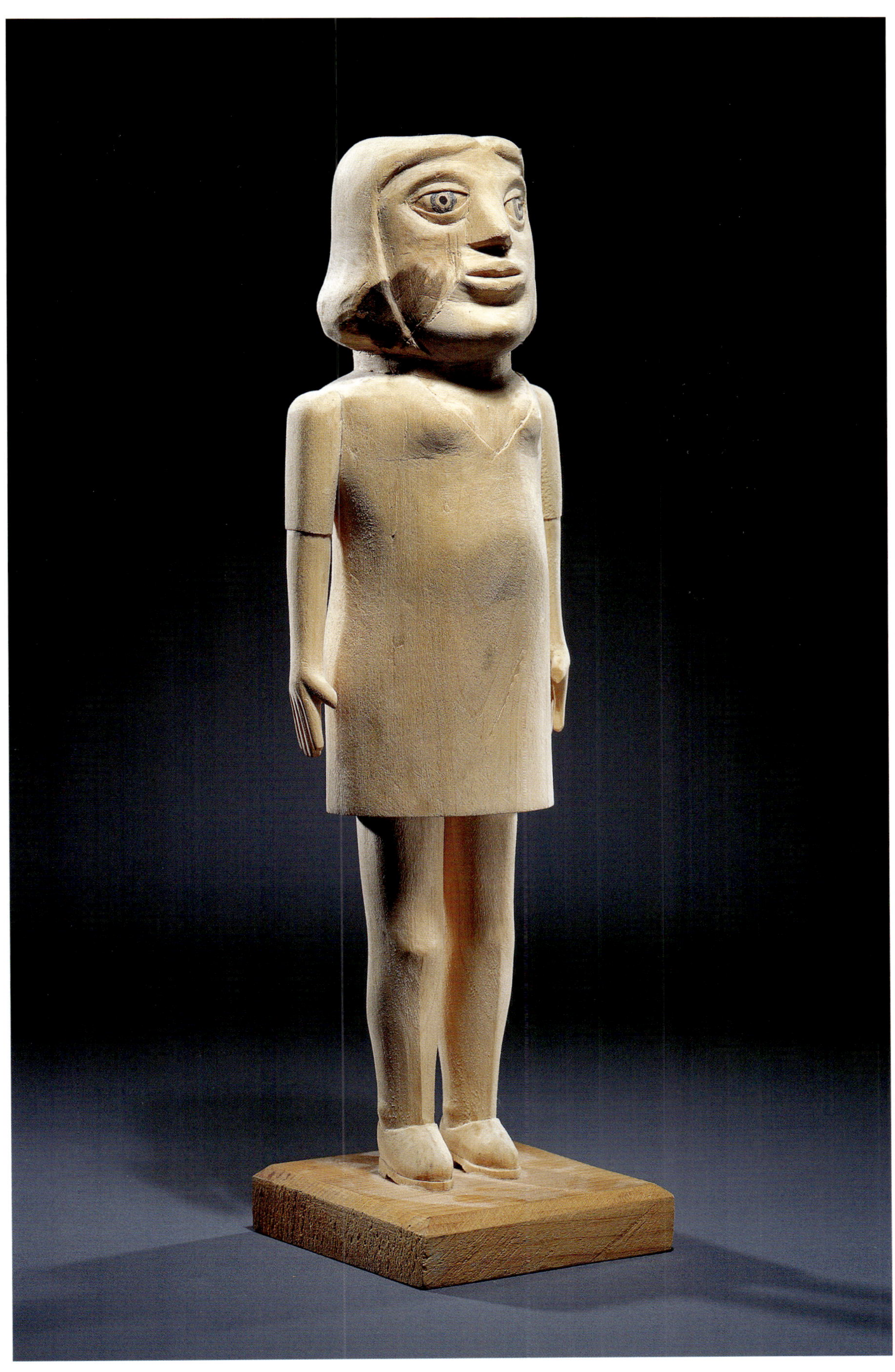

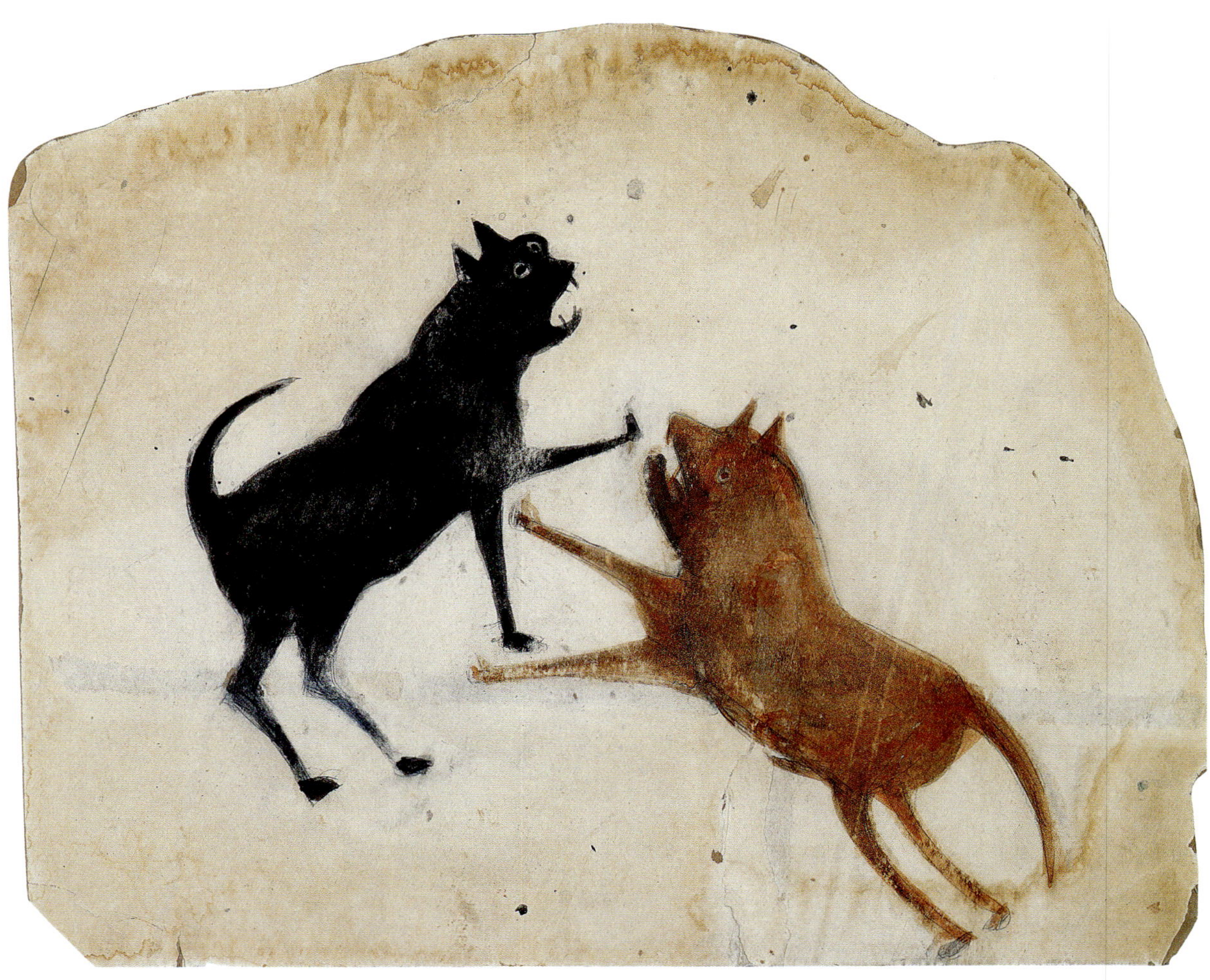

Cats. 79–82

Bill Traylor

ca. 1853–1949
Montgomery, Alabama

Untitled (Two Dogs Fighting), 1939–1948
Poster paint and pencil on cardboard
16½ x 21⅛ inches
Acquired from Ricco/Maresca Gallery, 1994
1997.116

Untitled (Black Elephant with a Brown Ear), 1939–1948
Poster paint and pencil on paper
14⅝ x 25¾ inches
Acquired from Ricco/Maresca Gallery, 1994
1997.113

Untitled (Man in Blue Pants), 1939–1948
Poster paint, pencil, colored pencil, and charcoal on cardboard
10⅝ x 7¼ inches
Acquired from Ricco/Maresca Gallery, 1994
1997.115

Untitled (House with Figures), 1939–1948
Poster paint and pencil on cardboard
13½ x 13⅞ inches
Acquired from Ricco/Maresca Gallery, 1994
1997.114

An economy of expression distinguishes the drawings Bill Traylor created on the streets of Montgomery during the final years of the Great Depression. A retired field hand in his eighties when he first picked up a pencil, Traylor called up on discarded cardboard the essence of things seen or remembered. While the radically simplified forms of Traylor's drawings seem familiar to viewers accustomed to the reductive tendencies of modernism, the witty vitality of his vision is striking.

Traylor depicted dogfights more than once. In the drawing of two dogs fighting, his taut line conveys a fury of bared teeth and stiffly arced tails. The animals' rigid forelegs increase the impression of frenzied activity frozen in paint. As is typical of Traylor, the figures float in space without groundlines to hold them to earth.

Traylor's line is eloquent in the subtle dorsal curve of an elephant. Its supple undulations add energy to this portrait of a calm but powerful beast. The repetition of ovals in the bulbous tail tip and feet sets up a rhythm interrupted by the color of the oval ear, whose startling brownness draws the viewer's eye into contact with the animal's keen round orb.

Traylor often left preliminary marks in his drawings that reveal both his working method and the structure beneath his forms. In the image of a man in blue pants, Traylor augmented the straight lines of legs and torso with the curves of buttocks and midriff. He appears to have drawn the body, then clothed it: legs are visible beneath the pants as is the head beneath the hat. Perched on tip-toe, one leg askew, the man may be dancing or expounding. The hat firmly planted

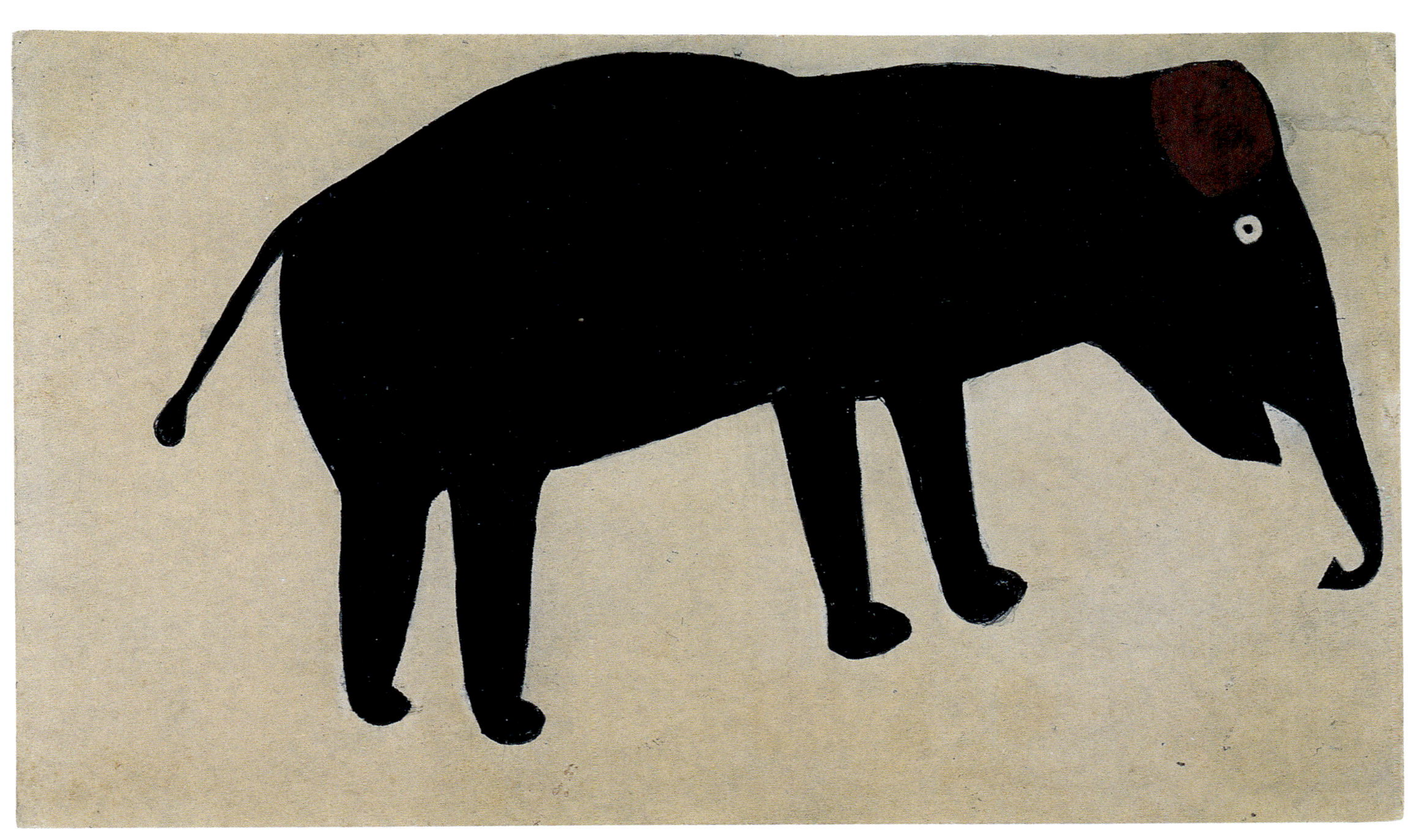

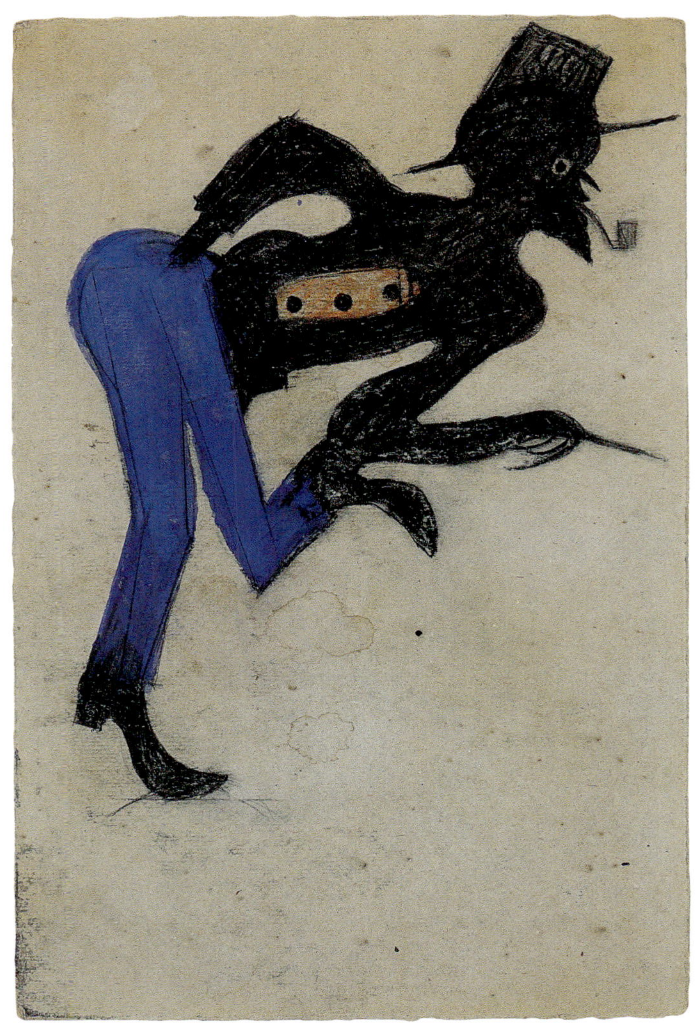

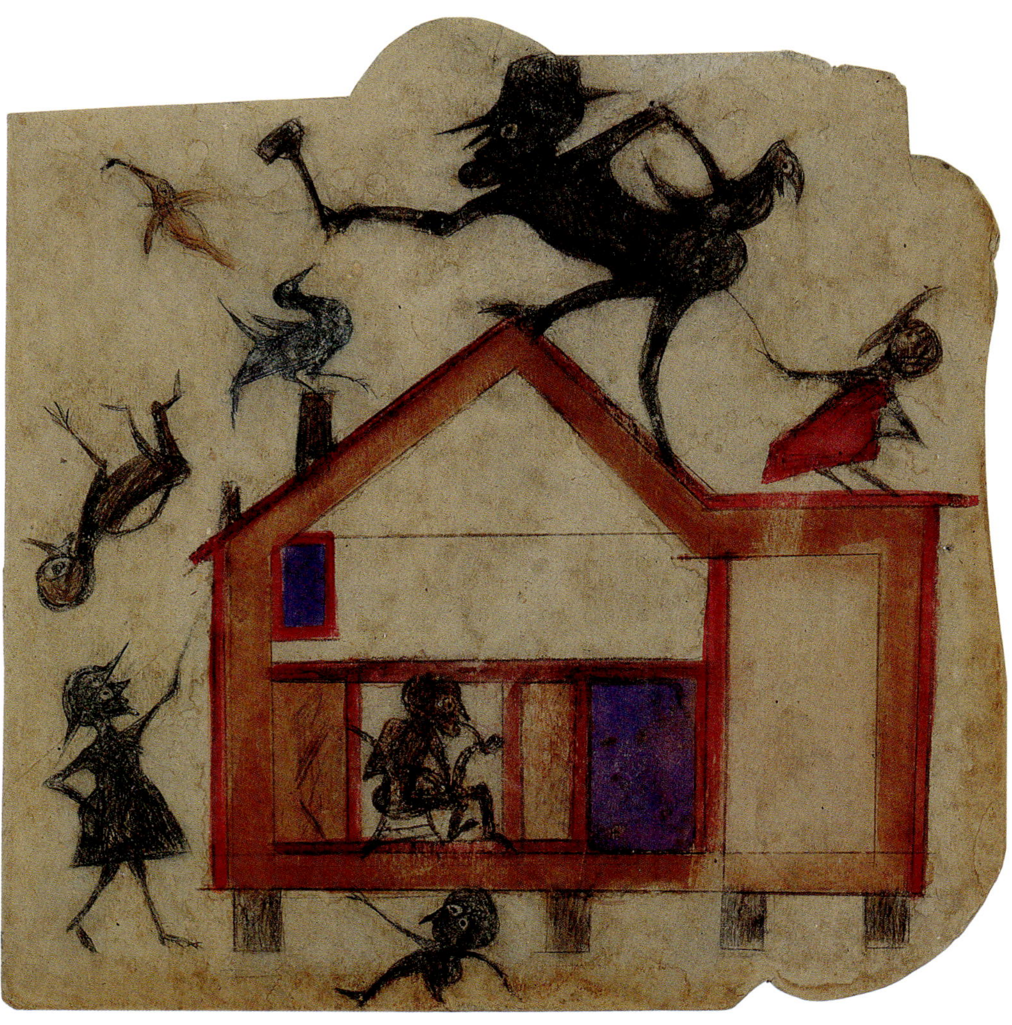

on his head could be a symbol of his status as a free man: in the antebellum South, slaves were not permitted to wear hats.

Nowhere is the ebullience of Traylor's drawings more apparent than in his multi-figure compositions, such as this drawing of a house with figures. Bustling with commotion, its figures exemplify Traylor's skill at storytelling through revealing gestures. Traylor's negative space takes on a character of its own, intensifying the tension of the scene, which is drawn together in a relationship of curving lines. The arcs interact subtly within each figure and correlate the figures to each other. The artist commonly drew attention to important elements of his works through adjustments in scale. Here, the man on the roof seems to provide the key to the action. This may be Traylor's account of an episode of poultry-pilfering remembered from his farming days. The oversized man atop the roof clutches a chicken behind his back as he brandishes a tool with which he has just knocked a pursuer off the housetop. A second pursuer lies stunned beneath the house. In the upper left, a bird flies off, its dinner clasped in its beak. Traylor perhaps emphasized the parallel between bird and man by bestowing avian attributes on some of the people in the scene. On the far right, a scolding woman's mouth gapes like a young bird's beak, while the man toppling from the roof sports enormous, bird-like eyes. Only the man smoking inside seems unaffected by the pandemonium encircling the building.

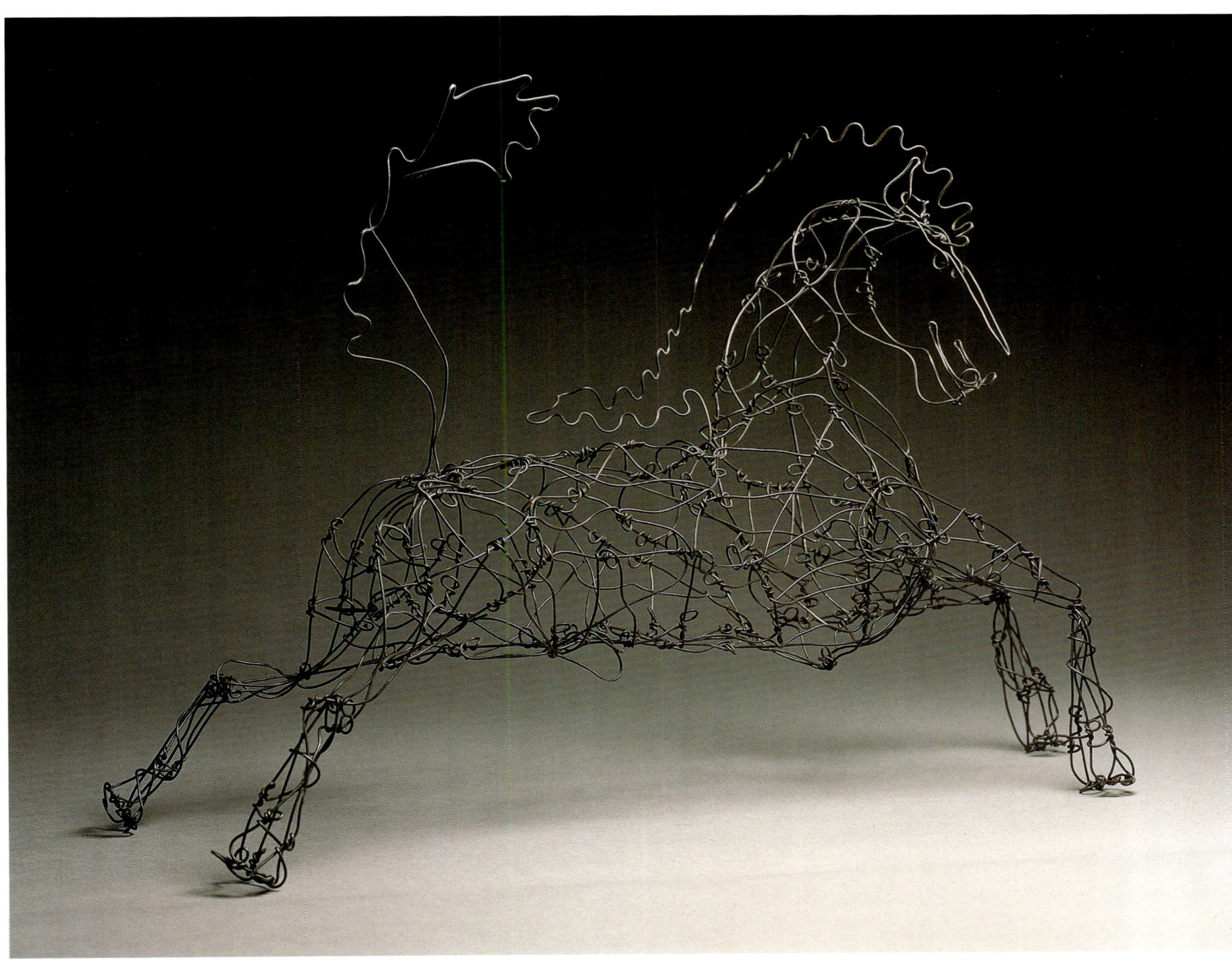

Cat. 83

Thai Varick

Born 1941
New York, New York

Horse, 1992–1993
Wire
16 x 22 x 8½ inches
Acquired from Bridges and Bodell, 1993
1999.102

Lyrical, light, and delicate, Thai Varick's sculptures are twisted from a single strand of wire. In his exploration of form, he has created animals, humans, and buildings, but always returns to reinterpret the horse. This stallion, lively in pose and line, displays the artist's technical ingenuity and keen sense of animal anatomy. Although the piece looks malleable, it is quite rigid. Both structural strength and integrity of form are produced by Varick's method of construction, in which long portions of the strand form the primary lines of limbs and torso, increasing the linearity produced by the continuously looping wire. Shorter sections connected to them add depth to the shape.

Varick starts by modeling the face because, he says, "That's where you find the character."[1] In this example, the mouth and nostrils are suggested by loops of a continuous filament that goes on to mold the elegant head, while another loop forms the eyes and the top of the muzzle. At the end of the strand Varick makes a knot, a heart that throbs inside the chest when the sculpture is moved.

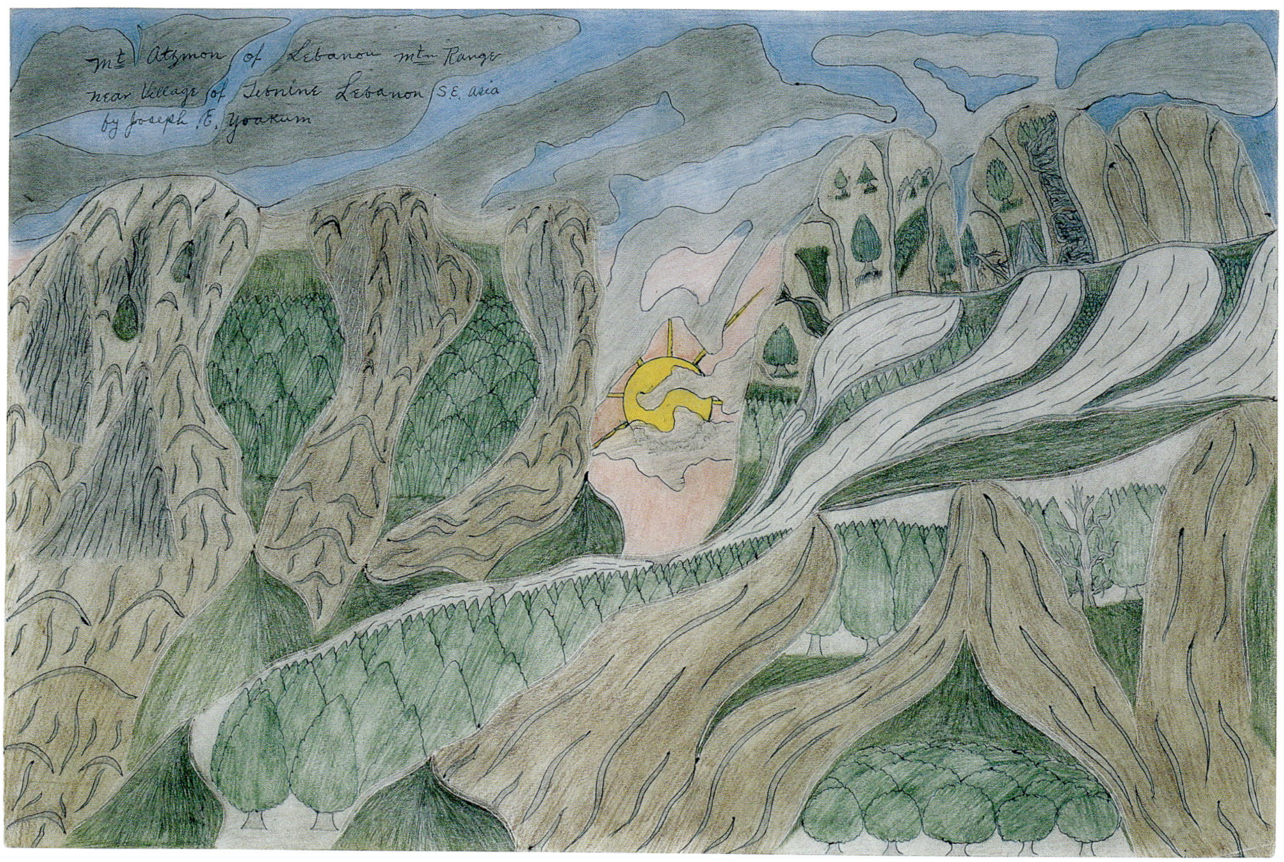

Cats. 84–85

Joseph Yoakum

ca. 1890–1972
Chicago, Illinois

Mt. Atzmon of Lebanon Mtn. Range near Village of Leonine Lebanon S.E. Asia, 1968–1971
Colored pencil and ballpoint pen on paper
11¾ x 18 inches
Acquired from Carl Hammer Gallery, 2000
2000.12

Mt. Uovz in Verkhoyansk Range near List Aldan S.E., U.S.S.R., 1968–1971
Colored pencil, ballpoint pen, and pencil on paper
12 x 18½ inches
Acquired from Carl Hammer Gallery, 2000
2000.11

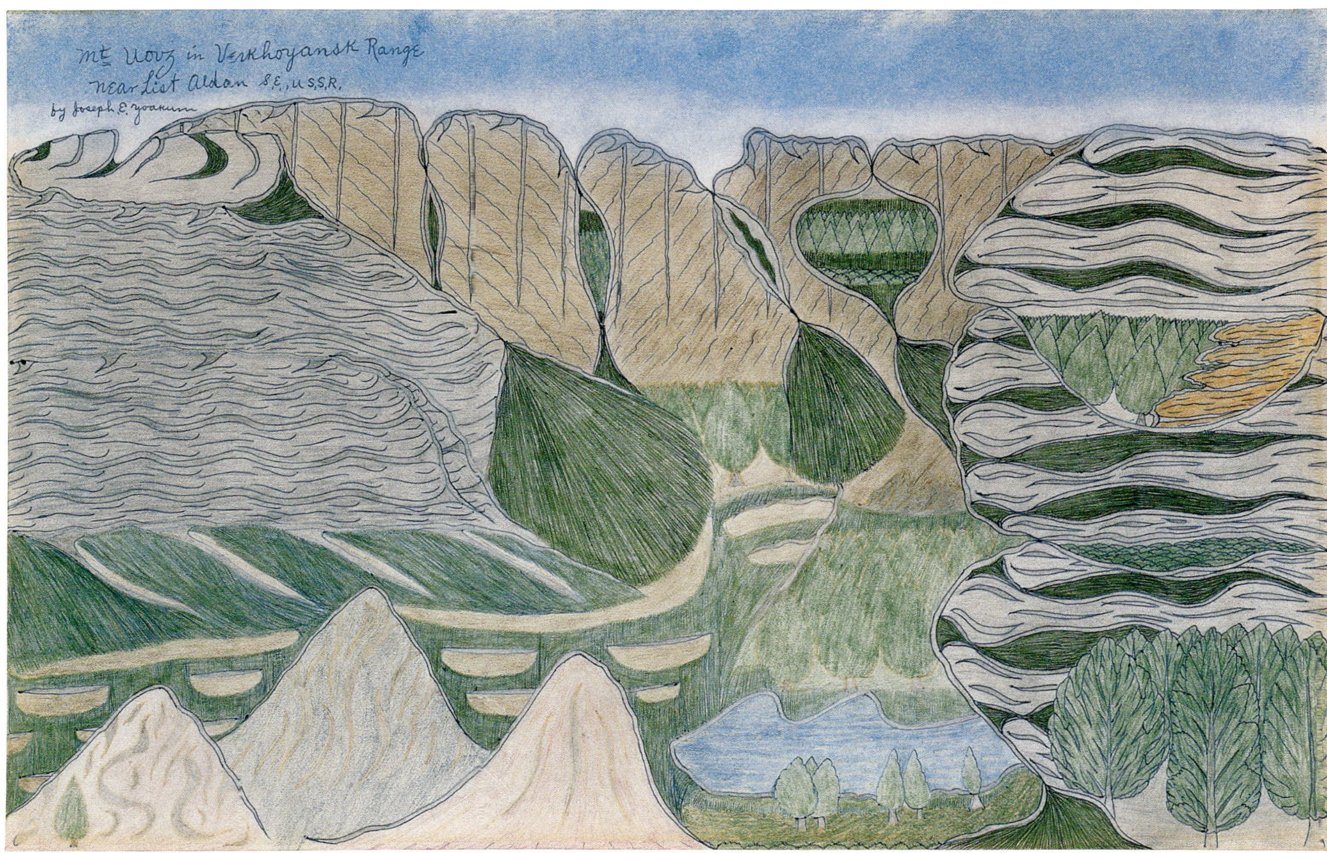

Joseph Yoakum's oeuvre occasionally included other subjects, but the vast majority of his abundant output consists of landscapes depicting far-flung places he claimed to have visited. Scenes of mountains and water were among his favorites.

The two works pictured here exhibit the confident drawing and subtle coloring that distinguish Yoakum's technique. The push and pull of delicate yet distinctly oriented pencil strokes produces a tension that unites the compositions' disparate elements. Harmonious greens and blues enlivened by light oranges and pinks contribute to the unity, with azure skies appearing above Yoakum's characteristically high horizon lines.

Yoakum was a master of pictorial rhythm and repetition. He filled pages with patterns created by such elements as regular clefts and rills and paradoxical trees, at once geometric and organic, whose patterns resemble textile designs. Geode-like pockets provide glimpses into other vistas within the scenes. However idiosyncratic his formal vocabulary, Yoakum crafted effective visual statements. As Hairy Who artist Phil Hanson saw them, "The drawings have a set of laws which he invented and they are rigorous, and yet infinitely varying."[1]

It is not known whether Yoakum visited the places he illustrated, but most of them exist. Mt. Atzmon lies in lower Galilee at the southernmost end of the Lebanon Mountains, making this one of several drawings Yoakum created of the Holy Land. Mt. Uovz may or may not be real, but its supposed location is. Curving between the Lena and Aldan rivers, the Verkhoyansk Range is a mineral-rich chain of mountains in eastern Siberia. He may have seen pictures of Mt. Uovz (if it exists) and Mt. Atzmon in the atlas, travel books, or encyclopedias he owned,[2] or he may have drawn them entirely from his imagination. He seems to have been as concerned with the spirit and energy of the landscape as with its physical appearance.

Notes to the Catalogue

To give a sense of the regional makeup of the Hahn Collection, the place where an artist lived while creating each work is identified in each heading. To give a sense of Hahn's collecting activities, the headings also include the person from whom or the gallery from which Hahn purchased the work.

Cats. 1–2

1. Metcalf 1996–97, p. 37.

2. Margaret Doan, facsimile transmission to Susan Crawley, 1 October 1999. Based on notes from her conversations with the artist in 1995, Doan provided information about the purposes for which Adkins designed these devices and deciphered his handwritten notes on the drawings.

Cat. 3

1. Williams S. Arnett, conversation with Lynne Spriggs and Susan Crawley, Atlanta, 3 August 1999.

2. Almon 1991, p. 13.

3. Catherine Fox, "Leroy Almon, Folk Artist, Dispatcher," *Atlanta Journal-Constitution*, 24 April 1997, sec. C, p. 10.

Cat. 4

1. Quoted in Chris Wohlwend, "Carving a Spiritual Niche," *Atlanta Journal-Constitution*, 11 August 1991, sec. N, p. 10. All subsequent quotations come from this article.

Cat. 5

1. Almon 1991, pp. 13–14.

2. Quoted in Chris Wohlwend, "Carving a Spiritual Niche," *Atlanta Journal-Constitution*, 11 August 1991, sec. N, p. 10.

Cat. 6

1. Almon 1991, p. 13.

Cat. 7

1. Quoted in Goreau 1975, p. 155.

Cat. 9

1. Quoted in Artists' Alliance 1992, p. 56.

2. Richard Gasperi, telephone conversation with Susan Crawley, 10 October 2000.

Cat. 10

1. Tom Patterson, "David Butler," in Trechsel 1995, p. 34.

Cat. 12

1. "Neither do men light a candle, and put it under a bushel, but on a candlestick; and it giveth light unto all that are in the house. Let your light shine before men, that they may see your good works, and glorify your Father which is in Heaven." (Matthew 5:15–16) This passage inspired the popular Sunday school song by Harry Dixon Loes: "This little light of mine/I'm gonna let it shine/. . . Hide it under a bushel? No!/I'm gonna let it shine."

2. Quotations from Ned Cartledge are from an interview by Lynne Spriggs and Susan Crawley, Atlanta, 2 December 1998, tape recording and transcription, High Museum of Art, curatorial files.

Cat. 13

1. Quoted in Westervelt 1986, p. 40.

2. The Strategic Defense Initiative (SDI), nicknamed "Star Wars" by its detractors, was the Reagan administration's space-based nuclear defense plan. Reagan's refusal to concede ground in this area was regarded by many observers as the primary obstacle to successful nuclear disarmament talks during his presidency.

3. Interview by Lynne Spriggs and Susan Crawley, Atlanta, 2 December 1998, tape recording and transcription, High Museum of Art, curatorial files.

Cat. 14

1. Interview by Lynne Spriggs and Susan Crawley, Atlanta, 2 December 1998, tape recording and transcription, High Museum of Art, curatorial files.

2. Cartledge, telephone conversation with Susan Crawley, 17 August 1999.

3. Illustrated in Westervelt 1986, p. 35.

Cat. 16

1. Tom Patterson, "Raymond Coins," in Trechsel 1995, pp. 38–45.

2. Ezekiel 37:1–14. At least two folk songs or spirituals by this title describe the events in the biblical Valley of the Dry Bones. The first begins, "Down in de valley de sperrit spoke" and contains a chorus that begins, "Dry bones gwinea gather in de mornin." The other is the song familiar to schoolchildren that begins, "Ezekiel cried, 'Dem dry bones!'" and contains the line, "The foot bone connected to the leg bone . . ."

Cat. 17

1. Quoted in Huffman 1994, p. 2. During the period when Coins worked there, the New Farmer's Warehouse was owned by the father of Atlanta art dealer Barbara Archer.

2. A photograph of Coins holding the framed newspaper photograph is in the High Museum of Art curatorial files.

3. Roger Manley, electronic mail message to Susan Crawley, 13 June 2000.

4. Quoted in Huffman 1994, p. 3.

Cat. 19

1. John M. MacGregor, facsimile transmission to Susan Crawley, 16 December 1999. (There is also a different, bound volume seven.)

2. Unbound vol. 7, reproduced with permission of Kiyoko Lerner and Michael Lerner. All quotations from the manuscript are from this volume. All descriptions of events recorded in *The Realms of the Unreal* and all quotations from the manuscript were provided by John M. MacGregor.

Cat. 20

1. Quoted in Kiah 1978, p. 273. Atlanta collector and dealer James Allen notes that Davis frequently sculpted works with African themes, although his symbols of U.S. patriotism and Christian subjects have been exhibited more often. James Allen, electronic mail message to Susan Crawley, 4 August 2000.

2. Kiah 1978, p. 277.

3. The busts of the presidents are displayed at the Beach Institute, King-Tisdell Cottage Foundation in Savannah, Ga.

Cat. 21

1. Except where noted, quotations from Thornton Dial are from an interview by Lynne Spriggs and Susan Crawley, Bessemer, Ala., 7 May 1999, tape recording and transcription, High Museum of Art, curatorial files.

2. Quoted in Goodman 1994, p. 137.

Cat. 22

1. Quotations from Thornton Dial are from an interview by Lynne Spriggs and Susan Crawley, Bessemer, Ala., 7 May 1999, tape recording and transcription, High Museum of Art, curatorial files.

Cat. 23

1. Quotations from Thornton Dial are from an interview by Lynne Spriggs and Susan Crawley, Bessemer, Ala., 7 May 1999, tape recording and transcription, High Museum of Art, curatorial files.

Cat. 24

1. Quotations from Thornton Dial are from an interview by Lynne Spriggs and Susan Crawley, Bessemer, Ala., 7 May 1999, tape recording and transcription, High Museum of Art, curatorial files.

Cat. 25

1. William S. Arnett, conversation with Lynne Spriggs and Susan Crawley, Atlanta, 3 August 1999.

2. Thornton Dial, interview by Lynne Spriggs and Susan Crawley, Bessemer, Ala., 7 May 1999, tape recording and transcription, High Museum of Art, curatorial files.

Cat. 26

1. Quotations from Thornton Dial are from an interview by Lynne Spriggs and Susan Crawley, Bessemer, Ala., 7 May 1999, tape recording and transcription, High Museum of Art, curatorial files.

Cat. 27

1. Spriggs 2000, p. 36.

Cat. 28

1. Pollitzer 1999, pp. 141–142.

2. Spriggs 2000, p. 19.

3. Interview by Jennie Summerall, tape recording, St. Helena, S.C., 1983.

Cat. 29

1. Spriggs 2000, p. 23.

2. Ibid., p. 21.

3. The lyrics of the wistful song, written by Noel Sherman and Joe Sherman, begin:

> Ramblin' rose, ramblin' rose
> Why you ramble, no one knows
> Wild and wind-blown, that's how you've grown
> Who can cling to a ramblin' rose?

Cat. 30

1. When Lynne Spriggs presented this image to island elders they began singing the spiritual. Virginia Green, Carolee Homes Brown, Samuel R. Brown Sr., and Marquetta L. Goodwine, interview by Lynne Spriggs, St. Helena, S.C., November 1999, video recording, Gullah/Geechee Sea Island Coalition, St. Helena, S.C.

2. Illustrated in Arnett and Arnett 2000, p. 323, plate 324.

Cats. 31–32

1. Personal communication to Susan Crawley.

Cats. 33–34

1. Quoted in Perry 1982, unpaginated.

Cat. 35

1. Similitudes are parables or allegories like the backward-gazing plowman. Finster often uses the visual equivalent of such devices in his paintings.

2. William Ferris has explored this phenomenon and its roots in "Folk Art and The American South," in Yelen 1993.

3. Quoted in Girardot and Viera 1994, p. 49.

Cat. 36

1. Quotations from Howard Finster are from an interview by Lynne Spriggs and Susan Crawley, Summerville, Ga., 23 February 2000, tape recording, High Museum of Art, curatorial files.

Cat. 37

1. Quoted in Finster and Patterson 1989, pp. 123–124.

2. When asked in a interview whether these buildings were of a heavenly or an earthly character, Finster replied, "Here on earth is where I've seen 'em."

Interview by Lynne Spriggs and Susan Crawley, Summerville, Ga., 23 February 2000, tape recording, High Museum of Art, curatorial files.

3. Ibid.

4. Finster 1989, unpaginated.

5. Spriggs/Crawley interview.

6. Quoted in Peacock and Jenkins 1996, pp. 106, 110.

Cat. 38

1. Interview by Lynne Spriggs and Susan Crawley, Summerville, Ga., 23 February 2000, tape recording, High Museum of Art, curatorial files.

2. Illustrated in Peacock and Jenkins 1996, p. 99.

Cat. 39

1. Cubbs and Metcalf 1997, p. 60.

Cat. 40

1. Frank Maresca, letter to Susan Crawley, 9 November 1999.

Cats. 41–43

1. See Parish 1974, p. 29. Arnold Lobel's illustration of the tyrannosaurus rex was unquestionably Hawkins's source for the painting and probably the source for the later drawing. His illustration of the stegosaurus (p. 9) was the source for Hawkins's drawing of that subject.

2. Schwindler 1989, unpaginated.

3. Frank Maresca, letter to Susan Crawley, 9 November 1999.

Cats. 44–45

1. Frank Maresca, letter to Susan Crawley, 9 November 1999.

Cat. 46

1. Schwindler 1989, unpaginated; and Gary J. Schwindler, "William L. Hawkins," in Ricco/Maresca Gallery 1990, p. 5.

2. Gary J. Schwindler, " 'You Want to See Somethin' Pretty?'," in Maresca and Ricco 1997, p. ix.

3. See Shapiro 1957, pp. 100–101.

Cat. 47

1. Frank Maresca, letter to Susan Crawley, 9 November 1999.

Cat. 48

1. Cubbs and Metcalf 1997, p. 62.

2. Gary J. Schwindler, "William L. Hawkins: A Biography," unpublished manuscript, Keny Galleries Archives, Columbus, Ohio, p. 191.

3. Cubbs and Metcalf 1997, p. 64.

4. Schwindler, "Biography," p. 191. Although most writers give a later date, Schwindler states that Hawkins first created a three-dimensional effect by applying a mixture of sand and enamel to a 1983 painting, *Funkenstein*, derived from the cartoon illustration on the front of a cereal box.

Cat. 49

1. Quotations from Lonnie Holley are from an interview by Lynne Spriggs and Susan Crawley, Harpersville, Ala., 7 May 1999, tape recording and transcription, High Museum of Art, curatorial files.

Cat. 50

1. Quoted in Raad Cawthon, "By Command of Spirit Flows her Louisiana Art," *Atlanta Journal-Constitution*, 19 May 1985, sec. H, p. 7.

Cat. 51

1. Lampell, Lampell, and Larkin 1989, p. 21.

Cat. 53

1. Quoted in Lampell, Lampell, and Larkin 1989, p. 248.

2. Illustrated in ibid., p. 249.

Cat. 54

1. Gary J. Schwindler, "Joe Louis Light," in Trechsel 1995, p. 121.

2. Quotations from Joe Light are from an interview by Melody Barnett Deusner, Memphis, Tenn., 28 August 1999, tape recording and transcription, High Museum of Art, curatorial files.

Cat. 55

1. Paul Arnett, conversation with Lynne Spriggs and Susan Crawley, Atlanta, 2 March 2000. Information about Lockett's iconography, technique, and links to the snipped tin and root sculpture traditions comes from this conversation.

Cat. 56

1. Paul Arnett and William S. Arnett, conversation with Lynne Spriggs and Susan Crawley, Atlanta, 2 March 2000. All information about Lockett's iconography, technique, and artistic development comes from this conversation.

Cat. 57

1. Paul Arnett, conversation with Lynne Spriggs and Susan Crawley, Atlanta, 2 March 2000.

2. William S. Arnett, conversation with Lynne Spriggs and Susan Crawley, Atlanta, 2 March 2000. See also Paul Arnett et al., "The Hidden Charms of the Deep South," in Arnett and Arnett 2000, pp. 102, 105.

3. Vincent Harding, " 'I Always Wanted to Be Free,' " in Arnett and Arnett 2000, p. 17.

Cat. 58

1. Quoted in Perry 1992, p. 145.

Cat. 60

1. Robert Bishop, introduction to O'Kelley and Bishop 1989, p. vii.

2. Quoted in Mark Childress, "Painting Memories of Georgia," *Southern Living*, August 1988, p. 89.

Cat. 61

1. Undated document, collection of the artist's papers, High Museum of Art.

2. Ibid.

Cat. 63

1. See Roberts 1992: *Three Ways to Send a Message: Telephone, Telegram, Tell-a-Woman* (1980), p. 145, colorplate 63; *Monday Morning Gossip*, p. 146,

colorplate 64; *Pilgrim's Progress*, p. 138, colorplate 56; and *Pride*, p. 225, cat. no. 150.

2. A shop in Carver's boyhood home in Diamond, Mo., sells seeds from the persimmon and ash trees he knew as a child.

3. Illustrated in Livingston, Beardsley, and Perry 1982, p. 118, cat no. 204 and in Roberts 1992, p. 139, colorplate 57. In style, technique, and composition, *Three Ways to Send a Message* resembles this piece and several others carved during the early 1940s, suggesting a similar date for the present work. See ibid.: *Presidents and Convicts* (1941), p. 101, colorplate 24; *Pearl Harbor and the African Queen* (1941), p. 139, colorplate 57; and *The Monkey Family* (1942), p. 147, colorplate 65.

Cat. 64

1. Quoted in Lynn Cline, "Folk Art from Venerable Lives, Deep Religion," *Pasatiempo*, 10 October 1997, p. 53.

2. Revelation 22:16; Revelation 22:2 and Genesis 2:9; Malachi 4:2.

3. "And his servants shall serve him: and they shall see his face; and his name shall be in their foreheads" (Revelation 22:4); "And there shall be no night there; and they need no candle, neither light of the sun; for the Lord God giveth them light: and they shall reign for ever and ever" (Revelation 22:5).

Cat. 65

1. "And there appeared a great wonder in heaven; a woman clothed with the sun, and the moon under her feet, and upon her head a crown of twelve stars" (Revelation 12:1).

2. Randall Morris, who has recently investigated Ramirez's *Inmaculada* figure, provided information about the traditional Mexican sources for the image as well as the ubiquity of the *Virgin Inmaculada* in Mexico. He has suggested that Ramirez may have used replaceable drawings like these in an altar that might have been vulnerable to confiscation or destruction in the hospital. Morris 1995–96, p. 44.

3. Randall Morris, electronic mail message to Janet Rauscher, 16 March 2000; and Morris 1995/96, p. 44.

4. Randall Morris, electronic mail message to Susan Crawley, 2 August 2000.

Cats. 66–68

1. Quoted in Alexander 1983, p. 9.

2. Telephone conversation with Lynne Spriggs, 17 July 2000.

3. Quoted in Alexander 1983, p. 11.

Cat. 69

1. Quotations from Mary Shelley are from a telephone conversation with Susan Crawley, 9 October 1999.

Cat. 70

1. Robert Knott, "Herbert Singleton: Between Good and Evil" (paper presented at the annual meeting of the College Art Association, San Antonio, Tex., January 1995), p. 4.

2. Quoted in ibid., p. 1.

3. Andy Antippas, telephone conversation with Susan Crawley, 9 November 1999. Antippas also provided the iconographical information concerning the New Orleans jazz funeral.

4. Quoted in Knott, "Singleton," p. 6.

Cat. 71

1. Quoted in Artists' Alliance 1992, p. 72.

Cat. 72

1. Illustrated in Arnett and Arnett 2000, p. 318.

2. William S. Arnett, conversation with Lynne Spriggs and Susan Crawley, Atlanta, 3 August 1999.

3. Quoted in Artists' Alliance 1992, p. 72.

Cat. 73

1. Quotations from Mose Tolliver are from an interview by Lynne Spriggs and Susan Crawley, Montgomery, Ala., 9 May 1999, tape recording and transcription, High Museum of Art, curatorial files.

2. William S. Arnett, conversation with Lynne Spriggs and Susan Crawley, Atlanta, 3 August 1999. The plaque is illustrated in Lee Kogan, "Mose Tolliver: Picture Maker," in Arnett and Arnett 2000, p. 343, fig. 166.

Cat. 74

1. William S. Arnett, conversation with Lynne Spriggs and Susan Crawley, Atlanta, 3 August 1999. Arnett believes Tolliver saw the Traylor drawing in the catalogue for *Black Folk Art in America* (Livingston, Beardsley, and Perry 1982). Tolliver's identification with Traylor's self-portraits on crutches may explain why he persisted in portraying himself similarly rather than with the walker he has relied on since the late 1960s.

2. Interview by Lynne Spriggs and Susan Crawley, Montgomery, Ala., 9 May 1999, tape recording and transcription, High Museum of Art, curatorial files.

Cat. 75

1. William S. Arnett, conversation with Lynne Spriggs and Susan Crawley, Atlanta, 3 August 1999.

Cat. 76

1. William S. Arnett, conversation with Lynne Spriggs and Susan Crawley, Atlanta, 3 August 1999.

Cat. 83

1. Quoted in Claude Solnik, "Sculptor Use [sic] a Single Wire to Create a Fanciful World," *The Villager*, 26 May 1993.

Cats. 84–85

1. Quoted in Allison 1997, p. 28.

2. That Yoakum owned these volumes is recorded by Whitney Halstead, unpublished manuscript, Department of Prints and Drawings, The Art Institute of Chicago, p. 33, quoted in Livingston, Beardsley, and Perry 1982, p. 165. Halstead also suggests that Yoakum may have been inspired by postcards (p. 38).

References

Alexander 1983
Alexander, Judith. *Nellie Mae Rowe: Visionary Artist, 1900–1982*. Atlanta: Southern Arts Federation, 1983.

Allison 1997
Allison, Diane Worfolk. "Joseph Yoakum at the Beginning: The Show at 'The Whole.'" *Raw Vision* 16 (spring 1997), pp. 24–28.

Almon 1991
Almon, Leroy, Sr. "Speakeasy." *New Art Examiner* 19 (September 1991), pp. 13–14.

Ardery 1998
Ardery, Julia S. *The Temptation: Edgar Tolson and the Genesis of Twentieth-Century Folk Art*. Chapel Hill: University of North Carolina Press, 1998.

Arnett and Arnett 1990
Arnett, William, and Paul Arnett. *Thornton Dial: Strategy of the World*. Jamaica, N.Y.: Southern Queens Park Association Inc., 1990.

Arnett and Arnett 2000
———, eds. *Souls Grown Deep: African American Vernacular Art of the South*. Vol. 1. Atlanta: Tinwood Books in association with the Schomberg Center for Research in Black Culture, the New York Public Library, 2000.

Artists' Alliance 1992
Artists' Alliance. *It'll Come True: Eleven Artists, First and Last*. Lafayette, La.: Artists' Alliance, 1992.

Baldwin 1985
Baldwin, James. *The Price of the Ticket: Collected Nonfiction, 1948–1985*. New York: St. Martin's/Marek, 1985.

Baraka et al. 1993
Baraka, Imamu Amiri, Thomas McEvilley, Paul Arnett, and William Arnett. *Thornton Dial: Image of the Tiger*. New York: Harry N. Abrams in association with the Museum of American Folk Art, the New Museum of Contemporary Art, and the American Center, 1993.

Bernard and Rice 1983
Bernard, Richard M., and Bradley R. Rice, eds. *Sunbelt Cities: Politics and Growth Since World War II*. Austin: University of Texas Press, 1983.

Berry and Blassingame 1982
Berry, Mary Frances, and John W. Blassingame. *Long Memory: The Black Experience in America*. New York: Oxford University Press, 1982.

Brownell 1975
Brownell, Blaine A. *The Urban Ethos in the South, 1920–1930*. Baton Rouge: Louisiana State University Press, 1975.

Cerny and Seriff 1996
Cerny, Charlene, and Suzanne Seriff. *Recycled, Re-Seen: Folk Art from the Global Scrap Heap*. New York: Harry N. Abrams in association with the Museum of International Folk Art, Santa Fe, 1996.

Corcoran Gallery of Art 1960
Corcoran Gallery of Art. *American Painters of the South*. Washington, D.C.: Corcoran Gallery of Art, 1960.

Couch 1935
Couch, W. T., ed. *Culture in the South*. Chapel Hill: University of North Carolina Press, 1935.

Cubbs and Metcalf 1997
Cubbs, Joanne, and Eugene W. Metcalf. "William Hawkins and the Art of Astonishment." *Folk Art* 22 (fall 1997), pp. 58–67.

Cullum 1998
Cullum, Jerry. "The Herod Paradigm." *Art Papers* (January–February 1998), pp. 26–31.

Dover 1960
Dover, Cedric. *American Negro Art*. Greenwich, Conn.: New York Graphic Society, 1960.

Driskell 1995
Driskell, David C., ed. *African American Visual Aesthetics: A Postmodernist View*. Washington, D.C.: Smithsonian Institution Press, 1995.

Ferris 1982
Ferris, William R. *Local Color: A Sense of Place in Folk Art*. New York: McGraw-Hill, 1982.

Finster 1989
Finster, Howard. *Howard Finster: Man of Visions*. Atlanta: Peachtree Publishers, 1989.

Finster and Patterson 1989
Finster, Howard, and Tom Patterson. *Howard Finster, Stranger from Another World: Man of Visions Now on this Earth*. New York: Abbeville Press, 1989.

Fuller 1973
Fuller, Edmund L. *Visions in Stone: The Sculpture of William Edmondson*. Pittsburgh: University of Pittsburgh Press, 1973.

Gates 1984
Gates, Henry Louis, ed. *Black Literature and Literary Theory*. New York: Methuen, 1984.

Gates 1988
———, ed. *The Signifying Monkey: A Theory of Afro-American Literary Criticism*. New York: Oxford University Press, 1988.

Girardot and Viera 1994
Girardot, Norman, and Ricardo Viera. "Interview with Howard Finster." *Art Journal* 53 (spring 1994), pp. 48–50.

Goodman 1994
Goodman, Jonathan. Review of *Thornton Dial: Image of the Tiger*, New Museum of Contemporary Art and the Museum of American Folk Art. *ARTnews* 93 (March 1994), p. 137.

Goreau 1975
Goreau, Laurraine. *Just Mahalia, baby*. Waco, Tex.: Word Books, 1975.

Gruber and Zed 1996
Gruber, J. Richard, and Xenia Zed. *Nellie Mae Rowe*. Augusta, Ga.: Morris Museum of Art, 1996.

Gundaker 1993
Gundaker, Grey. "Tradition and Innovation in African-American Yard Shows." *African Arts* 26, no. 2 (1993), pp. 58–71.

Gundaker 1998
———. *Signs of Diaspora/Diaspora of Signs: Literacies, Creolization, and Vernacular Practice in African America*. New York: Oxford University Press, 1998.

Hartigan 1990
Hartigan, Lynda Roscoe, ed. *Made with Passion*. Washington, D.C.: Smithsonian Institution Press for the National Museum of American Art, 1990.

Hartigan 1994
———. "Recent Challenges in the Study of African American Folk Art." *The International Review of African American Art* 11, no. 3 (1994), pp. 26–29.

Hartigan 2000
———. "Going Urban: American Folk Art and the Great Migration." *Smithsonian American Art Journal* (July 2000), pp. 26–51.

Hooks 1995
hooks, bell. *Art on My Mind: Visual Politics*. New York: New Press, 1995.

Horwitz 1975
Horwitz, Elinor Lander. *Contemporary American Folk Artists*. Philadelphia: J. B. Lippincott, 1975.

Huffman 1994
Huffman, Barry G. "Raymond Coins: Rock and Wood Worker." *Voices: The Newsletter of the North Carolina Folk Art Society* 3 (1994), pp. 1–3.

Kahan 1986
Kahan, Mitchell Douglas. *Heavenly Visions: The Art of Minnie Evans*. Raleigh, N.C.: North Carolina Museum of Art, 1986; distributed by the University of North Carolina Press.

Kammen 1993
Kammen, Michael G. *Mystic Chords of Memory: The Transformation of Tradition in American Culture*. New York: Vintage Books, 1993.

Kemp and Boyer 1994
Kemp, Kathy, and Keith Boyer. *Revelations: Alabama's Visionary Folk Artists*. Birmingham, Ala.: Crane Hill Publishers, 1994.

Ketchin 1994
Ketchin, Susan. *The Christ-Haunted Landscape: Faith and Doubt in Southern Fiction*. Jackson, Miss.: University Press of Mississippi, 1994.

Kiah 1978
Kiah, Virginia. "Ulysses Davis: Savannah Folk Sculptor." *Southern Folk Quarterly* 42 (1978), pp. 271–285.

Kirwin 1987
Kirwin, Liza. "Documenting Contemporary Southern Self-Taught Artists." *Southern Quarterly* 26, no. 1 (fall 1987), pp. 57–75.

Knott 1992
Knott, Robert. *Diving in the Spirit*. Winston-Salem, N.C.: Wake Forest University, 1992.

Kogan 1998
Kogan, Lee. *The Art of Nellie Mae Rowe: Ninety-Nine and a Half Won't Do*. New York: Museum of American Folk Art, 1998; distributed by the University Press of Mississippi.

Lampell, Lampell, and Larkin 1989
Lampell, Ramona, Millard Lampell, and David Larkin. O, *Appalachia: Artists of the Southern Mountains*. New York: Stewart, Tabori, and Chang, 1989; distributed in the U.S. by Workman Pub.

LaRoche 1989
LaRoche, Louanne, ed. *Sam Doyle (1906–1985)*. ArtRandom, no. 18. Kyoto, Japan: Kyoto Shoin, 1989.

LeQuire 1981
LeQuire, Louise. "Edmondson's Art Reflects His Faith, Strong and Pure." *Smithsonian* 12, no. 5 (1981), pp. 50–55.

Little 1957
Little, Nina Fletcher. *The Abby Aldrich Rockefeller Folk Art Collection: A Descriptive Catalog*. Boston: Little, Brown, 1957.

Livingston, Beardsley, and Perry 1982
Livingston, Jane, John Beardsley, and Regenia Perry. *Black Folk Art in America, 1930–1980*. Jackson, Miss.: University Press of Mississippi, Center for the Study of Southern Culture for the Corcoran Gallery of Art, 1982.

Longhauser and Szeemann 1998
Longhauser, Elsa, and Harald Szeemann. *Self-Taught Artists of the 20th Century: An American Anthology*. New York: Museum of American Folk Art; San Francisco: Chronicle Books, 1998.

Luck 1995
Luck, Barbara. *"Moving" with Mattie Lou O'Kelley*. Williamsburg, Va.: Colonial Williamsburg Foundation, 1995.

MacAdam 1990
MacAdam, Barbara A. "God's Green." *ARTnews* 89 (March 1990), p. 31.

Maresca and Ricco 1991
Maresca, Frank, and Roger Ricco. *Bill Traylor: His Art, His Life*. New York: Knopf, 1991; distributed by Random House.

Maresca and Ricco 1997
———. *William Hawkins: Paintings*. New York: Knopf, 1997.

McWillie 1987
McWillie, Judith. "Another Face of the Diamond: Afro American Traditional Art in the Deep South." *The Clarion* 12 (fall 1987), pp. 42–53.

McWillie 1988
———, ed. *Another Face of the Diamond: Pathways Through the Black Atlantic South*. New York: INTAR Latin American Gallery, 1988.

McWillie 1992
———. "Lonnie Holley's Moves." *Artforum* 30, no. 8 (1992), pp. 80–84.

Metcalf 1983
Metcalf, Eugene W. "Black Art, Folk Art, and Social Control." *Winterthur Portfolio* 18 (winter 1983), pp. 271–289.

Metcalf 1996–97
———. "William Adkins and the Art of Patent Drawing." *Raw Vision* 17 (Winter 1996–1997), pp. 34–37.

Milwaukee Art Museum 1993
Milwaukee Art Museum. *Common Ground/Uncommon Vision: The Michael and Julie Hall Collection of American Folk Art in the Milwaukee Art Museum*. Milwaukee, Wisc.: The Museum, 1993.

Morris 1995–96
Morris, Randall. "Martin Ramirez." *Folk Art* 21 (winter 1995/96), pp. 36–44.

Muller 1994
Muller, Joan. *Under the Cloak of Justice: The Work of Ned Cartledge*. Richmond, Va.: Anderson Gallery, Virginia Commonwealth University, 1994.

O'Kelley and Bishop 1989
O'Kelley, Mattie Lou, and Robert Bishop. *Mattie Lou O'Kelley, Folk Artist*. Boston: Little, Brown, 1989.

Oppenhimer 1995–96
Oppenhimer, Ann. "Ned Cartledge: The Injustice Collector." *Raw Vision* 13 (winter 1995–96), pp. 44–47.

Parish 1974
Parish, Peggy. *Dinosaur Time*. New York: Harper Collins, 1974.

Parish and Whitney 1974
Parish, James Robert, and Steven Whitney. *Vincent Price Unmasked*. New York: Drake Publishers, 1974.

Patterson 1993
Patterson, Tom. *ASHE: Improvisation & Recycling in African-American Visionary Art*. Winston-Salem, N.C.: Diggs Gallery at Winston-Salem State University, 1993.

Patterson and Ingram 1993
Patterson, Tom, and Lynne Ingram. *Not by Luck: Self-Taught Artists in the American South*. Milford, N.J.: Lynne Ingram Southern Folk Art, 1993.

Peacock and Jenkins 1996
Peacock, Robert, and Annibel Jenkins. *Paradise Garden: A Trip through Howard Finster's Visionary World*. San Francisco: Chronicle Books, 1996.

Perry 1982
Perry, Regenia. *What It Is: Black American Folk Art from the Collection of Regenia Perry*. Richmond, Va.: Anderson Gallery, Virginia Commonwealth University, 1982.

Perry 1992
———. *Free Within Ourselves: African-American Artists in the Collection of the National Museum of American Art*. Washington, D.C.; San Francisco: National Museum of American Art in association with Pomegranate Artbooks, 1992.

Pollitzer 1999
Pollitzer, William S. *The Gullah People and Their African Heritage*. Athens, Ga.: University of Georgia Press, 1999.

Porter 1969
Porter, James A. *Modern Negro Art*. 1943. Reprint, New York: Arno Press, 1969.

Ricco/Maresca Gallery 1990
Ricco/Maresca Gallery. *William L. Hawkins, 1895–1990*. New York: Ricco/Maresca Gallery, 1990.

Roberts 1992
Roberts, Norma, ed. *Elijah Pierce: Woodcarver*. Columbus, Ohio: Columbus Museum of Art, 1992; distributed by the University of Washington Press, Seattle and London.

Robinson, Foster, and Ogilvie 1969
Robinson, Armstead L., Craig C. Foster, and Donald H. Ogilvie, eds. *Black Studies in the University: A Symposium*. New Haven, Conn.: Yale University Press, 1969.

Saarinen 1958
Saarinen, Aline B. *The Proud Possessors: The Lives, Times, and Tastes of Some Adventurous American Art Collectors*. New York: Random House, 1958.

Schwindler 1989
Schwindler, Gary Joseph. *William Hawkins: Transformations*. Charleston, Ill.: Tarble Arts Center, 1989.

Shannon 1988
Shannon, Charles. "Bill Traylor's Triumph." *Art & Antiques* (February 1988), pp. 61–65.

Shapiro 1957
Shapiro, Irwin. *The Golden Book of America: Stories from Our Country's Past*. New York: Golden Press, 1957.

Spriggs 2000
Spriggs, Lynne E. *Local Heroes: Paintings and Sculpture by Sam Doyle*. Atlanta: High Museum of Art, 2000.

Stallybrass and White 1986
Stallybrass, Peter, and Allon White. *The Politics and Poetics of Transgression*. Ithaca, N.Y.: Cornell University Press, 1986.

Thompson 1984
Thompson, Robert Farris. *Flash of the Spirit: African and Afro-American Art and Philosophy*. New York: Vintage Books, 1984.

Thompson et al. 1999
Thompson, Robert Farris, Bobby L. Lovett, Rusty Freeman, Judith McWillie, Grey Gundaker, and Lowery Stokes Sims. *The Art of William Edmondson*. Nashville, Tenn.: Cheekwood Museum of Art; Jackson, Miss.: University Press of Mississippi, 1999.

Trechsel 1995
Trechsel, Gail Andrews, ed. *Pictured in My Mind: Contemporary American Self-Taught Art from the Collection of Dr. Kurt Gitter and Alice Rae Yelen*. Birmingham, Ala.: Birmingham Museum of Art, 1995; distributed by University Press of Mississippi.

Vlach 1991
Vlach, John Michael. *By the Work of Their Hands: Studies in Afro-American Folklife*. Charlottesville, Va.: University Press of Virginia, 1991.

Wadsworth 1976
Wadsworth, Anna, ed. *Missing Pieces: Georgia Folk Art, 1770–1976*. Atlanta: Georgia Council for the Arts and Humanities, 1976.

Weld, Serikawa, and Smalls 1992
Weld, Alison, Sadao Serikawa, and James Smalls. *Dream Singers, Story Tellers: An African American Presence*. Fukui, Japan: Fukui Fine Arts Museum, 1992.

West 1982
West, Cornel. *Prophesy Deliverance!: An Afro-American Revolutionary Christianity*. Philadelphia: Westminster Press, 1982.

Westervelt 1986
Westervelt, Robert F. *Ned Cartledge*. Atlanta: Nexus Press, 1986.

Wilson 1991–92
Wilson, Charles Reagan. "Southern Religion and Visionary Art." *Mississippi Folklore Register* 25–26 (1991–92), pp. 1–10.

Wilson and Ferris 1989
Wilson, Charles Reagan, and William Ferris, eds. *Encyclopedia of Southern Culture*. Chapel Hill: University of North Carolina Press, 1989.

Woodward 1951
Woodward, C. Vann. *Origins of the New South, 1877–1913*. A History of the South, vol. 9. Baton Rouge: Louisiana State University Press, 1951.

Yelen 1993
Yelen, Alice Rae. *Passionate Visions of the American South: Self-Taught Artists from 1940 to the Present*. New Orleans: New Orleans Museum of Art, 1993; distributed by the University Press of Mississippi.

Checklist of the T. Marshall Hahn Collection

Dimensions are given in inches, height before width before depth. In many cases it is difficult to determine an exact date of creation for folk art pieces. The dates given are often approximate.

Works purchased for the T. Marshall Hahn Collection with funds from the T. Marshall Hahn Folk Art Acquisition Fund are marked with an asterisk.

1. William Adkins
Addled Scratcher Fork, ca. 1995
Ballpoint pen on posterboard
22 x 28
1997.42
Cat. 1

2. William Adkins
Diphiore Dthuiore Feather Gamble, ca. 1995
Ballpoint pen on posterboard, envelope, feather, cashier's checks, money order, and dollar bill
22 x 28
1997.43
Cat. 2

3. Leroy Almon
God's Commandments to Man, 1980
Carved wood with paint and stain
33¼ x 23 x 3
1997.44
Cat. 3

4. Leroy Almon
The Prodigal Son, 1980
Carved wood with paint
22⅛ x 15¾ x 1
1996.157

5. Leroy Almon
The Sacrifice of Isaac, 1981
Carved wood with paint
11¼ x 16 x 1
1996.158
Cat. 4

6. Leroy Almon
The Baptism of Jesus, 1983
Carved wood with paint
16 x 13¼ x 1
1996.155
Cat. 5

7. Leroy Almon
Slavery Time, 1990
Carved wood with paint
36 x 22⅝ x ¾
1999.95
Cat. 6

8. Leroy Almon
Thomas Dorsey, 1994
Carved wood with paint
27½ x 35⅝ x ¾
1996.156
Cat. 7

9. Eddie Arning
Untitled (Pink House, American Flag), 1969–1973
Oil pastel and pencil on paper
22 x 16
1997.45

10. Eddie Arning
Untitled (Two Men, Tree, and Cloud), 1969–1973
Oil pastel on paper
19¾ x 25¾
1996.159
Cat. 8

11. Eddie Arning
Untitled (Two Men with Sheep), 1969–1973
Oil pastel, crayon, and pencil on paper
21⅝ x 31⅝
1997.46

12. Richard Burnside
The Man Climbing the Stairsteps, 1980–1994
Paint on board
17¾ x 23¾
1996.160

13. Richard Burnside
Untitled (Black Face), 1980–1994
Paint on metal and cardboard
15 x 23
1996.161

14. David Butler
Boat with Two Monkeys and a Squirrel, ca. 1984
Paint on metal
27¾ x 33¾ x 1½
1997.47
Cat. 9

15. David Butler
The Last Supper, ca. 1984
Paint, plastic, and nails on metal
27¾ x 42½
1997.48
Cat. 10

16. Ned Cartledge
The Flag Waver, 1970
Carved wood with paint
36¾ x 33½ x 2½
1996.33
Cat. 11

17. Ned Cartledge
Don't Hide Your Light Under a Bushel, 1986
Carved wood with paint
20⅜ × 23½ × 1
1996.32
Cat. 12

18. Ned Cartledge
The Reykjavik Rabbit, 1986
Carved wood with paint
22¾ × 17¾ × 1⅝
1996.165
Cat. 13

19. Ned Cartledge
Fundamentalist Preacher Negotiating with a Black Hoer, 1989
Carved wood with paint
20½ × 27½ × 1½
1997.49
Cat. 14

20. Ned Cartledge
The Rape of the American Taxpayer, 1992
Carved wood with paint
19⅜ × 21⅛ × 1⅝
1996.164

21. Ned Cartledge
Does Ross Perot Know Where His Bull Is Taking Him?, 1993
Carved basswood with acrylic paint
16 × 20¼ × 1½
1996.162

22. Ned Cartledge
Nixon, 1994
Carved basswood with acrylic paint
27½ × 12½ × 1¾
1996.163
Cat. 15

23. Raymond Coins
Valley of the Dry Bones, 1986
Carved steatite
17 × 19 × 1⅝
1997.50
Cat. 16

24. Raymond Coins
Best Friends, ca. 1988
Carved steatite
17⅞ × 13¾ × 3
1997.51
Cat. 17

25. Raymond Coins
Untitled (Dog), ca. 1988
Wood
36 × 30 × 20
1996.166
Cat. 18

26. Raymond Coins
Untitled (Turtle), ca. 1988
Wood
21¾ × 13 × 12½
1996.167

27. Karolina Danek
Untitled (Madonna and Child), 1992
Oil on canvas with rhinestones and plastic beads
27¼ × 21½
1996.168

28. Henry Darger
40 at Jenny Richee Facing attack by blengiglomeneans who mistake them for little Glandelinians because they wore gray uniforms [sic], *the only way to save save* [sic] *themselves is to undress & hide the Glandelinian uniforms* [Recto], 1910–1972

Long after Cromer Andren Jack Evans and Vivian girls mistaken for girl scouts by Abbieannan soldiers and held prisoners [Verso 1], 1910–1972

At Frances Atlanta a second Glandelinian rascal captured and forced to respect Vivian girl princesses [Verso 2], 1910–1972

At Frances Atlanta/The result of the persuit/ though they escaped 2 are injured Angelina Aronburg and Jennie Turmer with them [Verso 3], 1910–1972
Watercolor, pencil, and ink on paper
18¾ × 69¾
1997.52a & b
Cat. 19

29. Ulysses Davis
Untitled, 1970s
Carved wood with paint, glass beads, and toothpicks
13½ × 3⅝ × 4⅜
1996.31
Cat. 20

30. Ulysses Davis
Moses, 1960s–1970s
Carved wood with paint
17¼ × 12⅜ × 2⅜
1997.53

31. Thornton Dial Jr.
Jesus Christ of All the Races, ca. 1988
Wood, metal, paint, and industrial sealing compound
45 × 31½ × 12½
1996.172

32. Thornton Dial
Smooth-Going Cats and the Hard-Headed Goat, 1990
Oil on canvas
65⅞ × 78
1997.61
Cat. 21

33. Thornton Dial
Life and Love, 1991
Charcoal and watercolor on paper
22 × 30
1997.57

34. Thornton Dial
Rooster Picture, 1991
Pencil, watercolor, and oil pastel on paper
22¼ × 30
1997.62
Cat. 22

35. Thornton Dial
Heading for the Higher Paying Jobs, 1992
Enamel and oil paints, cloth, tin, wood, and industrial sealing compound on canvas, mounted on wood
64½ × 90 × 9
1997.55
Cat. 23

36. Thornton Dial
Love in the Hills and Mountains, 1992
Charcoal and graphite on paper
30 × 44¼
1997.58

37. Thornton Dial
Proud Cats Made to Climb, 1992
Paint, metal, carpet, and rope on canvas and wood
64⅞ × 65⅛ × 6½
1997.60
Cat. 24

38. Thornton Dial
Dressing Up the Dog, ca. 1993
Charcoal and pastel on paper
25¾ × 19⅝
1997.54

39. Thornton Dial
Holding the Dog, ca. 1993
Charcoal and pastel on paper
25¾ × 19⅝
1997.56

40. Thornton Dial
Peeping and Hiding, 1993–1994
Charcoal and pastel on paper
14 × 9¾
1997.59

41. Thornton Dial
Invention of the Chainsaw, 1994
Pencil and watercolor on paper
22 × 30
1996.170
Cat. 25

42. Thornton Dial
Old Projects, 1994
Paint, cloth, nails, wood, and tin on canvas and wood
32½ × 62 × 9
1996.171
Cat. 26

43. Thornton Dial
Flying with the Peckerwoods, Running for Your Life, 1995
Paint, wood, rope, and metal on canvas
40 × 30 × 6½
1996.169

44. Sam Doyle
Crab Man, 1975
Paint and pencil on paper
16 × 13¼
1999.96

45. Sam Doyle
First Doctor Y.B., 1970–1985
House paint on roofing tin
48⅛ × 25⅜
1997.63
Cat. 27

46. Sam Doyle
Frip, St. Helena's Best, 1970–1985
House paint on roofing tin
43⅛ × 52
1997.66
Cat. 32

47. Sam Doyle
John Chisolem, St. Helena's First Embalmer, 1970–1985
House paint on roofing tin
57 × 25¼
1996.29
Cat. 28

48. Sam Doyle
Onk Sam, 1970–1985
House paint on roofing tin
29¼ × 27½
1997.64

49. Sam Doyle
Rambling Rose, 1970–1985
House paint and beer can on roofing tin
48 × 25½
1997.65
Cat. 29

50. Sam Doyle
Untitled (Larry Rivers), 1970–1985
House paint on roofing tin
36 × 29⅜
1996.173

51. Sam Doyle
Welcome Table, 1970–1985
House paint on roofing tin
26¼ × 43½
1996.174
Cat. 30

52. Sam Doyle
Try Me, ca. 1981
House paint on roofing tin
41⅞ × 26⅝
1997.67
Cat. 31

53. Minnie Evans
Untitled (Composition with Two Yellow Scalloped Forms), 1944
Crayon, pencil, and pen on paper
13⅜ × 10¾
1997.3

54. Minnie Evans
Untitled (Three Faces Surmounting Landscape), 1963
Crayon and pencil on paper
11⅞ × 9⅛
1997.68
Cat. 33

55. Minnie Evans
Untitled (Face Surrounded by Foliage), ca. 1963
Crayon, pen, and pencil on paper
11⅞ × 8¾
1997.69
Cat. 34

56. Howard Finster
The Higher You Climb the Farther You Can See, #432, 1977
Paint on board with embossed wood
29¼ × 40
1997.76

57. Howard Finster
Take My Yoke Upon You and Learn of Me Saith Jesus, #1,060, 1977–1978
Paint on board with embossed wood
17½ × 48¼
1997.74
Cat. 35

58. Howard Finster
Find the Four Horses of the Revelation of the Bible, #1,128, ca. 1978
Paint on board with embossed wood
22 × 32¾
1997.70

59. Howard Finster
In My Father's House Are Many Mansions, #4,392, 1985
Plexiglas, plastic, beads, toys, and sequins
18 × 14⅝ × 9
1997.72
Cat. 36

60. Howard Finster
Jesus Is the Christ the Son of God, #4,189, 1985
Paint, Plexiglas, and plastic on wood
32¼ × 21¼
1997.73

61. Howard Finster
George Washington, #6,903, 1987
Paint on board
48 × 48
1997.71
Cat. 37

62. Howard Finster
The Angel of the Lord, #10,000, 1987–1989
Paint on plywood cutout
42 × 85
1997.75

63. Howard Finster
Coca-Cola Bottle, #38,348, 1995
Paint on prefabricated plastic bottle
65½ × 22 × 22
1996.175
Cat. 38

64. Lee Godie
Untitled (Profile of Woman), 1960–1994
Ballpoint pen and paint on canvas
19 × 17⅜
1997.77

65. William Hawkins
Con[q]uest of the Moon #1, 1984
Enamel paint on Masonite
48 × 56⅛
1996.27
Cat. 39

66. William Hawkins
State Office Building #2, 1985
Enamel paint on board
46 × 55
1997.82
Cat. 40

67. William Hawkins
Tyrannosaurus #1, 1987
Enamel paint on board
56½ × 48
1997.86
Cat. 41

68. William Hawkins
Elephant and Rider (Easel), 1988
Pencil on paper
14 × 11
1997.78
Cat. 44

69. William Hawkins
Flying Horse, 1988
Pencil on paper
14 × 11
1997.79
Cat. 45

70. William Hawkins
Indian Chasing White Man, 1988
Enamel paint on board
36 × 48
1997.80
Cat. 46

71. William Hawkins
Indian Courtyard, 1988
Enamel paint on board
48 × 48
1997.81
Cat. 47

72. William Hawkins
Stegosaurus, 1988
Pencil on paper
14 × 11
1997.83
Cat. 43

73. William Hawkins
Tyrannosaurus Rex, 1988
Pencil on paper
14 × 11
1997.85
Cat. 42

74. William Hawkins
Tiger and Bear, 1989
Enamel paint, paper, duct tape, and sand on board
42 × 48
1997.84
Cat. 48

75. William Hawkins
Buffalo, 1980s
Enamel paint on board
28 × 29¾
1997.87

76. Lonnie Holley
Blown Out Black Mama's Belly, 1994
Rubber, cloth, and wire coat hanger
84 × 22 × 4
1996.40
Cat. 49

77. Clementine Hunter
The Wedding, 1960
Oil on canvas
21⅜ × 27½
1996.176
Cat. 50

78. Howard Ivester
Untitled (10 wooden figures), 1993
Carved wood with paint
6⅞ × 2½ × 2 to 8 × 2½ × 2
1999.103.1–10

79. S. L. Jones
Owl, 1988
Carved wood with enamel paint
18 × 6½ × 6½
1997.88
Cat. 51

80. S. L. Jones
Untitled (Bust of a Man), 1990
Carved wood with enamel paint
18¼ × 11½ × 9¼
1997.89
Cat. 52

81. Charley Kinney
B'ar Tacked, mid-1970s–1991
Paint and crayon on paper
22½ × 28½
1996.177

82. Charley Kinney
Old Hanted Hoss, mid-1970s–1991
Paint and crayon on paper
21⅞ × 27¾
1996.178

83. Charley Kinney
Radler, mid-1970s–1991
Paint and crayon on paper
28½ × 22⅜
1997.90
Cat. 53

84. Charley Kinney
Wild Cat, mid-1970s–1991
Crayon, pencil, and paint on paper
22½ × 28½
1997.91

85. Joe Light
Untitled (Goat), 1985–1992
Paint on plywood
35 × 47¾
1997.92
Cat. 54

86. Ronald Lockett
Natural Habitat, ca. 1990
Paint, wire, wood, nails, and wood filler on plywood
48 × 48
1996.181

87. Ronald Lockett
Traps, ca. 1991
Paint, fabric, wood, metal, and netting on plywood
30 × 48 × 3
1997.93
Cat. 55

88. Ronald Lockett
Safe Return, ca. 1991
Paint on plywood
35 × 47¾
1997.92

89. Ronald Lockett
Cover of Night, ca. 1992
Paint, chicken wire, nails, photograph, and cellophane on plywood
47⅞ × 40⅛
1997.94
Cat. 56

90. Ronald Lockett
Facing Extinction, ca. 1994
Welder's chalk (?) on metal mounted on wood
49⅜ × 47⅝ × 3½
1996.179
Cat. 57

91. Charlie Lucas
Untitled (Yellow Figure), 1984–1993
Paint on wood
23 × 20
1996.182

92. Dwight Mackintosh
Untitled (Four Seated Figures), 1981
Ink and tempera on paper
26 × 39⅞
1997.97

93. Dwight Mackintosh
Untitled (Figure with Orange Hair), 1982
Pencil and tempera on paper
20 × 26 inches
1997.95

94. Dwight Mackintosh
Untitled (Four Orange Figures), 1988
Felt pen on paper
14¾ × 21⅞
1997.96

95. Dwight Mackintosh
Untitled (Three Orange Figures), 1988
Felt pen on paper
14⅞ × 22
1997.98

96. Sister Gertrude Morgan
Jesus Is My Air Plane (megaphone), ca. 1970
Watercolor, ballpoint pen, and pencil with heavy thread and safety pin on paper
17 × 4 × 4
*2000.10
Cat. 58

97. Mattie Lou O'Kelley
Untitled (Bowl of Apples), 1975
Oil on canvas
15¼ × 19¼
1997.99
Cat. 59

98. Mattie Lou O'Kelley
Georgia Farm, 1991
Acrylic on canvas
23⅜ × 31⅜
1996.184
Cat. 60

99. Mattie Lou O'Kelley
Mattie in the Morning Glories, 1992
Oil on canvas
39⅛ × 27⅜
1996.30
Cat. 61

100. Mattie Lou O'Kelley
Box of 92 works on paper, 1968–1996
63 pen and pencil drawings, 28 photocopies, and 1 photograph
5½ × 8½ to 8½ × 11
1996.183.1–92

101. John Perates
St. Peter and St. Paul, 1940s
Carved wood with paint
73⅞ × 39 × 5⅛
*1998.40
Cat. 62

102. Elijah Pierce
Three Ways to Send a Message: Telephone, Telegram, Tell-a-Woman, ca. 1941
Carved wood with paint
15½ × 18 × 1½
*1998.80
Cat. 63

103. Elijah Pierce
A Gifted Man of God, 1960
Carved wood with paint and glitter
17 × 17 × ¾
1997.100

104. Elijah Pierce
Christ and Lady, 1968
Carved wood with paint and glitter
21½ × 16½ × 1¼
1997.102
Cat. 64

105. Elijah Pierce
Bad Judgment, 1980
Carved wood with paint and glitter mounted on cardboard
21¾ × 15¾ × ¾
1997.101

106. Elijah Pierce
Two Dragons Flanking a Frog Surmounted by a Goat, 1981
Carved wood with paint, glitter, and rhinestones
14¼ × 21¼ × 1¼
1997.103

107. Martin Ramirez
Inmaculada, 1950s
Crayon, pencil, watercolor, and collaged papers
92 × 45
*1999.93
Cat. 65

108. Nellie Mae Rowe
Red and Blue Fish, ca. 1979
Crayon and pencil on paper
19 × 24
1997.107
Cat. 66

109. Nellie Mae Rowe
Woman in Orange and Red, ca. 1979
Crayon and pencil on paper
19 × 24
1997.108
Cat. 67

110. Nellie Mae Rowe
Blue Cat, 1980
Crayon and pencil on paper
18 × 24
1997.104

111. Nellie Mae Rowe
Joe and His Pigs, 1980
Crayon and pencil on paper
19⅞ × 15⅞
1996.28

112. Nellie Mae Rowe
Happy Days, 1981
Crayon and pencil on paper
18 × 24
1997.105
Cat. 68

113. Nellie Mae Rowe
Orange Lion with Broken Tail, 1981
Crayon, pen, paper, and pencil on paper
18 × 24
1997.106

114. Mary Shelley
Cow and Daffodil Buds, 1988
Carved wood with paint
21½ × 23 × 1½
1999.97
Cat. 69

115. Herbert Singleton
Hallelujah Door, 1993
Carved wooden door with enamel paint
115¼ × 48¾ × 1¾
1996.185
Cat. 70

116. Herbert Singleton
Abraham and Lot, 1970–1994
Carved wood with enamel paint
22 × 67¼ × 1¼
1996.186

117. Mary T. Smith
Untitled (Figure in Green and Black), 1980–1986
Paint on corrugated metal
49⅛ × 27
1996.187
Cat. 71

118. Mary T. Smith
Untitled (Figure with Halo), ca. 1986
Enamel paint on chipboard
48 × 27⅜
1997.109
Cat. 72

119. Jimmy Lee Sudduth
Untitled (Marine Creature), 1990–1994
Paint and pencil on wood
18 × 96⅛
1999.98

120. Mose Tolliver
Long Time Charlie, 1987
House paint on wood
31½ × 22⅝
1996.188

121. Mose Tolliver
Self-Portrait of Me, 1987
House paint on plywood
24 × 23¾
1997.110
Cat. 73

122. Mose Tolliver
Self-Portrait of Me on Crutches, 1987
House paint on wood paneling
33 × 18½
1996.192
Cat. 74

123. Mose Tolliver
Spot—House Dog, 1987
House paint on wood
22¾ × 31⅝
1996.191

124. Mose Tolliver
Wild Man, 1987
House paint on wood
35¼ × 16⅜
1996.193

125. Mose Tolliver
All the Way from Chicago Paul Ling Low 2. Annie Low 3. Charlie Bee Low 4. Chestafel Low, ca. 1987
House paint on wood
24⅛ × 31⅛
1999.101

126. Mose Tolliver
Chinese Fruit Basket, ca. 1987
House paint on wood
23⅞ × 24¼
1999.99
Cat. 75

127. Mose Tolliver
Hootin' Owl, ca. 1987
House paint on wood
27¼ × 26½
1999.100
Cat. 76

128. Mose Tolliver
Work of Bill Traylor, ca. 1987
House paint on wood
29½ × 20⅜
1996.194

129. Mose Tolliver
Magician Lady, 1988
House paint on wood
38 × 24⅜
1996.189

130. Mose Tolliver
Me When I Was Sick Trying to Make Section with Women and Dogs, 1988
House paint on wood
23¼ × 24⅛
1996.190

131. Edgar Tolson
Untitled, 1977
Carved wood with pencil and ink
12½ × 3½ × 3⅝
1997.111
Cat. 77

132. Edgar Tolson
Untitled, late 1970s
Carved wood with pencil and ink
12½ × 4⅞ × 4⅞
1997.112
Cat. 78

133. Bill Traylor
Untitled (Black Elephant with a Brown Ear), 1939–1948
Poster paint and pencil on paper
14⅝ × 25¾
1997.113
Cat. 80

134. Bill Traylor
Untitled (House with Figures), 1939–1948
Poster paint and pencil on cardboard
13½ × 13⅞
1997.114
Cat. 82

135. Bill Traylor
Untitled (Man in Blue Pants), 1939–1948
Poster paint, pencil, colored pencil, and charcoal on cardboard
10⅝ × 7¼
1997.115
Cat. 81

136. Bill Traylor
Untitled (Two Dogs Fighting), 1939–1948
Poster paint and pencil on cardboard
16½ x 21⅛
1997.116
Cat. 79

137. Bill Traylor
Untitled (Walking Woman with Handbag), 1939–1948
Colored pencil, pencil, and poster paint on cardboard
15 x 11½
1997.117

138. Thai Varick
Horse, 1992–1993
Wire
16 x 22 x 8½
1999.102
Cat. 83

139. Inez Nathaniel Walker
Untitled (Figure in a Striped Vest), 1973
Pencil and crayon on orange paper
17¼ x 11⅞
1997.118

140. Inez Nathaniel Walker
Untitled (Woman with a Green Collar), 1973
Pencil, pen, and crayon on paper
12 x 9
1997.121

141. Inez Nathaniel Walker
Untitled (Two Women), 1974
Pencil and paint on paper
19⅞ x 24
1997.119

142. Inez Nathaniel Walker
Untitled (Woman and Child), 1974
Pencil, paint, and marker on paper
19⅞ x 23⅞
1997.120

143. Inez Nathaniel Walker
Untitled (Woman with Red Lacy Collar), 1970s
Pencil and crayon on paper
12 x 9⅞
1997.122

144. Joseph Yoakum
Mt. Atzmon of Lebanon Mtn. Range near Village of Leonine Lebanon S.E. Asia, 1968–1971
Colored pencil and ballpoint pen on paper
11¾ x 18
*2000.12
Cat. 84

145. Joseph Yoakum
Mt. Uovz in Verkhoyansk Range near List Aldan S.E., U.S.S.R., 1968–1971
Colored pencil, ballpoint pen, and pencil on paper
12 x 18½
*2000.11
Cat. 85

Artists' Biographies

Following are the dates and venues of exhibitions mentioned more than once in these biographies:

Another Face of the Diamond: Pathways Through the Black Atlantic South, INTAR Latin American Gallery, New York, 1989.

Art Outsider et Folk Art des Collections de Chicago, Halle Saint Pierre, Paris, 1998–1999.

Black Folk Art in America, 1930–1980, Corcoran Gallery of Art, Washington, D.C., 1982; J. B. Speed Museum, Louisville, Kentucky, 1982; Brooklyn Museum, 1982; Craft and Folk Museum, Los Angeles, California, 1982–1983; and The Institute for the Arts, Rice University, Houston, Texas, 1983.

Common Ground/Uncommon Vision: The Michael and Julie Hall Collection of American Folk Art, Milwaukee Art Museum, 1993; The Nelson-Atkins Museum of Art, Kansas City, Missouri, 1993; Albright-Knox Art Gallery, Buffalo, New York, 1993–1994; Phoenix Art Museum, 1994; Delaware Art Museum, Wilmington, Delaware, 1994; and Abby Aldrich Rockefeller Folk Art Museum, Williamsburg, Virginia, 1994–1995.

Made with Passion: The Hemphill Folk Art Collection, National Museum of American Art, Smithsonian Institution, Washington, D.C., 1990.

Missing Pieces: Georgia Folk Art, 1770–1976, Atlanta Historical Society, 1976; Telfair Academy of Arts and Sciences, Savannah, Georgia, 1977; and Columbus Museum of Arts and Crafts, Columbus, Georgia, 1977.

O, Appalachia: Artists of the Southern Mountains, Huntington Museum of Art, Huntington, West Virginia, 1989.

Outside the Main Stream: Folk Art in Our Time, High Museum of Art at the Georgia-Pacific Center, Atlanta, Georgia, 1988.

Passionate Visions of the American South: Self-Taught Artists from 1940 to the Present, New Orleans Museum of Art, 1993–1994; University Art Museum, Berkeley, California, 1994; Portland Art Museum, Portland, Oregon, 1994; San Diego Museum of Art, 1994–1995; Corcoran Gallery of Art, Washington, D.C., 1995; North Carolina Museum of Art, Raleigh, North Carolina, 1995; and Bass Museum of Art, Miami Beach, Florida, 1995.

Pictured in My Mind: Contemporary American Self-Taught Art from the Collection of Dr. Kurt Gitter and Alice Rae Yelen, Birmingham Museum of Art, 1996; Southeastern Center for Contemporary Art, Winston-Salem, North Carolina, 1996–1997; and DeCordova Museum and Sculpture Park, Lincoln, Massachusetts, 1997.

Self-Taught Artists of the 20th Century: An American Anthology, Philadelphia Museum of Art, 1998; High Museum of Art, Atlanta, Georgia, 1998; Amon Carter Museum and The Modern Art Museum of Fort Worth, Fort Worth, Texas, 1998–1999; Memorial Art Gallery of the University of Rochester, Rochester, New York, 1999; and Wexner Center for the Arts, The Ohio State University, Columbus, Ohio, 1999; organized by the Museum of American Folk Art.

Souls Grown Deep: African American Vernacular Art of the South, City Hall East, Atlanta, Georgia, organized by the Michael C. Carlos Museum, Emory University, Atlanta, Georgia, 1996.

William Adkins

William W. Adkins was born in 1932 in Kansas City, Missouri. Adkins served briefly in the Army and worked construction jobs. He and his wife brought up ten children before divorcing in 1965. Around 1971 he became homeless and built a shack in an abandoned lot where he lived until the mid-1990s, doing odd jobs for neighborhood residents. Adkins drew obsessively, using ballpoint pen on posterboard. In the winter he delineated his complex inventions in the public library, where he found warmth, good light, and large worktables; in the summer, he drew outside. In 1995 his artistic production diminished after social workers moved him into an apartment, then a group home, and arranged for him to receive psychiatric drugs. Adkins now lives in a nursing home and draws intermittently. His art has been exhibited in several shows, including a solo exhibition at the Ricco/Maresca Gallery in New York in 1997, and *The End is Near! Visions of Apocalypse, Millennium, and Utopia* at the American Visionary Art Museum in 1997–1998.

Leroy Almon

Leroy Almon Sr. was born in 1938 in Tallapoosa, Georgia. From 1945 until he graduated from high school, he lived in Cincinnati and then spent six months in the Army. He studied at Kentucky State University and worked in sales for the Coca-Cola Company in Columbus, Ohio. While living in Columbus, Almon met Elijah Pierce at church. During the 1970s he managed Pierce's barbershop art gallery and learned wood carving from the older artist. In 1982 Almon returned to Tallapoosa, where he worked as a police dispatcher and continued carving. Almon died in 1997. He received the Georgia Governor's Award in the Arts in 1985, and his work has appeared in many group shows, including *Outside the Main Stream* and *Art Outsider et Folk Art*.

Eddie Arning

Carl Wilhelm Edward Arning was born in 1896 or 1898 in Germania, Texas, where he grew up on his family's farm. He attended school for approximately six years. After being diagnosed as schizophrenic, he was committed to a hospital in 1934 and spent the next three decades there. After he was transferred to a nursing home in 1964, the art teacher there gave him art supplies and encouraged him to draw. During the following ten years Arning produced nearly two thousand drawings, first in wax crayons and later in oil pastels, usually deriving his images from magazine advertisements and illustrations. In 1973 Arning left the nursing home to live with his sister and stopped drawing soon after. He died in 1993. His work has been exhibited often, including in *Self-Taught Artists of the 20th Century*.

David Butler

David Butler was born in 1898, in Good Hope, Louisiana. The son of a carpenter and a lay missionary, he quit school to help his family after his mother died. A sawmill accident in his early sixties forced his retirement, which gave him time to decorate his home and yard. His environment was composed of fancifully painted cut tin shapes, some assembled into whirligigs. He first concentrated on familiar scenes, later expanding his subject matter to include items from his dreams. Butler said that his ability to remember and reproduce his dream images was a gift from God. His artistic production continued until four years before his death in 1997. His work was included in many major exhibitions, including the seminal *Black Folk Art in America, Outside the Main Stream,* and a solo exhibition at the New Orleans Museum of Art in 1976.

Ned Cartledge

William "Ned" Cartledge was born in 1916 in Canon, Georgia. In 1930, after the banks in Canon failed, his father, a teller, moved the family to Atlanta. There, his mother opened a boardinghouse to help support her family. Cartledge, who began whittling as a child, worked as a carpenter's apprentice the year after he graduated from high school. He later managed the Cotton States Arbitration Board and sold tools. Cartledge began carving decorative items in 1947, but it was the Vietnam War that provoked his first political carvings. His Unitarian faith helped form his liberal viewpoint. Cartledge's work won second prize at the Savannah Arts Festival in 1969 and first prize the next year. *The Flag Waver* won the 1970 Atlanta Arts Festival Purchase Award. Cartledge has been the subject of several books and solo exhibitions in the Southeast during the 1980s and 1990s, including *Outside the Main Stream*. He has carved little since the death of his wife in 1996.

Raymond Coins

Willie Raymond Coins was born in 1904 in Stuart, Virginia. As a child, he moved to a North Carolina farm with his family and attended school through the fifth grade. Coins bought a farm in Westfield, North Carolina, in 1950. He grew tobacco and worked in a tobacco warehouse until he retired in the mid-1960s. After his retirement, he began carving imitation Indian artifacts from local stone; then he began to create larger works from his own imagination and took up wood carving. Coins died in 1998. His work has been shown in a number of group exhibitions, including *Outside the Main Stream* and *Art Outsider et Folk Art*. He received a North Carolina Folk Heritage Award in 1995.

Henry Darger

Henry Joseph Darger was born in 1892 in Chicago. When he was four, Darger's mother died after giving birth to his sister, who was immediately given up for adoption. After his tailor father became crippled, Darger was placed in a Catholic orphanage. A few years later he was sent to the Lincoln Asylum for Feebleminded Children because of his egregious behavior. Darger, who was not mentally handicapped (he was capable enough to skip the second grade), escaped at sixteen and found janitorial work at a Chicago hospital. He spent the remainder of his life doing menial work until ill heath forced him to retire in 1963. He attended mass regularly, sometimes several times a day, and collected cast-off objects. Around 1910 Darger began a massive apocalyptic novel, *The Story of the Vivian Girls, in what is Known as the Realms of the Unreal, of the Glandeco-Angelinian War Storm, Caused by the Child Slave Rebellion,* which he later illustrated with watercolor paintings. In 1972, after he was taken to the Catholic nursing home where he would die the next year, Darger's clandestine life's work was discovered by his landlord, photographer and designer Nathan Lerner, who preserved and publicized the hundreds of watercolors and thousands of manuscript pages he found. Darger's work was first shown in a solo exhibition in 1977 and is regularly included in exhibitions of self-taught and outsider art, including *Art Outsider et Folk Art* and *Self-Taught Artists of the 20th Century*. Fifty-eight of his paintings were shown in a retrospective organized by the University of Iowa Museum of Art in 1996 that traveled to the Museum of American Folk Art in 1997 and the High Museum of Art in 1997–1998.

Ulysses Davis

Ulysses Davis was born in 1914 in Fitzgerald, Georgia. He learned metalworking from his father, a blacksmith, and began carving when he was eleven. He left school after the tenth grade to help support his family by working for the railroad. After being laid off in the early 1950s, he began barbering in a shop he built behind his Savannah, Georgia, home. He decorated the outside of his barbershop, which became filled with his reliefs and freestanding carvings. Davis is best known for his series of busts of U.S. presidents. He died in 1990. His work was exhibited in *Missing Pieces*, *Black Folk Art in America*, and at the Library of Congress.

Thornton Dial

Thornton Dial was born in 1928 in Emelle, Alabama, and lived with a succession of relatives. He attended school through the third grade, leaving rural Emelle at thirteen for the industrial town of Bessemer, near Birmingham. There he was raised by his aunt, Sarah Dial Lockett, who also raised Ronald Lockett's father. In 1951 he married Clara Mae Murrow, and they had five children, four of whom have become visual artists. Dial has worked at many professions, among them carpentry, house painting, and ironworking. Using materials he found or had on hand, Dial first created decoys, then began makings paintings and assemblages dealing with social and political concerns. Among his first group shows was *Another Face of the Diamond*. He has been the subject of several solo exhibitions, including *Thornton Dial: Image of the Tiger* at the Museum of American Folk Art and the New Museum of Contemporary Art in the winter of 1993–1994 and *Thornton Dial: Remembering the Road* at the Michael C. Carlos Museum of Emory University during the 1996 Summer Olympic Games in Atlanta. His work was included in the Whitney Museum's Biennial of American Art in 2000 and *Self-Taught Artists of the 20th Century*. Dial was recently commissioned to create a tribute to Georgia Congressman John Lewis that will be placed in Atlanta's Freedom Park.

Sam Doyle

Thomas Samuel Doyle was born in 1906 on St. Helena Island, South Carolina. Doyle attended the island's Penn School, founded in 1862 to educate freed slaves. Although his artistic talents were recognized early, he left school after the ninth grade to work at a local store. He married, became a father, and began to paint in his twenties. His wife and children moved to New York City without him in the mid-1950s. Doyle's production increased dramatically after his retirement in 1967 from the Parris Island Marine Corps Recruit Training Depot laundry room, and he filled his yard on St. Helena with portraits of local characters and national heroes, painted with house paint on roofing tin. He also scavenged wood to create sculptural assemblages of animals, which may have been apotropaic. He died in 1985, three years after participating in *Black Folk Art in America*, the first of many group shows that have included his work. His art has been displayed in several solo shows, the largest and most recent of which was *Local Heroes: Paintings and Sculpture by Sam Doyle* at the High Museum of Art in 2000.

Minnie Evans

Minnie Eva Jones was born in 1892 in Long Creek, North Carolina. Her great-grandmother was a slave in Trinidad before she was sold to a Carolina planter. As a child Minnie began experiencing the visions that would continue throughout her life. She attended school through the fifth grade and then sold seafood door-to-door in Wrightsville Beach, North Carolina. In 1908 she married Julius Evans, and they raised three children. Her first drawing was completed on Good Friday in 1935. In 1948 she became gatekeeper at Airlie Gardens on the Pembroke estate near Wilmington, North Carolina, beginning her most productive period as an artist. Evans sometimes sold her works to the Gardens' visitors. Using wax crayons, pastels, ink, and, later, oil paints, on paper or cardboard, she made over one thousand drawings reproducing her visions or biblical scenes. In 1981, Evans moved to a nursing home, where she continued to draw until her death in 1987. Her work was first exhibited in New York in 1966 and has been included in several solo and group exhibitions, including *Outside the Main Stream*, *Art Outsider et Folk Art*, and a retrospective at the Whitney Museum of American Art in 1975.

Howard Finster

Howard Finster was born in 1915 in Valley Head, Alabama, and attended school through the sixth grade. He began preaching at the age of sixteen and supported his wife and five children through a variety of jobs, including mill work, making screened doors and windows, taxidermy, and repairing bicycles, cars, and lawn mowers. His Pennville, Georgia, environment—originally called the Plant Farm Museum—was constructed on land he purchased in 1961. Renamed Paradise Garden in 1975 as a result of an article in *Esquire* magazine, it contains fanciful buildings, including the World's Folk Art Church, and welded and modeled sculptures incorporating a variety of found and salvaged materials. Reverend Finster began painting in 1976, when he received a vision instructing him to "paint sacred art" in place of all other pursuits. At the turn of the millennium he had made well over 45,000 works of art for the purpose of spreading God's word. His work has been shown in such exhibitions as *Missing Pieces*, *Outside the Main Stream*, and *Self-Taught Artists of the 20th Century*. In 1982 Finster, who now lives in Summerville, Georgia, received a Visual Artist Fellowship in Sculpture from the National Endowment for the Arts. He has represented the United States in the Venice Biennale and has had many one-person shows. He has designed album covers for R.E.M. and Talking Heads and is the subject of and contributor to several books.

William Hawkins

William Lawrence Hawkins was born in 1895 on his family's farm in Madison County, Kentucky. He learned to draw on the farm, copying horse auction announcements and calendar pictures. In 1916 he moved to Columbus, Ohio, where he drove a delivery truck, collected and sold scrap metal and paper, ran numbers, operated a flophouse and brothel, worked as a carpenter and plumber, and built and painted houses. He sold drawings as early as the 1930s or 1940s, but he began painting in earnest in the 1970s, first using readily available materials, such as discarded house paint and scavenged wood. In 1981 he became friends with an artist who entered one of Hawkins's paintings in the Ohio State Fair, where it won first place. As his fame grew and his artwork brought in more money, his palette expanded, and he began to apply house painter's enamels on Masonite. He also started incorporating mass media images in his paintings to speed up his production. Hawkins died in 1990. His work has been shown in many solo exhibitions, including a 1997 retrospective at the Museum of American Folk Art, *William Hawkins Born July 27, 1895*, and in dozens of group shows, including *Made with Passion*, *Passionate Visions of the American South*, and *Art Outsider et Folk Art*.

Lonnie Holley

Lonnie Bradley Holley was born in Birmingham in 1950 and spent most of his youth in foster homes and reform school. At fourteen he went to live with his grandmother, who taught him to salvage usable items from other people's discards. In the late 1960s and early 1970s he worked as a dishwasher and short-order cook in Florida and Ohio. In 1972 he returned to Birmingham, where he continued to work in the food service industry. After his niece and nephew were killed in a house fire in the late 1970s, he carved grave markers for them from discarded industrial sandstone. By the mid-1980s, he was also making the semi-abstract paintings and assemblages with which he decorated his yard. Honoring the principles of recycling he learned from his grandmother, Holley combines found materials in constructions that express his philosophy of regeneration and transformation. Holley's environment was dismantled when an airport expansion forced him from his Birmingham home. He and the younger of his five children, several of whom are promising artists, now live in Harpersville, Alabama. Holley's work has been exhibited at the White House and in such group shows as *Outside the Main Stream*, *Passionate Visions of the American South*, and *Self-Taught Artists of the 20th Century*. A re-creation of his environment was featured in *Souls Grown Deep*.

Clementine Hunter

Clementine Rubin was born at Hidden Hill Plantation (now called Little Eva) near Cloutierville, Louisiana, in about 1886, the daughter of former slaves. She moved with her family up the road to Melrose Plantation, near Natchitoches, where she attended school for a few years before quitting to work in the fields. She married twice and bore five children. She was always good with her hands, quilting, making dolls, clothes, and baskets, and hand-tying lace. Her painting career began around 1940 when she was cleaning up the paints left out by a visiting artist. She told French writer François Mignon, a longtime guest at the plantation, that she could make a painting herself. He encouraged her to continue after he saw the result, painted on a window shade. Hunter painted with oils, watercolors, or house paint first on found materials and later on canvas or canvas board. She created murals (which are now in a private collection) for the well-known Africa House at Melrose. Hunter had to sneak into the closed gallery at segregated Northwestern State University in Natchitoches to see her own solo exhibition in 1954. Thirty years later she received an honorary doctorate from the school. Hunter died in 1988. Her work has been included in many group shows, including *Outside the Main Stream* and *Passionate Visions of the American South*.

S. L. Jones

Shields Landon Jones was born in 1901 in Indian Mill, West Virginia. He grew up with thirteen siblings on the small farm owned by his father, who probably taught him his first lessons about music and carving. He left school after the eighth grade to work for the railroad, and married Hazel Boyer, with whom he had four children. He took a painting class at the Y.M.C.A. before retiring from the Chesapeake and Ohio Railway Company, where he worked for almost fifty years. To stave off the loneliness and boredom that followed his retirement in 1967 and the death of his wife in 1969, Jones resumed the fiddling and carving he had enjoyed in childhood. His first pieces were miniature human and animal figures carved with a bowie knife from local woods. After he remarried in 1972, he began using wood chisels to make larger works, which he sold at craft fairs and a nearby state park. Jones died in 1997. His work has been seen in many group exhibitions, including *Outside the Main Stream*; *O, Appalachia*; and *Made with Passion*.

Charley Kinney

Charles Kinney was born in 1906 in Toller Branch, Kentucky. He attended school through the third grade. Weakened by a birth defect, he was unable to perform hard labor but acquired a collection of skills that allowed him to earn extra money and help on the Toller Holler farm owned by his younger brother Noah. He cut hair, baked, and made clay figures to sell in state park souvenir shops as well as split oak baskets known for their durability. He also played the fiddle in a small band in which Noah played guitar. They performed accompanied by dancing marionettes that Charley made from rags and found materials. Kinney had painted since first grade, but increased his production after Noah, a carver, stopped farming. Charley was a renowned storyteller, and the watercolors he painted on paper and cardboard often illustrate events from his life as well as local anecdotes. He died in 1991. His work has appeared in several group exhibitions, including *Outside the Main Stream* and *O, Appalachia*. His first solo exhibition, *Terrors, Holy and Otherwise: Works by Charley Kinney* was held in 1992 at the Rasdell Gallery of the University of Kentucky.

Joe Light

Joe Lewis Light was born in 1934 in Dyersberg, Tennessee. He attended school through the eighth grade and worked as a farm laborer before enlisting in the military for a short time. He served two prison terms; during the second, in the 1960s, he converted to the Judaism that informs both the moral commentary of his signboards and the symbolism of his paintings. After his release in 1968, he married Rosie Lee, also a painter, with whom he had ten children. Light also creates assemblages from found objects, and his house in Memphis is painted inside and out. His art often addresses current events and racial themes. Light's work was represented in *Outside the Mainstream: Folk Art in Our Time* at the High Museum of Art in 1988 and *Another Face of the Diamond*, *Pictured in My Mind*, and *Souls Grown Deep*.

Ronald Lockett

Ronald Lockett was born in 1965 in Bessemer, Alabama, where he spent his life. His great-grandmother, Sarah Dial Lockett, raised Lockett's father and his cousin Thornton Dial. Lockett showed skill at drawing and painting from childhood, and the Dial family encouraged him to devote himself to art after his graduation from high school. Lockett typically created works in series, exploring social, environmental, and autobiographical themes. He died in 1998. Lockett's work was included in *Souls Grown Deep*.

Sister Gertrude Morgan

Gertrude Morgan was born in 1900 in Lafayette, Alabama. After moving to New Orleans in 1939 she helped establish a small chapel, child care center, and children's shelter that Hurricane Betsy destroyed in 1965. She sang and wrote poems, sometimes set to music. In the mid-1950s she began to create evangelical crayon drawings and received a divine message that she would become the bride of Christ. From that point on, she wore only white, even as her art became more vibrantly colorful. Her career ended in 1978, after she received another vision directing her to stop making graven images. She died in 1980 at her home, the Everlasting Gospel Mission. Morgan's work was carried out in a variety of drawing and painting media on a vast array of supports, including plastic utensils, her guitar case, and pillowcases, in addition to paper. Her paintings were shown in *Louisiana Folk Paintings* in 1973 at the Museum of American Folk Art, *Black Folk Art in America*, and *Outside the Main Stream*.

Mattie Lou O'Kelley

Emily Mattie Lou O'Kelley was born in 1908 on a farm near Maysville in Banks County, Georgia, one of eight children. Her memory paintings depict the hardworking life of the farm and family she loved. As a teenager she read voraciously, although she attended school only through the ninth grade. She began to paint at age forty-seven, after the death of her mother. O'Kelley worked at various jobs before retiring in 1968, after which she took up painting full time. In 1975 High Museum of Art director Gudmund Vigtel bought *Spring Vegetable Scene* for the High and arranged to have some of her paintings sold in the Museum's gift shop. O'Kelley won the Georgia Governor's Award in the Arts in 1976, the same year her work was included in *Missing Pieces*. Her paintings were also exhibited in a show at the Abby Aldrich Rockefeller Folk Art Museum in Williamsburg, Virginia. She lived briefly in New York City during the late 1970s, then moved to West Palm Beach, Florida, before settling in Decatur, Georgia. O'Kelley produced several books illustrated with her paintings, including *From the Hills of Georgia: An Autobiography in Paintings* (1983), *Circus* (1986), *Mattie Lou O'Kelley: Folk Artist* (1989), and *Moving to Town* (1991). She also produced calendars and received commissions from collectors and museums. She died in 1997.

John Perates

John S. W. Perates was born in Amphiklia, Greece, around 1895. Trained to carve wood by his grandfather in his native country, he immigrated to Portland, Maine, in 1912 and became a cabinetmaker, eventually founding his own furniture company. After his sons were inducted into the armed services in World War II, he began to carve works derived from the icons of the Greek Orthodox Church. These works depict the life of Christ, the writers of the New Testament, and the earliest church fathers. In addition to his relief panels, he created an enormous altar. He never sold his carvings, giving many of them instead to his local church, where they remained in storage until Robert Bishop, later director of the Museum of American Folk Art, discovered them after the artist's death in 1970. Forty pieces were found in his workshop. His work was included in *Common Ground/Uncommon Vision*.

Elijah Pierce

Elijah Pierce was born in 1892 in Baldwyn, Mississippi, the son of a former slave. Pierce said that he was born with a caul (a membrane over his head), a sign that he was chosen by God to prophesy. As a child he began carving animal figures and walking sticks. Pierce became a barber and carved in his free time. He married and had a son. Shortly thereafter, his wife and father both died. Grief-stricken, Pierce wandered for a few years and then returned to Baldwyn, where he was ordained a minister around 1920. He moved to Columbus, Ohio, remarried, and took up barbering again. His wife's enthusiasm for an elephant he made as a gift for her encouraged him to begin carving more seriously, and he introduced religious messages into his art, along with autobiographical scenes, other animals, and famous Americans. Pierce carved and painted sculptures in the round as well as reliefs. During the 1920s and 1930s, he and his wife toured the South and Midwest, selling his carvings and using them to help spread God's word. Pierce displayed his art in the barbershop he built in 1954, which he eventually renamed the Elijah Pierce Art Gallery. He retired from barbering and turned to full-time carving in the late 1970s. He died in 1984. Pierce's carvings were first shown in a solo exhibition in 1971 at the Hopkins Hall Gallery of Ohio State University in Columbus. They were included in *Black Folk Art in America* and *Self-Taught Artists of the 20th Century*. His art was the subject of a retrospective, *Elijah Pierce, Woodcarver*, at the Columbus Museum of Art at 1992. Pierce received an honorary doctorate from Franklin University in Columbus in 1980 and a National Heritage Fellowship in 1982.

Martin Ramirez

Martin Ramirez was born in Jalisco, Mexico, in 1895.[1] He immigrated to California at an unknown date and worked on the railroad until 1930. That year, he was hospitalized for "catatonia." He remained institutionalized for the rest of his life under a revised diagnosis of "paranoid schizophrenia, deteriorated." It is possible that institutionalization intensified the worst of his mental problems. He never spoke after he was committed and reportedly had stopped speaking at around age fifteen. Ramirez began drawing in the late 1940s, manufacturing large sheets for his artworks from bits of paper pasted together with saliva or water mixed with starchy foods he hoarded from meals. His iconography combined motifs from his Mexican past and images from his experiences in America, sometimes collaged with magazine illustrations. He died in 1963 in Auburn, California. The Goldie Paley Gallery of the Moore College of Art in Philadelphia held a retrospective of Ramirez's work in 1985, and the artist's drawings have been included in a large number of subsequent shows, including *Self-Taught Artists of the 20th Century* and *Art Outsider et Folk Art*.

Nellie Mae Rowe

Nellie Mae Williams was born in 1900 in Fayette County, Georgia. As a child, she preferred drawing to the manual work she was expected to perform on her father's farm. She was required to withdraw from school in the fourth grade in favor of farm work. She married young and worked as a domestic. Rowe began to make art in earnest after the death of her second husband in 1948. She created an environment she called Nellie's Playhouse, using found objects, gifts, and her own creations inside and outside of the small Vinings home her husband had built. In addition to drawing, she sculpted chewing gum, created cloth dolls, and adorned photographs with drawing and collage. Rowe's artistic productivity ended only in the final months before her death in 1982. Her art was first exhibited in *Missing Pieces* and has been included in numerous solo and group exhibitions including *Black Folk Art in America* and *Outside the Main Stream*, earning several honors before her death. A retrospective, *The Art of Nellie Mae Rowe: Ninety-Nine and a Half Won't Do*, was presented at the Museum of American Folk Art in 1999, the High Museum of Art in the winter of 1999–2000, and the African American Museum, Dallas, Texas, in 2000.

Mary Shelley

Mary Michael Shelley was born in Doylestown, Pennsylvania, in 1950. Her father was a commercial artist and her Pennsylvania Dutch grandmother, a dedicated amateur artist. When she was twenty-three, Shelley (who studied to be a writer in college) was inspired to attempt carving by a relief carving her father sent her. Within a year, carving had replaced writing as her primary means of artistic expression. During the next two decades she sometimes supplemented her income by working as a sign painter. Shelley, who now lives in upstate New York, has carved and painted approximately five hundred wood reliefs since 1973. Her work has been exhibited in several solo exhibitions and many group shows in the United States and abroad, among them *Vision and Voice: Folk Art by Women of the 20th Century*, co-sponsored by the Museum of American Folk Art and Chubb Insurance in 1996, and the 1993 International Self-Taught Group Show at the Galerie Pro Arte Kasper in Morges, Switzerland, where she received the Prix Suisse et Prix Europe de Peinture Primitive Moderne 1993 and an honorable mention for best American work.

Herbert Singleton

Herbert Singleton was born in New Orleans in 1945, the eldest of eight children. His father, a municipal worker, deserted the family when Singleton was ten, leaving the children's mother to support them on her hospital worker's wages. Singleton left school after the sixth grade, becoming well acquainted with the world of drugs, gangs, and prostitution. He spent thirteen years in Angola State Prison on drug charges. In his youth, Singleton modeled snakes of

Mississippi river mud. After his release from prison, he resumed his practice of three-dimensional design in the sturdier medium of carved wood. In 1975 he began carving walking sticks from tool handles, but after one of these sought-after objects was used to commit a homicide he changed his focus to bas reliefs carved on old doors and driftwood. He also creates sculptures in the round. Singleton takes as his subjects the street life of his neighborhood as well as political, social, and biblical themes. His work has been exhibited in *It'll Come True: Eleven Artists First and Last,* at the Artists' Alliance, Lafayette, Louisiana, in 1992, *Pictured in My Mind, Art Outsider et Folk Art,* and other shows.

Mary T. Smith

Mary Tillman was born in 1904 in the community of Brookhaven in Copiah County, Mississippi. She attended school for five years. Her sister recalled that Mary preferred to draw in the dirt while the other children were playing. She married for the second time in the 1930s and sharecropped with her husband, John Smith, near Martinville, Mississippi. After that marriage ended, she moved to Hazelhurst, Mississippi, where she eventually settled into a house built for her by the father of her only child. It was in the one-acre yard surrounding that house along one of Hazelhurst's main highways that she created her renowned environment. She decorated the fence, her house, her son's garage, and the doghouse with paintings on tin and wood. Smith's subjects were local people, herself, spirit characters, and sometimes animals, and her paintings often include writing. She dedicated her environment, which flowered in the early 1980s, to the glory of God. She was the first American woman represented in the Collection de l'Art Brut in Lausanne, Switzerland, and her work was the subject of a retrospective at the Whitney Museum in 1995, the year of her death. She has been represented in many subsequent solo and group exhibitions, including *Outside the Main Stream* and *Art Outsider et Folk Art.*

Mose Tolliver

Mose Ernest Tolliver was born around 1920 in the Pike Road Community of Montgomery County, Alabama, one of twelve children of sharecroppers. He attended school through the third grade. His family moved to Montgomery in the 1930s. Tolliver did yard work, carpentry, plumbing, and painting and eventually worked for a furniture company, where in the late 1960s his legs were crushed by a load of marble, leaving him permanently disabled. Tolliver, who had occasionally carved and created root sculptures in his spare time, was encouraged to paint by his employer, who offered to pay for lessons. He declined, instead developing his own style through experimentation. He applies house paint to a variety of surfaces, including cardboard, found wood, Masonite, metal trays, furniture, and an occasional gourd. He has encouraged his daughter Annie and several of his sons to paint. His work was displayed in solo exhibitions at the Montgomery Museum of Fine Arts in 1978 and the Museum of American Folk Art in 1993. He participated in *Black Folk Art in America, Outside the Main Stream, Souls Grown Deep,* and many other shows.

Edgar Tolson

Edgar Tolson was born in 1904 near Lee City, Kentucky. He whittled as a child and attended school for at least six years. Tolson became a Baptist minister and worked a variety of jobs to support his numerous children. In 1961, recovering from a stroke and having left the pulpit, he began to carve full time. Although he created a few stone sculptures, he carved the bulk of his work in poplar with a pocketknife. His forms include walking sticks, single figures of humans or animals, and tableaux of two or more figures. Tolson died in 1984. He participated in the Smithsonian's Festival of American Folklife in 1968 and 1973, and his work was shown in the Whitney Museum's Biennial of American Art in 1973. His carvings have appeared in a number of subsequent shows, such as *Outside the Main Stream, Self-Taught Artists of the 20th Century,* and *Art Outsider et Folk Art.*

Bill Traylor

William Traylor was born into slavery near Benton in Lowndes County, Alabama, sometime between 1852 and 1856 and freed in 1863 by emancipation.[2] For more than fifty years he remained as a field hand on the plantation where he was born. Census records indicate that by 1910 he was living in rural Montgomery County, and by the mid-1930s he had moved to the city of Montgomery. He spent his nights in the back room of a funeral parlor and, later, a shoe shop. He spent his days on the city sidewalks, where he drew scenes from the plantation and the street life around him. In 1939 painter Charles Shannon met him. Recognizing Traylor's talent, the younger artist and other friends provided Traylor with art supplies and preserved much of his work. Traylor had a one-man show at Montgomery's New South Art Center in 1940, and in 1942 his work was exhibited in New York City. He spent the war years living with his children in the North and returned to Montgomery in 1945, when he resumed drawing. In 1947 he moved in with his daughter in Montgomery, but a further decline in his health soon forced him into a nursing home, where he died in 1949. The artist's short career was prolific; he produced more than fifteen hundred works in pencil, poster paints, and crayon. In addition to the exhibitions held during his lifetime, Traylor's work was represented in *Black Folk Art in America* and in many other group and solo exhibits, including *Outside the Main Stream, Self-Taught Artists of the 20th Century, Art Outsider et Folk Art,* and *Bill Traylor (1854–1949) Deep Blues* at the Kunstmuseum in Bern, Switzerland, and the Museum Ludwig in Cologne, Germany, in 1998–1999. The exhibition also traveled to the Robert Hull Fleming Museum of the University of Vermont, Burlington, in 1999.

Thai Varick

Louis Gladding Varick was born in 1941 in Brooklyn, New York. Varick dropped out of college to support his wife and child. He started woodworking while serving a prison term and sold the plaques he made for $100 apiece. After his wife and daughter left New York, he became an ironworker and began carving African-style masks on the side. During a break from working on the Brooklyn Bridge, he picked up a piece of wire and created his first sculpture. During this period, he taught woodworking and held art appreciation classes in a series of galleries he opened in Flushing. Varick lives on the streets of New York's Upper West Side, where he twists wire into animals, machines, ships, and landmarks. As he works he converses with admirers, using a screwdriver or metal rod to knot the wire into a strong framework. His work is on display at several New York galleries.

Joseph Yoakum

Joseph Elmer Yoakum was born in 1890 or 1891 in Missouri, to parents who were part Native American, part African American, and part European American.[3] He joined the circus in his youth and toured Europe and North America. His two marriages produced five children. He worked at various jobs, including one for the railroad. Yoakum served in World War I, after which, he said, he spent two decades traveling around the world. After his retirement in the early 1960s and the death of his second wife, his artistic output either began or intensified. Although Yoakum occasionally produced portraits, most of his works depict visionary landscapes. In 1972, the year he died, the Whitney Museum of American Art held a one-man show of his work, which was also included in *Black Folk Art in America* and *Art Outsider et Folk Art*. The visionary nature of Yoakum's art influenced the young artists of Chicago's Hairy Who, among others.

Notes

1. According to Randall Morris, Martin Ramirez's death certificate gives his date of birth as 31 March 1895 and his date of death as 17 February 1963. This information contradicts earlier assertions that he was born in 1885 and died in 1960.

2. Research into historical documents and conversations with Traylor's descendents by Miriam Fowler and Marcia Weber have uncovered new and sometimes contradictory information about Traylor's life.

3. Although earlier sources give his birth date as 1886 or 1888, Derrel de Passe states that Yoakum's Social Security and Veterans Administration records give it as 1890, while the 1900 and 1910 federal censuses give it as 1891. Yoakum usually said that he was born in Window Rock, Arizona, but he appears to have been born in Missouri, where he grew up. His son Peter's birth certificate says Joseph Yoakum was born in Ash Grove, Missouri, and his own V.A. records say he was born in Springfield, Missouri.

Index of Artists